SALFORD
PALS

15th · 16th · 19th & 20th Battalions
Lancashire Fusiliers
A History of the Salford Brigade

SALFORD PALS

15th · 16th · 19th & 20th Battalions
Lancashire Fusiliers
A History of the Salford Brigade

MICHAEL STEDMAN

LEO COOPER

Dedicated to Yvonne, Richard and Jonathan –
my closest family and greatest supports

First published in Great Britain in 1993 by Leo Cooper
Reprinted in this format in 2007 by
LEO COOPER
an imprint of
Pen & Sword Books Ltd
47 Church Street, Barnsley,
South Yorkshire
S70 2AS

ISBN 1 84415 520 X

A CIP record of this book is available from
the British Library

Printed in England by
CPI UK

Contents

The 1st Salford Pals, drawn up in parade formation on their training camp at the Morfa near Conway, North Wales. In the foreground is the band, destined to become the stretcher bearers once they arrived in France in December, 1915. At the rear of the parade are two field kitchens paid for by the wealthy industrialists who financed the initial raising of Salford's civic battalions.

Introduction & Acknowledgements

" **L**et All Nations Come And See How I Respect England – For 'U' See I Live In England's Richest Shire." Almost since its formation this mnemonic of the Lancashire Fusiliers had been drilled into the many thousands of recruits by soldiers who were proud of the regiment's history. But, by contrast, a great many of the original members of Salford's own Brigade of the county's fusiliers would come from one of the most notorious slums which Britain's Victorian culture and economy produced. Lancashire's industrialism always threw up stark inequalities in the distribution of wealth. Nevertheless, from within the overcrowded and smoke blackened confines of Ordsall, Regent and Trinity out to the less heavily industrialised parts of Worsley and Eccles the appeal which drew Salford's men to enlist was always the pull of dozens of work-mates whose livelihoods, like their own, were drawn from the textile, mining, brewing, engineering and commercial activities which were the stuff of working class life here.

This history of four unsung Fusilier battalions of the British Expeditionary Force, engaged in France and Flanders during the conflict of 1914–1919, portrays the passage of five years' unremitting struggle for those few original men and officers who survived the chilling watershed of war unscathed. During the years which followed on from their enlistment in late 1914 and early 1915 the character (of each battalion necessarily altered beyond recognition. Consequently, although I have initially referred to the battalions in the text as the 1st, 2nd, 3rd or 4th Salford Pals I have progressively changed towards the 15th, 16th, 19th and 20th Lancashire Fusiliers, reflecting the toll which war's attrition took of the original Salford Brigade's members.

During the assembling of materials and my research into this story I received enormous help and support from many people. Without doubt the greatest debts are to my wife, family and parents, and to

From their origins in Salford, the 1st and 2nd Salford Pals were destined to end their service in the German city of Bonn as part of the Army of Occupation. This photograph shows the consecration and presentation of the Battalion's Colours to the 15th (Service) Battalion, Lancashire Fusiliers, 1st Salford Pals. The ceremony took place in the Hofgarten, 1 March, 1919. Presenting the Colour is General Plumer.

Vincent Sleigh, whose encouragement has been instrumental in ensuring this story reached the fruition of publication. I am also indebted to Ian Lewis for the generous loan of his early research materials. Amongst the staff at Pen and Sword Books I should like to thank John Bayne and Toby Buchan for their initial encouragement at the start of this project. Nigel Cave's editorial work and Roni Wilkinson's humour and skill in producing the book have all been enormously helpful. Whilst my gratitude to all of these people is considerable, they should not be burdened with the responsibility for any errors which might appear within the text. Other people who have kindly given and lent photographs, documents, materials and the immeasurable wealth of their helpful advice include:

The Adelphi Lads' Club, Broughton, especially Len Lomax. Joan Aylmure. William Bailey. Evelyn and Joe Bamford. Mr Bannister. Lady Patricia Barnes. Mrs Lilian Benson. Cliff Blood. Don Bradshaw. Duncan Broady of the Greater Manchester Police Museum. Mrs Charles. Tony Conduit. Alan Davies of the Buile Hill Mining Museum. Monsieur Desailly. Mrs Donlan. Mrs Eckersall. Ron Evans. Mrs Fisher. Sergeant Joe Fitzpatrick. Mrs Flaherty. Ernest Gradwell. Private John Grainger. Mr E. Greenwood. Mr M. Hague. Major Hallam and the staff of the Lancashire Fusiliers' Museum at Bury. Keith Hallam. Terry Healey. Private Frank Holding. Alan Hopkinson. The staff of the Imperial War Museum, especially Peter Hart for his help in understanding the techniques of sound recordings and Nigel Steel of the Department of Documents. Bob Jackson. Diane Kenyon Jackson. Elaine Jones. Jill Jones. Herbie Knott. Les Lawton. Mrs Lee. Mike Lieber. Private George Lineker. Mrs Looms. Mrs Violet Massey. Sir William Mather. Joe Minogue. The staff of the Local Studies Unit within Manchester Central Reference Library. The staff of the North Wales Weekly News. Mrs Ogden. Derek O'Nions. Alan Powson. Private George Peake. Mr Platt. Mrs Maureen Pullen. Mr and Mrs M. Randall. Paul Reed. Jesse Robertson. Henry Sampson. Derek Seddon. Cindy Shaw, curator at Ordsall Hall Museum, Salford. The Salford Lads' Club, especially Jean and Kenneth Unsworth. Tim Ashworth, Tony Frankland, Sandra Hayton and Patricia Nuttall who are the excellent staff of the Salford Local History Library. The Salford Archives Centre. The Editor and Staff of the Salford Reporter newspaper. John Simmonds. Ken Smallwood. Private Bill Smedley, Klaus Spath. Mrs Stainton. Andy Taylor. Vic Tomlinson. Sergeant Bill Turner. Mrs Emma Walton. Terry Whippy, Mrs Willcock and Mike Walker. To all of you, and the many others whose help is unrecorded, I extend my sincerest thanks.

Such willingness to help and a genuine surprise that their own, their husbands', parents' and grandparents' story should now be told was a very great pleasure to me. As a consequence, the very hardest decisions came in making the choice of what to leave out of this story. To describe all of the dozens of actions, the tense patrols, the moments of humour and sadness and the many relatives' anecdotes was impossible within the confines of a history which attempted to depict the struggle for survival and victory engaged in by the many thousands of men who had served within the Salford Brigade.

Michael Stedman. 1993.

A short bibliography and selected sources

Although dozens of books and sources come to mind which proved very helpful in the preparation of this work, I most frequently consulted the following sources in my search for both guidance about and evidence of Salford's Pals:

* A Nation in Arms. (ed. Beckett & Simpson. Manchester University Press. 1985.)
* Geoffrey Bowen. A Memoir. (Privately Published, C1930.)
* The Classic Slum. Robert Roberts. (Manchester University Press. 1971.)
* Hansard Records of Parliamentary Debates. Record Office, House of Lords.
* History of the 16th Battalion. The Highland Light Infantry. (ed. Chalmers. John M'Callum & Co., Glasgow. 1930.)
* The History of the Lancashire Fusiliers. 1914–1918. Two volumes. Maj-General J.C. Latter. (Gayle and Polden. Aldershot 1949.)
* Historical Records of the 16th Battalion Northumberland Fusiliers. Captain C.H. Cooke. M.C. (Newcastle and Gateshead Incorporated Chamber of Commerce, 1923.)
* The History of the Royal Fusiliers. UPS. University and Public Schools Brigade. (Formation and Training.) Anon. (Times Publishing Company, London, 1917.)
* In Remembrance, The Adelphi Lads' Club Roll of Honour. (Hardman & Co. Manchester. C 1920.)

* *The Killing Ground.* Tim Travers. (Allen and Unwin. 1987.)

* *Kitchener's Army. The Raising of the New Armies, 1914–16.* Peter Simkins. (Manchester University Press. 1988.)

* *The Lancashire Fusiliers: The Roll of Honour of the Salford Brigade.* (ed. Sir C.A. Montague Barlow. Sherratt & Hughes. Manchester. 1920.)

* Captain E.B. Lord. The account of his service with the LF's Service Battalions during WW1. (Department of Documents. IWM.)

* Medical Officer of Health's Reports, Eccles and Salford. 1910–1920.

* Lieutenant C.S. Marriot's materials. (Lancashire Fusiliers' Museum.)

* *My Bit. A Lancashire Fusilier at War. 1914–18.* George Ashurst. (ed. Richard Holmes, Crowood Press.)

* *Official History of the Great War. Military Operations in France and Belgium,* Compiled by Sir James E. Edmonds. (Macmillan/HMSO 1922–1948.)

* *Lieutenant C.L. Platt. Account of the First World War – Manuscript letters to home.* (Department of Documents. IWM.)

* Salford Lads' Club Weekly News and Annual Reports and Minute Books, 1914–1919, Salford Lads' Club archives.

* *Soldiers Died in the Great War* and *Officers Died in the Great War.* The two vital sources of detail relating to the many thousands of men and officers who died during the Great War. (HMSO 1921 and 1919 respectively. Both reprinted by J.B. Hayward & Son. 1989.)

* *The Story of the Fourth Army in the Battle of the Hundred Days.* Major General Sir A. Montgomery. (Hodder and Stoughton. 1921.)

* *Youth Before the Flood.* Lieutenant R.A.S. Coke, 4th Salford Pals. (John Long Ltd, London. Undated.)

Contemporary local newspapers which provided an immeasurable wealth of detail:-

The Salford City Reporter.

The Salford Chronicle.

The Eccles and Patricroft Journal.

The Manchester Guardian.

The North Wales Weekly News.

Unit War Diaries and Operational Narratives held by the Public Records Office:

Amongst the many which have helped build the picture the following have proved to be the most significant:-

W095/2367, W095/2368 & W095/2372. 32nd Division HQ.

W095/2375, 32nd Divisional Artillery.

W095/2394. 19th Lancashire Fusiliers, (3rd Salford), including the *Account of the Operations at Mont Kemmel from 11th to 25th April 1918 compiled by Lieutenant-Colonel H.D. Bousefield C.M.G., D.S.O. West Yorkshire Regiment whilst a prisoner at Mainz from memory without any notes or memoranda, also held within the P.R.O.*

W095/2397. 15th & l6th Lancashire Fusiliers. (1st & 2nd Salford)

W095/2398. 16th Northumberland Fusiliers.

W095/2395 and W095/2396. 96th Infantry Brigade.

W095/2370. 97th Infantry Brigade.

W095/2484. 20th Lancashire Fusiliers. (4th Salford)

Sound Records.

The Sound Records department of the Imperial War Museum have a number of recordings made by both men and officers who served within the Salford battalions. These include:

George Ashurst, Frank Holding, William Turner, Wiiliam Tobey. These have supported the dozens of my own recordings of interviews with past residents of Salford. These people and the soldiers who were raised or later worked in the area have provided a rare insight into the social circumstances of the late Victorian and Edwardian era in Salford and have been crucial in setting the scene for this story.

Chapter One

A Quart From a Pint Pot

When we hate someone we are hating something that is within ourselves in his image. We are never stirred up by something which does not already exist within us.[1]

In 1913 no-one admitted to calling this place beautiful. But to equate the ancient borough of Salford with its more prosperous neighbours was to invite a frosty stare. Salford's people had a distinct heritage whose origins long pre-dated those of Manchester. Lying twenty minutes' walk to the west of Manchester's city centre, Salford's heartland had, during the latter part of the 19th century, become the definitive product of Britain's Industrial Revolution, boasting its own colliery, together with the cotton mills and the engineering, chemical, steel, copper, gas and dye works whose effluents were drained into the fetid River Irwell. Significantly, the borough also contained the Manchester Ship Canal Company's enormous and modern dockland which linked the area with world commerce.

That Ship Canal and the parallel Manchester to Liverpool Railway line revealed the vital importance of international trade to this area. Manchester's prosperity had long depended on an ability to by-pass Liverpool, bringing the raw materials which fed her voracious factories directly to Salford docks. Initially George Stevenson's railway line, completed in 1830, had carried out that task, but as the Victorian Empire had moved to the height of its industrial prowess the line had proved insufficient for Manchester's appetite. Between 1887 and 1894 the huge canal, capable of handling ocean going vessels, had been built, terminating in a vast array of bustling quays, cranes, wharfs, warehouses, railway sidings and customs' posts. 1905 saw the continual expansion of the port's capacity when King Edward VII opened the huge No. 9 dock.

Not that Manchester sullied her hands with much of the hard and often filthy work carried on there. Apart from the raw cotton, frozen meat, corn and engineering materials, cargoes of coal, iron ore, carbon black and charcoal often left the dockers with painfully raw skins. The thousands of stevedores,

Salford Docks – Manchester's link with the world's commerce. 1910. Salford Local History Library (SLHL)

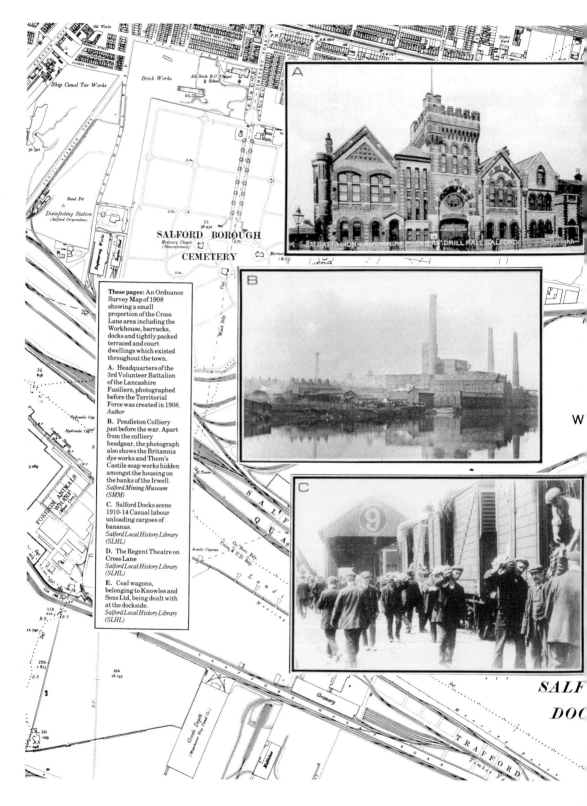

These pages: An Ordnance Survey Map of 1908 showing a small proportion of the Cross Lane area including the Workhouse, barracks, docks and tightly packed terraced and court dwellings which existed throughout the town.

A. Headquarters of the 3rd Volunteer Battalion of the Lancashire Fusiliers, photographed before the Territorial Force was created in 1908. *Author*

B. Pendleton Colliery just before the war. Apart from the colliery headgear, the photograph also shows the Britannia dye works and Thom's Castile soap works hidden amongst the housing on the banks of the Irwell. *Salford Mining Museum (SMM)*

C. Salford Docks scene 1910-14 Casual labour unloading cargoes of bananas. *Salford Local History Library (SLHL)*

D. The Regent Theatre on Cross Lane *Salford Local History Library (SLHL)*

E. Coal wagons, belonging to Knowles and Sons Ltd, being dealt with at the dockside. *Salford Local History Library (SLHL)*

Navvies working on the construction of the Ship Canal, about 1890. (SLHL)

dockers and labourers who worked the quaysides were Salford people, amongst whom the Ship Canal Company was the biggest source of employment.

Beyond its western boundary Salford looked out across the smaller communities of Irlam, Eccles, Patricroft, Pendlebury, Swinton and Worsley onto the peat-lands of Chat Moss whose boggy confines so tested Stevenson's engineering skills eighty-five years before. In parts these locations were almost rural in nature with substantial pockets of farmland interspersed among the spread of urban manufacturing, mills, collieries and housing. But the eastern side of Salford told a different tale. Here lay the tightly woven streets of Ordsall overlooking the docks. Lower Broughton and Trinity overlooking Cheetham and Strangeways, where poverty and deprivation stood in contrast to the nearby grand prosperity of Manchester's centre, the hub of regional commercial and industrial life.

The existence of close packed, verminous, terraced and court dwellings with the most elementary of sewerage systems, earth closets and open middens, meant that disease and infestation in the overcrowded and industrial parts of the Borough were part of daily life. Purveyors of remedies and pills ran a roaring trade from the corner shops among the tightly ranked slumland streets. Legions of lice and flies were countered with 'Klenzit Kleener' and thousands of fly papers every summer. Scarlet fever, typhus, diphtheria and tuberculosis were endemic here in pre-war years. In their school days many children were

Typically, people in Salford lived within the shadows of their employment. During the 1960s and 1970s almost every one of these simple dwellings were pulled down in Salford, to be replaced with a very different array of high rise flats. (SLHL)

Coal delivery cart operated by Andrew Knowles and Sons. Circa 1905. Salford Mining Museum (SMM)

the victims of an impoverished diet and the rickets which followed. Whilst people could expect to live as long as anywhere in semi-rural Eccles, the death rates of twenty-eight in each thousand in parts of Salford Borough were twice England's average.[2] This was real deprivation and the Salford Union Workhouse did grinding trade in dealing with poverty's casualties. Norman Blackett, one of the town's Registrars, recorded much of this as births, life, marriages and death passed into his records.

Among the gigantic mills, sweated workshops and dock quaysides an army of casual labour fought a daily battle against unemployment, excessive hours, low pay and the progressive inflation which corroded their tiny pay-packet's value. At the Hanover Works cabinet makers' labourers earned 12 shillings for a fifty-nine and a half hour week. In some of the local flax mills women were being paid 9 shillings for a fifty-five and a half hour week, with a l/6d bonus if no time was lost! Underground an army of miners laboured hewing the coal which gave energy to the region's industry. Their conditions

Armed London Police and Lancers on Cross Lane. (SLHL)

Uncle Norman Blackett. Eckersall

were brutal, dangerous and filthy, their employers openly exploiting the buyers' market for labour. The area's biggest and most notorious colliery owners were Andrew Knowles and Sons whose employees worked the Pendleton and Agecroft pits using equipment often scavenged second hand from other owners in the area. The Pendleton colliery was worked to a depth of 3,600 feet, down a seam gradient of 1 in 3. Apart from intolerable dust the face temperature was often recorded at 100 degrees Fahrenheit due to the inadequate air flow allowed by the very narrow entry and ventilation shafts.[3]

As a consequence of such exploitation and hardship the century's second decade had seen an undercurrent of unrest settle over the factories and docklands. In the torrid summer of 1911, disputes and strikes undertaken by seamen, dockers and miners had provoked bitter fighting between strikers and the scab labour. Armed police were billeted at the houses of colliery managers to forestall violence. These police were part of a small army of military force and police drafted from both nearby and distant boroughs at the request of the Chief Constable, Captain Cedric V. Godfrey. The local Territorial units, the 1/7th and 1/8th Lancashire Fusiliers with whom Godfrey had served, were ordered to return their weapons to Cross Lane Barracks, just in case they proved reluctant to use arms on behalf of the employers!

Part of the small army of military force brought in to quell the unrest in Salford in 1911. (SLHL)

Silcock's Shop, Harris Street, Salford. Typical of the pre 1914 shops which traded within the confines of many of Salford's less affluent districts. (SLHL)

The presence and behaviour of the Scots Greys, a battalion of infantry and the armed police had been much resented and remembered by the striking men's families. Significantly though, that extraordinary summer saw success for the combined workers of the town. Cabinet makers, dockers, miners, transport and textile workers, seamstresses and engineers all overcame lockouts, hardship and brutality to obtain considerable improvements to their hours of work and rates of pay. Employers had been forced to recognise both the reasonableness of their demands and their rights to be represented by unions, during what had been Salford's own General Strike.

On the 18th March, the following spring, the well known local Syndicalist[4] Tom Mann, was arrested. A few days earlier, during meetings at Salford and Pendleton Town Halls, he had publicly criticised the vicious Army and Police brutality which had occurred during strikes and rallies held in Liverpool the previous autumn. During those events dozens of innocents were injured by the police and two men had been shot dead by troops. After trial on a charge of incitement to mutiny Mann was sentenced to six months' imprisonment within the notorious local jail, Strangeways. The community in Salford were outraged.

Mann's ideas therefore gained a further currency amongst the local population and The Syndicalist's circulation received an unintended but substantial boost from the judicial process. Public meetings, organised by the many socialists campaigning against Mann's imprisonment, ensured that he only served seven weeks of the sentence. In this atmosphere it was clear that the main political parties of the Edwardian era were already coming under threat in the Salford area.

Further, these events also showed that the Army, at best, was not universally revered by the borough's people at this time.

Consequently Salford's clumsy sprawl was often despised by many Mancunians as a necessary but filthy, poverty-ridden and unstable testimony to industrialism, whose blackened acid air drifted unremittingly across Manchester's city centre. But to Salford men and women such a snub guaranteed the determination and community spirit which adversity and hardship bring. The truth was that Salford people hated to be seen as second best, even if the grimy view from their tramcar windows suggested otherwise. Here people were forced to recognise the real value of money.

George Peake, the son of a Broughton clogger remembered,

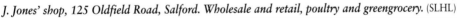

J. Jones' shop, 125 Oldfield Road, Salford. Wholesale and retail, poultry and greengrocery. (SLHL)

If we were playin' with a ball and it went through a window we'd all club up and tell our mothers what we'd done. The man would come round to put a new window in. These old Jews used to carry a big frame on their back with window glass in. If a window was broken they'd come along and put it in in no time. I think they charged ninepence!... ...and rabbits. The loveliest food in the world. They were plentiful and they weren't dear. Food was very, very cheap. You could get a big four pound loaf for tuppence ha'penny, and Woodbines, tuppence for a packet. I used to go to the shop for my father for half an ounce of thick twist tobacco and that was three ha'pence. And they'd give you a little bit extra. I'd bet there was nearly an ounce for three ha'pence![5]

The Lancashire Fusiliers had already established a considerable presence within this community. Two of the Regiment's Territorial battalions, the 1/7th and 1/8th, had their headquarters at the Cross Lane barracks in Salford. Along with two further battalions from Bury and Rochdale, these men formed the Lancashire Fusiliers Brigade of the East Lancashire Division. Throughout the years preceding the First World War the streets and homes of Salford were regular meeting places for these men.

... there were loads of men in Salford and Manchester who had rifles and bayonets, but there was never a casualty with them. We brought our rifles 'ome with us, and bayonets of course, all our own equipment and a suit of red with badges, the sphinx and the pyramids on a white collar, white cuffs, blue trousers with a red seam ...[6]

There was a considerable enthusiasm for the Terriers in the borough. The barracks and local drill halls were a part of many men's recreation and social life. During the Whit week of 1914 the Cross Lane Territorials were on their annual training camp at Prestatyn, but, in the early summer of 1914, it was not apparent that before a year had elapsed their destiny was to be part of the first Territorial Division to leave the country for active service at Gallipoli.[7]

In many ways, then, Salford was already well prepared for the coming of war. Its poverty and overpowering industrialism had always marked the area as a rich source of recruits for the Armed Services. The Lancashire Fusiliers had become the natural beneficiaries of this state of affairs but the growing Labour movement had, by contrast, found it difficult to sweep away the Liberal and Conservative Parties' predominance in the Borough's democratic Parliamentary politics.

The approach of high summer marked an increase in the intensity of left wing campaigning. Since the last week in July the National Clarion Campaign had been vociferously active in Salford's area. Local

Cross Lane Barracks, home of the Territorials in Salford and a constant reminder to the community of the Army's importance in the town's past and present. (SLHL)

Cross Lane, Salford, a seething bustle of commerce and trade which ran from the City's centre down into the dockland areas. Salford Local History Library (SLHL)

enthusiasts from the British Socialist Party had arranged a sequence of opportunities over the forthcoming fortnight for the community to hear the movement's best known speakers, including the London based lecturer, George Ebury. The targets for much of his rhetoric were the deferential working class men whose votes sustained three local Members of Parliament, Montague Barlow (South Salford, Tory), Sir George Agnew (West Salford, Liberal) and Sir William Byles (North Salford, Liberal).

> *If they had an industrial dispute, whether there was a Liberal or a Tory Government, they would use the forces of the country against the workers. They would use the Army and the Navy, and even the Boy Scouts (laughter). Socialism was a remedy for all the evils which the working classes suffered. The people must have the production, distribution and exchange of commodities in their own hands. It was time the working classes woke up and banded themselves together for their mutual benefit. The workers were combining industrially against the master class, but they still continued to send the latter to represent them in Parliament...[8]*

One of George Ebury's further meetings was held on the Bank Holiday, Monday 3rd August, little more than twenty-four hours before war was declared between Britain and Germany. On this day the Clarion Campaigners assembled at Broadway, next to the Salford docks. Ebury's address was a powerful indictment of the likely future cost of the war, but even the vigour of his oratory was incapable of stemming the tides of vehement feeling which were already sweeping the town.

Leading articles in National Press Newspapers, 5th August, 1914.

> *...Sir Edward Grey has spoken about morals. What cant and hypocrisy. It was enough to make one's blood boil. Was there anything moral in going to war? To blow to perdition, and to blow into pieces men, women and children against whom they had no quarrel? There were no morals in regard to war as far as he was concerned. He had no hesitation in saying that the present*

1/8th Lancashire Fusiliers drilling at Prestatyn, Whit 1914. George Peake

war had been fomented and engineered by the capitalists of Europe. Revolutionary Socialists and democrats recognised no economic difference between Liberals and Tories. One was just as bad as the other.... It would not be the working classes who would gain by it, but it would be the Army contractors and the armament firms. The armament rings were responsible for the war and they were the people who were going to benefit after the war was over. The working classes would not benefit in any way.[9]

A prescient speech, and reported in a way which did credit to the independence of Salford's local newspaper. Such a considered perspective revealed the Salford City Reporter's liberal heritage in publishing commentaries which questioned the imperative nature of going to war. The voice of dissent was, therefore, certainly present, though it was neither loud enough nor early enough to compel people's real attention.

A further public meeting held just hours before war was declared, took place two miles away in Milton Hall on Deansgate, Manchester. On the platform were many local figures and representatives, the Reverends and Vicars from many local churches as well as councillors from both Manchester and Salford. With only token opposition amongst those present, the meeting passed a resolution quite adamant in its feelings of dismay and regret about the impending conflict. The resolution's proposer, Councillor Windsor of Salford, suggested,

That this meeting of the citizens of Manchester is of the opinion that the Government should have maintained absolute neutrality in this crisis, and protests against the British nation being dragged into war, and that copies of this resolution be telegraphed to the Prime Minister and Sir E Grey.[10]

The reality of course was that they were too late. Britain's ultimatum had already been rejected by Germany.

Even as Councillor Windsor was speaking, that Tuesday evening, notices were being posted on the walls outside, announcing the mobilising of the Army Reserve and the embodiment of the Territorials. That night Salford's Post Offices remained open around the clock as Reservists identified themselves and presented their cash orders. By the following morning, the 5th August, the nearby Victoria and Central stations were already crowded with family groups saying goodbye to fathers, brothers and sons. Typical of the reservists who were departing were twenty-six members of the local police force, assembled in the Town Hall for a word of encouragement from their Chief Constable, who announced that each man's family would receive 15 shillings weekly with a further 2s. 6d. for each child during their absence. The Gas Department had already lost 28 men and the tramways 140! As people awoke that morning, the region's powerful newspapers were found to have given unqualified support to the object of dealing a blow to what was seen as Prussian Militarism.

18

In the chamber during that Wednesday's meeting of the Borough Council the Mayor of Salford reflected the media and popular interpretations of events when he said,

> We are face to face as a nation with perhaps the greatest calamity which has befallen Europe within the memory of man. That being so, if a demand is made upon our patriotism I am quite sure that the call which is made upon us will be responded to with that unanimity and enthusiasm which one always expects from the English race.[11]

In fact the call was already being answered in a chaotic throng which had gathered at the Cross Lane Barracks of the Territorials of the 1/7th and 1/8th Lancashire Fusiliers. Throughout Wednesday crowds had surged around the barrack's entrance, anticipating the departure of the Terriers. Mounted Police were drafted in to control the crowded streets and to allow some traffic to get through. Inside the building medical inspections and kit issues were taking longer than expected. The men were told to report again on Thursday morning. And Friday morning. And Saturday! These scenes, so close to the centres of both Salford and Manchester, produced an incredible spur to enlistment. Hundreds of men, including ex-soldiers as well as men with no military experience at all, enlisted into these two Territorial Battalions during these four days. In fact, for young men without military experience, the Territorials proved to be the quickest route out to the front lines. For example the 18-year-old Tom Winstanley with no military experience other than a place as drummer in the 1/8th Lancashire Fusiliers' band was out in Egypt and Gallipoli nine months before his father,[12] who would enlist in Salford's Pals, left the British Isles.

Seemingly it did not matter that Socialist or Syndicalist thinking before and at the outbreak of war suggested that this was a conflict out of which no benefit would come their way, the reality clearly was that Salford's working classes had neither the will, the organisation nor the desire to revolt. Indeed, for many men in this town the war had now become the opportunity for a great escape.

Within hours of the war's outbreak employment at the Salford and Pomona docks was under threat. The movement of German vessels was halted. The steamships *Providentia*, *Lubeck* and *Hornsund* with their cargoes of timber were impounded at the docks. The Dock Police were issued with pistols and placed on permanent guard at the locks to prevent any escape. Dockers, crane-men and gangers milled around the gates in search of non-existent work.

That same day the tension between the substantial German community in the town and their neighbours reached boiling point. It was a portent of very much more serious rioting still to come in 1915.

The Band of the 1/8th Lancashire Fusiliers, with its complement of youthful instrumentalists, before the war.
Jones

Enthusiasm grips Salford as thousands of people turn out to see soldiers marching past the Regent Theatre, along Cross Lane towards the Territorial Barracks. These may be men of the 1/7th and 1/8th Lancashire Fusiliers Territorials. (SLHL)

> An incident which might have proved more serious than it did occurred on Wednesday in Oldfield Road, Salford, which had a connection with the war. A German Army Reservist left for the front a few days ago and on Wednesday an Englishman who lived next door to him was leaving the house to join the British Army, he being an Army Reservist, when the wife of the German soldier passed the remark that she hoped he would get shot. The news spread around the neighbourhood and a crowd assembled and with bricks and other missiles they partially wrecked the premises, which consist of a shop and dwelling house. The police came on the scene and the crowd was dispersed. The shop has been boarded up and made secure, and the individual who made the foolish remark is now no doubt a sadder, if not a wiser woman.[13]

Such incidents were symptomatic of the personal bitterness and outrage which the outbreak of war had engendered in ordinary people's hearts.

Across the borough dozens of draught horses, usually employed in delivering the copious quantities of ale consumed in the town's pubs, were being requisitioned by the military. The Rochdale and Manor Brewery, controller of many such pubs, had only weeks before disposed of its horse drawn drays in favour of lorries, but they too were quickly snapped up for the Army. Veterinary inspections went on around the clock. People normally soundly asleep stayed out on the streets to witness the enormous bustle of activity. Butchers' assistants, milk roundsmen and grocers' boys paraded their horses across the stone sets. All the largest firms quickly lost the bulk of their horses. Fifty horses went from the Manchester Carriage Company with premises in Pendleton and Broughton. Even the undertakers' horses had gone by Friday.

Whilst the Reserve and Territorial troops were being mobilised, the town itself was in danger of being ground to a standstill.

On a practical and personal level there was evidence of considerable hoarding of foodstuffs as near panic stripped the shelves of local stores. Co-operative Societies across the borough imposed limits on each customer's purchases of flour and sugar, many anxious people initially besieging their premises hoping to acquire half sackfulls of these items. Shops in the Regent Road district were overwhelmed and the police were called to restrain groups of aggressive women demanding extra supplies of flour. By Wednesday afternoon the Co-op's ration had fallen to a 36 pound portion, further reduced by Friday to 12 pounds per person.

That same Friday evening a huge open air meeting off Ordsall Lane was addressed by Montague Barlow. The Borough's council supported the recruitment process with a clear statement of intent, announced by Councillor Williamson, before Barlow began to speak.

Salford people would be delighted to hear that the Salford Council had decided that any of the Corporation employees who joined His Majesty's forces would not lose a single farthing so far as their wages were concerned and their dependents would be amply provided for.[14]

As soon as he stood up to speak Barlow was met by a sensational swell of support. During his speech he exhorted everyone who heard him to prosecute the war with all in their power. His simple justification was that the war "was in pursuit of, common honour and decent justice between nation and nation (cheers)". His explanation was that, without war, the prosperity of every family, sustained by Britain's mastery over an Empire, would crumble.

War was inevitable if we were to remain an Empire. It was necessary from the point of view of self-interest that we should join in the war. If we had allowed Germany to encroach upon and probably absorb Belgium and Holland and beat France to her knees, capture the French Fleet and the French Colonies, all the wealth and resources that Germany had acquired by conquest would be turned against this country. By standing aside in a cowardly fashion we should have reaped the reward of those who did not carry out an honourable understanding (applause).[15]

Dock Policeman before the outbreak of war. *Salford Local History Library* (SLHL)

Barlow's populist appeal both created and captured the common sentiments of the time. Everybody in Salford could feel their working and personal lives being affected by the pressures of war.

Within ten days of the war's outbreak Salford Lads' Club, on the corner of Coronation Street and Oxford Street, was occupied by the Army and its recruiting effort. Along with the Adelphi Lads' Club in Lower Broughton these two extraordinary and caring institutions would provide hundreds of men for Britain's war effort, even before the idea of any locally raised battalions emerged.

The Police department in Salford's Town Hall had some other matters on their shoulders at this time. In one of the more light-hearted events during an otherwise tense and expectant month, Detective

Salford Territorials prepare for Active Service. Manchester Guardian 10/8/1914 (MG)

Salford Lads' Club Whit week camp at Ramsay, Isle of Man, 1914. (SLHL)

Mulraney's zealous pursuit of the regulations which prevented aliens from keeping telephones, cameras, cars and other means of perfecting the spy's art had created a considerable difficulty that week.

> *... a young German named Kurtwerner, who lives in the Seedley district, was arrested and taken to the Town Hall for a breach of the regulations in regard to the possession of carrier pigeons. Detective Mulraney was making enquiries in the neighbourhood, and in consequence of what he heard he went to the house where the man was living and found 25 homing and racing pigeons in the back yard. Police proceedings have not been taken, but the pigeons still remain in the possession of the police at the Salford Town Hall.[16]*

They were probably in good hands. Pigeon fanciers abounded in every street throughout and beyond the Borough! Some well informed wags pronounced that the Police department's fanciers had arranged a rather underhand nobble of some pigeons before the forthcoming race.

The end of August saw the Fusilier Terriers ensconced in camp at Turton and Chapeltown near Bolton. Reports in the local paper suggested an almost idyllic Pennine scene, bearing little resemblance to the reality of war.

> *... When I trained to Turton Station a brilliant sun was pouring down rays of beneficence upon the whole countryside, and the white tents of the Fusiliers and Field Ambulance, which are in full*

view from the station, reflected harmoniously with the green of the meadow-lands, the grey of the stone built village, the slate colour of the expanse of hills in the distance, and the blue and white of a sky that was threatening to become lowering...

A survey of the camp in the pleasant evening of Friday was enjoyable. The day had been hot and though the work had not been heavy, chiefly consisting of route marches in the morning, refreshing coolness was at a premium. Many were enjoying themselves in the streamlet that ripples down towards the station. Many others were bathing their heads, arms and shoulders. The horses had waded down to, and were sporting in, the water. Tea was finished by the general body of men – though I found Colonel King, the commandant, enjoying a repast under the verandah of his quarters, the tent connected with the bowling green behind the church – and evening scenes were unfolding. The little high street was crowded, and the retiring refreshment shops and Post Office were thronged. The window sill of the Post Office was a popular desk for the writing of letters and postcards to relatives and friends. Ice cream and banana vendors were reaping a rich harvest, and there were many alfresco parties on the grass by the roadside.[17]

This was just the sort of journalism guaranteed to sustain and swell Salford's enthusiasm. Families and sweethearts flocked to Turton, bringing back similar images of soldiering in a war still fully expected to be over within the year. Recruitment from the borough never wavered throughout August, even though it was known that Salford Borough Council was actively reconsidering their promise of making employees' service pay up to their pre-war wage rates. However, among all the argument about the merits or otherwise of enlisting, the trigger which Salford's pride and people really needed would be the establishment of the Liverpool and Manchester Pals' battalions.

Such rivalry was very real. This was a time when municipal pride was not stifled by the hand of Central Government. Industrial towns, which had expanded rapidly since the mid 1800s, had evolved their own identity, their blossoming civic pride spilling over as inter communal competition. That between Manchester and Liverpool was based on the right to pre-eminence in the region's economic life, and was reflected in both cities' profligate spending on civic buildings, cultural events, orchestras, museums, baths, tramways, waterworks, libraries, amenities and the huge administrative palaces known as town halls. However, the competition which Salford engaged in was the far less grand lifelong struggle for self respect and dignity.

On 27th August Lord Derby's influential letter appealing for men hoping to "serve with their friends and not be put in a battalion with unknown men as their companions" was published in the Liverpool press. Since Derby was an immensely influential figure in the industrial and political life of the North West of England, as well as being the Chairman of the West Lancashire Territorial Association, it took

The Lancashire Fusiliers' Territorials resting during a route march. Author

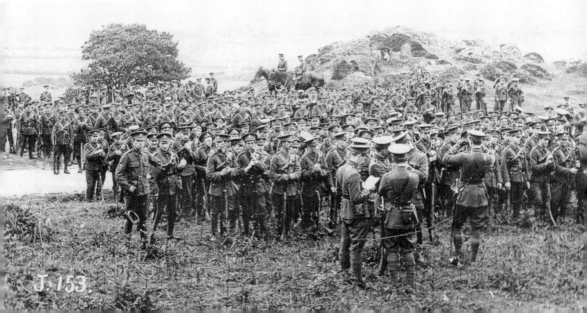

Soldiers at Station Road, Turton, September 1914. Author

no time at all for his suggestion to be taken up vigorously. Within two days a Liverpool battalion of pals was organised and another was planned. On 28th August a meeting in Manchester under the sponsorship of its Mayor established that the city would follow suit. On September 1st Lord Mayor Sir Daniel McCabe enrolled the first 800 men for the Manchester Clerks' and Warehousemen's Battalion (the First Manchester Pals) and the pressure on Salford became intense. Within days Manchester's fourth Pals' battalion was being enlisted and a drift of men from Salford's semi-rural western fringes started to travel across Salford to the recruiting stations near Manchester's Albert Square.[18]

Even without the attraction of their own 'battalions of pals', Salford's three recruiting stations[19] were still doing massive business. In the last week of August two hundred Salford men a day were being enlisted in return for the King's shilling. During the first week of September the pressure at Pendleton Town Hall was enormous:

> *Something like 500 intending recruits turn up each day and it may well be imagined that with only two doctors to pass the cases namely, Drs, Davey and Cantwell, a great deal of delay has been occasioned. In order to carry out matters fairly on the principle of first come first served tickets have been presented to the waiting volunteers which give them the right of precedence when they present themselves on subsequent days. Tired of waiting, however, many are said to have gone and enlisted in other places.[20]*

Further encouragement came from the work-place where the largest industrial employers were displaying prominent posters, promising weekly allowances to enlisted men's dependents, sometimes half pay, sometimes six shillings for a wife and six pence for each child as in the colliery's scheme. Mather and Platt's, together with the Broughton Copper Company, were allowing 10 shillings a week to the wives of employees on service.

The Right Honourable the Earl of Derby, KG, PC. Manchester City Battalion Book of Honour

If Salford failed to act soon the chance to raise proudly its own battalion would be lost in a welter of enlistments into the other units which were actively recruiting across the area. It was therefore impossible to imagine, in view of the events in the great cities either side of Salford, that the borough would not attempt to raise its own Pals' unit. The loss of civic pride would have been too great.

At this juncture, during the evening of Thursday 3rd September, the Salford Hippodrome on Cross Lane hosted the crucial recruiting meeting which established the Salford Pals' Battalions. The meeting was inspired by Montague Barlow acting under the auspices of the all-party Parliamentary Recruiting Committee whose purpose it was to stimulate enlistment through the efforts of local political parties and their agents. Speakers were to include the then Mayor, Alderman Desquesnes and Sir George Agnew, M.P., Sir William Byles M.P. and Barlow himself. The most prestigious figure present would be Lord Derby, the whole proceedings being supported by almost the entirety of the borough's Aldermen, its Councillors and the Chief Constable.

The seats and aisles from stalls to circle were packed in anticipation. Literally thousands were unable to gain access and assembled outside and in the Unitarian School opposite. Unfortunately, for the inception of Salford's municipal battalions, Lord Derby was unable to be present, bedridden by the overwork to which he had subjected himself during the previous ten days. Those present however were treated to a multiplicity of inducements to enlist.

> *Thousands, nay millions of men, were at the present moment being rushed into the bloodiest of wars, primarily, we had been told, for a mere scrap of paper. But on that scrap of paper was written the words, The honour of England (cheers)... That was indeed a fine idea, but we had also to remember that at the same time we were fighting for ourselves. We were fighting for our wives, for our children, for everything that was dear to us. We were fighting for our shores, the liberty of our country, for our hearths and homes. Let us not forget that. 'I said we were fighting, perhaps I ought to say that others were doing the fighting and that we, many of us, are sitting comfortably at home. It is quite true that we cannot all go to the war, but many of us who have not gone could. I want to speak to those men of Salford who are young and able-bodied and I want to say to them that we have no room for the unemployed with their opportunities. There is employment for all,*

> *and those able-bodied men at home who have no work to do can find work of a noble kind to do elsewhere.'[21]*

This inducement, by Alderman Desquesnes, was tantamount to the moral and economic blackmailing of the unemployed. Bishop Welldon[22], substituting for the indisposed Lord Derby, added the spiritual authority of the Church to these calls for enlistment, describing the German position as diabolical and having been put in the mouth of the devil himself. Drawing attention to the fact that one hundred clergy had already volunteered, he enthused the audience by saying that he had even offered to go himself!

Whilst Sir George Agnew contented himself with a political justification of the war, Montague Barlow got down to the serious business by embarking upon a wild tirade against German atrocities, believing that there could be no question about the truth of the allegations. The driving of women and children in front of their armies. The bricking

Salford Hippodrome, 1911. SLHL

25

up of mines containing Belgian miners. The ill treatment of wounded British soldiers. The despoliation of historic towns. The war against freedom. Having whipped up his gale of hatred Barlow put the question:

Who is for the King? I am going to make the same appeal to you tonight. Who is going to hold his hand up and volunteer to go from this magnificent meeting to fight for his King and Country?

Anything else said by the speakers who followed was irrelevant. The atmosphere of sordid hatred had already been created. From the platform speaker after speaker spoke of 'foul crimes towards both sexes', 'the hoardes of the German millions', impending invasion, the atrocities of the German Army and 'the gallantry of the little British Army'. The exits however were already swamped by hundreds of men seeking to put their names down.

Acting immediately, Barlow obtained permission from the War Office, in the form of their request to 'raise, clothe, feed and house' the battalion, 'provided at least 1,100 recruits come forward'. The battalion's existence was established on Wednesday 9th September, five weeks after the outbreak of war.

To draw on the many talents available within the borough Barlow set about establishing a Raising Committee. This consisted of the local M.P.s, together with councillors and industrialists who between them would co-ordinate the serious fund-raising and financing of the Pals' equipment, clothing and accommodation, until such time as they could be taken over by the War Office. The Raising Committee was very conscious of their role in ensuring that Salford's Pals took their place alongside the battalions already raised by their illustrious neighbours. The competitive nature of the movement was underlined by an article in Thursday 10th September's Manchester Guardian. The lengthy feature examined 'HOW THE BIG TOWNS HAVE RESPONDED' to 'Kitchener's call to Arms'.

London has furnished about 57,000 recruits. Manchester's total thus far is estimated at over 25,000. In Glasgow 22,000 recruits have been enlisted. Liverpool and the immediate district has contributed 20,000 for foreign service. Birmingham has supplied 23,000 and Sheffield 20,000.[23]

Pointedly, amidst over 3,000 words devoted to the question of comparability, the Manchester Guardian handily forgot the enormous contribution already made to that City's own figures by Salford men. Amidst many inches of column space given to Oldham, Grimsby, Rochdale, Crewe, Bradford, Bolton, Bury and many more towns Salford lacked even a mention!

However, once the news of a locally raised Pals' Battalion for Salford was out in the town a pause in the profligate enlistments elsewhere occurred, as the men now waited for their opportunity to join Salford's own Pals.

... recruiting for Lord Kitchener's Army was very brisk up to Tuesday last 8th Sept. Up to Tuesday the average number of recruits was 150 to 200 per day, but the numbers have dropped to about 40 since the new regulations in putting at once on reserve and paying them sixpence a day and liability to be called to the colours in ten days' notice came into operation. Recruiting will be quiet for a week or so. It can only be expected that the abnormal rush of recruits to the colours must come to an end some time. Recruiting at the Pendleton Town Hall has been much quieter during the last few days. On Monday 25 men of the Clifton Chloride Company's works came from there to Pendleton in a motor belonging to the firm and joined the colours. They waved the Union Jack and sang 'Rule Britannia' and other patriotic airs. At the Salford Lads' Club the numbers of recruits have diminished during the week.

The previous week [the first week in September] the recruiting numbers were 150 and upwards daily. There is no doubt the district has been fairly well absorbed of its young men. A large number of young fellows connected with the club, as well as old members, have joined the Army. Up to yesterday (Friday) week 1,160 recruits had been obtained at this depot and altogether about 1,500 have joined the colours. It must be remembered that hundreds of young men from Salford, Broughton and Pendleton have joined the Manchester Battalions.[24]

This pause in enlistment clarifies much of the initial enthusiasm for Salford's Pals. Since earlier that week it had been common knowledge in the area that the Army's depots were overflowing with recruits[25]. Many had been returned to the Salford area and posted to the reserve, after a nominal one day's service with the Army. Whilst this seemed superficially reasonable, in view of the fact that the men were free to pursue their normal jobs, the pay on reserve of 3s. 6d. a week meant real hardship for many who,

> ...on being posted to reserve, they find themselves without any employment to carry them over the intermediate period, without money, precariously assured of shelter, and even without food. Two hundred men who had been sent back from the Warrington depot yesterday morning turned up at the Manchester head recruiting office, many of them in so distressing a condition that Captain Walkley, acting on emergency, decided to distribute food tickets among them.[26]

Rather than risk just such a financial or social catastrophe it seemed a far better bet to wait one week and enlist into their own local Salford Pals' Battalion. That short pause ensured confidence that the arrangements being made would allow the men to be 'billeted on themselves', at the full pay and allowance rate of 21 shillings a week.

Until the emergence of the Pals' movement the bulk of Salford's recruitment had, for good reason, been taking place at the Salford Lads' Club. This crucial institution was located at the heart of some of the poorest and most needy parts of the borough's housing. The club's doors had been open for recruiting ever since the Army took over their premises on 15th August. Already the equivalent of two full battalions of Salford men had joined up in the general recruitment to the colours, very large numbers taking advantage of the Manchester Pals' organisation which had been actively enlisting men since 1st September.

It would prove a considerable feat, therefore, if Salford showed itself capable of raising a further whole battalion, beyond its already substantial commitment. The question being asked was whether the district had already, 'been fairly well absorbed of its young men'? Now, in the second week of September, the town abounded in debate about the merits of a local Pals' battalion. Lord Derby's acceptance of the role of Honorary Colonel, just as he had done in Manchester, ensured the status and charisma of the battalion. An appeal in the local press on Saturday 12th September, requesting that men arriving at recruiting stations state clearly if they wish to enlist for the Salford Battalion, was handily placed next to Sir John French's dispatch, detailing 'THE GREAT RETREAT', the actions at Mons and other accounts of daring by the Regular Army. In the opposite column were accounts of an extraordinary array of so called German atrocities:

> ... a mother who was forced to walk miles with her two day old baby at the point of a bayonet... a boy of 15 whom the Germans had forced to march in front of them for eight days.... Today there

Salford Lads' Club today. Sleigh

was brought in a baby which had had live coals thrown on it. It is burnt all down one side of its face and body. That is a fact…. The ghastliness of most of the German atrocities has been attested by soldiers in south-western Poland, who, returning to the battlefields from which they had retired, found unmistakeable evidence that their wounded comrades had been burned alive.[27]

It showed the extraordinary speed with which prejudice had spread its poison. What had always been a liberal and respectable newspaper now allowed itself to be used as a tool for the dissemination of, at the best, grossly exaggerated propaganda. Simple truth is always one of the first casualties in any war, and in the embittered climate of September 1914 such distortions helped to guarantee the success of the Pals, movement here in Salford.

The rush was on and recruiting for Salford's Pals began in earnest on Monday 14th September. Salford was only just in time. Manchester, the borough's infinitely larger and more prosperous neighbour, had by this moment already raised three full Pals' Battalions and was well on the way towards completing a fourth. By now the minimum height requirement for men enlisting throughout the country had been raised from 5'3" to 5'6", but Salford sought, and was given, War Office approval to enlist on the old standard in order to ensure parity with the Manchester City Pals who had been raised under the old 5'3" regulations.

Recruiting in the first week averaged, by contrast with Manchester's frenetic scenes, a more leisurely 40 men a day. The battalion's commanding officer was Lieutenant Colonel Moss from the l/8th Lancashire Fusiliers. His adjutant was Captain Charles Murray Abercrombie, a veteran of ten years with the Cheshires, including two years in the South African Transvaal with their 2nd Volunteer Service Company. Drilling initially took place at the Astley Street headquarters of the National Reserve and the Cross Lane Drill Hall. Their headquarters were established in Pendleton Town Hall, donated for the purpose by Salford Corporation.

Out of necessity these original Salford Pals were kitted in the handiest of uniforms. Civvies! Because the men were "billeted on themselves" their dress reflected the industrial and working class origins of the battalion. Quickly discarded were the best clothes in which many had chosen to enlist, replaced instead by stouter work-wear. The daily routine was quickly added to by running, along the Irwell's banks, drilling at the Racecourse and football at the John Lewis Recreation Ground. After each day's drill the men returned to their homes in Ordsall, Lower Broughton and Pendleton. Their presence in the trams and pubs which abounded served to support the recruitment of further groups of Pals into the Battalion. Some households prospered out of the home billeting arrangements. Each recruit into the Pals was paid one shilling a day together with a supplement of two shillings for food (whilst the battalion remained within Salford), making a weekly income of one guinea per week. It was luxury for some.

As the Borough was gripped by that fervour which was engulfing almost every northern town some men in the vicinity remained happy to join a local "Defence Corps". Out of their ranks many men would, however, subsequently enlist into the Salford Pals' Battalions. The Corps' organisation initially divided the borough into three areas, Salford, Pendleton and Broughton, within each of which men of "steady habits, trustworthy character and of good general health" intended to meet on a voluntary basis to prepare for their roles as special constables in the event of an "emergency"! The committee organisation was chaired by the borough's Chief Constable. A subscription of 2d a week was charged. The Salford section never succeeded in attracting support and quickly wound up its affairs, but the Pendleton section quickly enlisted 300 members, usually businessmen described as of "good class and standing".

Advertisement for 1st Salford Pals. Salford City Reporter 12/9/1914

SALFORD BATTALION
LORD KITCHENER'S ARMY,

Hon. Colonel, Right Hon. the EARL OF DERBY, K.G.
President, The MAYOR OF SALFORD.
Chairman of Committee, Mr. C. A. M. BARLOW, M.P.

LEAVE HAS BEEN GRANTED BY THE WAR OFFICE TO FORM A

Salford Battalion

IN LORD KITCHENER'S ARMY, PROVIDED THE NECESSARY NUMBER, VIZ.;

1,100 ARE ENROLLED.

WHEN THE BATTALION IS FORMED RE-CRUITS WILL BE ENTITLED TO FULL PAY OF 1s. A DAY, FROM THE DATE OF ATTES-TATION.

DURING FORMATION THE BATTALION WILL BE EQUIPPED AND WILL DRILL IN SALFORD, AND RECRUITS WILL BE ABLE TO SLEEP AT HOME, RECEIVING AN AL-LOWANCE IN PLACE OF RATIONS AT THE ARMY RATE, WHICH IS AT PRESENT 2s. A DAY. THIS IS IN ADDITION TO THE PAYMENT OF 1s. A DAY.

RECRUITS MUST STATE CLEARLY IF THEY WISH TO ENLIST FOR THE

SALFORD BATTALION.

RECRUITING STATION—

PENDLETON TOWN HALL.

'Pendleton Co-op Defence Corps 1914.' A rather defensive article in that week's Reporter pointed out that: 'A number of gentlemen in the Pendleton district have had the question of forming a Salford Volunteer Defence Corps, similar to that constituted in Manchester, before them, and in pursuance of the object a representative meeting of men was held in the Baptist Church, Nursery Street, Pendleton. Those present were composed of men precluded by age, family ties, business responsibilities and other satisfactory reasons from joining the regular forces. It was unanimously promised to form the nucleus of the corps for rifle practice, drill etc.' Salford City Reporter

Recruiting for Salford's Pals was boosted that Saturday afternoon, the 19th September, when Barlow organised a further drive at the Hippodrome Theatre where the first 150 men who had already been enlisted were assembled to form a guard of honour for Lord Newton from Lyme Hall in Disley. The Church was engaged to play a powerful role. Apart from Newton and the familiar array of political and military figures; Salford's Mayor, the local M.P.s and Councillors; Bishop Welldon, the Reverend Barry, the Reverend Cornibeer, the Reverend Thompson and the Reverend Hanson were all present to lend weight to the appeal, the Reverend Barry from the Broadway Docks Mission going as far as to describe the war as "a matter of religion. If ever there was a holy war, this was a holy war".

The enormous demands being made on the production of military woollen khaki at this time meant that none was available for what was

Two men from No. 2 Platoon, A Company. Sitting is Private William Bailey (10116), with Private John Howard[28] (10069) who were amongst the first day's recruits. Bailey

effectively a privately raised and run battalion, whose costs would only eventually, be underwritten by the War Office. At this time in September the War Office allowance to all municipal Raising Committees was £7 for the clothing and kit of each recruit. As with many other Pals' units the acquisition of articles of uniform and kit became a very tentative affair and it would be some months before the 1st Pals were fully equipped.

But arrangements were soon being placed in hand it was claimed,

> ... for the clothing and equipment to be proceeded with at once on a sealed pattern, which has been sent down by the War Office. The uniform presents a smart workmanlike appearance, consisting of a blue serge tunic, trousers, coat and cap, with regulation dress buttons and puttees.[29]

One example of the problems being faced by Barlow in trying to do the job of the War Office's procurement department was the acquisition of boots made to withstand the rigours of drilling and training. At this time, in the autumn of 1914, many disreputable and fraudulent suppliers were taking advantage of every Raiser's frustration and desperation. Montague Barlow explained his feelings towards these suppliers, and the difficulties he faced in supplying the Salford men with decent equipment.

> It is not only that the man is corrupt and defrauding the state, it means that many a good fellow's life may be sacrificed in consequence. Many a man on a long march, especially if it be a question of retreating under fire, may have to lag behind if his boots are defective, and that may mean the loss of his life. A much worse and stronger case could be made with regard to the supply of improper boots than anything else. May I just quote one instance which came under my own personal observation. Boots were supplied to a Battalion of which I have cognisance. They appeared to be excellent, they were passed by the local expert, and for them a high price was demanded. In appearance they were admirable boots. They were made of leather and looked charming. The only defect was that when they were put on the men's feet they would not hold together. The soles had a curious way of departing from the uppers – a practice which is not considered right in the best boot circles. After a good deal of struggle the contractor was forced to take the boots back. I cannot give their subsequent history, but a month or two later, a further supply of boots was required for the battalion, and they were ordered according to sample. The new contractor said he could not supply the whole 2,000 pairs according to sample, but 1,500 were coming along just as good as the sample, and the regiment would, he was sure, be quite satisfied. The 1,500 pairs were supplied in due course and they turned out to be a portion of the boots which had been rejected in the same warehouse for the same battalion.[30]

The only difference when the boots came around for the second time was that the price had risen by 1s 9d per pair!

The closeness of the community and the long standing influence of the Army and the Lads' Club within it ensured that the bulk of the Pals' recruits initially continued to come from the east of the Borough, around the docks, Cross Street and the heavily industrialised areas of Ordsall, Lower Broughton, Trinity and Regent.

The first to enlist in Salford's Pals were, therefore, men from the poorest parts of the borough. They had had plenty of time to think the issues through. Theirs was no thoughtless, headlong rush in response to one inspirational recruiting poster. The impoverishment which bedevilled the town's slums, the difficult personal economic circumstances caused by the casual and temporary nature of much of the town's employment, the long standing Army presence among the town's people, a compliant church, civic pride and a local press willing to print the distortions of popular war propaganda had all played their part.

Now it was becoming clear that the Town Hall at Pendleton, as the Battalion's headquarters, would become the natural centre of enlistment into these the 1st Salford Pals. Almost immediately, recruiting at the Lads' Club fell to a trickle.

Saturday 3rd October saw the first public appearance of the Pals on Salford's streets. Two contingents, each more than a hundred strong, marched to the Rugby matches being played at the

Pendleton Town Hall, 1914. (SLHL)

Broughton Rangers' ground and at Swinton. At the Broughton match the Mayor's well practised message was wielded again. At Swinton the crowd were spoken to by Montague Barlow whose prodigious efforts were now bearing real fruit. On their march back to Pendleton Town Hall both contingents were strengthened in the knowledge that more men would soon be enlisted.

During October A and B companies received 100 rifles per company for drilling purposes, but even by the end of the month only half of the men were equipped with their promised blue serge uniforms. These gradually turned out to be more practical than the worn and varied clothing in which many recruits preferred to be attired during their initial training. However "Kitchener Blue", as most people referred to the dark serge uniforms, was never popular with the men who now formed the 1st Pals, nor with their home community. The men hardly presented the confident appearance of being part of Lord Kitchener's Army! Regular appeals were made for socks and blankets to aid the men's comfort as autumn advanced. However, Salford's grim social circumstances continued to foster the steady recruiting figures. Since mid September the daily recruiting figures had been rising, lifting the average above 50 by early October. Since the last week in September the battalion's bugle band had been enlisting. In the hope of attracting boys from the Church Lads' Brigade's bands it was common knowledge that young men aged just 17 were being accepted.

Possible sites for the battalion's camp were being investigated at Rhyl and Conway.

Throughout this period Salford's unemployment continued to escalate. Jobs in the wharfs and warehouses of the Manchester Ship Canal Company had withered as trade not vital to the war's conduct collapsed. The numbers of children needing free dinners rose from five hundred to three thousand, some children needing an additional breakfast as well. Job losses and part time working were now commonplace among the middle classes who had previously thought of themselves as exempt.

By this time recruitment into Salford's Pals had become sufficiently well established to enable the Army to close the Lads' Club recruiting station that October 3rd. The seven week occupation of the buildings, during which the equivalent of almost two full battalions had enlisted there, resulted in a bill of £65 being sent to the War Office by the club treasurer for "expenses incurred through the occupation of the premises by the Military Authorities". From now on all enlistment in Salford was carried out in the Town Halls closely associated with the local Pals' units and their recruitment and esteem within the community benefited accordingly. By the 9th October the 1st Salford Battalion had over 850 recruits. 200 of them had even been issued with boots. Councillor Windsor, adroitly withdrawing from his earlier stance protesting "against the British nation being dragged into war", had been appointed "honorary adviser to the Battalion in regard to the contracts for the tents". It did not prove an arduous task. All accommodation at the forthcoming camp-site, now chosen for Conway, was being arranged in wooden huts.

The temptation to take advantage of the financial support, promised by employers, was overwhelming. Many of the men were enlisting in the belief that this would lead to an improvement in their family's economic wellbeing. In this atmosphere some of the recruits were prepared to make considerable personal sacrifice to get in. One of the oldest men to join the 1st Pals, Private William Campbell (10562)[31], had earlier been rejected during the period of general recruiting on account of his age. The problem had been overcome by a visit to the dentist's chair! Now equipped with a pearly set of new teeth, hair glinting under a proprietary darkener, he was duly enlisted into C Company, leaving his wife, six daughters and three sons to ponder why men were so enthused even at an age when they could safely, and without social stigma, have stayed at home.

On 10th October the bulk of the Battalion marched through the town, behind the South Salford Silver Band, to the Rugby match being played by Salford at their ground in Weaste. Again the men were paraded at half time and after the match active recruiting went on amongst the crowd who gathered in front of the stands to hear speeches by the Mayor and Captain Abercrombie.

On 19th October news broke in the town of the most extraordinary recruit to the Pals. That afternoon the Watch Committee heard an application from the Chief Constable of Salford to join the Pals. For some time he and Barlow had negotiated in secret, the outcome of which was an offer of a commission as a Major in the battalion. The committee acceded to his request and for his temporary replacement by a member of the Indian Civil Service, Mr J. A. Crawford from London. Cedric Godfrey was not without military experience having served in the Sherwood Foresters and later the Lancashire Fusiliers' Territorial battalions after his appointment as Chief Constable in July, 1909.

By 23rd October the battalion was nearing completion, with 1,074 men enrolled. Almost every man had boots and the battalion now possessed 400 rifles for drill purposes. C and D Companies had made their headquarters at Central Hall[32] on Broadway, next to the docks, where it was possible to get some shelter from the deteriorating weather. The Mayor's wife together with the daughter of the Liberal MP, Agnew, had by now collected 400 blankets and 100 pairs of socks for these men. It was the start of a long and sympathetic array of comforts provided for the men by their townsfolk.

On Sunday 25th October the 1st Pals, most of whose men were still without any uniforms, stepped out into a gale-lashed downpour to attend church parade. In front of only a tiny number of hardy souls A and B Companies left Broughton Town Hall behind the Salford Police Band. C and D Companies marched to the music of the South Salford Silver Band. The Catholic men went directly into the shelter of St. John's Cathedral, but the majority of men and officers attended at Christ Church where the service was given by the Reverend A.W. Thompson. Like many other churchmen in the borough his support for the pursuit of the war was reflected in his sermon, stressing the spiritual correctness of their purpose and the impossibility of compromise with what he saw as an essentially evil foe.

News of a contested election in the South Salford Parliamentary Constituency, appearing in the Salford City Record 17/10/1914 (SCR)

OCTOBER 17, 1914.

SOUTH SALFORD PARLIAMENTARY DIVISION.
The MEMBER & THE CANDIDATE.

MR. J. A. MONTAGUE BARLOW, M.P.   LIEUTENANT FRANCIS NORRIS,

Go forth from this place strengthened and resolved to fight not only your country's battles but the battles of the Lord against the world, the flesh and the devil, never disgracing your manhood, ever remembering that you are soldiers of the Cross, soldiers of the King of kings. Live for Him, and if needs be die for Him. Do the right, though the heavens fall and God bless you in doing it.[33]

The decision was now made by the Raising Committee to establish a further battalion. Even before the appearance of suitable advertising men were being recruited for the Second Pals, 100 by 30th October. The following day the football match between Eccles Borough and Northwich Victoria hosted a march by men from the now completed 1st Salford Pals, the 15th (Service) Lancashire Fusiliers[34]. After the game the crowd were treated to some well rehearsed recruiting by the Adjutant, Major Abercrombie, and Montague Barlow.

So, continued Mr Barlow, they had decided to form a Second Battalion, and it had been suggested that Eccles should form a 'Pals' company in connection with it. The 'Pals' would drill together, go to camp in North Wales together, and finally would take their places in the trenches side by side with the other gallant members of the gallant British Army (cheers)...[35]

The men who were moved by this challenge would become the First Eccles Pals (B Company, 16th Lancashire Fusiliers), with a special place in the hearts of that area. Three of this company's NCOs came from amongst the Eccles Co-operative Society's shop-workers, Sergeant A. Thompson (11972), Sergeant William Taylor (11532) and Sergeant Ben Broadhurst (11241)[36] who was an ex-member of the Pendleton Volunteer Defence Corps.

Lieutenant Thomas Tweed, transferred from the 1st Pals, was placed in charge of recruiting. Unlike many of his fellow officers though, Tweed was not a local man. He had been educated in Liverpool and graduated through the University's Officer Training Corps there. Interestingly he had been a member of the Police Specials during the Liverpool strikes and unrest of 1911, and had been injured whilst leading

An effective advertisement for the 2nd Salford Pals ... 'A Vacant Place for YOU' Salford City Record 7/11/1914 (SCR)

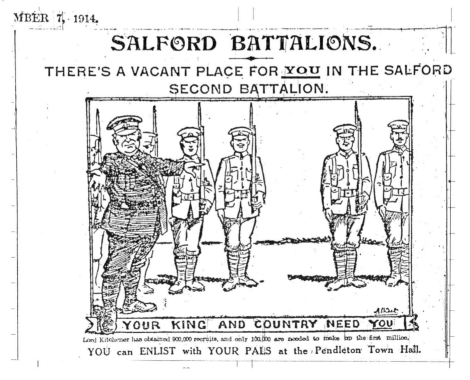

MBER 7, 1914.

SALFORD BATTALIONS.

THERE'S A VACANT PLACE FOR **YOU** IN THE SALFORD SECOND BATTALION.

YOUR KING AND COUNTRY NEED YOU

Lord Kitchener has obtained 900,000 recruits, and only 100,000 are needed to make up the first million.

YOU can ENLIST with YOUR PALS at the Pendleton Town Hall.

The Cliff, Higher Broughton, Manchester.

Although usually described as Manchester Racecourse, the tracks in the bend of the River Irwell just north of Salford were a favourite place of recreation for the townspeople before the war. During the period before the Pals' Battalions left Salford, the Racecourse, its slopes and open spaces became the natural location for the physical training of these men. (SLHL)

a baton charge against a group attacking a shop. Tom Mann's supporters, many of whom had recently been in his charge in the 1st Salfords, would certainly not have approved of Tweed's actions there. However, as Liberal Parliamentary Agent for the Eccles division since 1911, he was, at least in many working class minds, a political adversary of the Conservative Montague Barlow. Throughout the war Tweed would experience regular promotion, show extraordinary bravery and write a series of letters home, published in the Eccles and Patricroft Journal, under the pseudonym "Rien N'va Plus".

Friday 6th November was an important day for the 1st Pals. This was the Army's first formal look at the men who were, for the purposes of this day, divided into their companies at different locations around the area. Colonel Tudway, the Inspecting Officer, from Preston barracks, was accompanied on his route by Colonel Moss, Montague Barlow, Major Godfrey, Captain Stone and Sergeant Major Dunne, as well as Major Abercrombie on his last public appearance with the 1st Pals. At the Manchester Racecourse in Castle Irwell A and D Companies paraded. He saw the men worked in company, platoon and section drill before watching a small detachment with their rifles perform "musketry and skirmishing drills". He then proceeded to Broughton Town Hall where B Company was put through its paces. It would seem that Colonel Tudway was a little less happy here, "...at the close the Inspecting Officer spent some time in personally instructing the section commanders". His last port of call was the Lewis Recreation Ground to view C Company. They seemed to have passed the test with flying colours. "The inspecting officer was very favourably impressed with the appearance of the men and the manner in which they executed the different movements."

Overall the impression left was good, and Salford relaxed in the knowledge that its 1st Pals were deemed to be up to scratch by the Army.

The 2nd Salford Pals' Battalion was raised on the 5th November, their headquarters being established in Broughton Town Hall. Two of this battalion's companies were associated with close knit communities on the outskirts of Salford, one coming from Eccles and a further company, primarily from Swinton, Pendlebury and Clifton on the west of the Borough. This second area was home to many men who worked the Knowles' pits at Clifton Hall and Agecroft and the composition of the company was mostly miners and colliery employees. Major Abercrombie was promoted from his post with the 1st Pals to become the first commanding officer of the 2nd Pals. Before the end of the first fortnight in November his organisation had already enrolled 600 men into the battalion, including 150 into the Eccles' Company of whom 20 men were "poached" from the Eccles Athletes' Volunteer Force.

The first few of these men from the Eccles area were examined at the home of the local Medical Officer of Health, Dr. Hamilton, in Ellesmere Park, just north of Eccles' town centre. Undressing in the guest room they were treated to a very substantial and free supply of cigarettes which were gone in no time. The formal enlistment was undertaken at the Eccles Drill Hall in Cromwell Road. One of the men who enlisted here was Frank Holding. Like many of his contemporaries the thrill of participation far outweighed any considerations of age. Frank falsified his birth date as 1895 rather than the reality of 1897.

By now Salford's Raising Committee was appealing directly to the public for supplements to the War Office's very prescriptive kit and uniform allowances. The original £7 allowance was now inadequate and had to be raised, in line with the demand-driven price increases which now affected military clothing and stores material. By mid November the figure had risen to £8.15s.0d per man. A Guarantee Fund was established under the control of Alderman Frankenberg whose purpose it was to ensure fully adequate provisions of kit and medical care to the men whilst they awaited being taken over by the War Office. Very substantial donations to this fund, of £100 each, were given by local industrialist Sir William Mather and by Sir George Agnew, M.P.. In keeping with the values of the Edwardian era patrons of the organisation provided the instruments for the first two battalions' bands. Barlow himself paid for and donated the silver-plated bugles, whilst the rest of the Pals' instruments were paid for by Mr J.E.C. Lord, another member of the Raising Committee, at a cost of £70.

The indefatigable Montague Barlow and his committee had by now concluded the preliminary arrangements with Conway Corporation to establish a hutted camp at Morfa. Work had been put out to tender and a consortium of four firms[37], including the constructors of the Manchester Pals' camp at Heaton Park, were selected to carry out the work. On the 14th October Barlow and Colonel Moss had travelled to Conway and concluded those arrangements, much to the satisfaction of the people of the area who anticipated an influx of work and money to precede the soldiers. By the start of November

Frank Holding, one of the original Eccles Pals, B Company, 16th Lancashire Fusiliers, soon after he had enlisted in 1914. Looms And Frank Holding in 1989: "I went right through the war and never got a scratch."

construction was under way and it was anticipated that the felt covered wooden huts would be completed within three weeks.

On Tuesday 17th November Lord Derby himself, along with the Mayor, Lord Newton and Montague Barlow, spoke at one of the largest recruiting meetings held at the Hippodrome Theatre. By now any pretence at all of party participation in the recruitment process was over. Open hostility existed between Barlow and the Liberal M.P., Sir William Byles. Certainly Byles' manner and correctness was not suited to the turbulent methods which Barlow preferred to employ. Indeed Byles had, throughout the previous three months, taken stands against censorship and the sorts of distortions and lies, common in the press, which all too often originated in Barlow's recruiting speeches. Byles now alleged that Barlow was deliberately manipulating the process for party and personal gratification.

> I have remonstrated privately with Mr Barlow for not inviting me to the meeting, and I must now protest publicly against his attempt to ignore his colleagues in the representation of the borough and to twist this national effort to his party advantage. For example, though he never even informed me, the Member for the Division, that such a meeting was called, he made a special effort to get the presence on the platform of my respected opponent.
>
> [The] Joint Parliamentary Recruiting Committee ... has been completely set aside in Salford, and meetings have been called and managed entirely by the one Conservative Member for the Borough. I acknowledge, and have always recognised, that Mr. Barlow has done valuable service in Salford for the cause of recruiting; but he has no right to ignore his colleagues that the limelight may centre upon himself.[38]

However, the meeting, and the prestige which Derby brought to it, certainly added to the speed with which the battalion was completed. By the end of the month the Reporter let its readership know that,

> It is expected that the recruiting for the battalion will close today (Saturday) and that the remaining sixty men to complete the full strength will have been secured. This is very satisfactory indeed, as formal leave to raise the battalion was only granted to Mr Montague Barlow, M.P. on November 2. The rate of enlistment has been on average 30 to 35 per day. The question of raising a third battalion was considered at a meeting of the committee on Wednesday last, at which the Mayor (Alderman Worsley) was present. In this matter a difficulty has arisen owing

Soldiers of a Lancashire Fusiliers' Reserve Company engaged in the Swedish Drill. Author

to the fact that the War Office have refused to grant leave at present for the building of another hut camp...

Less than 40 men are now required to complete the Eccles' company of the 2nd Salford Battalion. Up to yesterday over 220 had been enrolled, and it is probable that the Battalion will be at full strength this weekend. Local men who are thinking of joining their pals must enlist at once to obtain a place in the company, which will be filled up from Salford recruits as soon as other companies are full. Each day the company is drilled at the Patricroft Drill Hall, or on the land adjoining the hospital, and the Swedish drill has already had a very noticeable effect on the appearance of the men.'[39]

As was the case with the 15th Lancashire Fusiliers, many of the 16th's junior officers were drawn from Manchester Grammar School O.T.C., the University O.T.C., and the University and Public Schools' Battalions, then in training at Epsom and Leatherhead.[40]

Mr. Mumford, who has been nominated as lieutenant, was with the Manchester Grammar School Officer Training Corps as adjutant... Mr Sidney Crossley, who has been nominated as second lieutenant, was for six years in the Manchester Regiment as private, and is now a platoon commander in the University and Public Schools Battalion at Leatherhead...' Second lieutenant J.S. Morgan was three years with the Manchester University O.T.C. and is also a platoon commander in the University and Public Schools' Battalion at Leatherhead.[41]

It was now, by the end of November, becoming clear that Salford had done far more than could reasonably have been expected from a town of its size. The seeds of a catastrophic disaster for the community had been germinated. The area had already given up many of its young men to the profusion of distant units who found the mean streets a prolific area within which to recruit. Yet now, as 1914 drew to a close, four further locally raised battalions, two Territorial and two Pals, would be making arrangements to leave the town, or had already left.

Montague Barlow could be well pleased with his work. However, he was not content to rest on his laurels and Barlow applied for, and was given, a commission with the rank of Major in one of the Lancashire Fusiliers' Territorial Battalions. Events, however, overtook him.

The fact was that still more extraordinary and willing enlistment was still waiting in the wings. Having equalled the record of many larger cities throughout the country, Salford now took stock before gearing itself to surpass all expectations.

This period, at the close of 1914, marked a lull in the recruitment of Salford's Brigade. Soldiers in the 1st and 2nd Pals worked on section, platoon and company drill, close order, extended order, route marches and fitness but more than ever wanted the freedom of open space to begin the real matter of battalion training. Their route marches across the rough sets with which the streets were paved were hard. When one company boasted a sixteen mile march through Salford and Manchester's streets, without one man falling out, that was no mean achievement.

The Morfa camp at Conway was nearly completed. In advance of the Battalion's expected departure the Sergeants of the 1st Pals held a smoker in the Griffin, the landlord of which, Mr Walmsley, had never seen the like in terms of attendance. The Commanding Officer of the battalion, Lieutenant Colonel Moss, Major Abercrombie as Commanding Officer of the 2nd Pals, the recently resigned Chief Constable of Police, Members of Parliament and the full complement of officers and sergeants. Entertainments included a song or rendition from each sergeant, pianoforte selections from Lieutenant Mandleberg, songs from local personalities and members of Dramatic Societies, a multiplicity of toasts, patriotic songs, speeches and responses.

Elsewhere, in the many smaller pubs which marked almost every street corner, smaller, less ostentatious, parties were marking the last weeks of the 1st and 2nd Salford Pals' presence within their community. 1914's Christmas parties were second to none in the town's history. Fortunately the Sunday Church Parades which featured regularly in the Pals' schedule during December were fixed for after dinner-time. Throughout numerous sermons Vicars lost no time in expressing their hopes, and fears, about the men's character and behaviour, often portraying them as Salford's representatives carrying the town's reputation with them. Drink, foul language and the corruption of the young men in the Battalion were seen as issues which could sour Salford's esteem amongst the population of Conway. As the pace

Men of the Royal Fusiliers University and Public Schools' Battalions, including men who would become officers with the 15th and 16th Lancashire Fusiliers. This photograph taken on October 13th, 1914, shows the King's inspection, when he was accompanied by Brigadier General R. Gordon Gilmour, taking place at Epsom Racecourse. This photograph was sent to friends by Edgar Lord, himself amongst the men and soon to be gazetted as a 2nd Lieutenant into the Lancashire Fusiliers. Like so many other UPS men, Lord was an ex-Manchester Grammar School student whose talent and ability soon ensured that the UPS' battalions would lose many thousands of recruits to commissions in other Regiments. Manchester and its surrounding areas had been particularly successful as a recruitment area for the UPS and large numbers formed the basis of the 20th Battalion of the Royal Fusiliers, the third of the four UPS' battalions. Wilcock

of preparation quickened Abercrombie's administrative responsibilities meant that Major Godfrey was often seen commanding the men, keeping a fatherly eye on their progress.

His men of course were proud that their Battalion was associated with a prominent local figure. One private in the 1st Pals discovered this feeling of belonging when he was able to provide a suitable defence when arrested for being drunk and disorderly and acting in an illegal capacity as tout and runner for bookmakers operating on the corner of Cross Lane and Regent Road. Alleging that the arresting plain clothes police officer "threatened me what he would do for me sooner or later" and that the charges against him had been fabricated in direct contradiction of witnesses' statements, the man had written to the paper in an attempt to clear his name and that of the battalion.

> *I have been a member of the Salford Battalion for eleven weeks, and we do our drills every day, except Sunday, which does not give me time to be touting for bookmakers. Before joining the Salford Battalion I worked for a gentleman (since last December) and was away in different parts of England. Previous to that I was employed by the Manchester Ship Canal Company as a delivery clerk, so that I cannot see how it would be possible for me to be shouting Hi, Hi! and touting for bookmakers as he says.*
>
> *Not satisfied with doing me all the harm he could in civilian life he states that I said Mr Godfrey was my so and so boss and not him, a statement for which I could be made to suffer if it were true (Mr Godfrey is an officer of my own Battalion). The witness for the police, whom I cross-questioned in the witness box said, after I had asked him if he thought I was drunk. No, he did not think I was. I also asked him if he saw a bottle in my possession, and he said No, and also that he did not hear me use obscene language. I seemed quiet enough whilst being taken to the police station. In conclusion I would like if you think it worth publication to use this letter as you think fit, and am also at your service whenever you want me. – I am &c., MERELY A COMMON SOLDIER. Salford, December 10.*

On 8th December a small party of 23 men, under command of Lieutenant Robert Smith, rather reluctant to depart and equally reluctant to be still dressed in Kitchener Blues, had arrived in billets at Conway to help in the final preparation of the Morfa site and the receiving of stores material. There they found that the electrical system was posing problems to the contractors, who were also being taxed by the need to rebuild the recreation hut, recently demolished by a violent storm.

In Salford last minute preparations included the raising of £125 to finance the purchase of 2,500 woollen balaclava helmets for the men about to depart, which would soon be added to the vast stock of equipment held at the Mandleberg warehouse on Cobden Street off Broughton Road.

During the third week of December the kit available for each man was now almost complete, including three shirts, three pairs of socks, woollen underwear, cardigan jacket, braces, towels, holdall, razor, brush, clasp knife, sewing kit, haversacks, belts, pouches, entrenching tools and caps. Also in store were huge quantities of woollen khaki, ready to be made up into greatcoats, and stocks of boots. Within this Aladdin's cave of material Montague Barlow was to be found every day, arranging contracts, pestering suppliers and directing the equipping of his battalions.

On Monday afternoon at 3 o'clock, three days after their last Christmas in Salford, the First Salfords were inspected by their Honorary Colonel, Lord Derby, at the Racecourse. Apart from the Reserve Company all the men were now dressed in blue serge. Having addressed these men Derby moved on to see the Second Battalion, still kitted in a rather worn array of civilian dress, at the Lewis Recreation Ground.

Tactfully he complimented both battalions on their appearance. That evening the men of the 1st Pals collected their kit from Mandleberg's warehouse, off Broughton Road.

Within 24 hours the 15th Lancashire Fusiliers, under the leadership of Colonel Moss, were ready to depart. The men of A and B Companies were drawn up in parade order within the confines of the Cross Lane Barracks, under command of Colonel Moss and the Adjutant, Captain Best. Unfortunately there was insufficient room to admit any of the men's families. That morning, in front of the many members

E Company, Platoon XIX, 1st Pals. Part of the last group of men to enlist into the original 1st Pals, before drilling, training and uniforms had an opportunity to transform their appearance. Photographed on 17th December at the Racecourse. Page 45, 'Salford Brigade'

Recruits of the Old Public Schools' (Manchester) Battalion. Just one of the many units raised within a stone's throw of Salford. A number of these men later returned to form the nucleus of the Salford Pals' Officers. Manchester Guardian 11/10/1914

of the Civic Authorities who had helped establish the battalion, and their raiser Montague Barlow, each man was told by the Mayor of his confidence that they would uphold the honour of the town at the front. A and B Company's march on the short distance from the barracks to the station was then conducted amidst a tumultuous outburst of good will and enthusiasm. But this was dwarfed by the scenes at the Town Hall in Bexley Square where the other two Companies were given a civic send off amidst the huge numbers of onlookers who could gather round. The battalion departed, as the two separate contingents, from Cross Lane station, one at 10.00, the second at 11.00 a.m. Once settled in the confines of their crowded trains however, few men had time to ponder on the significance of the Mayor's words or wishes.

The first stage in their terrible and tragic journey was underway.

Notes
1. Hermann Hesse. *Demian.* (1919) Chapter 6. pp 106, Granada Publishing Ltd. 1969.
2. M.O.H's Reports, Eccles and Salford. 1910–1914. By 1915 death rates in the central districts of Regent, Islington and Trinity were even higher, at 29.1, 32 and 29.8 per thousand, per annum, respectively.
3. The nearby Clifton Hall Colliery had been the scene of one of the region's worst accidents when 178 men and boys were killed in an explosion on June 18, 1885.
4. A revolutionary theory that Capitalism could be overthrown by industrial action, without Parliamentary activity. These ideas were propagated in a journal, The Syndicalist, first published in January, 1912.
5. George Peake. Interview.
6. Ibid.
7. See The 42nd Division. 1914–1918. Frederick Gibbon. Country Life Library. The Helles memorial at Gallipoli records the hugely disproportionate cost born by Salford, in terms of men killed, during that ill fated campaign.
8. Précis of George Ebury's speech (Sunday 26/7/1914) quoted in Salford City Reporter (S.C.R.) 1/8/1914.
9. S.C.R. 8/8/1914.

10. Ibid.
11. Alderman Desquesnes, quoted in S.C.R. 8/8/1914.
12. Corporal Jack Winstanley (10264) was amongst one of the first to enlist, in September 1914, into Salford's 1st Pals.
13. S.C.R. 8/8/1914.
14. Councillor A. Williamson. Friday 7th August, 1914.
15. Précis of speech by Montague Barlow on 7th August, quoted in S.C.R. 15/8/1914.
16. S.C.R. 29/8/1914.
17. Ibid.
18. Location of Manchester's huge Victorian Town Hall and scenes of huge enthusiasm once that City had established their own Pals' Battalions.
19. Located at Pendleton Town Hall, the Salford Lads' Club and at Cross Lane Barracks' Drill Hall.
20. S.C.R. 5/9/1914.
21. Alderman Desquesnes. 3/9/1914.
22. The Bishop of the Manchester Diocese. Bishop Welldon's sermons set the tone for many local clergy who provided constant support to the area's recruitment and its local battalions.
23. Manchester Guardian. 10/9/1914.
24. S.C.R. 12/9/1914.
25. See Manchester Guardian. Wednesday September 9th, 1914. Recruiting for the New Army...War Office Organisation Overwhelmed.
26. Manchester Guardian. 9/9/1914.
27. S.C.R. 12/9/1914.
28. Killed in Action, 1/7/1916.
29. S.C.R. 19/9/1914.
30. Montague Barlow's speech to the House of Commons during the Timber procurement debate, 4/3/1915. (Hansard, columns 1056–1057.)
31. William Campbell was Killed in Action, 1/7/1916.
32. Provided by the Reverend Barry and the committee of the Broadway Mission.
33. Reverend Thompson. Sermon at Christ Church, Salford. 25/10/1914.
34. Recruitment then started for the Reserve Company, the first 'Swinton Pals' . Given regimental numbers mostly in the 13000s these men were later drafted to many units scattered around the first three Salford Pals' Battalions, becoming the focus of much discontent that they had been split up from their friends, against the spirit upon which the company had been raised.
35. S.C.R. 7/11/1914.
36. Sergeants Broadhurst and Taylor were Killed in Action, 1/7/1916.
37. Peace and Norquoy, and Tinker and Young from Manchester, Garrard and Sons of Swinton and Cromwells of Liverpool.
38. Sir William Byles' letter to the S.C.R. 21/11/1914. Attached was the text of a further letter, to the Earl of Derby, which Barlow had omitted to read at Tuesday's meeting!
39. S.C.R. 28/11/1914.
40. See S.C.R. 26/12/1914 for names and background of many 2nd Pals' officers prior to departure to Conway.
41. S.C.R. 28/11/1914.
42. For a list of 1st Pals' officers accompanying the men to Conway see Salford Chronicle. 2/1/1916.

All the lads' clubs in Salford ran inter-club boxing tournaments. Here John Howard (left) spars up with Richard Johnson (right) both members of the 15th Lancashire Fusiliers (1st Pals).

Chapter Two

Them Bloomin' Hills

All men became as brothers. They thought it was patriotism and honour, but it was destiny into whose unveiled face they were all momentarily allowed to glance.[1]

The arrival of the 1st Pals in Conway marked a change for the men. Gone was the familiarity of evening meals at home and training at the Racecourse, along the banks of the Irwell, where weeks earlier they had been entertained, played football and walked out with friends and sweethearts. Here the reality was more ordered and severe. Alongside the encampment lay a railway siding, behind which steeply rising ground led away towards the North Wales hills and Snowdonia. In front of their felt clad wooden huts a view across the sandy flats stretched away towards the Irish Sea. The Morfa site was very open and exposed to all of the weather's vagaries, which for the next two months were relentlessly wet and cold, often shrouding the Great Orme headland to the north of Llandudno bay in low cloud.

In all sorts of ways these men's experience provided a better preparation than that undertaken by some of the other New Army battalions. The Morfa site included further huts under construction for the reserve companies and the Second Salford Battalion, a large hut for the YMCA, bath and shower facilities for up to 40 men at a time and a gas powered generator for the electrical lighting inside each of the wooden quarters which housed 30 men. Canteens, recreation rooms and NCOs' offices ensured that most needs were catered for. Outside space allowed for parade and drill, extended manoeuvres and ample rifle range facilities.

The Raising Committee were proud of the fact that their men's encampment had been constructed at considerably less cost than that allowed by the War Office. In a debate in the House of Commons on

Conway Castle and the road bridge. Author's Collection

War Office procurement policy, held in early March, Montague Barlow claimed that collusion between the firms recommended by the War Office would have resulted in profiteering on a grand scale, since,

> Those who were on the War Office list, by some very curious coincidence, tendered at a price which was within £2 of one another. Those off the War Office list put in perfectly proper tenders, which differed largely in amount, and I was enabled to get the work done at between 30 per cent and 40 per cent below the amount asked by the contractors on the War Office list. The coincidence was a curious one.[2]

On Tuesday 29th December two trains had delivered the men of the 15th (Service) Battalion of the Lancashire Fusiliers to Conway. The whole of this part of the North Wales coast had begun to fill with

Postcards showing 15th LFs' huts on the Morfa.

thousands of Kitchener's men. On the same day as the first Salfords arrived, eleven hundred men from the Gwent and Cardiff Battalions were billeted at Colwyn Bay. Thousands who turned out on the streets of Conway to welcome the Salford Pals were disappointed to discover that the trains from Salford deposited their men at the Morfa and not at the town's station as expected. Nevertheless, a civic welcome by the Mayor, members of the Council and local churches was arranged. The men listened, perhaps with some apprehension, as the Reverend David Davies described the Morfa as a fine training ground, but considered its climate to have 'boisterous weather'.

Local people had already showed considerable kindness. The Salford men soon discovered that,

> ... with the kind aid of friends and others, a full sized billiard table by Burroughs & Watts, piano by Brinsmead & Sons, and a large quantity of games and books have been placed in the Recreation Room at the Morfa camp.[3]

This was no bad thing. In truth the town and coast presented a forbidding face in mid winter.

The men were roused the following day at 6 o'clock. The routine was quickly established. Parade at 6.45. Then followed an ever expanding repertoire of running, drill and route marches.

In Salford the 2nd Pals were rapidly catching up in terms of their preparation. On Monday 4th January the Army made its formal inspection of the men at the Castle Irwell Racecourse. Brigadier General Thuillier[4] from Chester walked down the ranks of the 1st Pals' E Company, and of the 1,152 men of the 2nd Pals, drawn up in front of the stands. There was real pride in the town that these men had been raised so quickly in under a month's recruiting. This battalion also had the benefit of three Regular NCOs, who had been in India with the 1st Lancashire Fusiliers before the outbreak of war, Sergeant-Major McCann[5], Company Sergeant-Major Hargreaves (7667) and Company Quartermaster-Sergeant Greenhough (7174). Under their direction the 2nd Pals had established a reputation as the smartest and keenest group seen around the town. As with the 1st Pals the 2nd's companies drilled in separate locations; A at the Racecourse, B at Eccles' Drill Hall, C at the Tramways depot, D at Tenerife Street in Broughton and E at the Cross Lane Barracks. E Company, known locally as the Swinton and Pendlebury Pals, consisted almost entirely of miners from the Agecroft and Pendleton Collieries.

During January Major Abercrombie's rank as commanding officer to the 2nd Pals was upgraded, he being promoted to Lieutenant Colonel. His battalion's accommodation, in the extra 48 huts being built

Some of the 1st Salford Battalion at Conway, still dressed in their blue serge uniforms. January 1915. SLHL

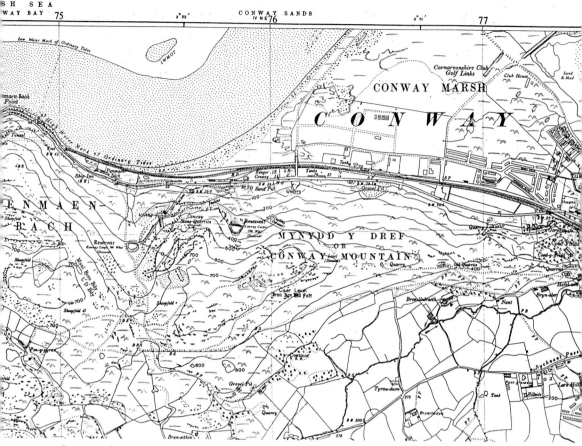

Morfa site. Ordnance Survey sheet, edition of 1915. Lewis

by Garrard and Sons of Swinton, was almost completed. Every man was subjected to a final medical in preparation for their departure from the town.

At Conway, as the 1st Pals' training gathered momentum through the dull days of winter, the chance came to ponder on the nature of the weather in France as the men did their best to keep warm in an inhospitable climate. It was sufficiently severe at the start of February, in fact, to destroy windows and rip roofs from the kitchens and Officers' Mess in the camp for the 2nd Pals which was, by then, nearing

Brigadier General Thuillier. Brigade Staff Group, Salford Brigade

The first to enlist in the borough's Civic Battalions. No. 1 Platoon, 15th LFs. Conway. Pawson

completion. Fortunately the sandy location was as suitable for the purpose of a camp as anywhere. The areas around each hut remained passable during wet weather, in stark contrast to the Manchester Pals' experiences at Heaton Park, where impervious rock, Manchester's notorious winter climate and heavy soil had given rise to a quagmire of filthy mud. Consequently most of the Salford men pronounced themselves well pleased with Montague Barlow's choice and reports continued to filter home of pleasant life at the seaside.

Those less delighted appeared before Mr P. W. Atkin, Salford's Stipendiary Magistrate! In the last week of January he dealt with 14 cases of men being absent without leave from the 1st Pals; 6 from Pendleton, 5 from Salford, 2 from Broughton and 1 from Manchester. In each case the men were held in cells to await escort back to Conway.

A further significant problem was that only a minority of men had weapons of any sort! Morfa's rifle ranges were silent. Battle training was done, with the few Canadian Ross pattern rifles available, in trenches which began to proliferate behind the camp on the slopes behind the quarry and the Hadley Holiday Home and in the open spaces around the town. The machine gun sections used wooden mock ups with football rattles to make an appropriate level of noise. Mobile night assaults in the open country of the Mynydd Y Dref completed the picture of 'training' which bore little, if any, resemblance to the reality already established in France. There was no doubt that the men had soon acquired an esprit de corps and were physically fit and hardened, but their military preparation in no way gave them an understanding of what to expect when they went to war for real.

Within a month of their arrival, the local paper had quite taken to the men from Salford.

> *'You've got to march till you're beat, and then double till you're bursting, and then march again and double again up them bloomin' hills that always go up and never down,' said one, and he ended with the pious wish that the Germans for their sins would spend eternity manoeuvering over the Welsh mountains.*
>
> *But it counts. The cold wind that blows from the bay does not seem to hurt them, and the muscles of their thighs are as tough as green ash. Except that Conway is a place of few amusements, they have no grievances, and the parson's stories in the canteen help to pass the evenings.*
>
> *There is nothing else to do except their business, and for all the world the battalion is like a university reading party or a Fabian school. These indefatigable embryo soldiers turn from drill to marching and from marching to another kind of drill, and then to night attacks, and in case they should get stiff in the joints they fill up the few intervals with gentle exercise at football.[6]*

Officers and men of 1st Pals at Conway, practising the arts of trench construction in the sunshine of spring 1915. Walker/Pawson

The Signallers of the 1st Pals. Jones

Small wonder that the men slept well. From the road which ran past the huts,

> The bass strings of the orchestra vibrate like stage thunder, and the wind that whistles over the dunes does not exceed in quality or shrillness the notes of the battalion's upper register.
>
> Enlistment is the finest cure for sleeplessness that ever was invented, and the words of one may show the contentment of the men: 'No,' he said. 'I don't want nothing else. There's good food and good fellows here, and plenty to be doing in the open air, and if it's sometimes cold on parade it's warm in the canteen, and one can sleep o' nights without worry and rise up in the morning without care. Only I hope the war won't be finished before we get a smack at them.'[7]

And the recruiting sergeant's encouragement of 'meat every day', which had been such a powerful inducement to many, had proved no idle boast. Colonel Moss' written reports to the Lord Mayor stated

Trenches in Maes-Y-Porth Gardens. 1st Pals. This etching made in the spring of 1915 gives a somewhat romanticised portrayal, to say the least! Lewis

that the men had so much to eat that 'they did not know where to put themselves'! Nor were they short of an after dinner smoke. At the Hare and Hounds in Pendleton the landlord's daughters, Sara and Gertie Perry, had affixed a collecting box to the wall of the bar. It bore the legend, 'Tabs for Tommies'. One postcard, written in thanks by Sergeant-Major Dunne, said simply, "Many thanks for your kindness in thinking of us: we all smoked your health in B Company on Sunday".

In spite of the tabs, the contrast with the unhealthy pallor induced by Salford's foul air was already apparent, especially when the Conway men, home on short leaves, were seen on the streets of Pendleton and Salford.

The 2nd Pals' Departure from Salford

It was Thursday 11th February when Salford said goodbye to this favourite group of sons.

In the still darkness before dawn the men of the 2nd Salford Pals had left their own homes, meeting up with friends before assembling at their respective company headquarters before 8.00 a.m. From there the men marched on towards the Lewis Recreation Ground for the last time. During these early hours few people saw the stirrings of the great body of soldiers, apart from numerous children fascinated by the sight of the men now fully kitted in their khaki uniforms, the issue of which had been completed the previous evening. From the Recreation Ground the men had marched through Peel Park and down the Crescent behind the Borough's mounted police and their own bugle band, to be met at the Town Hall by Montague Barlow, the Mayors of Salford and Eccles and an enormous crowd of well wishers. The Mayor's words to the completed battalion in Bexley Square had already been heard by the 1st Salfords and would be repeated a further five times as more drafts and battalions left the community.

> *You are now to proceed to Conway to take up the more severe duties of life in camp. From there in due course, if the war is not over, you will proceed, I suppose, to the Continent, and there, I know you will remember the great traditions of the British Army for courage and for valour, and*

No. 3 Platoon of the 1st Pals, soon after their arrival at Conway, still dressed in their Kitchener Blues. Bailey

No. 1 Platoon's bridge is completed across a rather dry stream-bed at the Morfa. Bailey

> *I know very well that Salford men and Eccles men and Swinton and Pendlebury men will do nothing to sully the flag of Great Britain. I am quite sure of that. Remember this that you have got the honour of Salford, Eccles and Swinton in your hands... We wish you good luck and every success. Don't forget that while you are away the people of Salford will constantly remember you and watch your career from day to day.*[8]

Well practised they might have been, but sincere and well meant for all to hear. Men listened and prepared to march in the town for the last time.

After this speech and the thanks expressed by Lieutenant Colonel Abercrombie the Battalion marched past the people thronging the streets around the Town Hall. These men were the Borough's pride and it showed. As the companies marched through the crowded confines of Bexley Square and away, through a Salford awash with colour, union jacks and singing which scarcely covered the regret and sorrow which simmered in the hearts of the town's people,

> *Round after round of applause burst forth as section after section passed in front of the Town Hall in a seemingly endless procession, and the spectators realised the significance of the Second Battalion as a fighting unit as they had never done before. The men were in new uniforms of khaki and no fear of partiality could justify the withholding of the opinion that they really presented a splendid appearance. Three months ago they were citizens with perhaps nothing to identify them specially for the military calling than a liberal show of patriotic spirit, but training has worked wonders in*

Bexley Square and Salford's Town Hall. As it was just before the war. SLHL

their appearance and now no-one could mistake them for anything but what they are – soldiers who, with a little more training and instruction in the use of the rifle, will be a more than useful addition to the fighting line when the time comes.[9]

One of the sights to arouse interest was a fine bloodhound, Bruce, destined to stay with the Battalion as mascot for more than two years. He had been presented to the men by a Mr Howarth of Pendlebury, and trained in the arts of tracking by a local breeder, Colonel Richardson. The dog's collar bore the Regimental number 15095. Also marching along were a number of company mascots including a bull dog and 'Cinders', a white terrier in the care of James Croft.

Back down the Crescent and along Cross Street they marched to the station. There was no police band for this Battalion's departure, far too many policemen had joined C Company of the 2nd Salfords to leave a worthwhile band, but the men sang out 'Its a long way to Tipperary' dozens of times as they wove their way through throngs of wives, children, friends, relatives and old soldiers who saluted. Personal greetings and goodbyes abounded, such as was consistent with some discipline, but everyone knew this was the real leave-taking of the finest the town knew and many men had to show fortitude to keep back the tears.

Some of these soldiers knew they were leaving wives and children who would not now find it easy to keep the bailiffs away.

Kirkham Street, off the Regent Road area of Salford. Sampson

This time three trains were assembled since the party totalled close on 1,700 men, made up of 1,350 from the Second Battalion, E Company of the First Battalion and a draft of 70 men, still dressed in civvies, ready to fill any vacancies.

> *[The] street was crowded with a dense mass of people mainly composed of relatives and friends who were anxious to convey to them final messages of farewell. Pathetic incidents were inseparable from such an occasion, but everyone prepared to put the bravest side on the matter and the troops could hardly have taken their departure under more cheerful auspices.*[10]

B, C, D and E Companies waited in the Drill Hall whilst A Company and the reserve company of the 1st Pals were entrained from the sidings in Windsor Street, beneath the Corporation Gas Work's towering gasometers and alongside the Egerton Iron Works. It was an appropriately industrial setting for the departure of a Pals' battalion whose whole upbringing had been within sight of such circumstances. The first men departed at 10.00 a.m. Within minutes the remaining companies were brought out and the police on duty had a difficult time preventing the crowds from pushing their way on to the railway sidings.

These further groups left on trains at 11 a.m. and 11.45. By midday it was all over. Now it was clear to everyone who witnessed their leaving that a formidable group of men had been given life by the Borough's households. But the collective contact was lost and all that the community could do now was wait.

Once their new huts were occupied and kit issued, the men flooded into Conway that evening, determined to forget the sorrow of leaving home. Clusters of friends who had been parted for weeks now met again, in high spirits and singing to the accompaniment of dozens of tin whistles and melodeons.

As their friends before had discovered, these men soon found that life at the Morfa was a world apart from the daily marches across town to the Broughton Town Hall headquarters of the 2nd Pals, now a distant memory!

The 2nd Salford Pals' camp.

> *Reveille was at 6.00 a. m., when we got coffee and biscuits and then we had to run to the top of the mountains behind the camp. The last two back to the camp were always given dirty fatigues so you made sure you weren't the last!* Pte. Frank Holding.

The Mynydd Y Dref hill was certainly run many thousands of times. Sometimes the fatigues and chores were the opportunity for light hearted relief outside the wooden hutments.

The Military organisation even allowed for the continued religious and moral education of the younger soldiers amongst the camp's inmates. These sessions were established after a visit by the curate of St. Michael's Church, who had arrived to see men of the 2nd Pals.

The Eccles Pals, potato peeling with bayonets. A very informal pose. The man in the centre, with the pipe, is Private (later Sergeant) Charlie Richmond, one of the minority of men from this group to survive the war.
Lewis

No. 5. platoon. 16th LFs. Conway. Many of the same men in more formal pose! The man holding the white dog, Cinders, is Corporal (later Sergeant Major) James Croft. Pawson

> *Well he arrived at camp on a Saturday morning, just after we'd been paid. He came over to our hut and knocked on the door. Well, no-one ever knocked so we wondered who it was. I was with a rum crowd in that hut and they told the knocker in no uncertain terms what to do. So the curate just walked in to find four or five card schools going strong. Pte. Frank Holding.*

Dressed only in vest and trousers the young Frank Holding extended an embarrassed welcome to the curate and later showed him around the camp's facilities. The curate was impressed by the need for action. As a later consequence, the Battalion's Chaplain, the Reverend Farnworth who had been the curate at St. Thomas' Church in Pendleton, began to organise confirmation classes behind a screen in the YMCA hut. Before leaving the Morfa, Frank and 23 other members of the Pals were confirmed in the camp's chapel by the Bishop of Bangor. The link with Pendleton Church was furthered when the congregation there bought a Communion Service for use by the Battalions at Conway. This was no mere gesture. The YMCA hut at Conway was extended by 50 feet in length, during February, to accommodate the increased numbers of men who wanted to attend the Reverend Farnworth's services together with the variety of musical recreations also on offer to while away damp February evenings. A further

Lieutenant Colonel Abercrombie. Destined to become the longest serving of all the Salford Pals' Battalions' commanding officers. Barnes

54

measure of its importance was the estimate of 20,000 letters having been sent from its confines and '300 pledges against intemperance and gambling made'.

During March the weather at last turned and the camp's advantage as a sports ground became apparent. Two football pitches were laid out parallel to the railway embankment. The Pals contained a double international in Dai J. Davies (12095) who had enlisted along with his brother Dan (12094). Dai's prowess in rugby for Salford, Warrington and Swinton[11] was also matched by his abilities as a footballer, having kept goal for Bolton Wanderers and being capped by his home country, Wales, at both soccer and rugby. Dai Davies revelled in the opportunity to organise and excel in those sports which had been his life until the outbreak of war.

On 17th March the whole camp was given over to celebration and recreation in recognition of St Patrick's day. That morning saw 600 of the battalions' Roman Catholic men attending the morning service, in the YMCA hut, given by Father Arkwright from Penmaenmawr. That afternoon the first inter battalion football match was played and was won 2-0 by the 1st Pals, Private Humphries (20 mins) and Private Murphy (78 mins) hitting the net. The football was followed by a series of boxing and wrestling bouts as the battalion champions pitted themselves against their counterparts. That night the YMCA hut was crammed with an even larger gathering as both battalions' concert parties entertained the men. Afterwards it was said that the cheers of support for Sergeant-Major Dunne, who had organised the day, could be heard in Conway itself.

Charlie Richmond and James Croft pose with two friends. Fisher

Eccles Pals of B Company, 16th LFs, with two of the Battalion's mascots which had been donated, before the men's departure, by Salford well-wishers. The bloodhound, Bruce, is Regimental Number 15095. Lee

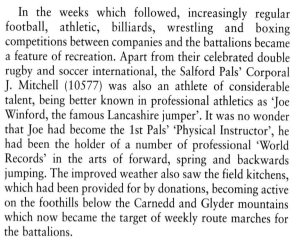

In the weeks which followed, increasingly regular football, athletic, billiards, wrestling and boxing competitions between companies and the battalions became a feature of recreation. Apart from their celebrated double rugby and soccer international, the Salford Pals' Corporal J. Mitchell (10577) was also an athlete of considerable talent, being better known in professional athletics as 'Joe Winford, the famous Lancashire jumper'. It was no wonder that Joe had become the 1st Pals' 'Physical Instructor', he had been the holder of a number of professional 'World Records' in the arts of forward, spring and backwards jumping. The improved weather also saw the field kitchens, which had been provided for by donations, becoming active on the foothills below the Carnedd and Glyder mountains which now became the target of weekly route marches for the battalions.

March also saw the return to camp, on Thursday 11th, of Solomon Archer. His family suffered the public humiliation of discovering his name in the local press, described as,

Private Ward's grave. Grave 686, Plot 31. Weaste Cemetery, Salford. Author

Corporal Mitchell. The 1st Pals' Physical Instructor. Salford Brigade

The deserter, G. [sic] Archer 10,638, C Company, 1st Battalion, who disappeared from camp some time ago in a semi-tragic manner, leaving some of his clothes on the mountains, has been arrested and brought back to camp in charge of Sergeant Harvey and Private Nutt. His colleagues were glad to see him, for he is a very popular and well respected young man.[12]

The previous Friday, 5th March, had seen the burial in Weaste of the first Salford Pal to die on military service. Private (10523) John Ward's body had been returned from Bangor Hospital, where he had died on 1st March. His body was accompanied by Chaplain Captain Farnworth and twenty of his Pals. He was from Pendleton, C Company 1st Pals.

The Raising of the Third Salford Pals

The popularity of Morfa camp and the constant presence of soldiers, visibly transformed by their training, continued to bolster recruitment in the town. During this period the Adjutant-General in London asked the Salford's raising committee to remain responsible for the camp, expenses, feeding and training of the first two battalions on the grounds that the War Office was unable yet to take them over. But more significantly it was known that Salford's record in recruitment was unsurpassed and Barlow was pressured into starting a Third Salford Pals' Battalion, leave for which was granted on 25th January.

This process was unlikely to be as speedily accomplished as the raising of the first two battalions, for a number of reasons.

The part-time working in the docks area had been overcome as traffic recovered to meet the demands of war. The local coal, iron, steel, copper and engineering works were now working flat out in the production of munitions and military materials. The loss of so many men from the area to both general recruitment and the Pals meant that employment prospects had improved beyond all recognition. The initial flush of war enthusiasm had been dissipated. If personal self interest prevailed it would be unlikely that Salford could raise a third Pals' Battalion.

Field cooking in action. Knott

Officers' Mess, 2nd Pals. Pawson

More in hope than faith, barometers to record progress were placed outside the Salford and Pendleton Town Halls. Incredibly, enlistment proved steady again. After four weeks nearly 400 men had been enlisted. The raising of this battalion was encouraged by far less strident recruiting meetings than had accompanied the raising of the first two battalions in the autumn of 1914. Sometimes the company officers appeared during the intervals at the local picture houses to make their appeal for volunteers. These appearances often followed the showing of a short 'moving picture'[13] which had been filmed of the 1st and 2nd Pals. More often a simple open air meeting with a suitable band to advertise their presence sufficed. The small meetings which did take place in Eccles and Swinton brought forward very few recruits. More effective was the competition for recruiting prizes. Bounties were being offered to men who 'brought in' recruits,

A group of Pals from C Company, 2nd Salfords, take it easy during a routine march in North Wales. Knott

C Company of the 2nd Salfords drawn up in the full heat of 1915's summer. Knott

Officers outside their mess at Conway. Knott

one worker supplementing his income by 15 shillings in the third week of March whilst winning the competition with nine recruits.

Nevertheless, during each of the nine weeks it took to raise this battalion an average of nearly 130 men joined their own Third Salford Pals. Again the area around Eccles gave birth to their own Pals' Company (B Coy. 'The Patricroft Pals'), enrolled by Lieutenant Lyon who was the manager at Parr's

Three photographs taken by Captain Roger Knott show his men at ease in the North Wales countryside. Knott

Officers of the 2nd Pals on the sports ground at Conway. On the right of the group is Captain Tweed. Walton

Bayonet drill for men of the 2nd Salfords. Knott

Bank. Again the Liberal connection was made. In his task of enlisting the Eccles and Patricroft men, Lyon had the assistance of 2nd Lieutenant Arundel Barstow who had been the Liberal Agent in the West Salford division to the area's M.P., Sir George Agnew. C Company was raised in the Swinton area by Captain Parkinson and 2nd Lieutenant F. W. Pilling and D were the 'Worsley, Walkden and Little Hulton Company', recruited by Lieutenant J. L. Freeman at the Bridgewater Collieries' company offices in Walkden.

Battalion training began immediately. The Salford Company, A, under the direction of Captain J. Ambrose Smith at the Racecourse and at the Astley Street headquarters of the National Reserve. Ambrose Smith had been a company commander in the 2nd Pals, being detailed to stay behind in Salford

Confidence and team building! Knott

to take charge of men who, for a variety of reasons, had missed the train to Morfa! The Eccles men in B Company were established at their headquarters in the Patricroft Drill Hall.

The Battalion's first commanding officer was Brevet Colonel L. C. H. Stainforth, 'late of the Indian Army. He has seen active service in the Mahmoud Campaign and two further frontier campaigns in India; holds two medals with clasps; and was mentioned in dispatches'.[14]

Just as their predecessors had, the men of the 3rd Pals returned home each evening to eat and sleep among their families and continue the extraordinary and close contact between the Pals and the people who gave rise to them. These men certainly quickly began to look like a military unit. By the second week in March the men were equipped with khaki uniforms and the bulk of their kit, including over six hundred rifles which were capable of being fired, as opposed to the 'drill purposes only' models with which the first two battalions had been part equipped.

Civic support for the men was considerable and continued the pattern established for the benefit of the first two battalions. The Tramways Committee provided free transport to men who lived some distance from their depots, the Baths Committee likewise. All the depots and training facilities had been given free of charge. The almost outrageous possibility

Not everyone who gained access to the camp was a soldier! Knott

The Walkden Offices, loaned by Lord Ellesmere, at which the Walkden men were enlisted. SMM

Bridgewater Offices, Walkden.

that a community of less than a quarter of a million people, together with its outlying villages, could raise its own Brigade, over and above the Territorials already in existence, now seemed much more than just an unlikely aspiration.

Kitchener's Review

On Sunday 21st March Liverpool and Manchester played host to Lord Kitchener. For both conurbations this was a day of enormous prestige and pride. More than ten thousand from Liverpool and Birkenhead were reviewed in the morning and the similar enormity of Manchester and Salford's commitment to the Pals' movement made comparison pointless.

The original arrangement was for only the 3rd Salford Pals to participate. Clearly this would have been unsatisfactory and Barlow made every effort to persuade the authorities at Chester to allow more representation for Salford at the review. Permission was extended, as late as 11.30 on the Saturday morning, for small detachments to travel from the Morfa. The following morning a train laid on by the London and North Western Railway Company left Conway at 9.20. Two groups of 150 men from the 1st and 2nd Pals arrived at Cross Lane, just before mid-day, under command of Major Stone and Captain Tweed. All the men carried full equipment and their rifles. They were accompanied by the band of the 1st Pals' battalion. After being greeted by Montague Barlow and the secretary to the Raising Committee, G. C. Mandleberg, the men were given a quick meal of pies and tea. By 1.00 p.m. the groups left to march on past the Racecourse towards Bury New Road where they met up with the Manchester Pals.

On a perfect spring day Kitchener had been met at London Road Station by the Lord Mayor of Manchester, then driven to the Town Hall where he reviewed the equivalent of twelve battalions. Four of those constituted the Manchester Pals' First Brigade, then in training at Heaton Park. A further four composed the Manchester's Second Brigade, brought from their billets in Morecambe. Behind them marched three Lancashire Fusiliers' battalions together with the small contingents from the 1st and 2nd

Manchester Town Hall. SLHL

Company Sergeant Major Elijah Suttle, (18655). Like many other NCOs, this was clearly not the first time that Sergeant Suttle had served in the Army. His wife was a local Salford midwife and delivered hundreds of the children who, in adulthood, became members of the Pals under Sergeant Suttle's command. Suttle had been the first Sergeant Instructor to the 1st Salford Pals, being forced to leave Conway after a serious attack of influenza and bronchitis. Jones

Pals and the almost completed 3rd Salford Pals who were already kitted in khaki uniform, unlike the 1st Pals' detachment. However, Salford's civic pride was marginally consoled by the fact that the 4,000 Manchesters from Morecambe were also attired in Kitchener Blue.

More than twelve thousand men paraded even though the majority of Salford's Pals were missing. The march should have exceeded fifteen thousand men and many people within Salford's community were heartbroken by the paucity of their representation when compared to that of Manchester's. After the review the Conway men marched back to Cross Lane Barracks to be received by the Mayor and his wife, who shared a welcome hot pot supper with all. The catering had been carried out by the Salford's school's canteen staff. The following day the Manchester Guardian put the area's feelings of pride, and with a rare dignity, in its leading article.

Only now and then in these months of war has it been forced fully home to us that we are living history, but the dullest could not see the march of the twelve thousand yesterday without knowing that of this his children's children will be told. Nor could he see it without a deep and quickening sense of his personal relation to the facts behind it. For Manchester's army is Manchester, and the New Army is Britain, in a way no soldiers ever have been before or, it is hoped, will ever need be again. The people who cheered and the people who marched were not spectators and a spectacle. They were kin in the truest sense, and every eligible man who watched the City Battalions swing by must have felt it an incongruous thing that he was not on the other side of the barrier.[15]

Within the week most of the 3rd Salford Pals had left the town. On the evening of Friday 26th March Montague Barlow entertained the officers and friends of this battalion at the Midland Hotel. Unlike the officers now serving with the first two Pals' battalions, the officers of the 3rd Pals were not predominantly local men, but represented a mixture of Public Schools' Officer Training Corps together with some pre-war military experience.[16] Apart from the Mayor of Salford, Eccles' Mayor, the Chairman of the Swinton and Pendlebury District Council and the Chairman of the Manchester Recruiting Committee, Mr Dixon, were all present to mark the impending departure of the men. As this was going on the men were being issued with completed kit bags from the Mandleberg depot in Cobden Street before making arrangements for their last night in Salford.

The following morning B company, raised in the Eccles area, and C Company from Swinton had their own civic send offs before marching towards the centre of Salford, to meet up with the rest of the men at Cross Lane. Those 330 other men from Walkden, together with A Company from Pendleton and the central districts, had marched from their assembly at Pendleton Town Hall to be reviewed by the Mayor in Bexley Square at 9.30. After the traditional exchange of wishes and hopes the men marched to Cross Lane. Their familiarity and lack of thorough training meant that many family friends and relatives marched with them along the route, speaking openly and wishing them luck. At the head of this rather informal procession walked 'Pongo', the battalion's Great Dane mascot, cared for by RQMS Penketh. Whilst waiting at the station dozens of girls climbed onto the walls hoping for a last glimpse of their sweethearts and relatives. At 10.55 a single train carrying this still incomplete battalion left from Cross Lane Station.

No permission had been received to build further huts at the Morfa so arrangements had been made for their billeting at Penmaenmawr, only four miles along the coast from their sister battalions, in an

The March past. Behind the platform party are the huge posters which recorded the progress of local and general recruiting in Manchester's Recruiting Offices. Manchester Local History Library. (MLHL)

arrangement which eventually allowed them to train and manoeuvre together as a complete brigade. During late April and early May two further detachments of 350 men each left Salford for Penmaenmawr, both occasions being marked by the now customary civic send off from Bexley Square and the march past the shopkeepers and onlookers to the Windsor Street sidings under the Gas Works at Cross Lane station. Soon after the first detachment of the 3rd Pals' arrival many of the Pals' Officers found themselves on a man-hunt in search of two German Officers who had escaped from the nearby detention camp. Officers on motorcycles, men on foot combing the hills and double guards set on the town's bridges created quite a local excitement for some days.

That same week after Kitchener's visit, on 23rd March, the War Office made it known that Salford was to be allowed to attempt to raise their fourth battalion. In view of the large numbers of miners in the area from Pendleton and Agecroft collieries, many of whom were short in stature, the decision had already been made to identify the Fourth Salfords as a bantam battalion on the 5'1" height standard.[17] Of all the battalions this proved the most difficult to enlist. The miners were working in an industry whose product was the essential raw material for the local armaments, steel and textile industries. Getting suitable officers at this stage of the war would prove difficult, as illustrated by this description of the expected first commanding officer, whose military experience stretched back nearly 40 years.

> *Bt. Col. H. H. Vaughan, late of the Indian Army. He formerly commanded the 7th Rajpoots, a fine Regiment which distinguished itself at the Relief of Pekin in 1900... Colonel Vaughan has also seen other service and holds the Egyptian Medal 1882, and was Staff Officer to the column on the Chin Lughai Expedition, 1891-92. A slight stiffness in one leg acquired in early life during service in India has in no way impeded his fine record of achievement in the field[18].*

By early June the 20th Lancashire Fusiliers were roughly 300 strong[19] but recruitment received a welcome boost from a review which was conducted by Lord Derby in front of the Eccles' Town Hall during the evening of 18th June. Consequently Eccles was again able to found another of its own companies, this time within the bantams, and Swinton also raised a strong contingent. Another factor

'K' on the steps at Manchester Town Hall, to his right is Colonel L. C. H. Stainforth. Like many other ex-Indian Army Officers, 'dug-outs' as such officers were sometimes justly called, Colonel L. C. H. Stainforth was not allowed to travel to France with his men. Nevertheless, he took great credit for having established the 3rd Pals as an effective unit in very much less time than had been given to the 1st and 2nd Pals.

which promoted the Bantam's esteem within the community was that this battalion was, almost from the outset, equipped with khaki uniforms, reflecting the easing of those shortages and difficulties which had beset the equipping of the first two Pals' Battalions in Salford. However, much of the slowness with which the battalion managed to enlist its complement of men was due to the intense competition in this part of Lancashire for soldiers of short stature. The Lancashire Fusiliers had already enlisted two further bantam battalions[20] in south east Lancashire during the early months of 1915 and long before their

Men of the Manchester Pals and a lone Salford Pal in immaculate new kit at Heaton Park. Fisher

Competition for the area's small men, mostly miners, came from other Lancashire Fusilier battalions being raised in the area. This photograph clearly shows No. 4 Platoon of B Company, 18th LFs, and clearly illustrates the short stature of these men. Lancashire Fusiliers Museum (LFM)

Montague Barlow with officers of the 20th Bn. The Salford Brigade

The Walkden Yard. Typical of dozens of small engineering premises in and around the Salford area where munitions work was carried on in improvised workshops, before the introduction of 'dilutees', unskilled women who flooded into factories from the summer of 1915 onwards. SMM

completion the recruiting net for the 20th Lancashire Fusiliers had to be extended into districts beyond the immediate Salford area. The 20th Lancashire Fusiliers became, therefore, the one battalion which maintained a slightly less intimate association with the borough whose name formed each man's shoulder titles.

Nevertheless, by the end of July the enlistment of sufficient men had been completed for Salford to announce the completion of its own Brigade.

For the first three of the borough's Pals' Battalions April and May were months of effort, physical work and commitment. Rules were stiffened. "Men having exceeded the limit of time allowed for visiting their homes, will cause a regrettable rigorousness in this connection." The trench system which now ringed the high ground around the camp was being equipped with parapets and dugouts, and the lengthening days caused the series of 'night attacks' to be moved back progressively from 6–9 to 8–11 and later 11.30. In terms of training the 1st Salford Battalion had the edge, but the 3rds made up in enthusiasm whatever they lacked in trained preparation. There was great optimism that their being brigaded together would see Salford's men kept together at the front and even the most recently enlisted men were motivated by the proximity of so many friends, throughout this period of their preparation. Already, though, some of the officers with specialist or previous military experience were being lost from the battalions as casualties in France and Belgium mounted. Both R.A.M.C. doctors attached to the 1st and 2nd Pals had left for the front as had the 2nd Pals' ex-Chief Constable, Major Godfrey. The battalion also lost a significant number of men during the first week of May, these were engineers who returned to their works in the Salford area where munitions work was being dramatically stepped up under the direction of the Manchester and District Armaments Committee.

One of the most telling episodes in the 3rd Pals' time at Penmaenmawr came with the prosecution of one precocious young man, Joseph Jones. Like many others, in all three of Salford's Pals' Battalions, Joseph Jones had been barely able to satisfy the authorities as to his age on enlistment. The combination of youth, a girlfriend at home and being billeted next door to the jewellers proved too much of a temptation for Joseph, and in the early morning of 26th April he had risen from bed to force an entry into the premises of Frank Williams next door. Three weeks later Private Jones was arrested on a charge of breaking and entering the shop in Penmaenmawr. The evidence which gave him away to the investigations of Police Constable Hughes was the broad and suspiciously empty band of pale skin across his wrist. When questioned Joseph Jones had broken down in tears, after which his billet was searched, revealing a letter from a girl in Eccles thanking Joseph for the 'beautiful watch' he had sent to her; together with two further watches hidden in the chimney! On his appearance in front of the town's magistrates, Dr. Morgan and the Reverend Phillips, the Juvenile Court was told by the Deputy Chief Constable that they would be surprised to learn that Joseph Jones was "only 15 years and nine months old, and he had given his age to the military authorities as 19 years".

He was sentenced to be bound over to be of good behaviour for six months, being spoken to severely by the Welsh Reverend who extracted a promise to 'be a good lad in future'.

The Salford Riots in May

Many employers in the Salford locality had suffered huge losses of manpower. The Manchester Ship Canal Co.; Nasmyth, Wilson and Company, Locomotive Engineers of Patricroft; Mandleberg's Albion Works; Agecroft Colliery and the Broughton Copper Company. The industrial and manufacturing heart of the area was under threat.

Consequently, this spring and early summer of 1915 was a disastrous period for community and industrial relations within the town. The loss of so many men from pivotal roles in the factories and the police, media, management and family life of Salford had a severe impact upon many people across the Borough. The tension boiled over in the midst of recruiting Salford's Bantam Battalion in early May. Following the torpedoing of the Liverpool based Lusitania on 7th May, rioting had broken out in that city.

Within days the poison had spread to Salford. Throughout Monday and Tuesday the wives and families of German tradespeople, businessmen and shopkeepers were forced to flee to sanctuary in local police stations. On the Monday night the shop of Mr Praz, a pork butcher on Eccles New Road, was the centre of an extraordinary scene.

> "I never saw anything like it," said a police officer who took part in the attempt to check the rioting. The premises were completely wrecked, and there would be many a breakfast table set better this morning than it has ever been before. One youth, picking up a side of bacon, remarked, "This is going to East Winford Street," and a collier carried off a brass curb and fireirons, saying they would look better on his hearthstone at Pendlebury than in the roadway. One woman

No 7 Platoon, 16th LFs. Winners of the inter platoon football knock out which ended in May. This group of Eccles men defeated the men of 20 Platoon (Swinton), in the final watched by over 900 spectators. After 90 minutes there was no score but in extra time the match was won by a goal from Private J. Johnson just before the turnaround. Albert Banks was the team's defensive stalwart. The winning team were; GK Private Crook (11951), LB Corporal Street (11956), RB Private Banks (11933), LH Private C. Smith (11689), CH Private Rigby (11874), RH Private C. Barrett (11615), LW Private Bethell (11764), IL Private Johnson (11762), CF Private Hambleton (11644), IR Platoon Sergeant A. Thompson and RW Private Welch (12017).

THE DAILY TELEGRAPH. SATURDAY. MAY 8, 1915.

LUSITANIA TORPEDOED : 1,400 LIVES LOST

complained to a policeman that she had only been able to secure a pot of dripping. When a piano was dropped from the window a man rushed forward and to the singing of the crowd he played 'Rule Britannia,' 'It's a long way to Tipperary,' and other popular ditties before the instrument was completely wrecked[21].

By Tuesday the rioters were sufficiently confident to come out during daylight. Their target was a shop known as 'Myerscough. Pork Butchers'. Unfortunately, his noticeable and incongruous accent revealed that the owner was of German extraction. Knowing this, the crowd of 'mill girls and apprentices and improvers', on leaving their works for a one hour lunch-break, were hell bent on destruction. Again the local press slipped from its normal standards of objectivity to revel in the rampant nationalism and distortion which was being used to justify 'the rioters' outlandish behaviour.

> *... they were hungry for reprisals for the appalling loss of life by the sinking of the Lusitania. They knew that anyone of German or Austrian descent rejoiced in the devilish accomplishments of the German submarine, and they were out for a limited time, not only to voice their resentment, but to demonstrate it effectively. At a few minutes after 1 o'clock there were unusually large and agitated crowds at the junction of Regent Road and Ordsall Lane. Their talk was not of the loom or bench, but of the fiendish work of the German pirates and how best they could exhibit their abhorrence of the foul deeds of the Kaiser's submarines.[22]*

They exhibited that abhorrence by a total gutting of the shop and premises whilst a crowd of followers smiled their acquiescence. Shopkeepers and their families were being systematically terrorised. Other disturbances continued throughout the day, and that night five shops in the impoverished Ellor Street district of Pendleton were

Daily Express cartoon showing the Kaiser and Admiral Tirpitz. This sort of xenophobic portrayal was at the root of the rioting. Author

wrecked including the businesses of local people whose property had been singled out for no conceivable reason other than to loot and steal.

A fourteen-year-old schoolgirl, Jesse Robertson, witnessed the scenes on Lower Broughton Road where crowds were attacking 'Porky Beck's', another German owned butcher's shop,

> *... breaking all the windows and stealing everything. People were watching but they couldn't do anything while the others were breaking in and stealing. There was a drapers shop, higher up, they were German Jews I think, Navinski I think their name was. Well their back doors came to our back doors where we lived. They were very nice people. They'd lived in Salford for years. They broke all their windows. They went in there and they was comin' out with rolls and rolls of cloth. It was heartbreakin' to see them 'cause they never did anybody any 'arm. They was all running 'ome with what they took.*[23]

The draper's family sought refuge in the Robertson home. Their terror made a lasting impression on the young girl whose brother was already fighting at Gallipoli with the 1/8th Lancashire Fusiliers and from whom she eagerly awaited news. Here in Broughton was the most violent of Tuesday's scenes. Although the police were out in force,

People mill around outside shops damaged during the Lusitania riots. SLHL

70

F. Praz is a German owned pork butchers. The buildings and premises next door have not escaped the rioters stones. SLHL

> *... they were powerless to cope with the thousands who by this time were present, and the crowd found little interference in their work of destruction. Windows were smashed and in some cases the contents were either destroyed or stolen. With each crash of glass the mob roared with laughter.*[24]

On Wednesday 12th May the Manchester Evening News reported the situation under a series of headlines, 'RENEWED RIOTING LAST NIGHT, ANTI — GERMAN OUTBREAK, PREMISES WRECKED, PROPERTY BURNED.'

> *Rioting directed against shopkeepers and householders supposed to be Germans or of German descent continued in many parts of Manchester last night.*
>
> *The disturbance was spread over an area even wider than that affected in the afternoon, and at numerous centres it was impossible to restore order, although the police had the assistance of almost every available special constable and in some cases of soldiers also.*
>
> *Much damage was done by the smashing of windows and the destruction of property, whilst the fire brigades of the city and the borough were called out several times to suppress fires which had been started by the rioters. Rain, which is often more effective than the police in dispersing a disorderly crowd, fell throughout the evening and night...*

Edgar Lord at Brocton Camp, Stafford, in April 1915. Within a year this fresh faced youth of 19 years of age would be in France with the 1st Pals. His age is typical of many subalterns then in training. What distinguished Lord however was that he took a camera with him to record a number of events which he witnessed during his career with the 1st and 2nd Pals. Willcock

During three days of violence any distant justification was quickly forgotten. In an orgy of racist intolerance many English wives and widows of naturalised German people were attacked and brutally terrorised. Homes were ransacked and buildings burned by cheering mobs in excess of 1,000 strong. Across the Borough the police were grossly outnumbered and powerless to restore order, being forced to stand and watch as angry men and women took the law into their own hands. The violence had been especially severe in the most impoverished parts of Lower Broughton, the Regent Road area and Pendleton.

The situation was restored when un-naturalised males were rounded up for internment. The Manchester Guardian spoke of the public's sense 'that justice had been done'. Well, perhaps.

Departure from Conway

Whilst Salford simmered in the summer of 1915, the Pals prepared to depart from north Wales. The men had built a considerable friendship with the community. A petition in early June, signed by the residents of Penmaenmawr, requested that arrangements should be placed in hand to extend the ties by having the Salford Bantams billeted there. A number of weddings cemented such bonds, including two involving men from C Company, Private Yates (10624) to Bessie Jones of Bethesda and Sergeant Fletcher (10718) to Miss Bridges, a Conway girl. Sergeant Fletcher's wedding, conducted by Chaplain Farnworth in Conway Parish Church, was a considerable occasion and was attended by his platoon commander, 2nd Lieutenant John Younger and Lieutenant Alfred Lee Wood together with many other 15th Battalion men including Sergeants Williams, Cotton, Hancock and Lewis and a guard of honour made up of all the men from No. 12 platoon. But the largest Church Parade of all occurred on Sunday 6th June when all three Pals' Battalions met for a service held on the Morfa camp parade ground. Many of the men's families were present and Montague Barlow had ridden with the 3rd Pals as they marched in from Penmaenmawr. In ideally sunny weather all the men were assembled in a huge square around which a large number of people from the local community gathered to watch as the Chaplain General's non denominational service was conducted.

Between 20th and 22nd June the Pals left north Wales for Catterick Bridge. During that last Sunday Conway's mayor addressed the men and complimented them all on 'being one of the finest bodies of men that would ever set foot on the field of battle. It had been a great pleasure to the inhabitants to have such noble men amongst them, and it was a greater pleasure to know that they had behaved themselves like men and soldiers'. First to depart were the 1st Pals whose two trains left the Morfa on Sunday evening. Late on Monday evening the 3rd Pals departed from Penmaenmawr where 'in some corners there were heartbreaking scenes where young girls were taking leave of their newly discovered sweethearts'.

Officers of the Sergeants Mess. 1st Salford Pals. Jones

Lieutenant Colonel Abercrombie of the 2nd Salford Pals at ease with other officers in the Welsh countryside. Knott

On arrival at Catterick Bill Turner, an ex-miner and Corporal (17486) in the 3rd Pals and son of a Worsley Brewery worker, remembered the contrast well,

> *That's where we started soldierin'. Comin' out of billets it were lovely! There were tents at Catterick Bridge when we got there. Six in a tent. The first mornin' as we'd got there we all got up and went to the place they'd built as wash-houses and shaved in cold water. So when they came round t' tent they called out, 'Ow many's in 'ere Corporal?'. 'Six' I replied. 'Right then ... one, two, three, four, five, six!' and 'e threw 'em in. 'Hey!' I said, 'What's your game man?' Then he shouted, 'You can pick 'em up, they're hard boiled!' I thought this is champion, and then they give us six pieces of bread.* Corporal Bill Turner.

By now the battalions were in effect beyond the control of the Raising Committee. Left behind in the Morfa camp, with the Bantams who began to arrive on 31st July, were the reserve companies occupying the old 1st Pals' hutments. The first three battalions at Catterick still had very few rifles and none of the service pattern Lee Enfield, but under canvas, with everything but a full complement of weapons and in perfect weather, this was an idyllic time for the cream of Salford's manhood. The fact that the weather was clear was a real blessing. However, in view of the limited water supplies, baths were often out of the question and the men became accustomed to regular bathing in the nearby River Swale.

The last complete battalion, therefore, to leave Salford was the 20th Lancashire Fusiliers, the 4th Salford Bantam Pals. Before departing Bexley Square for Cross Lane Station, each of the men had been given a red rose by women among the crowded confines in front of the Town Hall. Within hours they entered the camp at Morfa, just vacated by the 2nd Pals, soon to be taken over by the Military Authorities for general training purposes on August 3rd. However, the Bantams' association with the other Pals was broken and they were destined never to see action together. The Bantams in fact spent very little time at Conway. In mid August they moved on to

One of the last to enlist in the Salford Brigade. Private Ernest Groves (22440) enlisted on July 26th. As with many Bantams, his small stature was in part due to his age, 17 on enlistment. Ernest served with the Bantams until their disbandment in February 1918, when he along with the other men were transferred to two other battalions, the 17th and 18th Lancashire Fusiliers. Jackson

Parkhouse Camp on Salisbury Plain where they were brigaded, together with the 17th and 18th Lancashire Fusiliers from the Bury area and the 23rd Manchesters, into the 104th Brigade which was an all Bantam unit under the command of Brigadier General G. M. MacKenzie, itself part of the all Bantam 35th Division.

On 28th July the 2nd and 3rd Salfords went to Ponteland camp in Northumberland. Having received their service rifles, the 1st Salfords spent a fortnight at Whitley Bay, firing its first musketry proficiency course, then moving to Codford St. Mary in Wiltshire on 13th August. A week earlier the 2nd and 3rd Battalions had arrived there. Within a further fortnight, on 27th August, the War Office took formal control of the first three Salford Pals' Battalions. The First Pals' commanding Officer, Colonel Moss, who had been with the men since their inception as a battalion, was replaced by Lieutenant Colonel J. H. Lloyd.

The day before Minden Day and the Bantams leave Salford. Bexley Square. July 31st 1915. Salford Brigade.

The letter confirming these changes, received by Montague Barlow, gave a barely hidden insight into the clear purpose of the Reserve companies. Having thanked him and the committee for their magnificent efforts throughout the past year the letter went on to say that,

> *...I am to add that their success on active service will largely depend on the results of your efforts to keep the depot companies constantly up to establishment with men in every way fit for service in the field.*[26]

There was no lack of determination to maintain those depot companies.

This August saw that effort translated into the establishment of the last of the battalions associated with Salford. Whilst four active Service battalions had already been raised the Reserve or 'E' companies of each of the first three battalions were now brought together at Conway to form the 21st (Reserve) Battalion of the Lancashire Fusiliers, sometimes known as the 'Fifth Salfords'. This was fed by men from

The Bantams' Officers.

Men of B Company, Salford Bantams, in Camp at Conway. To the officer's left in both photographs is Company Sergeant Major J. Platt (21545). Pawson

Salford who continued to enlist voluntarily throughout 1915 and which was the object of a considerable recruiting effort in the borough for the entirety of this period. In November the battalion moved to Prees Heath as part of the 17th Reserve Brigade, eventually becoming the 72nd Training Reserve Battalion in September of 1916.

By this time the Brigade structure was established with the arrival of Brigadier-General Yatman[27] from France as commander to the first three Salford Pals' Battalions in the 96th Brigade. The Brigade was completed by the 16th Northumberland Fusiliers, another Pals unit raised from the quayside districts of Newcastle-upon-Tyne and Gateshead, the Tyneside 'Commercials'. The 96th Brigade was part of the 32nd Division, whose commanding officer was Major-General W. H. Rycroft.

From their huts, sixteen miles west of Salisbury, the apprentice soldiers launched forth on numerous exercises, digging interminable trenches and manning them for days and nights on end in strict trench

A rather different photo of men belonging to the 1st Salford Pals. This photo was almost certainly taken at Codford. All the men are now equipped with Khaki and their distinctive, brass, battalion shoulder titles. In the centre, with his hand under the mug, is Corporal George Charles (10794. Killed in Action, 1/7/1916.) with other men of Number 13 platoon. Charles

discipline. At night the field kitchens swung into action and the men from Salford had cause to thank their sponsors at home who had provided the cooking equipment.[28]

The desperate difficulties being experienced in equipping the New Armies with weaponry showed clearly in the experience of the 2nd Salfords. Their first Lewis gun arrived on 25th September and their service rifles on 20th October, almost a year since the men had enlisted and incredibly only a month before their departure. By now the men had become accustomed to sleeping out in their newly dug trenches and the onset of winter was hardening them to what awaited in France.

The men knew that time in England was short. Visits to Codford St. Mary by

A group of Officers pose in front of their mess at Codford in September 1915. (Left to Right) Top row; Barstow, Dixon, Wade, Gery. Middle row; Lyon, Wykes, Nightingale. Front row; Wood, Lee and Clifford Lowe Platt. Lying down, Whittles. Platt

members of the Raising Committee, home furloughs for the men and reviews on the downs by their Honorary Colonel and Lord Kitchener presaged their final days on Salisbury Plain. Before departure the men were issued with a full kit, two of everything. Their valises weighed in at 95 pounds. The 3rd Pals departed, via Southampton on the Princess Caroline, for France on 21st November, 1915. The following day the 1st and 2nd Pals left from Folkestone for their passage to Boulogne.

They had been just over a year in the making.

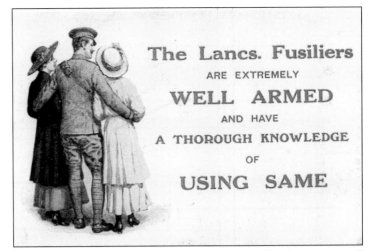

Humourous postcards depicting the Lancashire Fusiliers' prowess in all matters of both love and hatred were often sent home to their families in Salford before the men's departure to France! Fisher

Notes

1. Hermann Hesse. *Demian*. Chapter 8. pp 152.
2. Montague Barlow's Speech to the House of Commons, 4/3/1915, [Hansard. Column 1056.] and reported in the S.C.R. 13/3/1915.
3. North Wales Weekly News. [N.W.W.N.] 31/12/1914.
4. In command of 125th Infantry Brigade to which the two Salford battalions together with the 15th and 16th Cheshires were briefly, at this time, attached.
5. Gazetted as 2nd Lieutenant after the battalion's arrival in Conway.
6. N.W.W.N. 28/1/1915.
7. Ibid.
8. S.C.R. 13/2/1915.
9. Ibid.
10. Ibid.
11. Debut for Salford Rugby League Club in 1900, transferred to Warrington in 1903 as a talented half back. Also played soccer for Bolton Wanderers, appearing only months after playing professional Rugby League in the F.A. Cup final in 1904, which Bolton lost to Manchester City 1-0 (Billy Meredith).
12. S.C.R. 13/3/1915. Later promoted to Lance Corporal, Solomon Archer was killed in action on 1st July, 1916.
13. Now seemingly lost. If you know of its whereabouts PLEASE do get in touch.
14. S.C.R. 13/2/1915.
15. Manchester Guardian. 22/3/1915.
16. List of Officers' names, ranks and biographical detail in S.C.R. 27/3/1915.
17. The Bantams' history is very different from that of the other Salford Pals. Their active service is therefore a much briefer tale.
18. S.C.R. 17/4/1915. Although Brevet-Colonel H. H. Vaughan was a distinguished officer in his time he was replaced, before the Battalion was long established by Lt. Col. A. Reid.
19. See S.C.R. 5/6/1915 for officers then attached to the 4th Pals. List includes brief biographical details.
20. The 17th and 18th Lancashire Fusiliers, the 'First and Second South East Lancashire Bantams'.
21. S.C.R. and Salford Chronicle, 15/5/1915.
22. S.C.R. 15/5/1915.
23. Jesse Robertson. Interview.
24. Salford Chronicle. 15/5/1915.
25. Manchester Evening News. 12/5/1915.
26. Letter to Montague Barlow from the Army Council on transfer to Military Control of the first three battalions of Salford Pals.

27. Brigadier-General C. Yatman, C.M.G., D.S.O.. Previously Lieutenant Colonel to the 1st Northumberland Fusiliers. Took command of the 96th Brigade at end of August, 1915.

28. Four field kitchens and their equipment were provided by G. C. Mandleberg, Sir George Agnew M.P., C. Goodwin and Mather and Platt Ltd, a fifth being jointly financed by the Irwell and Eastern Rubber Company, Alderman Frankenberg and two smaller companies.

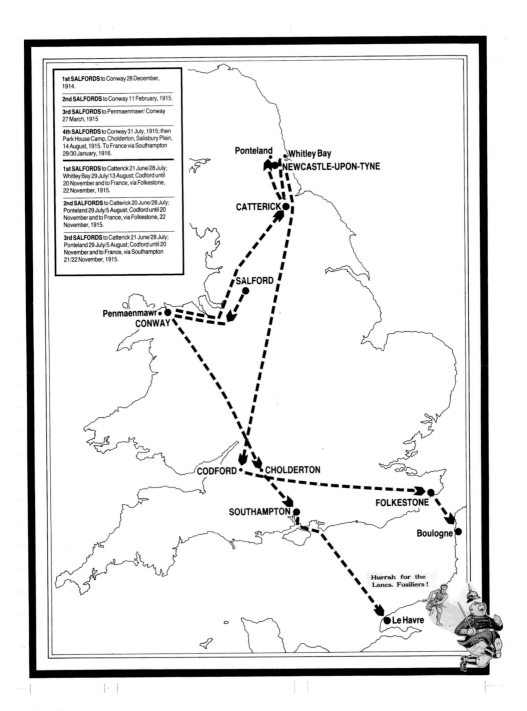

1st SALFORDS to Conway 28 December, 1914.

2nd SALFORDS to Conway 11 February, 1915.

3rd SALFORDS to Penmaenmawr/Conway 27 March, 1915

4th SALFORDS to Conway 31 July, 1915; then Park House Camp, Cholderton, Salisbury Plain, 14 August, 1915. To France via Southampton 29/30 January, 1916.

1st SALFORDS to Catterick 21 June/28 July; Whitley Bay 29 July/13 August; Codford until 20 November and to France, via Folkestone, 22 November, 1915.

2nd SALFORDS to Catterick 20 June/28 July; Ponteland 29 July/5 August; Codford until 20 November and to France, via Folkestone, 22 November, 1915.

3rd SALFORDS to Catterick 21 June/28 July; Ponteland 29 July/5 August; Codford until 20 November and to France, via Southampton 21/22 November, 1915.

Ponteland · Whitley Bay
NEWCASTLE-UPON-TYNE

CATTERICK

SALFORD

Penmaenmawr ·
CONWAY

CODFORD · · CHOLDERTON

SOUTHAMPTON

FOLKESTONE

Boulogne

Hurrah for the
Lancs. Fusiliers!

Le Havre

Chapter Three

That Village

Now I saw that many, indeed, all men were capable of dying for an ideal. Only they had no use for a free, self-chosen ideal; it must be shared and accepted[1].

An uncommonly dank bout of weather had already gripped this part of north eastern France. Not that the men were at all well equipped to face the rigours of winter. On arrival in Boulogne they had been relieved of 'one of everything'. It was the traditional way of building up stores and left Salford's 'sodgers' with no spare clothing save the socks, underwear and comforts which the Welfare Committees provided from home.

> *Our railway journey lasted until 5.a.m. the next morning, and from this terminus [Longpre] we had a fifteen miles' march, staying two days in barns at a small village [Coulonvillers]. After this rest we were off again for another fifteen miles' march and spent another night in barns [at Flixecourt]. After another day's march we arrived at a village which had been shelled, this being our first view of the effect of big gun and shellfire. We stayed at this village [Coisy] for two days, our lodgings being baths, ruined houses, and any other place which was fortunate enough to have a roof left.[2]*

En-route for the Somme, whilst meeting his Divisional General for the first time, Geoffrey Bowen who was the 3rd Pals' recently appointed adjutant heard General Rycroft re-assure everyone that they were going to the 'quietest part of the line, where it was very comfortable'.[3] Whilst his own experiences led him to a degree of scepticism and to make the most of each rest on the way up, Bowen noted that many of his battalion's men were filled with 'martial ardour' and keen to see the front lines. As his battalion marched in along the Grande Route Nationale towards the front one tired subaltern noted,

> *...the long double line of trees seemed to stretch away to an interminable distance, and whenever one rise was topped another appeared in front. So we marched on, heavily laden and weary, but eager to get on to see what this strange indefinite place was like – the Front of the Front. As we drew nearer to our destination the roar of an occasional gun could be heard more plainly: and when it grew dusk the whole sky-line was lighted up here and there by the brilliant flares. So bright were these, that we thought ourselves much closer than we really were, and when we at last plodded into the battered and deserted streets of Albert we were surprised how the flares lit up each other's excited faces.*
>
> *The whole adventure was weirdly exciting – the march in the glowing darkness – the flares – and last of all the dark and deserted gloom of the stricken town.*
>
> *And then our first shell! How we enjoyed it! What a joke we thought it![4]*

Albert's famous Basilica, past the wreckage of which almost every soldier who served on the Somme marched. (LFM)

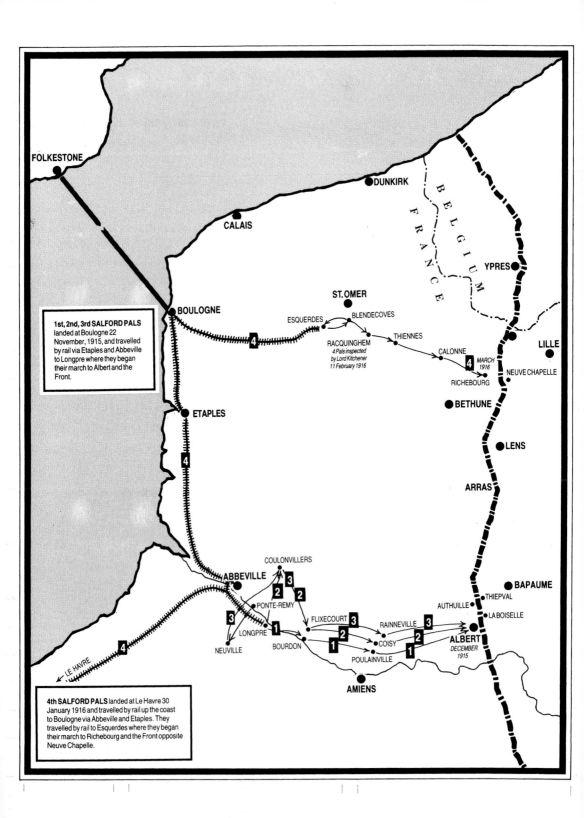

FOLKESTONE

DUNKIRK

CALAIS

BELGIUM
FRANCE

YPRES

ST. OMER

BOULOGNE

ESQUERDES
BLENDECOVES

THIENNES

LILLE

1st, 2nd, 3rd SALFORD PALS
landed at Boulogne 22
November, 1915, and travelled
by rail via Etaples and Abbeville
to Longpre where they began
their march to Albert and the
Front.

RACQUINGHEM
*4 Pals inspected
by Lord Kitchener
11 February 1916*

CALONNE

4 *MARCH
1916*

NEUVE CHAPELLE

RICHEBOURG

ETAPLES

BETHUNE

4

LENS

ARRAS

BAPAUME

COULONVILLERS

THIEPVAL

ABBEVILLE

2 **3**

2

AUTHUILLE

LA BOISELLE

PONTE-REMY

3

FLIXECOURT

3

RAINNEVILLE

3

ALBERT
*DECEMBER
1915*

3

1

2

COISY

2

LONGPRE

1

BOURDON

POULAINVILLE

1

4

LE HAVRE

NEUVILLE

4th SALFORD PALS landed at Le Havre 30
January 1916 and travelled by rail up the coast
to Boulogne via Abbeville and Etaples. They
travelled by rail to Esquerdes where they began
their march to Richebourg and the Front opposite
Neuve Chapelle.

AMIENS

Thus, at the end of November, 1915, the Salford Pals were making themselves familiar with the town of Albert. The 32nd Division was assembled, 'somewhere in France'.

The town itself had long ceased to bear anything more than a passing resemblance to its pre-war tidiness and style. The central streets were deserted of almost all civilians except those too infirm or old to face a journey from their homes. Few of the town's substantial buildings retained more than a broken outline of their roofs and windows. Those windows not smashed through were shuttered, casting an unwelcoming scowl to Salford's men. Albert's basilica had become the regular target of German 77s whose purpose was to deny the advantage of the tower's outlook to the British Army. The surrounding area was a chaos of rubble, dust and weed-ridden dereliction. Away from here, towards the west of the town, a few estaminets and patisseries served the many passing soldiers whose billets occupied every available house, barn and shed.

For the rest of their life, as a unit composed of original battalion members, the savage desolation of once prosperous farmland which surrounded the town was to be home to the Salford Pals.

North east of the town an arrow straight road headed for Bapaume, running between the nearby villages of La Boisselle and Ovillers. Within the E2 sector trenches, facing La Boisselle, and the E3 sector astride the Bapaume road the trenches had already acquired a notoriety for their slimy wet conditions and the tense proximity of the enemy. On their left a group of trenches known as the X7 sector snaked away west of Ovillers.

Three miles to the north lay three areas of shattered woodlands; Aveluy, Authuille and Thiepval. Dominating the ridge above and to the east of these woods lay immensely powerful defences, below which two spurs descended into the valley. The northern spur fell towards Thiepval Wood, already in British hands but overlooked by the network of strongpoints which constituted Schwaben Redoubt. The slopes above the wood were enfiladed by a score of machine guns, hidden in the village's desolation of rubble. The larger southern spur was dominated by trenches which formed the Leipzig Salient, above Authuille Wood. The British trenches here below Thiepval and in front of the Mill Road were known as the G2 sector, drier than those at La Boisselle and well served by Thiepval Wood which sheltered the trench railway, considerably easing the burden of carrying parties.

Authuille Village as the Salford battalions found it on their arrival in late 1915 before the real destruction wrought by the Battles of the Somme. Reed

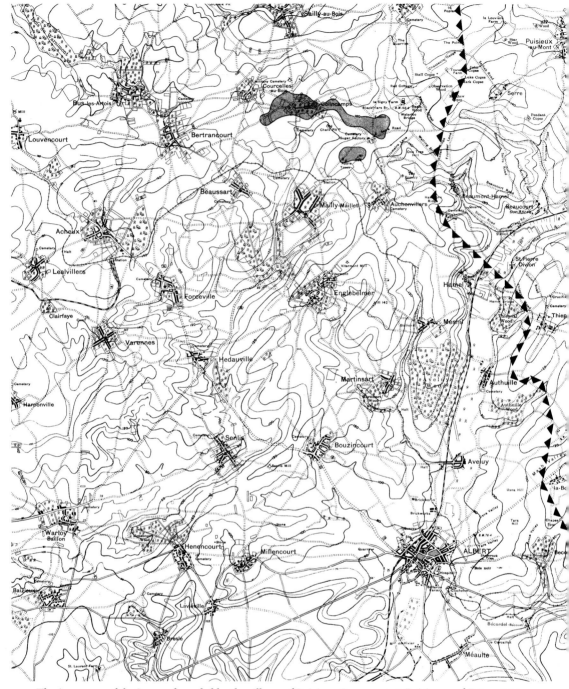

The Ancre area of the Somme, bounded by the villages of Baizieux, Louvencourt, Puisieux and Fricourt. Map 1. Military Operations France and Belgium, 1916

Along the valley below, the River Ancre stuttered through its shell pecked and putrid marshes, past the wreckage of Authuille village en-route for Aveluy, Albert and beyond to its confluence with the River Somme.

2nd Lieutenant Clifford Platt[5], with the 3rd Pals, quickly found time to write home. This officer was an exceptionally literate and well educated man, having been educated at Malvern College and Corpus Christi College, Oxford where he obtained a double first in Classics. His letters and account show an astute awareness of life with the Battalion, describing the daily filth into which his platoon were thrust, and, initially, the relief he felt at having had the foresight to bring his own waders, when he was taken up to the lines for the first time.

Soldiers prepare for a working party. Taylor Library

La Boisselle, astride the Albert-Bapaume road. This location provided the Pals' first experience of close trench warfare. The area was already pitted by craters caused by instant mining. At some points the lines were less than 30 metres apart in this location.

Lieutenant Clifford Platt's hand drawn map of the E3 sector behind the 'Hot'.

… It was the most remarkable – & in some ways the most entertaining – December 4th I have ever spent. Part of my twentieth birthday – the first complete twenty-four hours spent in a real front line trench – was passed in slushing about in beastly narrow ditches, with water and mud in most places over one's knees – it's always 'waists' in Tommy's letters – and spiteful little bullets cracking harmlessly overhead now and again, the monotony being occasionally relieved by an 'oilcan', a 'sausage' or a 'whizz-bang'… …The Friday night I only had one hour's sleep, as I was on duty part of the night and too wet the rest: creeping up to sentries in advanced post on craters and places was really quite exciting. But this morning's journey down a trench called Berkshire Avenue, which leads from the trenches to Albert, was the worst part of the whole show. It is just a mile long, and we took four solid hours to get to the end: nearly the whole way along there is thick sticky clay up to one's knees and on this occasion I had on a Burberry stretching nearly down to my ankles! Now I know what real mud is! Today I had my first real hot bath in France, and didn't I just enjoy it?…[6]

Experience quickly taught Clifford Platt that the elegance of his smart Burberry, whilst splendid at his family's home in Bexley, made no sense at all inside the trenches in front of Albert. Within days he had cut it down, saying,

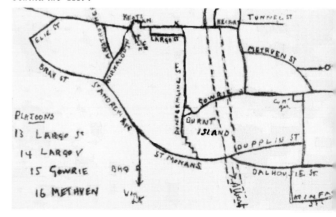

...it catches the mud on your waders and works it all up inside as far as your waist, which is unpleasant to say the least of it. And besides the extra length is quite useless, as what need is there for protection to the lower limbs from rain, when they are already under mud and water?[7]

It was all part of the process of learning.

The Pals' 'Course of instruction in Trench Warfare' was undertaken at the hands of men drawn from hardened units such as the 7th Royal West Kents and the 7th Buffs. During the first two weeks of December 1915 all units in the newly arrived 32nd Division went through similar experiences. The purpose was to familiarise and sharpen the men and officers to the lifesaving routines which were essential in the hostile and subterranean environment of the Somme trenches.

By 11th December the 3rd Pals were launched alone into the line at La Boisselle. Conditions on the way up to this area were loathsome, men constantly becoming entrapped in the glutinous clay which lay ever thicker in every communication trench. Often it was necessary to dig the men and their kit out. Captain Bowen watched as 2nd Lieutenant Platt's men struggled for hours in utterly impossible conditions to free the trapped men, and later themselves.

> *'Words fail me to describe it... there we found this line of men down the trench with mud over their knees, just standing there, unable to move forward or back. One really could not help laughing at them. To get them out we had to take off their equipment and greatcoats, and pass them along a line of men. We could not even get out of the trench, as it was about 10 feet deep. After we had got them all out, we had to get out three of the fatigue party who had stuck firmer than any of the original lot. It took about an hour to get the last three out. I lost a pair of thigh waders, and had to walk back along a mile of trench with bare feet.'*[8]

Privates Street and Hamer. (E & PJ 7/1/1916)

That 'fatigue party' had been waiting in support for just such an opportunity.

Captain Bowen. (Bowen Memoir p. 16)

...A message came through to say that another of our companies was completely bogged and that we had to turn out to help. Two platoons of us were there from 6pm to 11pm in the pouring rain, thick mud and water well up to the waist, working like navvies hauling out these men and their kits and overcoats some of which were lost entirely...

... You can't get out of this mud anywhere. The trenches communicating with the town are the worst. They are dug in clay, which in many places reaches over the knees and everywhere over the ankles and sticks like nothing on earth. In my sector the fire trench is pretty nearly as bad; so that it is pretty hard work moving about. I'm simply covered in mud at present. It all works in over the top of my long thigh waders, through my feet scraping together in the narrow trench. Then of course my tunic is caked all over. Any coat longer than a tunic really is hopeless as it collects mud at the bottom and weighs a ton...

...Here one is rather apt to forget there is a war on. I mean, when you have got used to the banging of the guns and other occasional noises, you are wholly taken up with the trench routine and trying to keep as warm and as dry as possible.

This particular bit of the trench system is called the 'Ilot, and what adds to the weirdness of the scene there, especially by night, is that it is all chalk and dead white, relieved here and there by some black mass of debris, thrown up by some mine, then a little further to the left the line crosses what was once a great main road, [the Albert-Bapaume road] but what is now a desolate waste, with a clump of broken trees, surrounding an absolutely untouched Crucifix, on one side and a battered French cemetery on the other. In our trench stand the remains of the last lampost of La B-[oisselle] on the Albert road.[9]

Ingenious carrying techniques were developed to cope with the worst of the mud. In the 3rd Pals' trenches a small punt was designed, capable of carrying rations whilst being pulled by rope along the 'navigable' trenches!

On 17th December, Private James Holt (11695) had become the first Eccles Pal in B Company of the 2nd Pals to be killed.

'... a chap called Holt, whose family kept a butcher's shop on the corner of Barton Lane and Boardman Street, was killed by a sniper. There were notices all over the trenches telling you to keep your head down – he didn't.' Pte. Frank Holding (11407), B Company, 2nd Pals.

Mining activity in the E2 and E3 sectors was an accepted part of life and death here. The Ilot and its immediate surrounding area was notorious for the close presence of the enemy trenches, sometimes less than a cricket pitch distant from each front line. On the 18th December three miners and a member of the 2nd Pals were killed below ground when two German mines were detonated during the day, causing damage to the underground galleries and the trenches. During the late afternoon of the 19th the detonation of another mine gave the 2nd Pals a further experience of this hideous and random form of attrition. At 3.15 the men were listening to the roar of a heavy strafe of the La Boisselle positions when the Duhollow Street trenches (at X13d4/2), were themselves rent by an enormous explosion. Three listening posts were destroyed. Five miners were buried underground.

Immediately after the explosion under the most advanced of the listening posts, Sergeant A. Smith (12019) crawled to the wreckage, seeking its seven occupants. He found five shocked and bruised men. Having brought them in Sergeant Smith again went out, in search of voices heard crying 'Sergeant' in the darkness which had gathered. Only when the voices came from three different directions did the Germans' pretence betray itself.

It proved impossible to recover the bodies of Privates Samuel Hamer (11614) and James Street (15216), even though their pals searched the area for two further nights.[10] Before the war Sam Hamer had been an employee of Westinghouse and had only married whilst on home leave from Codford the previous autumn.

Already the men's letters to home talked about the casualties incurred at the 'Ilot'. Captain Tweed of the First Eccles Pals (B Coy. 16th LFs), already well known in the area for his efforts in having raised the men, now began the heart-rending task of reporting their deaths in front of the forbidding village of La Boisselle.

La Boisselle in 1916, clearly showing the destruction wrought in the area of the Ilot.

> *I regret to have to inform you that your husband was killed in the first line trenches [at La Boisselle] on December 23rd, at about three o'clock in the afternoon. The Germans were shelling our trenches, and he was struck in the head by shrapnel and killed instantaneously, just as he was entering his dugout. Writing as I am on Christmas Day, I feel most acutely how terrible your grief must be…*
>
> *Captain Tweed to the wife of Private Harold Furguson (15097). Harold was the first man from the 'Swinton, Pendlebury and Clifton' Company to be killed. Before the war he had been a miner at the Clifton Hall Colliery.*

In a straight exchange, the 1st Pals moved out from Albert to spend their first Christmas in France in the filthy confines of the E3 sector trenches astride the Albert-Bapaume road at La Boisselle. This tour in the line was shared with half of the 3rd Pals. Writing on that Christmas Eve one group of men's letters made a poignant appeal for some simple form of entertainment.

> *…I am writing to see if any of your readers have got such a thing as a melodeon (sic) to spare to brighten up the hearts of some of the Salford 'Pals' on these dark and lonesome evenings as there's absolutely nothing to enjoy ourselves with here. No doubt some kind hearted individual will see this appeal and forward the above named article to 'The Knuts,' No. 7 Platoon….. (Signed) Jimmy Lupton, William Searle, Jack Finch, George Washington, all 'Salford Lads.'*[11]

The following morning,

> *At Christmas 1915 we all 'ad a parcel from Queen Mary. Well, it passed through that many hands before it eventually got to the Battalion that I made a standing joke out of it. I said I was going to write to the Queen and thank her for that parcel sayin', 'Dear Mary, I thank you very greatly for that parcel you sent. I'm writing this by the light of the candle that was my share of it. That was all I got out of it'.* Pte. (later Sergeant) Bill Button. (10897) D Coy, 1st Pals.

Other anticipated Christmas parcels proved equally disastrous for the recipients. Under a lighthearted headline, **'TRAGEDY OF A CHRISTMAS PARCEL. A SOLDIER'S COOKING EXPERIMENT',** one Swinton Officer explained how a letter had forewarned him to expect a cooked chicken on the 25th's post. Not until the 30th did it arrive!

> *I was curious to see how it had fared. After sniffing all round the parcel, I decided to risk opening it without putting on my respirator. Mick (my Irish Chum), was more cautious, and stood as far away as possible, with his revolver ready in case the contents proved to be lively! Well, I cut the string, and on opening the paper, found the box all burst, and the inside a regular mix-up of crumbs of cherry-cake and nuts. After saving a tin of cream, I recognized, wrapped up in cloth, the chicken. By this time I began to feel the effects of asphyxiating gas, and was almost putting on my helmet, but on*

Harold Furguson. Harold Furguson was desperately unlucky. On Christmas Eve hi battalion was withdrawn into reserve at Albert. Whilst the odd shell in that forsaken town usually aroused little interest, that night, in a grim impersonation of the traditional Christmas message the German Army arranged th systematic shelling of the town for two hours. This made certain that there was no Christmas truce in 1915. Miraculously, although many of the men's billets were hit by shell fragments, there was not single casualty in the 2nd Salford Pals that night. (E&PJ 7/1/1916)

Bill Button in 1988.

second thoughts decided to chance it. Holding it out as far away as I could (Mick had bunked outside), I cut a little of the cloth away. Phew! what an odour... a closer look showed the poor chicken to be as green as grass, and jolly near walking... so we buried it with military honours in the dust heap.![12]

Other forms of humour took the form of verse. The Scout section of the 1st Pals, Lance Corporal W. Peters, Privates George Leeming, A. Charleson, W. Royle, H. Barker, E. Wall, R. Shenton, S. Blore and Bill Button, passed some of the time in the darkest hours of 1915's winter by writing a parody to the tune of 'My little grey home in the West'.

Bill Turner.

*We are the Salford Battalion you know,
We are anxious to get at the foe,
 And the lads they were gay
 As they went on their way,
To the trenches by night and by day,
And Fritz, with his machine gun,
Provides us with plenty of fun
 And the Scouts they did shout
 When they saw Fritz knocked out,
From their little dug-out in the West.
In our little dug-out in the West,
There were nine little Scouts having rest,
 And the Corporal he came,
 And said, 'What a game,'
There's a big German sniper gone West.
It was late when he came and told us,
But that made no difference to us,
 There were whizz bangs a ringing,
 And sausages singing,
O'er our little dug-out in the West.[13]*

Early in 1916 the Pals' brigading arrangements were altered, removing the 3rd Pals from the 96th Brigade to the 14th Brigade of the 32nd Division, their place in the 96th being taken by the 2nd Royal Inniskilling Fusiliers. This was part of the reorganisation, completed on 5th January, which was conducted throughout those parts of the B.E.F. composed entirely of New Army units. Their 'stiffening' by a regular battalion was thought necessary after some service battalions were, mistakenly, deemed to have shown lack of resolve during engagements in 1915.

The 'Skins' were splendid fellows, friendly and helpful, and of course magnificent to have next to you up the line. Naturally, we didn't attempt to compete with the Regulars as parade troops!.[14]

Already 'trench foot' and frost bite were becoming a serious problem and officers were constantly appealing for more socks to maintain the health of their men's feet. Grease was the best known protection,

...and the officers have to see personally that every man washes his feet in cold water, and has the grease well rubbed into feet and legs. When in very wet trenches the men have served out to them rubber boots reaching well up to the thigh. These are a great protection, but when the mud and water is waist deep, they are useless, as once filled they are the most uncomfortable things imaginable. To be absolutely free from damp one would have to be dressed almost as a deep sea diver. [15]

When out of the trenches the men foraged as best as they could amid the haphazard fields and villages behind the lines. Everyone found it impossible to maintain their kit in the filthy confines of the front lines, seeking every opportunity to rid themselves of the pestilential lice when back in billets,

...I'd been in the trenches for a fortnight at a time. Well when we come out we'd get in the houses and cellars what was left and we used to make a fire with wood and we used to put a brick on until it got very hot and then take our shirts and trousers off and go up the seams with this hot brick to kill the lice. We was alive with lice. Then we all started with scabies. We didn't know what the devil they was. Corporal Bill Turner. 3rd Pals.

Propaganda postcard carried by one of the Salford Pals to France. The inscription on the reverse says, 'Condemned to death by a military tribunal in Belgium, under the charge of having favoured the evasion of British soldiers. Miss Edith Cavell, of Norwich, a voluntary nurse, is taken to the execution ground on the 12th of October at daybreak'. Sampson

In the search for food and a real meal, borrowed pairs of wire cutters from stores proved the most handy of all implements in view of the fact that Bill and his mates were,

...skint, 'adn't a penny. One bloke, Worthington his name were, 'e got killed poor lad, said, 'We've nothing to eat, 'ave you owt?'. I said, 'I've nothing.' 'Well', 'e said, 'We'll 'ave to 'ave somethin'. What can we get?' I said, 'There's a potato field down there. Take your tin 'at and fill it. There's a shop down 'ere.' They said, 'We've no money for eggs.' I said, 'You and 'im go in shop and I'll go and get these wire cutters. Keep arguin' with 'er. You don't understand French and she doesn't understand English. Keep arguin', talkin' to 'er while you see me come back.' So we got sixteen eggs. I'd cut the wire, put 'em in me tin 'at. Put the wire back again. Off! We'd only just come off guard. Well 'ere we are stood with boiled potatoes in a bully beef tin with some water in, no peelin' 'em. When we'd done we got the eggs out, no bread, and we had a good feed. Corporal Bill Turner, 3rd Pals.

Behind the lines very few precious opportunities presented themselves to make a little on the side.

'... Talkin' to an old farmer and 'e wanted a ground sheet. I said to one of the lads, 'Sell 'im one of your groundsheets.' So one sold 'im a sheet for a franc. So 'e said, 'Ow will I go on come kit inspection?'. I said, 'Watch where 'e puts it and we'll pinch it back!' Oh dear, if ever I'd got caught with tricks I'd done in the Army I'd 'ave got shot, but you got that road that you didn't give a damn what come or went. Corporal Bill Turner, 3rd Pals.

Behind their front line trenches the Salford Pals all billeted at Martinsart, in reserve, during the January of 1916.

...a horrible smelly place. Though not very much strafed, it is almost a desert. The back garden of our billet is pitiful to see. It is all broken down and dug up in various places and smells of nothing on earth: and yet several patches of snowdrops are struggling to break through the awful desolation.[16]

On 17th January the founding sponsor of Salford's Brigade came to visit the 3rd Pals who had recently taken over in the G2 subsector. His men were really pleased with the 'exceptionally good and well drained' trenches which they had now inherited. One of the 'Trench Stores', always handed over on relief, was a cow! When he visited the site of their newly acquired trenches, here in front of Thiepval, the Member of Parliament for South Salford became the last civilian to see his Pals complete. Although the enemy was active in the use of rifle grenades and trench mortars on this day the borough's Tory MP was shown the wire which surrounded Thiepval and the 'very strong position commanding the valley as [well as the] several MGun emplacements [which] can be observed by telescope'.[17] Montague Barlow then travelled to meet the men of the 1st and 2nd Pals in their Bouzincourt and Henencourt billets.

German airborne reconnaissance photograph taken over Authuille during the spring of 1915 shows the relatively undamaged landscape, clear field patterns with uncut crops, the trees within Authuille Wood and the Leipzig Redoubt, east of the village. Desailly

During the afternoon Barlow kicked off a football match between the officers and sergeants. In the evening the whole of these two Battalions gathered for a concert and to hear Barlow convey the hopes and wishes of their families and friends back home in Salford.

> *The concert was given in the barn of a Chateau, the owner of which – a French Countess – occupied the chair. To present her with a bouquet various cabbages and cauliflowers had to be requisitioned.* [18]

However, no matter what organisational changes were effected and whatever brief recreational opportunities were afforded, the nightly fatigues and repairs had to continue unabated.

Henencourt Chateau, in whose outhouses and barns the Salford Pals were sometimes billeted during the spring of 1916. Reed

At the junction of the roads running between Authuille and La Boisselle, and Aveluy and Ovillers stood Crucifix Corner. Every one of Salford's Pals came to know this place as intimately as Chapel Street or Blackfriars Road at home. Here at the foot of the exposed convex slopes leading up from the Ancre, an old quarry provided shelters, dugouts and dumps for R.E. stores. Running past this hive of silent activity, balanced on the edge of the flooded and blasted pastures, the Authuille road was the scene, every night, for men to assemble as a 'working party' with stores drawn from 'The Brigade' at Lancashire Dump, Bapaume Post or Crucifix Corner itself.

...Fifty steel helmets stand in two rows perched upon fifty bodies hidden in fifty leather jerkins, which just conceal the tops of fifty pairs of rubber waders. Company Sergeant Major Y- stands upon the other side of the streak of white liquid mud which was once the main street of a prosperous French hamlet, and is now possibly known as 'Piccadilly'; he stands in semi-darkness with the air of a man whose arduous task is nearly done. Suddenly he stiffens and shouts, 'Party, 'shun!': salutes another figure, who has just appeared and reports 'Fifty other ranks all present, sir!' This last figure is the 'one officer'. It is now his move. 'Right-o, sergeant-major!' he says and then 'Party, slope ... up! Move to the right in fours, for...m fours! Right! By the right, quick – march! March at – ease! Good night sergeant-major! Tea be ready at 12 o'clock? Right. Good night!' 'Good night, sir!' replies the SM and disappears into the cheery warmth found nowhere else than in the SM's den, be it dugout or billet. The party swings off with a buzz of subdued conversation, chiefly consisting of remarks as 'Blinking sappers' orderlies', 'All for a tanner a day' etc.

After extracting with great difficulty sufficient tools from the Brigade, or rather from its worthy representative, a sleepy, surly storeman, the party will at last arrive at Crucifix Corner, expecting (if they have not been out very long) to find 2/Lt. X-of the R.E. If on the other hand they have been out some time; our 'one officer' and his sergeant will scour the surrounding dugouts for the inevitable lance-corporal of the sappers. When found he will conduct the party by dirty, devious and possibly dangerous paths to the various 'jobs' alloted to them. 'I'd like four men here, sir, please.' 'First four here, sergeant,' says the subaltern, 'and L. Cpl Q-.'And so it goes on. Possibly at 7.30 (if so soon) the subaltern will find himself accompanied only by his sergeant and the L. Cpl: of sappers, asking of each in turn where it is that the second party of six men are working: they may be able to tell him or they may not!

The next four or five hours he will spend trudging round his various parties seeing that they are doing their work, and occasionally dropping in on an hospitable Company Head-Quarters with a laconic 'Good Evening, Fatigue Party' as the only explanation of his sudden appearance. In the course of his wanderings he will also probably meet 2/Lt X – of the R.E. whom he will accompany round all his parties, pointing out how hard the men are working and in the same breath inquiring how long he will be required to stay. 'Oh, knock 'em off about 11.30, they're working pretty well tonight,' will probably be his orders.

So when 11.30 is getting near our subaltern will tell his sergeant to collect the parties to a certain spot and will himself make a last tour round to see if any men or tools are left behind, and then the whole party hurry off down the trench; jolly glad to think that 'That's that'. As soon as the road is reached, they form up and swing off, dump the tools at the 'Brigade' and are then dismissed at their billets. The cooks bring up to the Company Headquarters a steaming 'dixie' of tea and by the time the '50 other ranks' are fallen in again with their mess tins, the 'one officer' has poured the rum in and the sergeant is ready to dish it out. That goes down well, very well. 'Exeunt ommes' gratified if tired; and so to bed! The game is over.[19]

Nighttime activity was always the men's accustomed lot.

Sentries on duty noted the occasional 'burst of rapid rifle fire' in F1 or G3; spotters counted the flashes and reports as shells launched from St. Pierre Divion rumbled overhead en-route to their destination in Albert or Aveluy Wood; wiring working parties witnessed silently to the dull crunch and glare of the reply as howitzer shells fell on the Chateau's wreckage opposite. Officers moved quietly among the sentries, stepping round the sleeping platoon members who had avoided tonight's working party. Newly dug machine gun posts were frequently attacked with 'six rounds of Minenwerfer'. Teams with spades and revetting material then sweated their way forward to make good the damage to parapet or dug-out. 'Our Bombing Officer fired several rifle grenades at DIAMOND WOOD.....fired rifle-grenades from MAISON GRIS. Enemy replied with the same sort of missiles – wounding 4 men.' A perpetual activity was being undertaken to gain the supremacy of No Man's Land from the men whose furtive activities opposite they nightly tried to identify and despoil. During the night of February 14th, Lieutenant Nightingale's patrol left Maison Gris sap to investigate the state of the wire. Just twenty-five yards away a new German sap was discovered.

Pte. J. TAYLOR,
Barlow-lane, Winton,
Lancashire Fusiliers.

Pte. WM. LOVATT,
54, Broomhall-rd., P'bury,
Lancashire Fusiliers.

> A sentry was fired at by our snipers at point R25C62. He did not appear after second shot. His hat appeared to be slate blue and similar to a 'Glengarry'.[20]

The sunken Mill Road, running from Thiepval down towards the Ancre in front of the Hammerhead and Peterhead saps, was the perpetual scene of nocturnal activity, designed to deny the area to the enemy. Sometimes small groups went out under cover of the early darkness but the frequent, sudden illumination of flares and the attentions of the machine guns in Thiepval's cemetery, just north of the village at R25b7/7, always made this risky. Far better to wait until the tired depths of night when patrols often left these trenches into the

Sergt. J. CARTER,
1, Paradise-st., Eccles,
Lancashire Fusiliers.

Pte. T. SMITH,
12, Crawford-st., Monton,
Lancashire Fusiliers.

frosty blackness of 3 or 4 o'clock in the morning. If the cloud was thick enough a few Mills bombs would be thrown to see what the response would be. Usually another lazy rocket flare and a desultory shot rang out. Sometimes the nights were still and without incident. On other occasions the German machine gunners tried a new location; in the trees opposite Thiepval Point North; the church belfry; sometimes the recesses of Schwaben Redoubt, and a brief bout of trench mortar rounds and Vickers gun fire would disturb the silence again.

cc-Cpl. A. BLUER,
Worsley-st., P'bury,
Lancs. Fusiliers.

Corpl. H. DAWSON,
103, Pendlebury-rd., S'ton,
Lancashire Fusiliers.

Surrounding this surreal life at the 'Front of the Front' there was a constant succession of movements out of the line, into support, into reserve and the never-ending provision of carrying and repair parties followed by reliefs back into the line. As a consequence the rest billets were much anticipated. But, in Senlis, Bouzincourt, Henencourt, Montigny and as far back as Rainneville the accomodation was often terrible.

-Cpl. J. BEBBINGTON,
ligher Croft, Barton,
Lancashire Fusiliers.

Pte. F. CROMPTON,
40, Park-st., Patricroft,
Lancs. Fusiliers.

> ...the weather was bitterly cold, and when it was not freezing and snowing, it was certainly raining. The room also had a stone floor and a stove that no one could light or keep alight for more than a quarter of an hour. It was owned by an awful specimen of humanity, whom we dubbed 'Jimmy' (why on earth, I cannot tell) and his wife who was known as Mrs Jimmy. Jimmy would always insist on trying to light the stove, which was even more unruly with him than with us. He spoke an almost unintelligible 'patois', and all the time slobbered at the corners of his mouth – altogether he was a most disgusting sight; and his clothes were filthy! Mrs Jimmy was almost as bad, but occasionally made us some very good coffee. Whenever we retaliated with a tot of rum or a tin of ration tobacco, their delight would be almost ape-like. Indeed I should be sorry for

Pte. S. PRICE,
25, Earl-st., Swinton,
Lancashire Fusiliers.

Pte. H. WORTHINGTON,
11, King-st., Eccles,
Lancashire Fusiliers.

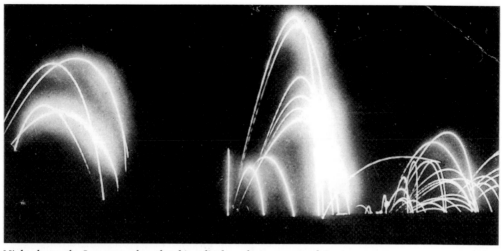

Night sky on the Somme – a breath-taking display – but men were dying.

rural France if they were the ordinary type. And so for all the time we were there we sat and shivered, stamping our feet and glaring at the smoking stove – that was another of its little foibles – while the old couple jabbered and slobbered and cast more unspeakable filth upon the already disgusting midden, just under our window.[21]

He was in clover.

The men often did without a roof or 'smoking stove', throughout the piercing cold of that winter.

By the end of January life in the 'quiet sector' of the Somme had become progressively more belligerent. On the 26th of that month the 3rd Pals re-entered the lines at Authuille, as relief to the 16th Northumberland Fusiliers, only to discover that their trenches had been shelled all day.

'Authuille. 27th. Kaiser's birthday, slight anxiety as to what the enemy might do. Our guns gave them a birthday present at 6 p.m. – this necessitated the Battn taking refuge in dugouts – 400 men working all day. 28th. Large working parties – quiet day until 6 p.m. when the enemy returned with thanks our birthday present of the 27th. Result – 3 G.S. waggons of the R.F.A. broke away, one horse killed, 2 others wounded. One of these waggons upset 'A' Coys rations which were fortunately retrieved later. Transport had lucky escape as they shelled AVELUY as it passed through – no casualties. 29th. Enemy bombarded our Trenches in G2 subsector opposite their village of Thiepval, trenches and wire badly damaged...[22]

Pte. A. H. COLDWELL,
40, Charlton-av., P'croft,
Lancashire Fusiliers.

It was into the depths of the coldest period of this winter that the 35th Division, including the last of Salford's active service battalions, arrived. The 4th Pals had left Park House Camp on Salisbury plain on 29th January 1916, crossing the Channel on the 30th from Southampton to Le Havre. A week later, in what must have been an arrangement made in the true English tradition of theatrical farce, representative parties of officers and men from Salford's Bantams were attached to the Guards' Division for initial instruction in the arts of trench warfare! On their arrival at the farm buildings which were to be their 'bedder',

'They skirted the side of the building and turned into a large courtyard. From a cesspool in the centre came an indefinite, unpleasant smell of damp rubbish and sewage. Round the cesspool ran a narrow brick causeway, on to which gave a door and several windows. Across the cesspool was an open barn full of tall men, lying, sitting and playing cards by the light of candles.'[23]

Pte. T. JONES,
15,South King-st., W'ton,
Lancashire Fusiliers.

The Kaiser's birthday, Kaisersgeburtstag, *27 January, 1916. This building behind the lines in the Somme sector is decorated to celebrate the occasion. British artillery observed the day with suitable bombardments.*

For a few of the 4th Pals it was their first introduction to the world of reserve billets which were often to be their lot for the next three years.

Shortly after this incongruous meeting between the tallest and shortest of Britain's Army the 4th Pals had the privilege of an inspection by Lord Kitchener, undertaken on 11th February at Racquinghem. Since the Bantam Salfords had not been established on the occasion of his visit to Manchester, in March of 1915, the inspection at Racquinghem completed the process by which Kitchener, instrumental in raising the New Armies, had now inspected or reviewed each of Salford borough's civic battalions.

By the end of February the rest of the 4th Pals were undergoing their first tour of front line trench duty and instruction under the guidance of the 19th Welsh Regiment at Richebourg.

One of the regular War Effort processions, held through the streets of Salford, which resulted in so many of the 'comforts' sent to the town's Pals' Battalions. (SLHL)

At home in Salford the published descriptions of conditions at the front were carefully sanitised, with no reference to 'unspeakable filth', 'cesspools' or 'disgusting middens'. Whilst details of individual deaths and other casualties were reported in the local press with sensitivity and care, the preoccupations of many column inches were the surviving soldiers' comforts and welfare. The Pals were the community's favoured sons and benefitted accordingly.

> Nobody but those who have been out here in the winter know the value of them. The, socks are the very best I have had on, and they were welcome. As for the helmet, I hardly know how to thank you for it. I never put on anything so warm and cosy in my life. It makes you feel you could do an extra turn when you feel so comfortable.[24]

By stark contrast, men who enlisted into other units told a different story. It was a constant complaint from local men outside the Pals' fraternity.

> ... A sapper in the Royal Engineers, who says he gets the 'Journal' every week, says it would seem as if only the 'Pals' needed anything. 'I have been away,' he says, 'for two Christmasses, and have not received a single present from anyone yet....Surely someone will look after such chaps as us.'[25]

Letters in the Journal from Pals' Company commanders were carefully structured to throw a much more reassuring light on the men's status, always claiming to be in fine spirits, and anticipating the receipt of further comforts.

Sometimes the men's letters claimed a divine intervention which ensured adequate protection. Private W. Moran (10058 No. 1 Platoon, A Coy 1st Pals) wrote that,

> 'Up to now we have had only two deaths, one killed by a sniper and one died of wounds, and very few wounded. We are known by the 2nd and 3rd Salford Battalions as 'God's Own,' and we hope we may continue to keep lucky.'[26]

German Raid, 10th March

Late on the evening of 10th March the 2nd Pals had their first taste of close contact with the enemy. A wiring party in front of the Battalion's trenches was driven in by a ferocious bombardment which extended beyond their own lines. It was the start of a raid, the like of which the men had not seen before.

For the first time the whole battalion stood to during the terrifying ordeal of 'minnies', rifle grenades, 'oilcans' and shells,[27] launched from the fortifications which stood starkly above. Many sentries were killed or injured. Amongst those was Sergeant Percy Machell (12589), hit by a large fragment of shell whilst encouraging his men to stay calm and collected in the face of the bombardment which straddled their firing lines. Percy Machell was the first of the Salford policemen, who had enlisted with such enthusiasm into Salford's Pals, to be killed.

This event was, if anyone there or at home needed it, a reminder that this area did not always provide the relatively quiet trenches with which the men had become so familiar. Lieutenant Colonel Abercrombie wrote at once to one young officer's parents, Mr and Mrs Rylands of Worsley.

> 'I am sorry that your son was amongst the wounded on March 10th, but hasten to tell you that his hurt is not serious, and should not be very long before it is all right. Your son was hit early in the action, but refused to go to the dressing station, and stayed at his post until the shelling ceased before he would consent to have his wound attended to. We cannot afford to lose such a cool and devoted officer as your son has shown himself to be.'[28]

For other people at home the news would be far worse. Bloodstained caps and equipment in and at the entrance to the C.S.M's store in a front line dugout had provided evidence of fierce hand to hand fighting. One officer, 2nd Lieutenant N. H. Anderton, and seven men were missing. 2nd Lieutenant A. Jarvis was wounded, as was 2nd Lieutenant Harold Rylands. 2nd Lieutenant Robert W. Sharratt, an original officer who had gone to Conway with the 2nd Pals, was killed during this action. His brother was serving as an officer with the 1st Pals.[29]

Watching from reserve, behind the same lines at Authuille, one 15th Battalion machine gunner, Private J. Hughes, witnessed the scene and later wrote,

They started bombarding us at 11 p.m., and kept it up until 12.30 a.m., and I don't think there has been anything worse for the time being in any part of the line. I should think we had 2,000 shells all about our little place. The flare from the shells so illuminated the place that we thought the village was on fire.... We had to sit in our cellar, with no help for ourselves and trust to luck. We expected a shell dropping in every second. The noise of the bursting shells, especially the big ones, was deafening, and as they came through the air they sounded like engines coming along. We dare not venture out, as shrapnel was bursting in front of us, and there were holes all around where shells had dropped. One of these holes is about 16 feet in circumference and on what is left of the walls are marks where they were struck by the shells. Men said their prayers who, perhaps, had never said them before. I can tell you that we are most exceptionally lucky fellows, and we congratulated outselves later when we sat down to breakfast. The Huns also shelled the trenches, and I can assure you that they found their billets. The trenches and the dug-outs were blown up. I am sorry to say that from what I hear the casualty list will be a large one.[30]

One officer who experienced the ordeal and survived, C. S. Marriot, photographed near Albert, April 1916. (LFM)

It had been a daring and well executed raid.

When the clearing up was done and the trenches restored, these events were discovered to have cost the 16th battalion of the Lancashire Fusiliers many shell shocked men, incapable for some time of continuing in the line, the missing who were probably now prisoners and many dead and wounded. Outside their trenches a tape marked the route which their opponents had followed, across No Man's Land, into a crater just outside the Salfords' parapet. Once again the fortunate 1st Salfords, 'God's Own', had escaped the worst. Actual casualties in the 2nd Pals were as follows:

	Killed	Wounded	Missing	Shock
Officers	1	4	1	–
Men	12	31	7	16

1 Officer and 2 men died from their wounds during the next two days. (Details from the Bn. War Diary. 1–17th March 1916. PRO reference: WO 95/2397.)

During the next few days the 2nd Pals moved down to so called 'billets' in the utter devastation of Authuille. Hardly a building stood as more than a vestige of its previous structure. Throughout the night of the 13th they were shelled continuously. On the 14th the shelling continued during the day. On the 15th the village was again subjected to a barrage throughout the night. On the 16th they were back in the misery of the front line.

Such was the constant awfulness of trench warfare.

For 2nd Lieutenant Anderton these events had become the start of three years' imprisonment. The conditions to which officers were subjected were relatively relaxed, without the forced working parties which the men would be exposed to throughout the later years of the war.

Memorial Silk to Herbert Feeney (27452), 1st Pals. Killed February 11th, 1916. Pullen
Along with the other early casualties of the Salford Pals, Herbert Feeney is buried in the Authuille Military Cemetery on the steep slopes south of the village where shelters provided cover for soldiers in support behind the front lines. Although the whole area was devastatingly shelled, the steepness of these slopes ensured that only a few early graves were destroyed by that shelling.

During a lighter moment, a group of officers share some of the benefits of their greater affluence. On the right, pouring wine, is Walter Sharratt, whose brother Robert was also serving in the Salford Brigade. LFM

To the right of the 2nd Pals the 3rd Pals had watched and listened to the 'bombing stunt', whilst engaged in their continuing nightly rounds of duty, listening and digging. Their first tour in the X7 subsector at Ovillers, ending on 15th March, had revealed the intensity of preparations which were going on below the trenches and saps opposite. Many of the hidden machine gun nests were being strengthened with sections of the narrow gauge railway lines which abounded behind the German lines and which had served the outlying farms and villages in the Albert hinterland before the outbreak of war. Writing to his father, Geoffrey Bowen identified the hectic schedules of this front line tour of duty.

> We came out of the trenches last night after rather a strenuous time as regards work, as the General, the C.O. and the Second in Command all came round and told us to do different things. The General wanted some saps deepened, as he is thinking of digging another trench out in front of our firing line and using the saps as communication trenches. The C.O. wanted us to clean out an old support trench which he had reported passable, but which had so fallen in that it would not hide a boy, and the Second in Command wanted to make traverses. The General and C.O. were quite pleased with us, as we showed them work other units had done for us, but the Second in Command was not taken in at all. The German was very quiet, as he had just built a new trench just in front of us, and we could hear him working away practically night and day. We could hear him talking and hammering on iron, and throwing iron girders about. We turned the artillery on to him, which stopped him for a time. He must have been making some beautiful dugouts. We had some snow one night, which made it very cold for the men. They have to be out on the fire-step all night

British prisoners being marched away from the Front where they have been captured during one of the many trench raids.

2nd Lieutenant Anderton, with other prisoners of many nationalities.

2nd Lieutenant Norman Anderton.

Signed card guaranteeing not to attempt escape.

565

Lt. W. H. Anderton

By this card I give my word of honour, that during the walks outside the camp I will not escape nor attempt to make an escape, nor will I make any preperation to do so, nor will I attempt to commit any action during this time to the prejudice of the German Empire.

I give also my word of honour to use this card only myself and not to give it to any other prisoner of war.

W. H. Anderton (2nd Lt.)

16th Lancs. Fus.

and are not allowed in their dugouts between dusk and dawn. After 'stand-to' in the morning, they have their breakfast and sleep till lunch. During the afternoon and most of the night they work.[31]

1st Pals' Raid, Authuille

Revenge for the Pals was not swift. But on the night of the 5/6th May the 1st Pals' own raid achieved a notable success. Moving up from reserve dugouts at Black Horse Bridge some fifty men and four officers arrived at the 16th's trenches in Boggart Hole Clough (in Xla) south of the Leipzig salient at 11.00 p.m. At the same time the G.O.C. 32nd Division, Major-General Rycroft, arrived at the advance report station on the Bouzincourt road to watch the bombardment. Immediately the scouts moved out into No Man's Land, quickly reporting that in view of the dark and stormy weather conditions there was no German patrol activity in the area.

All was set for a successful raid.

Within minutes parties were taking out a Bangalore Torpedo[32] and layers were feeding guiding tapes out under the direction of Captain Ernest MacLaren, who along with Sergeant J. Pollitt had reconnoitred the ground the previous night.

They were protected on their left, from the tip of the salient, by two Lewis gun teams led by Sergeant Pollitt and by an enormous barrage fired by the artillery of 32nd Division and which began to fall on the blunt nose of Leipzig salient at midnight. To either side of the raid 'dummy' bombardments from the flanking division's heavy howitzers were fired to deceive the salient's defences as to where the raid would fall. The trenches which were to be the object of this raid, just east of Leipzig redoubt around Xla9/8, were saturated with shells from an 18 pdr battery, four 4.5″ howitzers, four 6″ howitzers and five 2″ trench mortars.[33] Under cover of this very specific artillery barrage the first group of men under the command of Major Robert Thomas had moved up to within sixty yards of the German trenches and the precision of the shellfire was inspiring confidence among the men, none of whom had been in this sort of exposed position before. It was easy to see in the light of hundreds of explosions, yet no retaliation was forthcoming. However, at 12.25 the first Bangalore Torpedo failed to explode. A second was hurriedly brought up and this detonated, causing the initial one to explode as well, smashing a gap of ten yards through the concertina wire and apron fencing. By 12.33 a.m., the raiding parties, commanded by Captain Smith, Lieutenant Heald and 2nd Lieutenant Younger, rushed into the enemy trenches whilst the bombardment continued on the support trenches to the rear.

Five prisoners, belonging to the 109th Reserve Regiment of the 28th Reserve Division, were brought out of their dug-out by Lieutenant Heald and perhaps thirty more were killed as grenades were thrown into other dug-outs. Resistance was minimal, seemingly vanquished by the ferocity of the artillery, which had damaged a number of these structures. Up to this point, at 12.45 a.m., not one Salford man had been injured and the parties of men began to withdraw. However this was the moment when the German counter barrage began. Whilst waiting in a depression before returning to their own trenches in front of Aintree Street Captain Robert J. Smith, Second Lieutenant John Younger, Sergeant Thomas Brooks (11035) and Private Ernest Wall (10924) were killed by the German artillery's response which was sweeping No Man's Land, Private George Looming (10096) dying of his wounds soon after. Captain Ernest C. MacLaren escaped with the help of his steel helmet which was smashed by shell fragments, leaving him dazed but with no more damage than cuts to his forehead.

An officer of the 1st Pals poses with an unexploded shell at Aveluy during March 1916. Willcock

But these isolated hours of terror and tension which shattered the drudgery of trench routine were a real foreshadowing of far greater events whose terrible timetable was already set in motion. Those plans centred on the opportunities which would unfold when a massive combined assault, at the junction of Britain and France's Armies, fell on the German lines, astride the River Somme and its tributary, the Ancre.

In the epicentre of the expected holocaust, up some of the steepest slopes which the Ancre ran past, the Salford Pals were an integral part of that Division whose task it was to assault and take that crucial village, Thiepval. The key to unlocking the defences of the Pozieres-Bazentin Ridge.[34]

Beyond lay the villages of Martinpuich and Courcelette in an almost untouched countryside. From the plateau's heights observation of Bapaume and its crucial road and rail links would be possible. To the south, east of Albert, were Mametz and Montauban, which if successfully captured by the Manchester and Liverpool Pals would leave the Pozieres-Thiepval ridge observed and under direct fire from both ends, and therefore indefensible. On 7th June the G.O.C. 32nd Division, General Rycroft, came up to each battalion headquarters in the Authuille sector to explain his hopes for a successful outcome and to detail the assault training which Salford's Pals were confident would ensure success.

One letter from John Howard (10069) to his father, posted a month before the forthcoming events, predicted a sudden end to the war, allowing him to be home soon. *[Bailey]* The text reads:

> 'Dear Father. Just a few lines to you Hoping to find you in the Best of Health as it leaves me at present. Dear Father I received your kind and welcome letter and Parcel and I thank your very much for it tell our Nelly I thank her very much for the Papers and toffee tell our Polly I have had a letter of Billy and he is doing alright, well I hope you are looking after and I hope you are having some nice weather for we are having Champion weather at Present tell our Maggie I have seen nothing of Joe yet. well Dad we are having it alright here at Present for we do about eight days in the trenches and then we have twenty four out so you see we are not having it So bad for when we first came out we use to do eight in the trenches and eight out and it use to be rotten.

A last postcard sent to Lance Corporal George Aspden (27344, 3rd Salfords) from his wife and seven children. Below: The account, which appeared in the press soon after he was killed by shellfire whilst in Brigade reserve trenches at Crucifix Corner near Aveluy, is reproduced here:

Mrs Aspden, 7 Dumbell Street, Pendlebury, has this week received the sad news that her husband, Lance-Corporal George Aspden, has been killed in action. He was in the Second Swinton Pals' Company of the Lancashire Fusiliers, and had been on active service about six months. The information was sent by his company officer, Captain Haywood. "It is with deep regret," wrote Captain Haywood, "that I write to inform you of the death of your husband. We were subjected to a heavy bombardment last night (14th May), and at the time your husband was in the front line. I am sorry to say that he was hit in the head with a piece of shrapnel, and killed instantaneously. He was such a bright and good soldier, and will be sadly missed by us all. He was later buried in a cemetery just in the rear of the line, along with the other men of our battalion who were killed. We express our deepest sympathy with you in your great loss. You will be comforted to know that he died a soldier, doing his duty for his King and country." The deceased soldier, who was 34 years of age, was married and leaves a widow and seven children. Before enlisting he was employed at the Clifton Hall Colliery. Two of his brothers are also on active service, John being at Salonika, and Thomas in France.

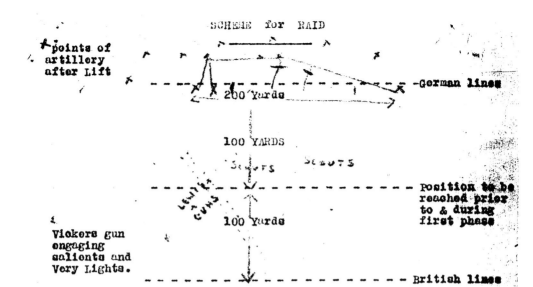

SCHEME for RAID

↗ points of
artillery
after Lift

200 Yards — German lines

100 YARDS

Scouts   Scouts

— Position to be
reached prior
to & during
first phase

LEWIS GUNS

100 Yards

Vickers gun
engaging
salients and
Very Lights.

— British lines

The General Idea is as follows:-   Zero time 12 midnight

Hrs.	Min.	Sec.	
0	0	0	Start bombardment on Right Flank of the position to be attacked
0	5	0	Start bombardment on Real point
0	10	0	Start bombardment on Left flank
0	24	30	*Lift* Right bombardment on Real point
0	25	0	Continue bombardment round Real point

Barrage

After this ½ minute pause - Raiders go in

| 0 | 45 | 0 | Raiders start coming out if they have not already started back with prisoners or other prizes |
| 0 | 60 | 0 | Cease fire |

The Special Idea for Infantry:-

The party will consist of 10 groups -

in each group   4 persons

Total:-   40

Scouts, Vickers & Lewis
guns:-   18 persons

Grand total   58

Plans for the raid on the German trenches taken from documents now available clearly showing the method employed during this raid. (WO 95/2397)

Detail of groups:-

		Off	Sgts	Men
Group 1	Advanced patrol		1	3
" 2	Leader and tape layers	1		3
" 3	Torpedo		1	3
" 4	Sentry tacklers & Blockers	1		3
" 5	" " "		1	3
" 6	Dugouts and Snatchers		1	3
" 7	" "	1		3
" 8	" "		1	3
" 9	" "		1	3
" 10	Bell ringers and clearing out party - bring up the rear coming back, after counting every one out.	1		3

(Reinforced by the torpedo men 1sgt 3 men)

.................;

Movements and dispositions.

Advanced patrol parties out and watchers.

Groups go out of trench in order, and take up positions towards half-way or thereabouts as circumstances allow - the head of the column pushing as near as out preliminary bombardment will permit.

(During this bombardment 2" trench mortar places 15 bombs as near the spot of entry as possible. This will guide leader and help to keep direction)

At 0. 25. 0 leaders guides torpedoes to point of entry - sets torpedo and retires.

at 0. 26. 0 torpedo explodes.

Group 4 now finds itself at the head of the tape and rushes in.

Group 5 follows in.

The remaining groups are now coming along the tape in rear, and push in outer trench, and seize prisoners, or any objects of military importance.

A group is to be satisfied if it can secure and bring away 2 prisoners or a machine gun, and having obtained such success will at once withdraw reporting to the clearing officer (Group 10) who remains at the exit with his party on guard.

Group 10 commences bell-ringing and trench clearing at 0. 45½ 0 or sooner as circumstances dictate.

The leader is to explore and send back 3 messengers, at 5 minutes intervals, from the time of entry reporting progress.

A pass-word will be given and told to our troops holding trenches so that anyone getting back off the tape line can shout it out on approaching our line.

the only thing that is rotten out here is that they only pay us once in the twenty four days we are out and we get five franks and that is only three shilling and two pence so you see they dont give us much they have enter your Credit up in our Books up to December 31st and I am 3 pound 3 shillings in credit and I am going to transfer it to you if I can. Dad ask our Minnie how is it Dick never thinks of writting to Me? for it is ages since I heard how he was going on well Dad. I think the war will come to end all of a sudden so cheer up for I am expecting it wont belong before I am home with you. give Mr Eamshaw my best respects and the Manglers at the [bleach and dye] works hoping you are keeping in the pink. So Good night and God Bless you all. John.

Lce. Cpl. G. Aspden.

For Salford's men the months of waiting in squalid bleakness below Thiepval was soon to end. There was an optimism about the cause, and a desire to get the sacrifice and effort done. It percolated all of the Pals' battalions at this time. And it was clear to every man, from the massive preparations, the munitions dumps, the road strengthening and growing

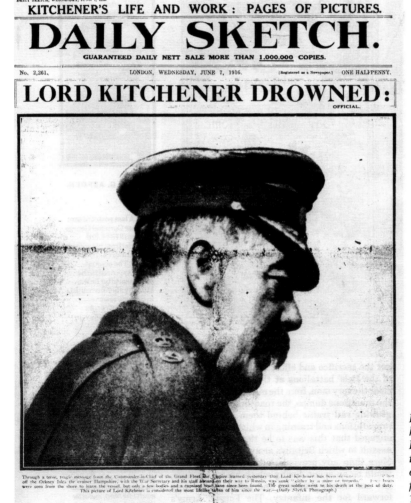

Remember Kitchener! Newsp. headlines announce the dea. Lord Kitchener, drowned u. the cruiser Hampshire was s. off the Orkneys whilst en r. for Russia. (Daily Sketch, June 1916)

rail traffic behind them as well as the preparations and training in which they were now engaged that this was to be the most enormous assault to which Britain's army had yet been put. More than any previous battle of the war, this would be an event during which heavy artillery, gas and mines smashed and prepared the way forward for the infantry. The Fourth Army's aspirations were revealed by Rawlinson's declaration in April that, 'The capture of a system of hostile trenches is an easy matter compared with the difficulty of retaining it'.[35]

This was real opportunity. Salford's sons had enlisted in the hope the war would not be over before they did their bit. Now these soldiers felt they had the opportunity to hasten the end, even win it, and with luck be rid of Authuille's dreadful circumstances. One man was already out. On 21st June he and another officer had been wounded by the explosion of a rifle grenade in their trenches. His wound consisted of broken bones but he was still surprised to be sent home. Every hospital in France was now being cleared in preparation for the 'big push', and two days after his operation to reset the bones "of his right hand Clifford Platt was crossing the Channel on the hospital ship Asturias, en-route to Stoodley Knowle Officers' Hospital in Torquay.

Notes

1. Hermann Hesse, *Demian*, Chapter 8, p 152.
2. Sgt. Ben Broadhurst, 2nd Pals, letter home, quoted in S.C.R. 18/2/1916.
3. Geoffrey Bowen, Memoir. Privately printed c1930. Captain Bowen had been invalided home earlier in the summer of 1915, following an attack of jaundice contracted whilst serving with the 2nd Battalion Lancashire Fusiliers.
4. 2nd Lieutenant Platt's material. Imperial War Museum. Reference 78/72/1.
5. Ibid.
6. Ibid.
7. Ibid.
8. Geoffrey Bowen, Memoir, p 34.
9. Platt's op cit. The "Ilot" was a series of craters, blown on the Albert-Bapaume road, immediately in front of the E3 sector British trenches at La Boisselle.
10. A full description appears in the Eccles and Patricroft Journal, 7/1/1916, written by "Rien n'va Plus".
11. S.C.R. 30/12/1915.
12. E&PJ. 7/1/1916.
13. S.C.R. 30/12/1915.
14. Lieutenant C. S. Marriot's account, written in December 1964. Lancashire Fusiliers Museum. Bury.
15. Captain Lyon. B Coy. 3rd Pals. in letter to Mr Brookes, J.P., quoted in E&PJ. 11/2/1916.
16. Platt op cit.
17. PRO. WO 95/2394. Intelligence Report, Jan 17/18th, 19th LFs.
18. Salford Chronicle, 22/4/1916.
19. Platt op cit.
20. PRO. WO 95/2394.
21. Platt op cit.
22. PRO. WO 95/2394.
23. Lieutenant R. A. S. Coke, 4th Salford Pals, from his book *Youth Before the Flood* pp 189-190.
24. Pte. C. Mather. 3rd Pals. E&PJ. 4/2/1915.
25. E&PJ. 31/3/1916.
26. Salford Chronicle. 19/2/1916.
27. E&PJ. 31/3/1916 contains "Rien n'va Plus" account.
28. E&PJ. 24/3/1916.
29. A. W. Jarvis was an ex-Manchester 'Pal', later commissioned in the 2nd Salford Pals. R.W. Sharratt was an ex-Manchester Grammar School and University O.T.C. member. See Salford Chronicle, 18/3/1916. Harold Rylands would be Killed in Action at Beaumont Hamel on 23/11/1916. His brother, Captain R.V. Rylands, had already been killed at Gallipoli. 2nd Lieutenant John G. A. Scott had been commissioned into the 2nd Pals from the Sportsman's Battalion, he died soon after from the wounds he received during the raid. The Salford Chronicle of 25/3/1916 carries a number of letters and accounts dealing with the events of 10–11/3/1916.
30. Pte. J. Hughes quoted in E&PJ. 24/3/1916.

31. Geoffrey Bowen, Memoir, p 34.
32. An explosive charge whose detonation was designed to tear gaps in barbed wire defences.
33. The 8th Division's barrage 5 minutes beforehand, the 36th Division's barrage 5 minutes after the raid started. See PRO, WO 95/2367, WO 95/2375 and WO 95/2397 for details. Ammunition expended by the 32nd Division's artillery during the raid included 2,633 18 pdr rounds, 490 4.5″ howitzer rounds, 70 6″ rounds and 138 2″ trench mortar rounds.
34. Standing roughly 70 metres above the floor of the Ancre valley at Authuille. In reality a broad, flat plateau rather than a defined ridge.
35. Fourth Army, "Tactical Notes". Often referred to as "that bloody pamphlet, the bible". (Marriot papers).

Chapter Four

The First Days of Battle
'Be of Good Courage.'[1] ...

... he wanted to go over the top with the company.[2]

The Chairman of the Eccles 'comforts' fund, H. J. Albrow. Salford Museum.

The men were confident and well satisfied that everything was being done to ensure success. From home a torrent of 'comforts' continued to sustain and aid most of these civic soldiers. Earlier in June the 1st Eccles Pals had received 500 soap cakes, 500 candles, 500 tins of insect powder, 240 packs of boracic powder, 200 sulphur bags, 240 pairs of socks, 240 khaki handkerchiefs, 240 writing pads and envelopes, 6 collapsible wickless stoves with refills, magazines, 80 tins of Oxo cubes, 40 tins of cocoa, tea, sugar, dried milk cubes and books! Indeed all of the Eccles Pals' Companies were sustained by an incredibly vigorous comforts committee which made them the envy of other units!

The build up of munitions in the area was staggering. Beneath Thiepval ridge Authuille Wood was now home to dumps of nearly 5,000 trench mortar rounds, 22,000 grenades and 2,000,000 rounds of Small Arms Ammunition, (SAA). The village of Authuille itself sheltered identical dumps, themselves backed up by vast stocks in the area of Lancashire Dump on the edge of Aveluy Wood. A further 2,000,000 rounds of SAA were dumped in Thiepval Wood behind the 96th Brigade's front, again together with 4,500 Trench Mortar rounds and 22,000 grenades. Water filling stations, prisoner cages, debriefing centres, R.E. dumps, HQ posts and

Build-up on the Somme front in preparation for the 'Big Push'. Taylor Library

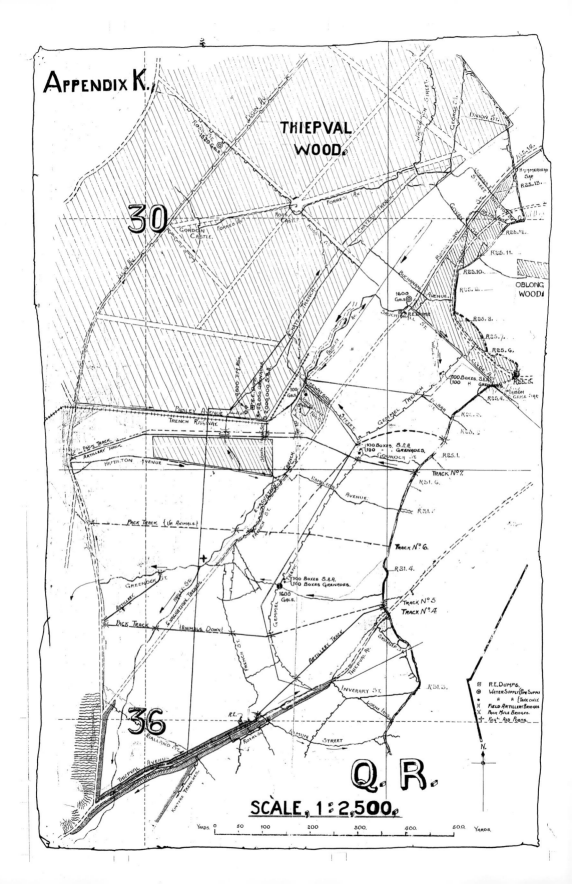

APPENDIX K.

THIEPVAL WOOD.

30

36

Q. R.

SCALE, 1:2,500.

YARDS 0   50   100   200.   300.   400.   500. YARDS.

artillery pits proliferated in any declivity along the Ancre's banks and in Blighty Valley below Authuille Wood. Evacuation trenches were identified[3], leading to the dressing stations at Tramway Corner and the Black Horse shelters. Divisional collecting posts for casualties were established at Black Horse Bridge, with an advanced Corps Collecting post on the Bouzincourt road out of Aveluy. Casualty Clearing would be further back at Warloy-Baillon. All this was required to service the attack by the 96th, 97th and 14th Brigades on a front measuring little more than a mile in width. Fortunately for the 1st Salfords much of the carrying required to get the huge weight of munitions across the Ancre's flooded valley was done by other battalions.

June had been the month during which the Pals had spent their longest period, so far, out of the lines. On the hillsides which surrounded Warloy-Baillon for two weeks, from the 14th to the 27th of June, the 1st Pals rehearsed their role as an assault battalion in the forthcoming battle. The 2nd Pals managed nine days at Senlis, between the 13th and 21st, but the 3rd Pals were less lucky, just four days at Warloy-Baillon from the 24th to the 27th. This training was conducted according to the rather wooden principles contained within the 'Tactical Notes', written by Henry Rawlinson, G.O.C Fourth Army. Those

Thiepval Chateau Chapel in 1915, before the intense shelling of 1916 reduced it to rubble. The officer is General Leutnant Freiherr von Soden, c/o 26th Reserve Division. Reed.

comments and instructions which dealt with attacks upon 'Defended Localities, such as Woods and Villages' were of special relevance to the battalions being prepared to carry the assault at Thiepval.

> *(e) The offensive action of the defenders of these localities can be entirely neutralized by heavy bombardments of H.E. shells, smoke, and lacrymatory projectiles, combined with a shrapnel barrage on the outskirts, and troops can advance on either side of the locality with little loss or interference.*
>
> *(f) To complete the neutralization, the attention of defenders of the front of the locality facing our lines must be held by an infantry attack, either by the fire or direct assault of a limited number of men.'[4]*

So, here on the hills behind the front lines Salford's men walked forward, rifles at the slope, occupying the imaginary and bereft wreckage that was thought of as having once been German trenches. Beyond each day's assault lines, tapes marked out their fanciful routes forward, towards Mouquet Farm and beyond.

The stark reality was that 'neutralisation' would prove impossible.

A maze of passages, running between the underground shelters, fortified cellars and machine gun emplacements, existed beneath the shattered brickdust, mortar and tumbled timber-work of Thiepval. These subterranean structures provided a prodigious test of the destructive power of the Royal Garrison Artillery's high explosive shells. Many of the smaller buildings had their own wells, additional to the three communal wells which served the village. 'The water supply of the chateau is considered abundant'[5], its cellars providing accomodation for in excess of 1,200 soldiers. The German soldiers who took shelter within these cellars and tunnels opposite the Pals were from Alsace-Lorraine, the Wurttembergers of Elsab-Lothringen. They had faced the Pals throughout and boasted that their stretch

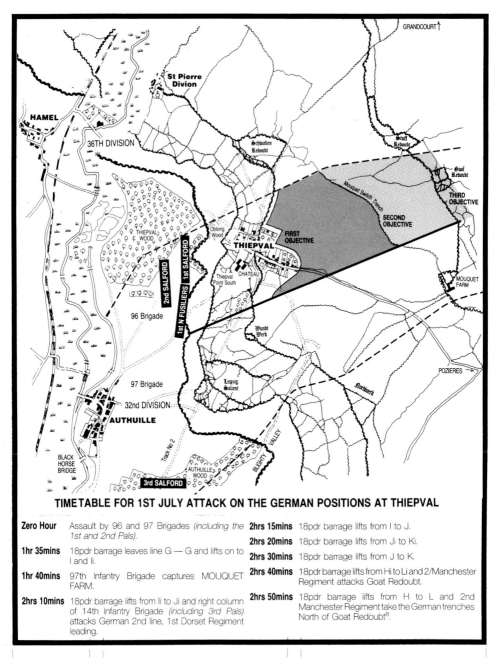

TIMETABLE FOR 1ST JULY ATTACK ON THE GERMAN POSITIONS AT THIEPVAL

Zero Hour	Assault by 96 and 97 Brigades *(including the 1st and 2nd Pals)*.	**2hrs 15mins**	18pdr barrage lifts from I to J.
		2hrs 20mins	18pdr barrage lifts from Ji to Ki.
1hr 35mins	18pdr barrage leaves line G — G and lifts on to I and Ii.	**2hrs 30mins**	18pdr barrage lifts from J to K.
1hr 40mins	97th Infantry Brigade captures MOUQUET FARM.	**2hrs 40mins**	18pdr barrage lifts from Hi to Li and 2/Manchester Regiment attacks Goat Redoubt.
2hrs 10mins	18pdr barrage lifts from Ii to Ji and right column of 14th Infantry Brigade *(including 3rd Pals)* attacks German 2nd line, 1st Dorset Regiment leading.	**2hrs 50mins**	18pdr barrage lifts from H to L and 2nd Manchester Regiment take the German trenches North of Goat Redoubt[8].

of line could never be taken. These men belonged to the 26th Reserve Division[6] whose frontage extended across the line to be attacked by X Corps. Apart from the protection afforded by their underground shelters, these men had the defensive superiority of a layered and interlocking network of fields of fire which their machine gunners knew intimately. Three Maxims in particular, opposite Thiepval Wood, were especially well placed to cover the entirety of the slopes up from that wood to the fringes of Thiepval itself. Moreover, behind and to either side of Thiepval's deceptively chaotic ruins, a number of other self-contained positions of enormous strength were located. Their intention was to check any breach of the front line in a maze of trenches which provided the opportunity for phased retirement, without risking the loss of the whole of the Granatloch-Leipziger-Graben.

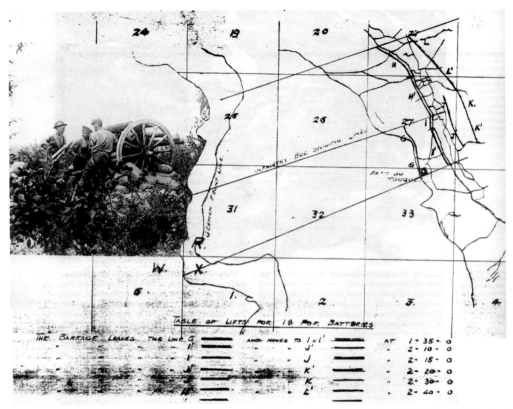

Such preparations were both fantastic and mechanically unreal in their lack of elasticity. This lack of flexibility could cost the men from Salford dear. Map showing the artillery lifts and distances. Public Record Office WO95/2394. Taylor Library

South lay the enormous Leipzig Salient, jutting threateningly into the British lines along its spur. Behind and above it lay the Wundt-werk, itself protected by the machine guns of the Nord-werk on the Ovillers spur. At the tip of the salient the Leipzig Redoubt's machine guns were an especially dominant weapon. Three guns at this point covered a 280 degree arc past Boggart Hole Clough towards The Nab or Krone-werk and from there round northwards to enfilade the slopes of No Man's Land crossed by the Authuille-Thiepval road. Above the front line trenches, 50 to 100 yards further back, equally strong

Mouquet Farm in 1915. Out of sight to the Pals in their positions below Thiepval but centrally located on the road from Thiepval up to Pozieres and an important objective during the early hours of the anticipated 'Big Push'. Reed.

fortifications such as Hindenburg Stellung, Lemberg and Zick-Zack Stellung were all equipped with deeply concreted dugouts and numerous machine gun emplacements.

North of the entanglements which stretched at crazy angles across Thiepval's surface, the Schwaben Redoubt topped the spur pointing towards Thiepval Wood. It was guarded along its lower slopes by the fortifications of St. Pierre Divion. This in turn was protected by the machine gun nests of the Beaucourt Redoubt across the Ancre marshes, whose fire could enfilade the north and north western slopes of the Thiepval plateau.

A mile to the east of Thiepval lay Mouquet Farm and the powerful defences whose trenches marked the German intermediate positions running between Pozieres and Grandcourt. Mouquet Farm was the Regimental Headquarters for the 99th Reserve Regiment whose 1st and 2nd Battalions were directly opposite the 32nd Division's front. It also housed the telephone exchange and artillery control for the area. A pipeline carrying unpolluted water ran from Mouquet to Thiepval.

Clearly the task for Morland's X Corps was enormous, but so great was the degree of observation afforded from the heights of Thiepval, south to Pozieres and north to Serre, that even the most naive could visualise its importance. It was the kingpin of German defence on the Somme. Its geographical features were the most dominant for miles around. It glowered impregnably, entreating any to attempt its capture. Loss of this position would threaten the security of the entire German position in front of Bapaume.

X Corps consisted of the 32nd, 36th and 49th Divisions. The 36th were Ulstermen. The 49th were mostly Yorkshiremen, the Corps reserve, and earmarked as part of Gough's 'Army of Pursuit' in the event of a breach in German resistance. The plan envisaged a breakthrough by the 36th towards Grandcourt, through St. Pierre Divion and the Schwaben Redoubt, whilst the 32nd broke through Thiepval and past Mouquet Farm, linking on their right with III Corps' anticipated advance through Ovillers and La Boisselle in the direction of Pozieres and beyond.

German engineers, in the grounds of Thiepval Chateau, prepare another of the tunnels which networked the ground underneath this area. The determined attempts to ensure permanence are well illustrated by the man in the centre who is carrying a spirit level and bricklayer's trowel. Reed.

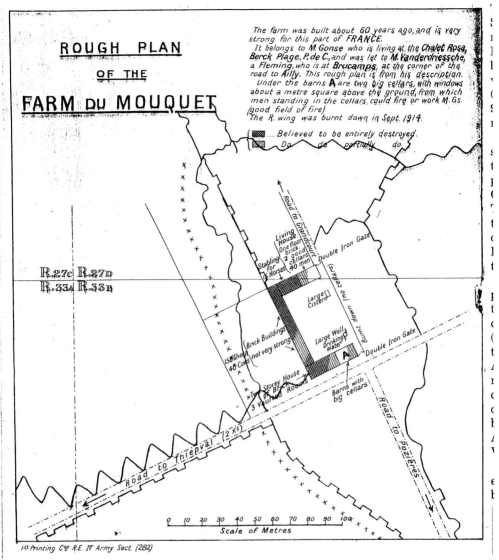

Plan of Mouquet Farm. This document, taken from the 3rd Pals' Operational Orders for 1st July, illustrates the sort of optimistic preparation which had overtaken the planning process. PRO WO95/2394.

Major-General W. H. Rycroft of the 32nd Division had every confidence in the men from Salford. The 96th Brigade's two assaulting battalions would be the 1st Salford Pals and on their right the 16th Northumberland Fusiliers. In support to these two leading battalions would be the 2nd Salford Pals. The 96th Brigade's frontage ran from Skinner Street (R31a1/3), opposite the Wundt-werk, northwards to Queens Cross Street at Hammerhead Sap (R25a4/3), the 1st Salford Pals being directly opposite the Chateau and Thiepval village from Hammerhead to Maison Grise Sap (R25c3/3). On the right of the 96th Brigade the 97th Brigade would attack and to their left the men of the 36th Division.

Immediately in front of the 1st Pals' trenches a semi-circular track cut across No Man's Land. In the midst of this natural amphitheatre a sap provided the opportunity for men to move up into Oblong Wood without being exposed to direct fire. To the right Thiepval Point South was the closest the lines were together in this sector. On the left of Oblong Wood scattered trees enclosed Hammerhead Sap where it had been dug out towards the crossroads north west of Thiepval.

View forward from British trench in Thiepval Wood. IWM

Once Thiepval fell, the 2nd Pals' task was to push through to form two defensive redoubts in the rear of the village. Those redoubts were to be constructed on the Mouquet Switch lines (R27c25/75 to R20c85/15) which ran from the farm to the Schwaben redoubt. This reflected the Fourth Army command's concern to make the advance methodical and proof against expected heavy counter-attacks. Thus consolidation was becoming of paramount importance as the idea of total breakthrough evaporated in the heat of the French Army's catastrophic conflict with Germany at Verdun.

For their part, in what the men still fully expected to be the 'great advance', the 2nd Pals' Battalion strength was four companies, each of 120 men including the Lewis Gun teams. 40 men, including signallers, messengers and a party of bombers were attached to Battalion Headquarters. The Battalion had the services of a party of men from 206 Company Royal Engineers who were to help in the construction of the redoubts. C and D Companies were detailed for the construction work and apart from their already overladen packs, each of these men were further burdened by R.E. stores and engineer material. A and B were ordered to support the assaulting battalions, although a small party of C and D would move over the top with these companies to mark out the ground in preparation for the work of the construction parties.

Further south, two hours later in the day, the 3rd Pals would traverse No Man's Land out of Authuille Wood in their march across the Blighty Valley Area. This move by the 14th Brigade was drawn up to a complex and precise timetable which entailed their passing through the 97th Brigade who would, by then, have overcome the defences of that salient. It was therefore not thought necessary to assault the southern face of the Leipzig salient since it was believed that those trenches would fall automatically once the lines to the west and north of them had been taken. The process of consolidation begun by the other two Brigades would be completed by the 14th Brigade who would then work northwards past Mouquet farm, the 3rd Salfords taking the trenches (R27b55/15 to R27b20/75) just south of Goat Redoubt on the German second line, or intermediate positions, running from Pozieres to Grandcourt. The 14th Brigade's move across Blighty Valley was divided into two columns, the right being ordered to

Spring, 1916, the objective of the Salford Pals' attack – Thiepval village. This photograph shows the ruins of the chateau – photographed from a window of the Church. Within weeks these crumbling ruins were shelled to mere rubble, but the surviving network of tunnels and cellars provided shelter and protection for the village's defenders. Right: troops observing the German lines at Thiepval prior to the attack on 1st July, 1916.

take the intermediate lines behind Mouquet Farm, whilst the left column, headed by the 2nd Manchesters, would attack and take Goat Redoubt to the north. The right column was placed under the command of Lt. Colonel Graham of the 19th Lancashire Fusiliers and included his 3rd Salford Pals, the 1st Dorsets, a half section of 206th Company Royal Engineers and the bulk of the 14th Brigade's Machine Gun and Trench Mortar Companies together with four Stokes Guns for smoke barrage purposes. Once installed in these intermediate lines the 1st Dorsets and 3rd Salford Pals were expected to construct further redoubts, with the help of the Engineers, and to garrison them with two platoons, each equipped with one Vickers and one Lewis Gun carried up for the purpose. Each platoon detailed to garrison a redoubt would carry an

Dugouts near Thiepval where men pass the time awaiting the day of the 'Big Push'. Taylor Library

113

extra burden for the engineers of 20 picks, 20 shovels, 2 hand axes, 4 wire cutters and 250 sandbags! In moving forward the leading battalions of the 14th Brigade were instructed to maintain close contact with the rearmost unit of the 97th Brigade, the 11th Borders.

Assembly trenches capable of housing thousands of men were dug within the confines of Authuille Wood. Twenty-four inches of space per man was allowed for each of the battalions which would assemble here! Surrounding these trenches was a proliferation of munitions dumps, engineers dumps, aid posts, artillery tracks and water tanks, an indication of the meticulous optimism which sustained the preparations.

No pessimism, or contingency permitting the possibility of failure, was allowed to figure in preparatory orders. Within an hour and forty minutes Mouquet Farm would fall to the 97th Brigade. The 14th Brigade would then take the Germans' second line defences. Nothing was left to chance in more than forty pages of mechanically detailed instruction, even down to the numbers of buttons permitted to remain open:

> 11. (a) Fighting kit will be worn. The mess tin to be inside the haversack, and to contain pack of iron rations.
> Steel Helmets. Water bottles filled.
> 2 Bandoliers S.A.A. (100) in addition to 120 rounds carried in pouches. Waterproof sheet.
> 2 Sandbags under flap of haversack. Unexpended portion of day's rations. 1 Iron Ration.
> 1 Tin meat and 4 biscuits. (b) Two gas helmets will be worn, one attached to the shirt as already demonstrated, the other slung over the left shoulder in the usual manner. The satchel for gas helmet attached to shirt will be placed in the haversack.
> The top three buttons and hooks of the tunic will be left undone so as to facilitate the adjustment of helmets ...
> (d) Each officer, NCO and man will carry 2 detonator bombs (No. 5) in his pockets. Except in the case of Bombers, these will not be used by the carrier but will be dumped under platoon arrangements, when the final position has been taken up. From this dump the bombers will replenish their supply ...[7]

Even any possibility of gaining advantage by choosing to attack from the western darkness before sunrise was thrown away. The full glare of daylight at 7.30 a.m. would do nicely.

18 pounder gun crew hard at work during the Battle. Taylor Library

The Final Preparations

On 24th June the massive barrage which presaged the Battle had begun. Its purpose was to so utterly smash the wire and defences in front that even the relatively untrained and inexperienced soldiers of Kitchener's Army would be able to walk through to their objectives. In the sheer volume and profligate use of shells nothing like it had yet been seen on the British Front. Two days later, however, the weather deteriorated and for two further days thick mist and heavy showers made artillery observation all but impossible. In the midst of this drizzle and gloom the 1st Pals moved up to Bouzincourt on the 27th, where they stayed for four days before the offensive. Already the 2nd Pals were in their accustomed trenches at Authuille. The 3rd Pals moved up to shelter trenches in Aveluy Wood, ready for the expected attack on the 28th.

> The shriek of shells passing overhead, the crash and vibration as huge 'crumps' burst on the enemy's trenches and villages was awe inspiring. At night the sky was lit up as if it were day as far as the eye could see.[9]

But, by contrast, rations were none too plentiful at this time.

> We were always starved. Before the Battle of the Somme when it was cancelled for 48 hours, and the six days previously, we were on bully beef and biscuits, tea and sugar. No milk of any description. Sgt. Bill Dutton. 10897. D Coy. 1st Pals.

Although the 27th had been a fine day, it was followed by a night of persistent and saturatingly heavy rain. Under the cover of the cloud and rainfall an officer's patrol had left Thiepval Point North and entered the German trench opposite. Although the trench was not occupied it was, ominously for the Salford Pals who were due to attack here, found to be 'not much damaged'. The patrol then worked northwards along the deserted front line trench, across the route which the Pals were expected to stream over, to where the Thiepval Road crossed the German front line trench outside the village. Here the trench was more severely damaged although loose barbed wire was lying about outside the parapet. Just

ansport mule belonging to the 1st Pals Mesnil Church, across the Ancre •posite Thiepval. Willcock.

in front of this patrol a trench mortar was firing towards Thiepval Wood (from R25 central) as was an undetected machine gun just north of the village. Another patrol found some 'chevaux de frise'[10] in front of Thiepval. Just to the south in the area to be attacked by the 16th Northumberlands the patrols reported that 'the wire about R31a60/32 is only slightly damaged and few gaps cut'. In some places here thick coils of concertina wire had been thrown over the German parapet.

Early on that morning of the 28th Haig's decision to delay was made and at 12 noon 32nd Division's headquarters were told by X Corps that Z day was postponed until 1st July. This was not surprising in view of the heavy rain which had continued to fall all morning. The 3rd Pals were immediately taken back to Senlis, where they would stay for those two days. By the afternoon, however, the weather began to clear. Later, during the early evening, roughly 50 German shells were ranged on Johnstone's Post and two further hostile machine guns were located in Thiepval (at R25c75/45 and in a sap at R31a55/85). On the 29th the dawn broke on much clearer weather and, although a little rain fell, the ground quickly began to dry. 4 Squadron of the R.F.C., who were observing above this sector, were now able to report that 'the enemy front line wire has been cut in a great many places and that the enemy's line appeared to be damaged'. Anticipating the coming assault the German artillery were observed registering their guns on their own front line trenches in the vicinity of the Wundt-werk and the Hindenburg trenches in the Leipzig Redoubt. As if to confirm that the German front line troops were desperate for water and supplies, some were observed collecting fresh rainwater from pools on their own parapets in the Leipzig salient. Patrols by the 2nd Inniskillings in the Thiepval subsector that night confirmed it, 'the enemy wire is practically non existent'.

The following morning at 8.30, an enormous barrage erupted on the German lines in front of the whole of the Fourth Army's front. It lasted for 50 minutes and careful observation noted where the German counter-barrage fell. Although reported as weak in the neighbouring 8th and 36th Division's areas, so many German shells fell in the Authuille sector that almost all telephone communication wires were cut in the 96th Brigade sector. It was also noticed that far less high explosive was fired in the German counter-barrage, but that large numbers of air burst anti-personnel shrapnel shells 'covered our front line trenches on this sector'.[11] Clearly the German artillery was very alert and active and not in any way subdued by counter-battery fire.

However, the less substantial buildings of the village and chateau at Thiepval had been systematically erased from the map, but of the 66

96th Infantry Brigade Staff.

houses which existed in the village before the war it was clearly known, by Brigade and Battalion Commanding Officers immediately before Z day, that at least 13 had fortified cellarage, providing protected accommodation, along with that in the chateau, 'for 1,500 men underground'.[12]

> *The village is in ruins but from latest reports and from aeroplanes it may be deduced that many of its less fragile buildings are still so little damaged as to afford valuable protection against attack.*[13]

So, although the German wire was known to be broken in many places in front of Thiepval, it was clear that Thiepval's cellars provided protective shelter for very many men. South of Thiepval, on the west face of the Leipzig salient, the wire was still strong in places.

Water supply was considered quite abundant to the men sheltering in Thiepval, but less so for the men at Leipzig.

The remaining parts of substantial buildings in Thiepval still afforded 'valuable protection against attack'. Unless the bombardment had physically destroyed the considerable number of machine guns and the munitions available to the 26th Reserve Division, the prospects for a successful assault were bleak.

Nevertheless, the Pals would be expected to show indifference to any of their comrades injured in the coming assault. 'Men in the trenches or in the assaulting Brigades, will not fall out to bring back wounded', spoke the battalions' orders. The collection of 'souvenirs' was expressly forbidden.

Catastrophically, every senior figure at Fourth Army HQ and GHQ was being swept along upon the tide of false optimism. Rawlinson knew by the eve of battle that slaughter was almost inevitable in front of the uncut wire to the south of Thiepval, but felt disinclined to confront Haig with such an unpalatable truth. Rawlinson's Tactical Notes, issued two months earlier in May, had always insisted throughout the men's training on the methodical style which had to be employed. The maintenance of regular infantry 'waves', the fixed adherence to an artillery timetable, the denial of initiative to junior officers and the achievement of specified objectives within too rigid a timetable – all of these were now combined within a disastrous inevitability.

The 1st and 2nd Pals' Attack

On the night of 30th June the 1st Pals moved up from Bouzincourt. Every few yards the platoons were momentarily lit by the flash of explosions. Even shouted orders proved impossible to hear. Nevertheless, the men moved into the familiarity of their line under the cover of darkness and the crashing sounds of shellfire, being in position by 1.00 a.m. The trenches which they took over from the 'Skins' had been

Dawn breaks on the Somme and the 'Big Push' is about to begin.

badly shattered by the persistence of the German shelling and provided only minimal shelter. Simultaneously the 2nd Pals moved out of Black Horse dugouts into support in the French Street evacuation trenches and around Johnstone Post, roughly three hundred yards behind the two assault battalions; the 1st Pals and the 16th Northumberland Fusiliers. As this move got underway,

Private T. H. (Harry) Potter 15166

> *there was a ruined village [Authuille] to traverse, where shells had set fire to one of the ruined houses, and the red glare added a further awesomeness to the scene. Leaving the village we proceeded along the communication trench, and shells began to fall about us in greater number, but we kept steadily on. At last we entered the communication trench leading to the assembly trench. This lay through a thick wood [Thiepval], and enemy shellfire had brought down heavy trees, which partially blocked the way and made progress slow. We were almost at our rendezvous when a crash in front warned those behind that things were not well. The party halted and the order was passed down: 'Officer wanted at the front at once.' An officer started off brushing past the crouching men, and then whizz crash, a whizz bang fired enfilade along the trench fell amongst us, followed by others.[14]*

This relief cost the 2nd Pals four killed, including Sergeant W. Taylor and T. H. [Harry] Potter (15166), together with seven wounded, including Lieutenant Waugh of D Company and 2nd Lieutenant Powell which necessitated Captain Tweed taking command of both support companies behind the 1st Pals.

Throughout that cloudless night a thick ground mist rolled through the trenches and valleys. Very few of the men could sleep through the erratic din and glare of shelling and the damp cold of their contemplation.

One man who had been anguished that night was Bill Dutton. Earlier in June his great friend from Salford, Peter Fensome, had been shot in the leg. By contrast with some of the more dreadful sights which he had seen this was a relatively minor wound and Bill had been pleased to think that his mate would miss today's events. Since their days in Conway the boys had been great friends, although once arguing so fiercely that their mothers had to issue instructions to patch things up! Now, in the blackness of the night of 30th June, they unexpectedly met again.

> I saw Peter coming along and we put our arms around each other. I said, 'What made you come back Peter?' He said they were clearing the hospitals for the coming battle and if you weren't too badly wounded, well, you volunteered to come back. He said he wanted to go over the top with the company. Sergeant Bill Dutton. 1st Pals.

German machine-gun team in action. Along with accurate artillery fire they proved most effective in stopping the attacking British infantry on the Somme.

As daylight began to break, the sky above Thiepval was uncluttered by clouds and ominously blue. In the sodden Ancre valley and the shattered woodlands out of which Salford's Pals would attack the air was damp, misty and still.

In front of Thiepval the Germans clearly expected a dawn attack and their defensive barrage was initially heavy, lasting for an hour after first light at 3.30 a.m. As the sun then began its climb above the Thiepval ridge a deceptive lull in the cacophany of noise existed, shattered at 6.25 a.m., when the British bombardment intensified into a another pulverising series of explosions which seemed to make the very air bounce and resonate[15]. Under their feet the men could feel the vibrations and shock waves. Simultaneously gas was released from cylinders placed in No Man's Land. It drifted slowly over the rubble in front. If nothing else it proved the continued presence of men opposite as the clanging of gas alarm bells was heard during momentary gaps amidst the blasts of explosion. Between Maison Grise and Hammerhead the Pals' officers were visibly tense and anxious. Far too much of the wire was still clearly visible in front of Thiepval, although at 6.37 a.m. the 97th Brigade to the right telephoned Divisional HQ with word that,

> the enemy wire on their front [west of Leipzig] completely cleared and all are satisfied there will be no hitch.[16]

With just ten minutes to go, as the final bombardment thundered into Thiepval, A and C Companies of the 1st Pals, under command of Captain Alfred Lee Wood and Lieutenant H. C. Wright, crept forward to within a hundred yards of the village, beyond the trees east of Hammerhead sap, either side of Oblong Wood and down past Thiepval Point South. In support, in Thiepval Wood, were B and D Companies, commanded by the recently promoted Captain Geoffrey Heald and Captain Ernest MacLaren[17]. The violence being wrought by the shellfire on Thiepval in front of them convinced some that no-one could

Landscape at Thiepval during the Somme Battle.

possibly continue to live in that inferno. But shockingly, and contrary to all the men's expectations of this point in time, German machine guns were already being heard, firing over the thunderous sound of shells falling on Thiepval.

There would be no respite from their deadly attention.

At 7.30, the first waves from A and C Companies stood up and began to walk forward. As soon as they breasted the rise in front of Thiepval and showed themselves, scores were cut down by the inevitable, scything, machine gun fire. Within minutes a heavy barrage began to fall on the British front line and casualties began to occur among the runners trying to maintain communication between Lieutenant Colonel Lloyd's Battalion headquarters in Bromielaw Street and the attacking companies. All the meticulous planning was as nought.

Private Hutton (10204) provided one of the few eye witness accounts from the midst of this disastrous scene. Speaking of Captain Alfred Lee Wood, from Lake Hospital in Ashton-under-Lyne, he said that,

> Barely fifty yards had been covered when he was hit by a bullet, which grazed his head, whilst I got one in the arm. Without pausing we went on a little further, when a second bullet struck the captain on the head, causing a nasty gash, and almost at the same moment I was shot through the leg. Turning to me Captain Lee Wood asked, 'Are you badly hit?' and I replied, 'Yes Sir, I can't go on this time'. He then ordered me to try and get back to our trench, and although I begged him to come back with me, since he was badly wounded, he said, 'No, I will get that machine gunner.'[18]

On their left the 36th (Ulster) Division's attack was going well, the 9th and 10th Royal Inniskilling Fusiliers crossing No Man's Land and sweeping across the front and support trenches towards the Crucifix and Schwaben Redoubt. This vital distraction on Thiepval's right flank gave a pitiably small number of the 1st Pals in A Company a chance to get through the wire and enter the German trenches in front and to the north of the village. Unfortunately, no attempt at mopping up the dug-outs was possible and those Salford men who had crossed the first German line then made their way to the north of Thiepval, in the direction of the Ulstermen's success south of Schwaben Redoubt.

Nevertheless, behind those first companies, the following waves of men from B and D Companies tried desperately to get up to the enemy's trenches through the counter-barrage now sweeping No Man's

The ground over which the Salford Pals attacked on 1st July, 1916. Taylor Library

Land but all efforts simply resulted in the almost instant killing or wounding of the parties moving forward. At this point the 96th Brigade still believed that the advance was going smoothly although communication had become impossible.

> *The leading and support Companies kept their proper distance and all lines got into the enemy trenches. At 7.45 AM connection between Bn. H.Q. in BROMIELAW STREET, which had been maintained by a chain of messengers, was broken owing to several casualties due to M.G. fire both from front and flanks.*[19]

In No Man's Land those soldiers who had survived the first shattering moments were in a desperate position. Many of the men were being pinned down and picked off by very accurate machine gun and rifle fire.

> *As soon as we got into No Man's Land the Germans opened fire with their heavy machine guns. We dropped like nine-pins. I was the same as everyone else. I dropped into a shell hole. One officer realised how futile the attack was and told us to stay there 'till nightfall. You were shot down if you made any movement at all. We spent the day in shellholes, talking and swearing.* Sergeant Bill Dutton. 1st Pals.

One of the men with whom Bill Dutton shared that shellhole was 'Boxer' Wilson. Bleeding profusely Wilson had been lacerated by his own barbed wire as he struggled to find safety from the constant machine gun fire.

Of the four gun Vickers section from 96th Machine Gun Company, supporting the 1st Pals, all guns bar one were knocked out trying to cross No Man's Land. The remaining gun's team by then consisted of one Private who brought the gun back to the front lines. Two teams of the 96th Trench Mortar Battery[20] moved forward to Hammerhead Sap, one officer moving forward from there in an attempt to ascertain the situation of the 1st Pals but was unfortunately killed.

Private George Right (10163) then serving in the machine gun section, from C Company, 1st Salfords, who was amongst those killed. Simmonds.

In the shell-pecked and cursed acres in front of Thiepval hundreds of khaki clad figures lay, some breathlessly motionless, some in terrible agony, some simply still, under the increasing heat of a clearing blue sky. The minutes trickled by and the sound of exploding shells dulled as the bombardment lifted and began to fall on the intermediate positions beyond the near edge of Thiepval plateau. As that barrage moved uselessly into the distance the machine gunners in square 25 were set for revenge after seven days of waiting in a terrible anticipation under the 32nd Division's enormous preparatory bombardment. Their situation was even further improved when one of the two British 9.2" howitzers, detailed to fire on enemy machine gun posts in the Thiepval area, suffered a premature shell burst, putting itself and its partner out of action for the duration of the day.

Within minutes of their attack going in it had become impossible for the 32nd Division's observers to see what was happening.

> *At 7.55 the Mesnil OP reported that it was impossible to see owing to smoke. Very little shelling but a lot of machine gun fire.*[21]

The trench mortars remained silent. It was already thought inadvisable to redirect their bombardment onto Thiepval in view of the uncertainty surrounding who was in the vicinity of the village.

One hour after the start of their assault, and more in hope than certainty, the 1st Salford Pals' Adjutant reported to 32nd Divisional Headquarters that the Battalion's men had taken the German front lines. In fact, all that Lieutenant Colonel Lloyd now commanded, apart from his Adjutant, was his Lewis gun officer and some 20 to 30 men held back from the attack. However, air and artillery observers now reported seeing isolated parties of British troops in and to the north and east of the village, but not one

Thiepval from the air. This reconnaissance photograph reveals the strength and depth of the defences within Thiepval village. Reed

man or officer from the 1st Pals who got there would live to tell that tale. Behind those parties of the 15th Lancashire Fusiliers' men who had broken through, the German troops quickly emerged from the protection of their dugouts on the right of the Salford's attack to re-establish themselves in their own front line.

On the 1st Pals' right zero hour had seen the utter obliteration of the 16th Northumberlands, to the south of Maison Grise Sap. As their own barrage had lifted from the German trenches opposite the leading waves of Newcastle men had set off,

> *A and B Coys moved forward in waves and were instantly fired upon by Enemy's M.G. & snipers. The Enemy stood upon their parapet & waved to our men to come on & picked them off with rifle fire. The Enemy's fire was so intense that the advance was checked & the waves, or what was left of them, were forced to lie down.*[22]

Line after line of men from each subsequent company had leaped out of their trenches only to meet with the same fate as their predecessors. It was not until 8.20 that it became known at Division that the situation here was desperate and that more barrage was required on the German frontline. Behind the 16th Northumberlands their machine gun section was brought into the front line to provide direct supporting fire across the unfolding catastrophe in front of them.

The failure of the Tynesider's attack meant a day of unremitting horror and difficulty for the few surviving men of the 96th Brigades' assault battalions and their support, the 2nd Pals. The behaviour of the 2nd Salfords that day was both tragic and exemplary, motivated as much by the plight of their pals as by the tactical military imperative of taking Thiepval.

A and C Companies were in support of the Northumberlands, in French Street trench behind Gemmel Trench. B and D Companies were behind their own 1st Pals. When the men from Newcastle were so savagely cut down, Lieutenant Nelson Allen brought A Company into Gemmell Trench at 7.55, just behind the Northumberlands' front line trenches. At 8.10 Allen's A Company moved into the front lines, between Maison Grise and Hamilton Avenue, from where No. 1 Platoon went over the top at 8.20 under the command of 2nd Lt. W. E. Foss, in a vain attempt to support the failed attack made by the 16th Northumberland Fusiliers. One man who was there, Sergeant E. Wild (12167), later recounted his experiences whilst recovering, in a Stockport hospital, from bullet and shrapnel wounds[23]. Sergeant Wild was one of the men from No.1 platoon of the 2nd Pals who had gone over to support the 16th Northumberland Fusiliers at 8.20. He initially took shelter against the road bank leading from Skinner Street in the direction of Thiepval. Subsequently he and four others found a shellhole more effective. All five were already struck by bullets. Further injuries were sustained as shrapnel continued to tear into the earth around the group. They were joined in the hole by a solitary German prisoner who was desperately making his way to the British lines. Like many other men that day one of this group, looking over the rim of the shellhole in search of further prisoners, was immediately shot through the head, so severe and accurate was the machine gun and rifle fire.

Seeing this disastrous situation in front, Captain Roger Knott ordered his men in C Company to dump their R.E. materials whilst he sought Colonel Ritson, commanding the 16th Northumberlands in their front line. It was clear that the 16th Northumberlands were so depleted that they would be unable to effectively man their own front line. Within Captain Knott's company 2nd Lieutenant Charles Marriot was therefore ordered to take his men down into the chaotic confines of the front line trench.

I sent a message to A Coy on our left to say what I was doing, and started to lead up a communication trench between us called Hamilton Avenue – or rather what was left of it. Gerry was plastering the whole sector with H.E., and already it was less a trench than shellholes and hummocks. Our scrambles over these were speeded by the German machine-gunners above, who weren't missing much that morning. After all these years I still clearly see certain gruesome sights, burnt into the memory, as we struggled up to the front line. Hands, feet and shin bones were protruding from the raw earth stinking of high explosive. A smallish soldier sitting in a shellhole, elbows on knees, a sandbag over his shoulders: I lifted it to see if he were alive, and he had no head. Further on, a corporal lying doubled up and bloody; just in case anything could be done for him I bent down to raise him a little, and his head was only attached by a bit of skin. The front trench was so blown up and gouged by H.E. that only bits of it remained, and it took some time to deploy out along it.

Meanwhile I was told that a badly-wounded officer was lying in it about twenty yards along. I got to him over a great blown-in block, bullets whizzing like wasps, and found a tall young Northumberland Fusilier Lieutenant, shot through both knees, one wrist and one shoulder: the moment he got up onto the parapet the impact of the bullets had flung him backwards into the trench. I tried to bandage him up a bit (his courage was so superb I think I was weeping as I did so, which wasn't really much help) and sent an urgent call for stretcher-bearers. But there was too much to see to, I had to leave him, and never knew what happened to him. We found others like him shot straight back off the parapet, one, a sergeant, drilled through the forehead, his brains spread like hair over the back of his neck. At last we were ready, and I was bracing myself for the hideous decision to go over the top when we were saved from further massacre in the nick of time by a sweating runner with a message from the C.O. to stay put. My God, what a moment! No Man's Land, covered with bodies, was a sight I can never forget: the whole of the 16/N.F. seemed to be lying out there.[24]

Nelson Allen. Knott

In this position the men of A and C manned the shattered Northumberlands' line, suffering casualties throughout the day from the high explosive and shrapnel being rained on these positions.

Meanwhile, on their left, B and D Coys had been brought into the front lines twenty minutes after zero when news already suggested that men of the 1st Pals were in trouble in the area of Thiepval. Since early hours officers had awaited the moment when the courage of their men would be put to the test, anxiously consulting watches and marking the progress of the Ulstermen who could be seen on their left.

Above our heads an enemy machine gun kept spitting away defiantly. Skillfully hidden behind a wood, in the ruins of a village which was to be taken by us, it had braved the bombardment and its team of to be quite fair – very brave and capable soldiers, fired with a deadliness and accuracy which was amazing. It was drawing towards the time of our going forward. Every second we expected our first troops to silence the gun. Five minutes before eight the gun was silent. Then the Captain's voice, 'Fix bayonets,' a few pregnant minutes, and a further order, '5 and 6 over the top, and good luck, boys'.[25]

Under the command of Captain Tweed both companies needed no encouragement to get forward to do their bit. It was however both desperate and hopeless. The instant the Eccles men left their trenches and revealed themselves the machine guns restarted.

Some, like young Grindley, were killed getting over, and rolled back into the trench, but through the perfect storm of lead the company went on. Ignoring the rain of death that whistled about them, they kept running from shell hole to shell hole, on and on. Pals of years' association dropped, others fell riddled with bullets never to rise again. But the cry was always 'On!'. Lieut. Walton was wounded and left behind; Lieut. Brooman who had charge of 5th and 6th platoons, was well ahead [at the cross roads beyond Hammerhead sap], and had already been hit twice. [Tweed] rushed up to the 7th and 8th platoon, who had lost nearly all their N.C.O.s, and leaping out of a shell hole urged them to follow. A few seconds hesitation to face the lightning death above them, and then Private Bradshaw leaped out and called again, to be followed by all the others. Forward, ever forward. But by this time a very few men were left, and a sheltering bank in 'No Man's Land' became a haven of refuge. What was left of the company stayed there for two hours unable to move.[26]

A succinct entry in the battalion War Diary recorded just how few of the Eccles Company had in fact made it to the shelter of the road embankment.

At 8 o'clock the first line of B Co advanced but came under M.G. fire whilst crossing QUEEN'S X BANK, the other lines and D Co followed. The front line reached the crossroads beyond HAMMERHEAD SAP but had suffered severely from M.G. fire from direction of THIEPVAL, Captain TWEED reckoning that his Coy was only about 40 strong at this point.[27]

This tiny force of men had, as yet, only covered fifty yards in the direction of Thiepval and a further hour would elapse before they would be ordered to reinforce the 1st Pals. Behind them three of the officers and many men with D Company were already casualties from the intense air bursts of shrapnel being hurled at the Queens Cross Trench and bank area. Tweed initially had run back to tell the remaining 2nd Lieutenant, Jones, to keep his men under cover until B Company could be seen to make progress.

At 9.10 a.m., Major-General Rycroft ordered the 96th Brigade to use the supports to push round the northern edge of Thiepval to meet up with the 1st Pals and the right of the 36th Division at the 'Crucifix' on the southern tip of Schwaben Redoubt. Unfortunately the 2nd Royal Inniskillings were not as yet available. Their headquarters and two companies arrived at Johnstone Post at 10.00 a.m. One further company was being held in reserve at the Bluff. Only one company of the 'Skins' was in the area of the 2nd Salfords, sheltering within French Street since 8.55. This clearly meant that what was left of B and D Companies of the 2nd Salford Pals would be responsible for the attack on their own.

The remaining small numbers of B Company tried to get forward through the trees towards the edge of the village. Immediately the intensity of machine gun fire from the Thiepval Fort area became overwhelming. Small groups of men were pinned down outside the wire by the machine gun fire which tracked above their heads. Some desperate men took their lives in their own hands in attempts to reach their friends. They were simply cut down as they bunched to get through the one obvious gap in the wire. Other men, under the extraordinarily brave command of 2nd Lieutenant Edward Brooman who had already been twice hit by bullets, stayed under the wire all morning in the search for a way through. Under the road embankments, around Hammerhead Sap, and in any shell hole around Oblong Wood dozens of men crouched and swore and prayed for darkness.

Three of the Eccles Pals' Platoons, 5th from right in the top row is Frank Holding, last survivor of Salford's civic battalions.

124

Captain Tweed tried to work a number of parties forward himself after having reconnoitred possible routes through the trees. Corporal Sharples (11757) and Privates Howell (10266) and Jones tried and were almost immediately cut down.[28] As soon as Private Fiddes (12491), Tweed's orderly, left the safety of the embankment to obtain instructions from Battalion Headquarters he was instantly shot, but was pulled back into shelter. Whilst writing his next message Tweed's notebook was hit by a bullet and flung from his grasp. Brooman was hit for a third time.

Capt. A. LEE WOOD, Formerly of Oldham, Lancashire Fusiliers.

Taking enormous risk Tweed dragged Brooman back to the comparative safety of his front line trenches in search of orders to pull the men out. By 10.30 a.m., orders were received from Major-General Rycroft requesting the men to hold fast whilst attempts were made to capitalise on success by the 36th Division and turn the Thiepval defences from the north. The Ulstermen had made incredible inroads into the German defences north of Thiepval even though their right flank was being eroded by the persistent and deadly storm of machine guns firing in enfilade from Thiepval village. By 9.30 the 36th Division were believed to be moving on point Cl2 (R13d6/9), north of Schwaben Redoubt and north east of St. Pierre Divion. An hour later the German prisoners from the Schwaben redoubt area were running into 36th Division's lines 'with hands up in considerable numbers'. By 10.45 the two machine guns firing from close by Thiepval Chateau were still causing heavy casualties amongst the Ulstermen's 107th Brigade. Nevertheless, by 11.00 a.m., men from that Brigade were up at the Mouquet Farm-Grandcourt lines and the German situation in Thiepval was becoming critical.

Pte. H. LEACH, 125, Blantyre-st. M'side, Lancashire Fusiliers.

Unfortunately the artillery reports reaching 32nd Divisional Headquarters were geographically rather vague, although positive about the presence of Salford men in Thiepval at R25cd.

> At 10.55 am the artillery report that 16th N.F. are over the front line and 15th Lancs Fslrs are somewhere in THIEPVAL. There is no information from Northumberland Fusiliers.[29]

By 11.40 Major-General Rycroft at last managed to contact Lieutenant-General Morland in his observation tree at Engelbelmer. Between them a plan was devised to extend the attacks on Thiepval by a further artillery bombardment, including heavy howitzers, of the reverse of the spur, the Wundt-werk, the Nordwerk and the trenches at the head of Blighty Valley. By noon X Corps had arranged the bombardment of these positions from 12.16 until 1.30 p.m. Rightly or wrongly the shelling of Thiepval itself was again postponed in view of Brigadier-General Yatman's continued belief, at 11.45, in the presence of the 1st Pals there. Morland was told by Rycroft that Brigadier-General Yatman had already arranged to send companies of the 96th Brigade's reserve battalion, the 2nd Royal Inniskilling Fusiliers, to prepare to penetrate north of the village, with orders then to turn south, taking the position of Thiepval in reverse and cutting off the route of any reinforcements moving along Zollern Graben (Lancashire Lane) from the direction of Goat Redoubt and Courcelette.

Pte. O. JACKSON, 18, Ham-han-st. Green. Lancs. Fusiliers.

The reluctance of Thiepval to fall was having a disastrous impact on the 36th Division's chances of holding on to the gains at Schwaben Redoubt. At 11.50 the 109th Brigade headquarters reported that machine gun fire from Thiepval was preventing all movement across the German front and support lines, making it impossible for them to get any fresh troops, ammunition or water forward to the men who were clinging on in the redoubt. Along the Thiepval Road above Hammerhead Sap piles of bodies, Ulstermen, Inniskillings and Lancashire Fusiliers were literally heaped in lines where the machine guns in Thiepval had cut them down throughout the day.

Pte. A. HIGGINS, 12, Queen's-pl., f-o th'-H., Lancashire Fusiliers.

Those men from the 2nd Salford Pals who were still left alive, and able to crawl back, had been withdrawn into Queen's Cross Street trench, to regroup and prepare to attack again with the Inniskillings. At 1.30 two companies of the 2nd 'Skins' together with the parties of the 2nd Salford Pals attacked towards the north west corner of Thiepval in a desperate attempt to close the gap on the 36th Division's right flank. They met with exactly the same fate as the Pals had earlier in the day. A further attack, by men of 1/6th and part of the 1/8th West Yorks[30], mounted during the afternoon at 4.00 p.m., also met with disaster. At best, these attacks by the 146th Brigade of the 49th Division could be said to have lacked coordination. The other two Brigades were ordered to circulate aimlessly behind the Thiepval Wood area throughout the day. Anything that moved in front of the wood became an easy prey to the enemy machine gunners in Thiepval. Writing later, to the family of Private Fiddes, Captain Tweed said that the orderly had been bandaged. However,

> When the surviving members of the Company retired he appeared to have been hit again, and was unconscious. A number of wounded were lying in the open, and the enemy later in the afternoon riddled them with bullets. Another attack was made by fresh troops with no better success, and some hundreds of bodies lay in the open,...[31]

Brigadier-General Yatman, whose belief in the presence of the Salford Pals in Thiepval had a profound effect on the battle for control of this area throughout the 1st July. Historical Records of the 16th NFs, p. 19.

West of the Ancre, watching from the 32nd Division's Advanced Report Centre on the Bouzincourt road, 2nd Lieutenant (later Captain) Edgar Lord of the 15th LFs pondered the circumstances which had forced him to miss these events. As an officer attached to the Battalion since mid May, Lord had had little experience with the unit, having been injured by an explosion at the trench mortar demonstration a month earlier, in which Major Robert Thomas, the Second in Command, was killed.

> A broiling hot day without a breath of wind and down the dusty road came men with wounds of every description. A few of the worst cases came on the ambulances, which were in very small supply, but carts, wagons, lorries, limbers, water tanks and any vehicles which would give a lift were crammed to the utmost. The walking cases were choked with dust, staggering along between the timbers, sometimes helping each other forming human crutches, most of them wearing blood stained bandages, and many in improvised splints. The agony on their weary faces told a weary tale of experiences well-nigh beyond recounting, as all had only just escaped the longest Journey of all.[33]
>
> I helped as I could by buying chocolates, biscuits and giving draughts of water from my bottle, but all along the road men laid down for the last time, being wounded worse than they knew.

North of Thiepval the men of the Ulster Division were gradually weakened throughout the day's fighting.

During the morning patrols had been driven away from the village by grenades and the intensity of fire, but other patrols towards Mouquet Farm along the switch trench had shown that it might well have been possible to take Thiepval in reverse since this area was not occupied by the enemy. However, it was proving impossible to sustain the 36th Division's advanced supplies of ammunition and water because of the curtain of machine gun fire which swept Mill Road and the slopes in front of Thiepval Wood. During the afternoon two infantry counter attacks from the directions of Grandcourt and Goat Redoubt, combined with a prolonged bombardment of the Schwaben Redoubt, exhausted the dwindling band of

The British trenches filled up with wounded within minutes of the offensive getting underway.

men. The elements of the 49th Division now detailed to support the Ulstermen came up too late to effect a change in the tactical balance of power here. By 10.00 p.m. the Ulstermen retired from the Schwaben Redoubt positions to the old German front line positions.

When the 2nd Pals from B and D Coys were brought together for rollcall in their trench below Thiepval that night, only Tweed and 17 others remained uninjured. By contrast, A and C Companies were still comparatively intact. As the 2nd Inniskillings moved into the trenches to relieve the Salfords that night at 11p.m., C Company of the 2nd Pals were moved right to hold the front line between Greenock Street (R31a1/5) and Skinner Street (R31a2/2).

The 1st Pals were decimated, having only 3 officers and 150 men left in the entire Battalion. That night these remaining men were withdrawn to the Bluff at Authuille. Writing in his own Battalion's diary within hours of these events, the 2nd Pals' Lieutenant Colonel Abercrombie already knew the cause of the catastrophe.

2nd Lieutenant Laurence Price. 18 years of age and only with the 2nd Pals since June 1st, having been posted from the 4th Lancashire Fusiliers[32], he survived the events of 1st July. On his left shoulder are the distinctive battalion recognition stripes of the 2nd Salford Pals. Whippy

> *It is evident that the bombardment failed to dislodge the protected M.G.s in the Thiepval defences and it is probable that some of these were in advanced positions nearer to our lines than we had supposed; there must also have been some M.G.s with a high command as our men crawling were instantly detected and fired on. During our bombardment before the attack enemy M.G.s could be heard firing from several positions.*[34]

These were the machine guns which had been sited within strengthened saps, just a few yards in front of the German front lines at Thiepval. The menace of these guns was now clearly understood and accounted for, although that knowledge was too late to stem the continuing impetus behind the Somme offensive which was now destined for four further bloodied months' duration.

Most of their machine-guns were in steel rail and concrete nests, proof against anything less than a direct hit by a 12-in., cunningly camouflaged in No Man's Land, and superbly sited for crossfire.[35]

Thiepval had proved to be a quite impenetrable fortress. The attacks this day were all too clearly destined for failure in view of the village's commanding position, the strength of the defences and the rigidity of the assault's timing which ensured that the Salford men here would attack with little more hope than that of perishing bravely. This they had most certainly achieved.

Throughout the remainder of the night the men of the 2nd Pals dug in and sheltered as best they could from the continuing bombardment of 77s and 4.2s. Parts of No Man's Land were searched and as many of the wounded as could be found were carried in.

At dark a few survivors and slightly wounded came in, but the dead were everywhere. We spent the night searching for the badly wounded and bringing in all we could. One of my chaps, Corporal Chidgey, carried in seven on his own back.[36]

The following day was spent clearing the dismembered bodies and discarded equipment from the trenches, and repairing the parapets and revetments which had been virtually destroyed by shellfire. A further heavy bombardment of Gemmel trench and the front positions opposite Thiepval again caused casualties at 5.30 p.m. that afternoon. The 2nd Pals were relieved from their trenches by the 2nd South Lancashires at 3.00 a.m., on 3rd July, marching back to Aveluy Wood and thence on to Warloy-Baillon. Their casualties during the previous two days had been 223 men and 9 officers.

The 3rd Pals' Attack

At 9.30 p.m. during the evening of 30th June the 3rd Salford Pals left their billets at Senlis and marched to the shelters at Blackhorse Bridge, below Authuille.

... it would be close on 1 o'clock before we were all settled. In a dugout meant for 20 there would be 50 of us, and we were in the most uncomfortable positions. Very little sleep was possible, and we were not sorry when dawn broke on 1st July. We were up by 5.00 am., washed in a lake just at the rear of the dug-outs, breakfasted on biscuits and 'bully' and were then ready waiting orders. It was a beautiful morning, and at the time of getting up not a sound could be heard, not even a rifle shot ... At 6 a.m. you could not hear yourself speak; the bombardment had commenced. Our gunners were working like niggers. It was the most intense bombardment I have yet heard. Every gun available was firing, including two or three batteries of French 75s and a number of guns of the South African artillery. You could feel the ground vibrate beneath your feet.[37]

An advanced dressing station taking in walking wounded on the Somme.

The column was assembled in order of advance, being led by the

1st Dorsets which were followed by the Trench Mortar Battery, the Stokes Guns, the 3rd Pals and in the rear the half section of 206th Company Royal Engineers.

In advance of the 3rd Pals the 97th Brigade were due to take the Leipzig Salient, within minutes of zero. In an extraordinary rush close behind their artillery barrage the men of 17th H.L.I, charged into the redoubt in the small quarry at the tip of Leipzig Salient, killing or taking prisoner almost all of the defenders. Their success was aided by a heavy smoke barrage which the Divisional Artillery fired on the German lines east of Blighty Valley, preventing any volume of aimed machine gun and rifle fire from the direction of the Nord-werk. However, the H.L.I.'s further and very brave attempts at advance, towards Hindenberg, across the exposed ground behind the tip of Leipzig Salient proved impossible and by 7.55 a.m., the Germans had begun to shell their own front line at the quarry. Under this shelling the H.L.I.'s men found themselves pinned down at the south western tip of the redoubt by persistent machine gun fire from the Hindenburg Stellung itself, the Lemberg Stellung and Wundt-werk above and from the Nordwerk on the Ovillers spur.

Private Herbert Douglas Strachan, 11254, B Company, No 5 platoon, 2nd Pals. Killed in action, 1st July. Although Scottish born, Herbert Strachan was an original Pal, enlisted in Salford after having been living at Eccles. Irlam and Cadishead's Roll of Honour. 1914–1917.

To their left the assault by the 16th H.L.I, on the western face of the salient was virtually stopped in its tracks by the severity of the machine gun fire, only a handful of men getting through to join the 17th H.L.I, in Leipzig Redoubt. Throughout the morning any attempt to move in this area of No Man's Land west of the salient caused immediate and very accurate machine gun fire from the direction of Thiepval Chateau. Even three hours after these events the 97th Brigade Headquarters in Blighty Valley still had no news of the 16th H.L.I.

An hour and a half later the 3rd Pals were due at Mouquet Farm, a mile and half behind one of the most complex and heavily entrenched strongpoints on the Western Front!

At 7.10 am the 3rd Pals set off on their desperate journey, marching along the Ancre's banks for 1,000 yards before they turned east into Blighty Valley. The men advanced in columns of platoons in fours, with 100 yards between each platoon, entering their assembly trenches on the southern edge of the splintered, shrieking confines of Authuille Wood. (Trench Map reference W6c55/06.)

The Ancre Valley behind Thiepval Wood from where the 1st and 2nd Pals attacked. Taylor Library

At 7.30 a.m., [sic] prompt the order was given to move into 'Blighty Wood,' so called because so many have been wounded there and sent to England. In front of us was the 1st Dorset Battalion. We had hardly got into the wood when the cry of 'stretcher-bearers' was heard. The Germans had evidently seen us advancing or they already knew the time and place from whence we were to advance. Case after case passed us on the way back to the dressing stations, some on stretchers, and some on foot. The Germans had opened fire with machine guns, and the Dorsets in front were losing a great number of men. Advancing further on to the wood we came across a large number of dead, and others seriously wounded awaiting attention. And we had not as yet commenced any attack.[38]

British big guns' pounding of the German positions prior to 1st July should have made the attack a 'walk-over'.

In front of them, at 8.30 a.m., in the belief that the Salient was then in British hands, the 11th Borders had set off to cross No Man's Land. Their right flank was still totally exposed by the failure of the 8th Division's attacks across the Nordwerk and towards Ovillers.

> The 11th Borders which, seeing that the right was held up should have been kept back in AUTHUILLE WOOD, debouched into the open about 8.40 a.m. and immediately came under heavy machine gun fire from enemy works in front of the left Brigade of 8th Division. They suffered heavy casualties, Hachell being killed and 2nd in command and Adjutant wounded. Few if any of this battalion reached the enemy trenches.[39]

They had been practically annihilated, their bodies forming a further intimidating image of the sacrifice to be risked. Only a tiny handful of men, on the left of the Borders, had got across to join their comrades in the 17th H.L.I, in the redoubt. From their right the machine gun fire from the Nordwerk had been devastating. Fifteen minutes later the 1st Dorsets went over the top, seemingly incapable of stopping the inexorable slaughter when faced with a clear catastrophe in front.

> 9.30 14th Brigade report their 2nd Battalion 1st Dorsets have left the WOOD under cover of smoke. The 3rd Battalion is being held back till the position of Dorsets is clear. Enemy M.G. fire from X 2 central and Lachrymatory shells have been fired at exit of DUMBARTON TRACK. They think the left of 8th Div cannot have progressed far.[40]

Attacking across No Man's Land at the start of the 'Big Push'. The failure of the 8th Division near Ovillers left the 3rd Salford's right flank very exposed.

Of the 1st Dorsets just sixty men from the first companies covered the ground to Leipzig's shelter. The rest took cover, either in the wood or the ever more crowded British front line. What was happening here proved that the meticulous planning had taken on an impetus of its own which prevented even relatively senior Brigade staff effecting any change in the plans. The 14th Brigade's G.O.C., Compton, whose HQ was also little more than half a mile away in Blighty Valley along with 97th Brigade's HQ, was unable to call halt. Again the Divisional Commander, Rycroft, was critical.

> *The 1st Dorsets, the leading battalion of the 14th Brigade which, seeing that the leading Brigade was held up, should have remained under cover but also debouched into the open...[41]*

Inside the confines of the wood, moving up Dumbarton track, the 3rd Pals were,

Pte. F. G. BROOKSBANK, 5, Mabel-avenue, Worsley, Lancashire Fusiliers.

> *... moving very slowly and we were getting restless. It was painful. We wanted to charge for all we were worth. Under ordinary circumstances the sights of the wounded would have sickened us, but now everything was different. We just merely smiled. We could hear the continual 'ping-ping' of the German machine gun and the continual whistle of the bullets through the wood. The noises of cracking and falling branches, the thud as the bullets penetrated the bark of the trees, the occasional cry of a wounded man, and the continual cry for the stretcher bearers. On we went through the wood, tears rolling down our cheeks, caused by the gas shells sent over by the Germans.[42]*

Sergt. E. CROFT, 23, Garden-st., Eccles, Lancashire Fusiliers.

Lieutenant Colonel Graham surveyed the carnage between the tip of Authuille Wood and the British Front Line.[43] In front of him the communication trenches

No Man's Land was covered in dead and wounded.

Lieutenant Colonel Graham. Lewis

were utterly blocked with the dead and wounded from previous attempts to move forward towards and across Boggart Hole Clough. If his men were to get across Blackpool Street, up to their own front lines and cross the exposed glacis in front of Leipzig Redoubt some more radical tactics were necessary. It was clearly time to throw Rawlinson's 'Tactical Notes' out before more lives were squandered needlessly!

Graham decided that the prescribed mechanical advance, rifles at the slope, was futile. Lieutenant Huxley's A Company were sent out in platoon rushes but many were mown down. Another smoke screen was requested from the Brigade's Stokes Mortar bombers to obscure the right of the route forward and to give some respite from the machine gunners firing from the Nordwerk.

> We were now ready for the mad rush from the 'Gap', which was at the extreme end of the wood. Before us lay the open country, a country devastated and blackened with fire, and innumerable trenches and shell holes.[44]

Signaller Handley was looking across an area bounded on its left by the artillery track, No. 2, which left the top of Authuille Wood behind the British front line trench, here called Boggart Hole Clough just south east of the tip of Leipzig Salient. On his right lay No. 1 track and beyond that the upper reaches of Blighty Valley and the Brigade's boundary with III Corps. No. 2 artillery track was the merest fragment of the farmtrack which led out of Authuille Wood towards the quarry forming the snout of the Salient. These two tracks constituted the right and left limits of the 3rd Pals' attacks across No Man's Land. The whole of this zone was already littered with the dead and injured.

> We crouched in a springing attitude at the 'Gap' waiting for the command. The colonel stood, cap in hand, cheering on the platoon who had just left. We saw them falling, and no wonder, it was sheer murder. Incessant machine gun fire was on them, also rapid rifle fire from each flank; but on they went clean over our first line and then down. Then our order came 'Advance', followed by a volley of machine gun fire from the back. My heart leaped; the word 'Advance' seemed to strengthen me. Grasping rifle and bayonet firmly, on we flew, bloodthirsty and desperate, down and then on again. We had reached our own trench breathless, and had lost half the platoon.[45]

German dead sprawled around trenches flattened by artillery fire.

Under concealment of the swirling greyness of smoke and covering fire from Lewis and Vickers guns, but still suffering heavy casualties, some more men from B Company, commanded by Captain Hibbert, and half of C Company made it as far as the British front lines, below the Leipzig Redoubt opposite. The advance had been made in 30 to 40 yard rushes, the men taking shelter in shell holes before gathering themselves for the next sprint. When Captain Hibbert arrived in his front line trenches they were so grotesquely congested with men that word was sent back to prevent any further moves of men out of Authuille Wood until space could be made available. At this point the remaining half of C Company and all of D were kept back in Authuille Wood. The right column of the 14th Brigade, seeing the disaster unfold to its left, had also been ordered by Brigadier General Compton to stand fast in the shelter of Authuille Wood, a decision which undoubtedly saved many lives from the untroubled attentions of the Nordwerk's machine guns, which-enfiladed the whole of No Man's Land here.

Nevertheless, the Salford Pals in the front line were not to be deterred and efforts to get forward were continued without hesitation at the front lines. Lieutenant Huxley's attempts were shot to ribbons, Huxley being the only surviving, but wounded, officer left alive from A Company. Only 4 of his 40 men got within ten yards of the German trenches. The next wave led by Captain Hibbert was more fortunate, and his attack was followed into the German trenches by groups led by Lieutenant Musker of C Company and 2nd Lieutenant George of B Company who between them brought forward roughly 140 men, disentangled from the chaotically crowded confines of their own fire trenches.

> One Lewis Gun was carried over into the German trenches, but of the others, the carriers were either killed or wounded.
>
> Of the bomb carriers very few got across the fire-swept zone with their buckets. This was due to the fact that the men could not advance quick enough with the loads they had to carry, and they, probably being more conspicuous, were singled out.
>
> The smoke barrage thrown out on our right flank ... considerably aided our advance, and that together with the machine gun and Lewis Gun fire from point X1c35/75 certainly helped in reducing our casualties.[46]

Those who had survived the perilous crossing,

> had reached the first line of German trenches, or what was left of them. Our artillery, who were still firing, had levelled them to the ground. German dead bodies were strewn all over; ...By this time our ranks had been terribly thinned and we were feeling very weak and exhausted. The Germans' guns had started in earnest, and were playing on our first line, and we were also losing heavily there. Numerous gas shells were sent over, and to escape the gas the men were staggering over the parapet for safely and occupying the nearest shell holes.[47]

These men of the 3rd Pals were located at the angle of the salient[48] with groups of men from the 1st Dorsets on their right and from the 11th Borders on their left. Using up the stock of 800 German grenades which had been found, Captain Hibbert and his men then resolutely defended against repeated attempts by German troops to re-occupy their trenches at the tip of the salient. During the early afternoon seven or eight Germans were found still hiding in the dug-outs and they were then sent down to Blackhorse bridge via the Russian sap, opposite Sanda Street, which linked with this western corner of the salient.

As part of the plan to pinch out the Thiepval defences by launching attacks round the northern side of Thiepval and through Leipzig men of the 2nd Manchesters were ordered to make a further attempt to enter the redoubt and reinforce the units already there. Unfortunately the 85 minute barrage put on the German trenches at the top of Blighty Valley and the Nordwerk proved too thin, and again failed to knock out the machine guns in these positions. However, under the protection of the final intense minutes of this barrage the two companies of Manchesters were able to get across at the point where the Salford Pals had entered the salient, managing to incur relatively few casualties from the Nordwerk's machine gunners en route. Predictably, the combined attempts of all these groups then to make progress towards Hindenberg Street were blocked by bombing, hand to hand fighting in the communication trenches and a renewed hail of machine gun fire from Lemberg and the Nord-werk when any men showed themselves above ground.

These events which unfolded in front of the south face of Leipzig Redoubt had become a catalogue of inevitable errors. What was designed to be a walk across positions that should already have fallen became a nightmare frontal assault on strong defences which were fully in control of a panoramic field of fire and which had not even been subjected to an earlier attack co-ordinated with the launch of the main offensive. At least three battalions, the 3rd Salfords included, were wasted as successive waves were launched across the desert of blackened shellholes with imperfect knowledge of what was now their new objective or any real hope of success. These troops who had rehearsed assaults on Goat Redoubt and Mouquet Farm therefore floundered with incredible fortitude and guts across a battlefield littered with the dead and dying from each previous assault. In front of them the monstrously complex and well developed trench network of Leipzig Salient remained almost untouched. To its right the junction between X Corps and III Corps, which ran along Blighty Valley, on the left of the 3rd Pals' attack, meant that the German defences at the top of the re-entrant were unmolested by co-ordinated artillery fire and were able to utterly decimate the attacks on the south of Leipzig by the Borders, Dorsets and Salfords. The outcome had become quite predictable. At 9.30 that evening the 3rd Pals were ordered to pull back from the Leipzig Redoubt and Authuille Wood below it. Because of continued hostile artillery this

Thiepval defences taken from the original German map showing the location of front line machine guns, their angles of fire and effective range. SPATH

relief by the unused companies of the 2nd Manchesters took some time and it was not until midnight that the 3rd Pals were withdrawn from the sector, having lost half their strength. Unlike the disastrous situation in front of Thiepval, where wounded were left in agony in No Man's Land with little if any chance of rescue, the 3rd Pals were able to pull back with their injured comrades.

> *It was terrible to see the sights on our way back, and then again it was wonderful the number that did get back under such fire. The ground we had advanced on, and were now going back over, was a battleground I'll never forget. Dead and wounded were lying all over the place. Equipment, rifles and bayonets, ammunition and bombs which had been thrown off and left by the wounded were strewn everywhere. It seemed impossible to reach the wood again or even our own trenches. I managed it with a few others …We were now at the rear end of our first line, and had got down for a rest. I went down to the dressing station for water. The stretcher-bearers and R.A.M.C. were working like niggers, and as they dressed the men they were despatched with as much speed as possible to the advanced dressing station, and from there to the various hospitals. At dusk we were taken out of the trenches and marched to Authuille road…*[49]

By 1.00 a.m., the men passed Black Horse shelters on their way to man the Authuille reserve trenches. The signallers took shelter under the steep road embankment which ran from the mouth of Blighty

Bapaume. The British High Command expected this German-occupied town to fall in Haig's 'Big Push' – at the middle of November, 1916, when the fighting on the Somme finally petered out, it was still two and a half miles behind German lines. Here a German observation balloon is seen flying over the undamaged town in 1916.

Valley towards Authuille. It was here that, later in the night, Signaller Handley's party was hit by shrapnel. Within days his description was being penned in Bangour Hospital in Scotland.

Throughout the 2nd July the 3rd Pals were in reserve in Authuille and then moved back into the lines above the village, finally being taken back to rest billets in Senlis on the 4th July, having been awake, in action and under almost constant shellfire for a period close on a hundred hours.

We are gaining ground fast

For the men from the docklands, engineering workshops, mines and mills of Salford it had been a deplorable and pointless end to their eighteen months of preparation. For the 1st Pals the events had been particularly catastrophic. Five hundred days in the making, they had been a mere few hours in destruction. Never more would men of the 15th Battalion of the Lancashire Fusiliers be able to survey a sea of their pals' faces at parade. From now on the Battalion took on a more cosmopolitan character.

2nd Pals' 1st July casualties killed in action.

Pte. JESSE ROYLE, Hazlehurst, Worsley, Lancs. Fusiliers.

Pte. J. L. ROUTLEDGE, Eccles, Lancashire Fusiliers.

Pte. D. S. POTTS, 50, Earl-st., Swinton, Lancashire Fusiliers.

Pte. J. ORLEDGE, 24, Renshaw-st., P'croft, Lancashire Fusiliers.

Pte. W. F. MURDEN, 10, Knowsley-av., Eccles, Lancashire Fusiliers.

By midnight on 1st July it was clear that X Corps' casualties were catastrophic. Over 5,000 in the 36th Division, of whom more than 1,800 had been killed. Nearly 4,000 in the 32nd, of whom more than 1,280 were dead and 2,500 wounded. In all, in excess of 9,000 soldiers of the Corps were put out of action this day. Although the Liverpool and Manchester Pals of XIII Corps had successfully opened up the southern end of the British sector of the Somme battlefield, the failure of X Corps' attack meant that it would now be weeks before British soldiers would be able to look down over the Bapaume area from the broad expanses of its highest ground.

Within this deluge of casualties Salford and its surrounding districts would suffer accordingly. On this one day the 1st Pals lost 21 officers and 449 men (out of 24/650), two thirds of them 'missing'. Almost to a man this battalion had enlisted in Salford and were resident there or in nearby communities. An extraordinarily high proportion of those who went over the top had been killed; in the case of the 1st Pals' officers every one who went over had been killed or wounded. The 2nd Pals lost 9 officers and 223 men (out of 20/480), mostly in B and D Companies whose casualty rates had been disastrous. The 3rd Pals lost 11 officers and 270 men (out of 20/577). The casualties incurred by the 2nd and 3rd battalions were spread rather further afield and reflected their community origins in the Pendlebury, Swinton, Eccles and Patricroft districts.

More than 60% of the officers had become casualties, 55% of the men.

When Lieutenant Lord first saw the men who had survived the ravages of their experience in front of Thiepval he was shocked and dismayed. The remnants of the 1st Pals were on their way back to rest, at Warloy-Baillon,

What a sight this small band presented when we met them; weary, haggard and drawn faces, bodies exhausted and legs that almost could not carry their burden, but their thoughts were too tragic for words. All had lost many friends on that awful day and as I marched along with them trying to cheer them on, I felt like a warder escorting a condemned prisoner. The band joined us, and as it played 'Keep the home fires burning till the boys come home' I nearly wept with impotence and sadness. For the first time I fully appreciated the horrors of war, the futility and madness of it all and realised that nothing but dishonour could justify such senselessness.[50]

The expenditure of munitions had been equally profligate, and to similarly little gain. Between the evening of 30th June and noon on the 2nd July the artillery under control of 32nd Division fired 33,932 18 pdr. rounds together with 5,509 4.5 howitzer rounds. Of more than 13,000 Stokes Mortar shells available the vast majority had been expended.

During the next few days the tiny number of remaining officers were presented with the unenviable task of writing hundreds of letters to relatives. It was an impossible duty in view of the numbers and the lack of first hand knowledge concerning what had happened. In a huge number of cases the letters attempted to suggest a hope that the missing were, in fact, prisoners. The seeds of months of uncertainty in Salford were being sown, quite innocently and with the best intention. At the same time the 1st, 2nd and 3rd Pals' Battalions were reconstructed into temporary units of two companies, pitiably thin in the case of the 1st Pals, and made up of the shocked survivors, the Battalion Reserves and men of the

2nd Lieutenant R. I. Doncaster killed in action at Thiepval on 1st July, 1st Pals. Ivan Doncaster had journeyed to France with Edgar Lord, when they were sent out to join the 1st Pals, in the spring of 1916. They had become close friends since their time together at Brocton Camp, where this had been taken the previous summer. Willcock.

transport sections and quartermaster's staff, but whose presence could not disguise the truth that the character of these Battalions was now irretrievably changed.

> *After lying for three days in No Man's Land a private of C (Doncaster's) Company returned, telling me that he had seen Ivan hit in the wrist about twelve yards from the German wire, and whilst sitting in a shell-hole to bind it was hit through the head by a bullet. As the man's mind was wandering after his ordeal, we could not rely entirely on this story, but as it was the only evidence, I sent the news to his people. His mother never completely recovered from the shock, and the loss of a friend was a very severe blow to me throughout the war.*[51]

At least Ivan Doncaster's family had a tentative confirmation that he had paid the ultimate price. By stark contrast, the majority of officers' and men's families from the 1st Pals were left in a terrible state of apprehension, wanting above all to believe the letters suggesting that the men were 'missing'.

Just occasionally the existence of close relatives in one of the battalions helped clear possible confusion. Edward Rydings' (17254) brother, William, wrote to their sister with the explicit news that,

> *... our Ned got killed in action. We had a lively time, and a rough one, too, but we took a lot of German prisoners. I wish we could have taken them all. I don't think it will last long, as we are gaining ground fast. Ned was brave to the last. He said to his pal, 'Let's go and fetch him out that's throwing them oil-cans'. But before they could get the chance to use the bayonet he was shot down.*[52]

Like many of the other casualties in the 3rd Pals, Ned had been a miner at Wheatsheaf Colliery in Pendlebury. Both Ned and William had enlisted in the same battalion.

Like many other letter writers William saw a very clear need to give justification for the death by explaining the speed with which the conflict would, almost certainly, soon now end. William's letter says as much by what it omits as anything spoken of directly. 'A lively time... a lot of German prisoners... we are gaining ground fast.' The conspiracy of silence and self-imposed censorship was necessary to prevent friends and people in the streets at home from knowing and understanding the awful truth.

The war was squalid, and these soldiers were treated like the dirt they were forced to live, fight and die in.

Less than a fortnight after the Pals' denouement, the old hands were back at Ovillers. By now the British front line had moved forward, marginally, towards Pozieres. The Battalion diary of the 1st Pals states, laconically, 'Remained in support, collected equipment, buried dead'. The truth, of course, was far more sordid.

> *Our work was to salvage as much equipment as we could; packs, rifles, bayonets, ground-sheets, Lewis guns, ammunition. Very pistols, revolvers and such like were transported to a central dump to be sorted.*
>
> *Corpses lay everywhere, and the stench from the decaying bodies was very unpleasant. A blackened hand protruding from the ground was gruesome to say the least. One night I was detailed with a dozen men to bury some of our dead near our new front line. As some of them had been doing this the day before, they were feeling sick and groggy, so I ordered them to dig holes in the ground and make wooden crosses whilst I went with a Lewis gunner to handle the corpses. It was a ghastly job in the dark, feeling for their identity discs and effects, as most of them were bloated, having been killed some days earlier. One man whom we handled had lost both feet and the hand wearing his identity disc had been so badly smashed that the disc was mixed with the putrefying flesh; after a vain attempt to recover it, we interred him as 'unknown'. Before we had finished our labours, Jerry gave us a very warm half hour with high explosives and we crouched in the nearest shell hole till the strafe was over. When I found out where I was, I found I had been lying alongside a dead stretcher-bearer who was still clasping his stretcher; the experience was revolting. When we returned to the place where we had left the others, we found that they had bunked, we were dead as far as they knew, and in a cowardly moment had left us to our fate.*[53]

On the 11–14th July the 16th and 19th Battalions were involved in heavy fighting, centred upon the utterly smashed confines of Ovillers' main street, towards the church (at X8a9/l). Like many other battalions which had passed through the events of 1st July, the 3rd Pals only consisted of two companies, the first under Captain Haywood, being in trenches just south of Ovillers, the second under Captain Palk occupying trenches on the village's western side, with the 2nd Salford Pals on their left. Having advanced through the rubble and tangled woodwork which marked the street, on the night of

Salvaging and dreadful burial duties became the inevitable task of many Pals during the early days of July 1916.

12/13th, Captain Palk's men dug in in front of the remains of the Church. The severe fighting here involving Number 1 Company under Captain Haywood, just to the south of the Church, ebbed backwards and forwards throughout the early morning of the 13th, within the confines of a lattice work of trenches and barricades which criss-crossed the surface of the village. 40 of Haywood's men were killed or wounded, mostly the bombers who bore the brunt of the fighting within the claustrophobic passages. Of Haywood's four subalterns, 2nd Lieutenant Young was wounded and 2nd Lieutenants Longley and Mahoney were killed. Eventually the survivors succeded in joining up with No. 1 Company's advance and when it became clear that these men of No. 2 Company and the 2nd South Lancs to their right were in control a retiring party of Germans were brought under machine gun fire by Number 1 Company's men. The report on this operation drawn up by Lieutenant Colonel Graham says that this enemy detachment then,

> *...surrendered to Captain Palk, who went out personally – and brought these men in – although the Germans had begun to turn their own machine guns on to them. Thirty-seven prisoners belonging to the Guards Fusiliers' Regiment were thus captured by No. 2 Coy.*[54]

138

The rate for the job is illustrated by Bill Dutton's Pay Book. Private Dutton, as he then was, carried this document during his part in the attack at Thiepval. Half the pay of one shilling a day was sent home to his family, leaving him with sixpence for his labours in front of Thiepval on 1st July. The officer commanding D Company, whose signature appears on the book, is Captain E. G. MacLaren who was the brother of the famous Lancashire cricketer, Archie MacLaren. Paybook loaned by Ken Smallwood

This was the last occasion that the 3rd Pals saw action whilst operating strictly as an infantry battalion. On the 29th July the 3rd Pals became Pioneers, being transferred to the 49th (West Riding) Division. By now all three Pals' Battalions had left the Somme, the first two units remaining with the 96th Brigade. These changes and departure mark a watershed in the men's history. Not many of them were sorry to see the back of Authuille, Thiepval and Albert.

But at home their story had, as yet, barely begun to unfold.

Captured German trenches at Ovillers. July 1916. Taylor Library

Notes

Pte. JOHN JONES,
13, Peel-st., Eccles,
Lancashire Fusiliers.

Pte. J. GORING,
1, Moor-st., Swinton,
Lancashire Fusiliers.

Lce.-Cpl. L. RILEY,
69, King-st., Eccles,
Lancashire Fusiliers.

L.-Cpl. FRED MORTON,
4, Bolton-rd., P'bury,
Lancashire Fusiliers.

Pte. H. SIMPSON,
16, New-lane, Winton,
Lancashire Fusiliers.

*Some 3rd Pals'
casualties killed in
action 1st July, 1916.*

1. The annual motto, for 1916, of the Adelphi Lads' Club, Salford.
2. Bill Dutton, speaking of Peter Fensome.
3. Blighty Valley Tramway in area of 14th Brigade, Oban Avenue for the 97th Brigade and Greenock Avenue for the 96th Brigade.
4. Fourth Army 'Tactical Notes'. Issued May 1916.
5. PRO. WO 95/2394.
6. The German 26th Divisional headquarters were at Courcelette, 3 miles east of Thiepval.
7. 19th LFs' Operation Order. No. 37. PRO. WO 95/2394.
8. Ibid.
9. Rien N'va Plus.
10. Logs set with spikes.
11. PRO. WO 95/2367.
12. PRO. WO 95/2394.
13. Description of Thiepval in 14th Brigade Operational Orders for Z Day. PRO. WO 95/2394.
14. Captain Tweed. Rien N'va Plus.
15. See PRO WO 95/2375 for Divisional Artillery details and WO 95/2368 for 32nd Divisional Diary of events.
16. 32nd Divisional Diary. PRO. WO 95/2368.
17. Clarence Wright was employed at Frasers' merchants in Manchester. His MGS friend, Geoffrey Heald, worked on the actuarial staff of the Refuge Assurance Company in Manchester. Alfred Lee Wood worked at Lancashire Dynamo and Motor Company, Trafford Park. A Company's platoon commanders were Lieutenants Noyes, Freeman and Clegg. B Company's were Lieutenants Lodge and Aird. C Company, Doncaster and Jackson. D Company, Robinson, Wrong, Hampson and Audaer.
18. Pte. G. Hutton. (10204) 1st Pals. S.C.R. 15/7/1916.
19. PRO. WO 95/2395.
20. Unfortunately a number of the Brigade's Stokes Mortar guns had already been knocked out by direct hits on their emplacements and only four were able to fire during the last five minutes of the 'Hurricane Bombardment'. The two guns supporting the 16th NFs were later ordered to cease fire because of the German 5.9 fire they were attracting.
21. PRO. WO 95/2368.
22. The battalion diary of the 16th NFs is in PRO WO 95/2398. See also Historical Records of the 16th Battalion Northumberland Fusiliers. Captain C. H. Cooke. M.C. (Pub. Newcastle and Gateshead Incorporated Chamber of Commerce. 1923.)
23. See E&PJ. 14/7/1916.
24. Lieutenant C. S. Marriot's account, written in December 1964. LFM.
25. Rien N'va Plus. E&PJ. 21/7/1916.
26. Ibid.
27. 2nd Salford Pals' Battalion War Diary. PRO WO 95/2397.
28. Corporal Sharples being killed and the two Privates surviving their wounds.
29. 32nd Divisional Diary. PRO WO 95/2368.
30. These were part of the 146th Brigade of the 49th Division. The dilatory management of this whole Division on 1st July led the Official History to comment, 'The piecemeal employment of the 49th Division by X. Corps headquarters had accomplished nothing.'! p 416. Military Operations. France and Belgium. 1916. Macmillan. 1932. 96th Brigade Diary (WO 95/2395) records that, 'The 5th West Yorkshire Regiment did not arrive until the attack had failed. These Battalions of 49th Division were late in arriving and there seems to have been some misunderstanding as to whether they were acting under my orders or those of their own Brigadier'.
31. Captain Tweed. E&PJ. 11/8/1916.
32. The 4th LFs were a home service battalion. At the start of the war Laurence had enlisted as Private L. C. Price (1916) in the 6th Seaforth Highlanders, at the age of 16.
33. Captain E. B. Lord.

34. 2nd Salford Pals' Battalion War Diary. PRO WO 95/2397. What the 1st Pals C.O., and Adjutant thought of their battalion's destruction was more difficult to know since that day's diary has been stolen from the Public Records Office. I am in the debt of Tony Conduit who provided a photocopy made by the P.R.O. before that act of vandalism took place.
35. Lieutenant C. S. Marriot's account, written in December 1964. LFM.
36. Ibid.
37. Signaller W. Handley. 18637. B Coy. 19th LFs. Quoted in E&PJ. 1/9/1916.
38. Signaller W. Handley. 18637. B Coy. 19th LFs. Quoted in E&PJ. 1/9/1916.
39. General Rycroft's comments in the 32nd Divisional Diary. PRO WO 95/2368.
40. 32nd Divisional Diary. PRO WO 95/2368.
41. General Rycroft's comments in the 32nd Divisional Diary. PRO WO 95/2368.
42. Signaller W. Handley. 18637. B Coy. 19th LFs. Quoted in E&PJ. 1/9/1916.
43. He was located at Trench Map reference Xlc38/75.
44. Signaller W. Handley. 18637. B Coy. 19th LFs. Quoted in E&PJ. 1/9/1916.
45. Ibid.
46. Lieutenant Colonel Graham's 'Report on Operations Carried out by 19th Lancashire Fusiliers from 1st to 4th July, 1916'. PRO WO 95/2394.
47. Signaller W. Handley. 18637. B Coy. 19th LFs. Quoted in E&PJ. 1/9/1916.
48. Trench map reference R31c30/30.
49. Signaller W. Handley. 18637. B Coy. 19th LFs. Quoted in E&PJ. 1/9/1916.
50. Captain E. B. Lord.
51. Ibid.
52. Letter home, quoted in E&PJ, 14/7/1916.
53. Captain E. B. Lord.
54. PRO. WO 95/2394. Report on the Fighting in Ovillers.

Chapter Five

Life Must Go On

At home in the grim and dusty streets of an expectant Salford, the events of 1st July were by no means clear. Censorship maintained a firm grip on all that appeared in newspapers and would continue to do so until the war's end. In advance of any firm news, in the form of letters, the local newspaper groped through the correspondents' dispatches which found an uncritical place in many columns early that week.

Seven days after the start of the Battles of the Somme the Salford City Reporter was able to describe the events as,

> OF GREAT INTEREST TO SALFORD PEOPLE
> VICTORY FOR OUR BRAVE BOYS
>
> *The great struggle began at the end of last week, and at the time of writing all goes well with our brave Army. Around Albert – La Boisselle, Ovillers, Thiepval – Salford people will have a peculiar interest.*[1]

Initial accounts of the fighting described the episode fancifully, the Tommies having 'swept through the little town of Thiepval'. Half a dozen regiments were portrayed as having won universal praise for their bravery and achievements.

> *...Northumberland Fusiliers, the Royal Irish Rifles, the Suffolks, the Royal Scots, the Lancashire Fusiliers, the Warwickshires, all of these, and others no less, when all is known, will be found to have done magnificently.*[2]

But amidst all of this ill-advised and crudely founded optimism, the galling and fatuous ambiguity of the Daily Mail's writer foretold of the dread and distress which the Borough would have to endure.

> *The losses of some units are very heavy, but what stirs a man's spirit more than all is to find in the relic survivors an ecstasy of sacrifice, an exhilaration of mind, as the men who have outlived the human measure and transcended human effort. The price of immortal courage was paid in this fighting by all parts of Great Britain (including the Lancashire Fusiliers). We trust that as they fell they knew that they helped to win the victory of the others, British and French, in the south, as well as a victory for humanity.*[3]

In a week when 4,000 Salford dockers were on strike for an additional penny an hour, an event which would normally have dominated community life, the question raised throughout the town, its newspapers and pubs was 'what had happened?'.

Images for public consumption contrasted sourly with the soldiers' knowledge of reality. This image, suggesting the easy conquest of a vanquished foe, appeared on July 15th, 1916, in the Illustrated London News.

The 1st Weaste Boy Scouts who would be so shattered to hear of the death of Cyril Crossley. This photograph was taken in 1915 and mirrors the military pose so often struck by groups of adult men who had just enlisted. SLHL

The so called 'ecstacy of sacrifice' was soon to be translated into an immense personal tragedy, whose impact spread without favour across the entirety of Salford and its outlying districts. By 15th July the Reporter carried many lengthy and extensive obituaries detailing the lives and brief military careers of a number of officers from the Pals units.

> *The Scout movement has lost one of its most ardent supporters, and indeed one of its early pioneers, by the death of Second-Lieutenant Cyril Crossley (25 years of age) of the Lancashire Fusiliers. He was killed in action on July 2 [sic] in the great British offensive. Before his enlistment he resided at 57, Seedley Road, Pendleton. He was Scoutmaster of the Salford Scouts, and also latterly of the St. Thomas' Boy Scouts. He was also secretary of the Salford and District Scout Association. He received his education at Manchester Grammar School. He enlisted...*[4]

Significantly, far more were described as 'missing'.

The community's fervent belief, fuelled by letters from the front, was that these men would turn out to have been taken prisoner. In an attempt to sustain this hope the Reporter openly suppressed details, saying that absence of news from Salford men 'may mean good news eventually'. Their attempt to put a gloss on the disaster clutched at the straw of German telegrams which,

> *... should give encouragement and hope in Salford homes that mainy of their boys are prisoners – bad as that may be. The telegram states: 'The number of unwounded Englishmen taken prisoners during the last few days on the right bank of the Ancre amounts to 43 officers and 867 men.' Thiepval is on the right bank of the Ancre and is without doubt the place indicated. We have ascertained also that many officers of the First Salford Battalion were missing after the battle.*[5]

Of course many feelings of burden and guilt were bound to surface among the men who felt in some way responsible for the concentration of grief caused by this disaster. Montague Barlow worked without stinting in trying to find details of the missing. However even by the end of July the War Office would claim to have no information on the missing, nor of how many, or if any, were prisoners of war.

Although a number of officers were already known to have been killed, a list of thirteen missing from the 1st Pals was published on 29th July in the Reporter, saying,

We were requested to ask soldiers who were in the battle and can give any information relating to these officers to forward same, addressed to 'The Editor'...

Lieutenant-Colonel J. H. Lloyd, who had commanded the 1st Pals since August 1915, admitted in his letter to the parents of Lieutenant Robinson that he had no news of what had happened. It was clearly no easy task to write of such an oppressive state of affairs. Speaking of his hope that the Lieutenant was now a prisoner, Lloyd said,

... he would be well treated because the Germans opposite us were a good soldierly lot. I had a fine lot of officers and men. I never saw a Battalion during all my experience which was better. We were like a family, and I used to feel just like a father to all those boys, and I really think many of them felt like sons almost. I know they would have gone anywhere for me; in fact, they did. At 7.30 a.m., we started and by 8.30 a.m., we were finished.[6]

Captain Thomas Tweed went as far as to issue a statement to the relatives of the men from his company. In it the burden of responsibility weighs heavily on his mind and clearly shows the impossibility of his position.

... That I feel the loss of so many gallant men need not be stated. Most of my men I personally persuaded to join the colours and I felt the burden of responsibility for their welfare, as a matter of both honour and duty, and now so many of them have made the supreme sacrifice, I wonder with what feelings their loved ones regard myself. For my men, both those wounded in hospital and those few who still form the Eccles Company, I know that they will acquit me of responsibility... I feel certain that, apart from my own men, the mothers, wives and sweethearts of those who willingly and gallantly laid down their lives for their country, will also acquit me of any blame for persuading those dear to them to enlist.[7]

Already the pitiable notices, in memory, had begun to appear in the local press. Frequently these took the form of simple verse, espousing a deep rooted patriotism even in the face of anguished loss.

Casuality list which appeared in the Eccles and Patricroft Journal 4 August 1916.

One of the first to hear the call,
For the land he loved he gave his all,
Somewhere in France in a nameless grave
Lies our boy amongst the brave.

Sadly mourned by

FATHER, MOTHER and SISTER.
Memorial notice to Lance Corporal Charlie Westhead.
(12060) K in A 2/7/1916. D Company, 2nd Pals.

Those fortunate enough to have survived the experience with only a 'Blighty' injury came back to hundreds of hospitals across the country. This photograph, believed to show some Somme casualties, was taken inside Hope Hospital, Pendleton, 1916.

Could we have raised his dying head
or heard his last farewell,
The grief would not have been so great
For those who loved him well.
Sleep on; dear son, in a far-off grave,
In a grave we may never see;
But as long as life and memory last
I will always think of thee.

From his sorrowing

Lieutenants Edgar Hampson and Harold Robinson. Both were officers of the 1st Salford Pals, K in A 1 July 1916.

MOTHER, SISTER and BROTHERS.
Memorial notice to Lance Corporal Albert Brearley of Lower Broughton, Salford. (11786) K in A D Company, 2nd Pals.[8]

Trones Wood

This was the particular location on the Somme which produced one indelible record of the 4th Salfords and their activities throughout the long hours of the 24th and 25th July. For more than two weeks, since early in the battles for the Somme area, Trones Wood and the nearby Bernafay Wood had been the scene of bitter fighting, constant churning shellfire and a determined defence by the German Army. Since the 21st July the 4th Salfords had been pushed up into the ill-defined chaos of trenches which marked the front at Bernafay Wood. Three days after their arrival there the Battalion was moved up, at 4.30 a.m., to the notorious sunken lane below Trones Wood. Twelve hours later three companies, including that under the command of Captain R. A. S. Coke, were ordered to advance into the wood. One was retained there in support whilst the two other companies reinforced the intermittent trenches running from the light railway line on the east of the wood towards its northern tip (S24c4/3 to S24a2/2), facing Guillemont and Waterlot Farm.

Richard Coke's account of this action emerged some years later in the form of an autobiographical novel, 'Youth Before the Flood'.[9] This dealt with a Manchester upbringing in 'Cottonopolis', public school life and a military service which mirrors Coke's own circumstances and service with the 4th Pals. Coke was an ex-Repton Public School pupil and had spent 1 year at Pembroke College

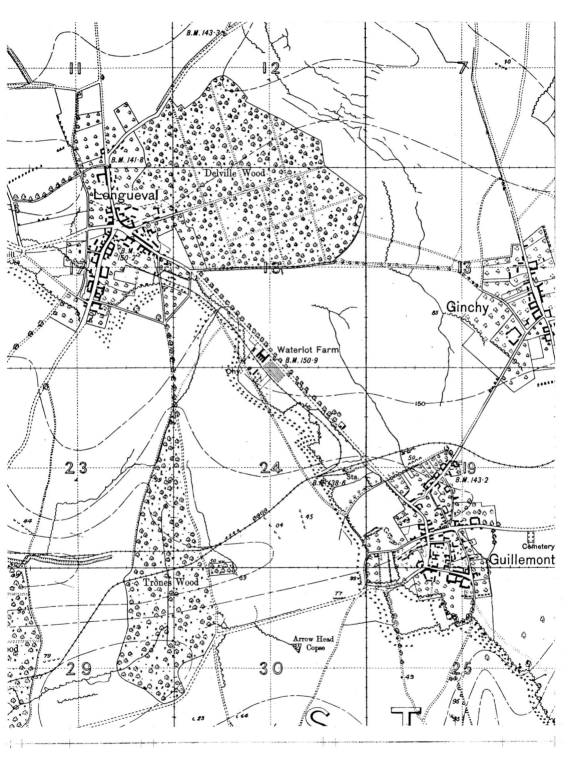

The Trones Wood area showing the trenches corrected to the 24 July 1916.

Cambridge. He had been commissioned into the 4th Pals as a 2nd Lieutenant and was a friend of 2nd Lieutenant Alexander Berry of Pendlebury (the son of Dr Berry) whom he buried in a roadside grave soon after these events at Trones Wood. The actions he describes here are a straight autobiographical account of his own Bantam Battalion's grim experience in Bernafay and Trones Woods. Whilst his writing did not portray a soldier's lot with the same power as Frederic Manning's 'Her Privates We', Coke's book deals with the events he experienced on the Somme at Trones Wood in a clear and evocative style.

As his men were guided into the remains of Trones Wood,

By the time the Salford Bantams arrived in Trones Wood, fighting in this area had already cost many hundreds of lives. Taylor Library

> *... there was no trench at all, but a low, uneven parapet of earth which had been thrown up by somebody as a kind of rough, desperate protection. It was noticeably darker in here, and the charred tree stumps, their foliage and branches burnt as with fire, looked like the ghosts of trees in some demented forest. Shells burst more frequently now, with a loud mocking echo that seemed to jump at one from tree to tree. A damp, unpleasant smell obtruded itself; sweet, nauseating, clinging as the dust along the road. The smell of burnt powder; the smell of tear gas; the smell of dead men lying, not in ones and twos but in scores and hundreds; human flesh and blood blown to bits, scattered, trodden underfoot; capable of leaving no memory but this, a last, sickly, pungent protest.*[10]

As soon as Captain Coke and his men left the dubious shelter provided by the woodland, C Company was subjected to a torrent of shells as they raced for the cover of the shallow trench which they were due to extend northwards. The trenches here consisted of three short sections, with shell holes between. Within minutes the barrage caused the collapse of the shallow trench and yet, although himself injured by a shell splinter in the back, Coke continued to lead his men, organising the connection of shell holes into a viable trench, tending the wounded and digging out men buried by the shellfire throughout the thirty torrid hours that they remained there. As the hours wore on German high explosive shells combed the area and the men killed by air bursts of shrapnel were simply incorporated into the parapet. As Coke observed,

> *...they picked up the recumbent body and placed it on top of the small bank already built. Quickly they commenced to cover it*

Stark wreckage marks the site of Waterlot Farm, opposite Trones Wood. By this stage of July the constant pounding of artillery had reduced the landscape to "a mass of churned up earth..... like a gigantic cheese".

with earth. In a little while it had disappeared and, the parapet was already taking shape. Every little helps, like.[11]

Looking out across the sea of desolation towards the Germans' lines in front of Guillemont little could be made out of the scene.

> In the dim moonlight he peered carefully across what he took to be No Man's Land for a glimpse of the German front line. But he could make out nothing. The entire landscape seemed to be, so far as he could see in the darkness, a mass of churned-up earth, formed into waves of monstrous, fantastic shapes, and full of little holes, like a gigantic cheese. It reminded Roddy of a pit-head, of pictures he had seen of country round volcanoes, or pieces of the moon seen through telescopes. In such an uneven maze of mounds and hollows it was impossible to distinguish the enemy trench line, or even to guess where it was. No very lights were to be seen, no rifle or machine-gun fire to be heard.[12]

For the leadership, bravery and endurance which he showed throughout these events Richard Coke was awarded the Military Cross. In the first four hours here at Trones Wood the 4th Salfords lost 10 officers and a further 120 casualties amongst the men. The 4th Pals were eventually relieved from Trones Wood at 1.30 a.m. on the morning of 26th July. Throughout the remainder of that month and August the Bantams were moved in and out of many locations along the southern arm of the Somme battlefield, Carnoy, Montauban, Maricourt and Guillemont but September saw them established in the lines at Arras. Already the unique character of this battalion was waning. It proved impossible to replace their losses with a supply of small stature men from the Reserve battalion and drafts were now just as likely to be men of average height.

Men of the 1st Pals in 'Old Boots Trench' at Cambrin (Map reference A27). The man wearing the tin helmet is Private Barnes, 'chatting' lice from his equipment. Wilcock

Minden Day, 1916. The 2nd Salford's No. 11 Platoon's survivors of the Somme Offensive. LFM

149

Bethune

For the men of the 1st and 2nd Pals, July had already marked their departure from the awfulness of the Somme. Their marching for fifteen miles a day took them north beyond Arras, into the trenches in front of Bethune, Cambrin, Cuinchy and opposite La Bassee.[13] Once the scenes of intense fighting during 1915, the area was now a cracked and broken industrial landscape of shattered coal miners' cottages, brickworks, spoil heaps and derelict pit heads. Through their trenches at Cuinchy ran the filthy La Bassee canal. In the trenches along the banks of that canal the months of August and September were passed, training and preparing the Derby Men who had been drafted into the battalions as they passed through Marles-les-Mines. On 8th August the 2nd Pals were strengthened by a 'Draft arrived of 100 men from 2/8th Lancs Fus, direct from England – Good men'.[14] As with all battalions who had passed through the sorrow and anguish of terrible loss on the Somme, the Pals took time to come to terms with these men. Although they were familiar as local men from the borough, the drafts were initially regarded as intruders, with none of the experience which bound the surviving veterans together. This was a haunting time for the new members of the battalion, who could only guess at what their comrades had seen, survived and of which they had resolved to speak so little.

Cambrin itself proved to be rather better than Authuille. It was, admittedly, a filthy and rat infested hole where the stagnant refuse of two years of war lay in abundance around the whole noisome scene. But it was also, by contrast with the intense preparation for battle on the Somme, a relatively quiet sector. When out of the lines the Divisional Reserve billets were located within what was left of Bethune. Brigade Reserve billets were at Annequin and Brigade support trenches at Maison Rouge, just outside Cambrin (at A26b). As the battalions marched out of front line duty they often passed the many coal miners, rising early to labour in the nearby collieries.

> Our training here started at 5.00 a.m. as the heat became unbearable in the middle of the day, so we performed the physical tasks whilst it was yet cool. Bathing in the muddy filth of the la Bassie [sic] canal was our chief recreation; nudity was de rigueur. Captain Morton was swimming one day when two Tommies came along. 'Hello Ginger, it warm in there?' 'Quite', said he, in his best Oxford accent. 'Blimey, it's a blinking officer', and they beat a hasty retreat.[15]

By the end of August the new men were sufficiently well prepared. The weather had deteriorated and German activity resulted in the blowing of a number of mines at the location of Railway Point's craters (A28c2/7), and numerous smaller ones further north in the area of Cuinchy brickstacks and the canal. On occasions when shelling was fierce, the men were sheltered in the tunnels being dug as counter-mines in this area. At night numerous wiring parties operated within twenty yards of their enemy's lines.

In the darkness of 30th August a party from C Company of the 2nd Pals went out to reconnoitre the German wire, in front of the trenches occupied by their sister battalion, in preparation for a raid being

La Bassee. Reed

Cuinchy. Both photographs show the devastation duplicated behind both the German and British lines. Reed

planned for the following night. The group consisted of Lieutenant C. W. Smith and 2nd Lieutenant Charles Marriot together with two NCOs, Sergeant Tommy Lawton (11476) and Corporal Bertram Barlow (15043). When only yards from the German wire the party were heard, flares were sent up and the first shot fired hit Tommy Lawton, badly wounding him. Smith, Marriot and Barlow began to carry the N.C.O. towards safety when Barlow himself was also hit. Marriot and Smith then pulled the two desperately wounded men down into a shell hole and tried to staunch the flows of blood. Whilst Smith crawled back for help, Charles Marriot cared for the two men and stood guard as the minutes ticked by, still only fifty yards from his opponents' trenches. Incredibly Tommy Lawton and Bertram Barlow were recovered by men of the 1st Pals. Tragically Tommy Lawton died before he could be brought into their trenches. On the fire step Bertram Barlow was treated by Lieutenant Lord.

> I was busy for an hour trying to staunch the bleeding from his abdomen and at last succeeded. Perhaps inadvisedly we tried to get him to the dressing station and as the trenches were too narrow we had to carry him on one man's back, whilst another held his legs. He was half-demented with pain, trying to kick furiously all the time. All our efforts were in vain, however, as he died just as we got him to the door of the dressing station.[16]

Corporal Bertram Barlow was eighteen years old. That night the 2nd Pals' Battalion War Diary recorded three casualties, the two caused by German fire and one further, a self inflicted wound. These figures were fortuitously light. At 6.16 a.m. on the morning of 31st another German mine was detonated under Railway Point.

A week later Lieutenant Smith led his raiding party up to the German wire (at A28a1/0), but was forced to return when he discovered that the artillery had failed to cut the wire entanglements. Three days later a further attempt was made under the direction of Captain Tweed, on the night of 10/11th of September. Although this was a night of full moon the whole scene was shrouded by a dense cloud. Zero was set at 2.30 a.m. This time the artillery was accurate, initially bombarding the German trenches for no more than fifteen seconds before forming a box barrage around the party of 71 raiders under command of Lieutenant Smith and 2nd Lieutenants Marriot and Bill Foss. Under its protection two Bangalore torpedoes were detonated to blast a passage through the wire. On their right a diversionary attack on the Railway Craters, led by 2nd Lieutenant Sydes with 18 men, covered that flank. The left flank was guarded by one of the battalion's Lewis Gun teams. In the trenches opposite the raiding party found the German lines almost deserted. Four prisoners were taken for identification purposes, one of

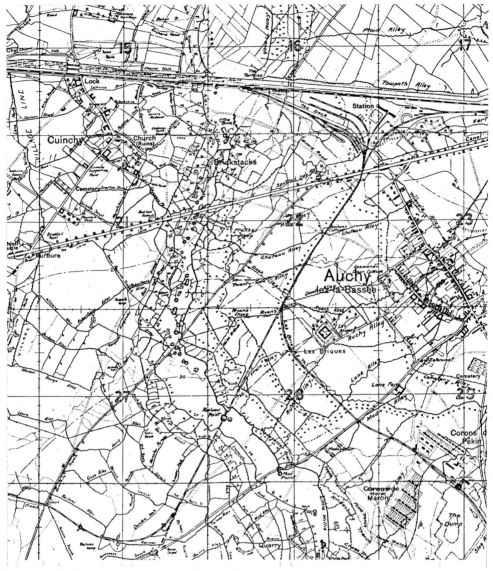

Lieutenant Charles Marriot's trench map showing the 'Cambrin and Cuinchy' (Brickstacks) Sectors, August 1916. LFM

whom died soon after from his wounds. During the whole action virtually no fire was brought to bear on the raiders and no S.O.S. flare was sent up. Casualties amongst the 1st and 2nd Salford Pals amounted to no more than 7 men with slight wounds from shell splinters resulting from the proximity of their own barrage.

It had been a textbook operation. Not one man had lost his life whilst the raid had been carried out in its entirety with complete success.

Smith and Foss were awarded the Military Cross for their persistence and gallantry during these events. One of three men to win the Military Medal during this action was Lance Sergeant Enoch Holland. His brother, Sergeant Joe Holland, would also win this decoration with the 2nd Pals within weeks of Enoch's accomplishment.

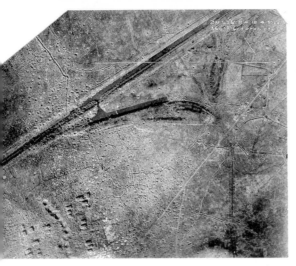

The Cuinchy brickstacks area from the air. Amidst the brickstacks can be seen the series of craters which scarred this area just south of the La Bassee canal and dock. LFM

For 2nd Lieutenant Charles Stowell Marriot there was no reward for the bravery and coolness he displayed in bringing in the two wounded N.C.O.s. His public recognition came on a different field. Between 1919 and 1921 he represented Lancashire, that year being picked to play for the 'Gentlemen' at Lords. He later played for Cambridge University and then qualified for the county of Kent. In 1933 he represented his country again, this time against the West Indies, taking 11 wickets for 95 runs! He retired from first class cricket in 1937.

During this late summer period the pressure of attrition was maintained by the persistent use of mortars and *minenwerfers*. Although men had been killed before when their dugouts had been blown in, the most horrific incident which occurred that summer followed an occasion when a dug-out entrance in D Company's section of the 1st Pals' line was completely blocked by the simultaneous explosions of two 'minnies'. The men dug desperately, for four hours, eventually pulling the grotesquely twisted shapes of two of their pals out. Both died soon after.

The following morning,

> *... we extricated the others who had died of suffocation. There was evidence that they had become insane and attacked each other with their entrenching tools; what a ghastly death.*[17]

Almost imperceptibly the unique character of the Battalions was being leached away. It was still quite possible to find men present from those who had originally enlisted in the heady days of autumn 1914. Those numbers were limited in the 1st Pals, rather greater in the 2nd and 3rd battalions. A year in training, they were now approaching the first commemoration of their arrival in France.

For the 3rd Pals this autumn and winter of 1916 and the spring of 1917 saw their work as the pioneer battalion of the 49th Division take them back to trench lines on the Somme around Martinsart and Thiepval, thence on to Arras and Laventie. They had converted to their new role at Capelle during the

Guerre de 1914-15 — *Église de Cambrin.*
A.-M. Béthune.

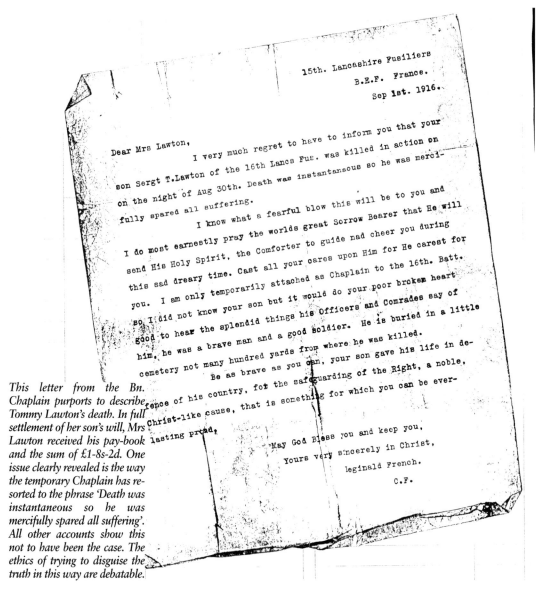

```
                                    15th. Lancashire Fusiliers
                                          B.E.F. France.
                                        Sep 1st. 1916.

Dear Mrs Lawton,
              I very much regret to have to inform you that your
son Sergt T.Lawton of the 16th Lancs Fus. was killed in action on
on the night of Aug 30th. Death was instantaneous so he was merci-
fully spared all suffering.
              I know what a fearful blow this will be to you and
I do most earnestly pray the worlds great Sorrow Bearer that He will
send His Holy Spirit, the Comforter to guide nad cheer you during
this sad dreary time. Cast all your cares upon Him for He carest for
you.   I am only temporarily attached as Chaplain to the 16th. Batt.
so I did not know your son but it would do your poor broken heart
good to hear the splendid things his Officers and Comrades say of
him, he was a brave man and a good soldier. He is buried in a little
cemetery not many hundred yards from where he was killed.
              Be as brave as you can, your son gave his life in de-
fence of his country, for the safeguarding of the Right, a noble,
Christ-like cause, that is something for which you can be ever-
lasting proud,
                             May God Bless you and keep you,
                                Yours very sincerely in Christ,
                                        leginald French.
                                              C.F.
```

This letter from the Bn. Chaplain purports to describe Tommy Lawton's death. In full settlement of her son's will, Mrs Lawton received his pay-book and the sum of £1-8s-2d. One issue clearly revealed is the way the temporary Chaplain has resorted to the phrase 'Death was instantaneous so he was mercifully spared all suffering'. All other accounts show this not to have been the case. The ethics of trying to disguise the truth in this way are debatable.

week prior to August 6th. That transformation ensured that life for them would now be little short of a hard labour sentence as they dug their way across much of north eastern France. These were tough men and their background in the mining communities of Salford provided the men with invaluable stamina.

The Somme Again

During October the 1st and 2nd Pals returned to the Somme area, where battle was still raging. On the 23rd of that month the men found themselves back at Bouzincourt and by 14th November were in support, below Thiepval, for an attack expected to be made by the 56th Brigade of the 19th Division. The persistent rain which was now falling eventually ensured its postponement and gave the opportunity which, once and for all, squared the debate about the missing which had continued so fervently in Salford since 1st July.

For three short days in the middle of that wet November, many men of the 15th and 16th Lancashire Fusiliers searched the ground below Thiepval for the corpses of their pals. Often the bodies found were unrecognisable after so long in the summer heat but, where possible, a soldier's identity tags, pay-book or even medal ribbons were used to identify friends.

Sergeant Tommy Lawton.

It rained so incessantly that the attack was postponed and finally cancelled. I decided to look at the Thepval [sic] battlefield where the 15th were decimated on 1st July, thinking as a vain hope I might look for Ivan Doncaster. A miracle took me to the place where he lay; I might have been a mile away in any direction as I had not been on the ground before. What a sad task it was identifying his skeleton by his hair, shirt, breeches and lastly by his identity disc, which I removed to send to his people. With a volunteer or two we fashioned a shell-hole into a form of a grave and reverently laid him to rest, covering his body with earth and saying a prayer for his parents who were even yet, possibly, hoping he was a prisoner. We found him about thirty yards from the German wire along with many of his comrades. They must have gone steadily forward to their deaths amid a murderous hail of machine gun bullets. I fashioned a cross from pieces of wood, inscribed his name and regiment and took a photograph of his grave in front of the Bosche wire... We found and buried the bodies of several more officers and men, but time prevented us from spending more than one afternoon, besides which it was indeed a melancholy task. A skeleton hanging on a wire with a tattered shirt fluttering in the breeze made a very grizzly background to the scene. There but for the grace of God was I! About a hundred yards to the rear was a clump of trees smashed to bits by shell-fire, whilst in the centre was a crucifix hardly touched at all. Symbolic perhaps. We had to collect salvage for a day or two and took a snap of a tank which had been knocked out, but had been repaired. Possibly this was the first photograph ever taken of a tank which had been in action.[18]

Lieutenant C. S. Marriot. In 1933 he represented his country again, this time against the West Indies, taking 11 wickets for 95 runs. He retired from first class cricket in 1937.

The chaplain to the 1st Pals wrote to Montague Barlow, telling him that more than seventy bodies were identified, and that arrangements were made to bury them together. Many years later Sergeant Bill Dutton would also claim that the bodies found were buried in a mass grave. No evidence exists today except a small number of the Pals whose graves are scattered in the area.

Another 'minnie' about to be launched. The huge projectile is clearly visible in the arms of this Minenwerfer *team member.*

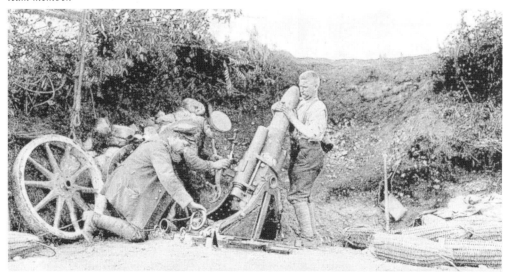

By 25th November the Salford Reporter was confirming the deaths of many men, previously hoped above all to be missing. Included in these reports were photographs of Lieutenants Robinson and Hampson, the latter being the only Broughton man to become an officer. He was the son of the Reporter's proprietor and was always described, even seventy years on, as the officer who enjoyed the closest and most fully trusting relationship with all the men.

In a letter dated 30th November one 'high officer' spoke to the Reporter about his having searched for the missing from the 1st Salford Pals on the battlefield below Thiepval:

> … upwards of 150 of our brave lads were found lying exactly where they fell in their terrible advance across 'No Man's Land'. Many were half buried by mud and debris and were quite unrecognisable, but the searchers were able to identify ten officers and 87 men.[19]

Lieutenant Colonel Stone, newly appointed to command the 1st Pals in October, was quoted as being,

> … anxious to express my deepest sympathy with the families of those whose fate is now known, and even more with those whose anxious uncertainty can now be relieved by so little hope.[20]

Further letters in the Salford Reporter from 2nd Lieutenant Norman Blackett confirmed the news.

> Bearing in mind your appeal for information regarding any of the 'missing' officers of the Battalion I carefully scrutinised the ground, with the result that I found one grave, marked with a wooden cross, bearing the following inscription –

> R.I.P.
> Lieutenant C. H. Wright.
> 15th Lancashire Fusiliers.
> Killed in action,
> 1st July, 1916.

> Lieutenant Wrights relatives and friends have not previously learned of this; it will be some consolation to them. It was nearing dusk when I came to this spot so I had to abandon my search, but tomorrow I will again take it as a duty to try and find traces of any officers and men of the Salford Battalions who took part in the first advance of the 'Big Push.'[21]

Blackett wrote further letters confirming his location of other graves, including those of Lieutenants Edgar Hampson and Harold Fletcher Robinson as well as Private Herbert Dorning (10644).

In Broughton and other parts of the town telegrams confirming that the missing were known to be dead were now arriving every day, in their dozens. Arrangements were put in hand by the Mayor, Councillor J. Higson, to hold a

This is the only known photograph of one of these battlefield burials at the site where the Salford Pals were decimated below Thiepval. It was taken by Edgar Lord in November 1916 and shows the cross which he constructed to mark the grave of Ivan Doncaster. Willcock

Lord's 'snap' shows men of 1st Pals surrounding the tank which had been disabled at Johnstone's Post and which had only recently been repaired. This photograph, from November 1916, was taken in the hollow below Thiepval where so many Pals had died four months earlier. These men are one of many small groups who were searching the area for both salvage and the bodies of their pals. Willcock

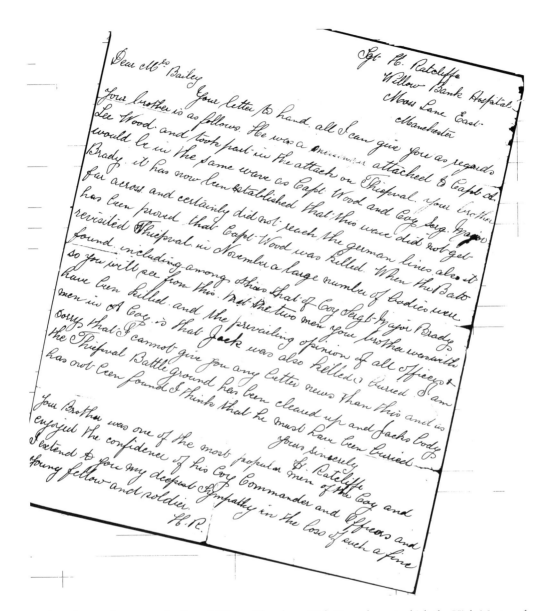

Sgt. H. Ratcliffe
Willow Bank Hospital
Moss Lane East.
Manchester

Dear Mrs Bailey

Your letter to hand. all I can give you as regards your brother is as follows. He was a member attached to Capt C. Lee Wood. and took part in the attack on Thiepval. your brother would be in the same wave as Capt Wood and Coy Serg. Major Brady. it has now been established that this were did not get far across and certainly did not reach the german lines. also it has been proved that Capt Wood was killed. When the Bat revisited Thiepval in November a large number of bodies were found. including among others that of Coy Serg Major Brady so you will see from this. that the two men your brother were with have been killed and the prevailing opinion of all officers & men in A Coy. is that Jack was also killed & buried I am sorry that I cannot give you any better news than this and is the Thiepval Battle Ground has been cleaned up and Jacks body has not been found I think that he must have been buried

Your Brother was one of the most popular men of the Coy and enjoyed the confidence of his Coy Commander and Officers and I extend to you my deepest Sympathy in the loss of such a fine young fellow and soldier.

H.R.

Yours sincerely
H. Ratcliffe

service of remembrance at the Sacred Trinity Church on 10th December, at which the High Master of Manchester Grammar School, J. L. Paton, would read the lessons.

Council business came to be swamped by the community's sense of loss. The General Purposes Committee meeting, held on Wednesday 22nd of November, was now forced to recognise the finality of the loss. Speaking of men who were known to have been killed, the Mayor quoted from the War Office telegram which informed of one such certainty,

> The Military Secretary presented his compliments to Mr. T. Fletcher Robinson and deeply regrets to inform him that a report has been received which states that the body of Lieutenant H. F. Robinson, 15th Battalion Lancashire Fusiliers, who was previously reported 'missing', has now been found and identified. The Military Secretary is desired by the Army Council to express their sympathy.
>
> As the Mayor of the Borough, I am sure you will be sorry at the sad news, although you will be the first to recognise that the men of Salford have well maintained the honour of the borough, because

Lieutenant Norman Blackett with soldiers of No. 3 Platoon, Lancashire Fusiliers. Certainly many of these men were engaged with Blackett in the search below Thiepval for the bodies of men from the 1st Pals. Eckersall

several hundred men followed their officers heroically and paid the same sacrifice, of their lives without flinching.[22]

Afterwards motions expressing the deepest sympathy, to all the families who had lost menfolk, were passed by the committee members who stood in silence. These citizen soldiers' deaths, combined with the further casualties which continued to mount in the coming two years, would produce an incalculable loss to the borough.

A chapter in the life of Salford was about to be closed. Meanwhile in France life had to go on. For seven days, after their return to Thiepval, until 25th November 1916, the wreckage of Beaumont Hamel and the billets at Mailly-Maillet were home to the Salford Pals. In the midst of this period two companies of the 2nd Pals were commandeered to provide carrying parties out of Colincamps for the 14th Infantry Brigade. The other two companies remained in support of the 97th Infantry Brigade. Without remission the rain teemed down. Many of the carrying parties were literally bogged down. Those in support who were excused the enormously draining fatigues shivered without shelter, saturated and miserable.

Card in circulation in the Pendleton area of Salford towards the end of 1916. Bailey

In
Loving Memory
of the
Fallen Lads
of
This District

Who answered their Country's call.

The homestead gleams in sunset rays,
The Parents sit alone,
Lost in the light of other days
And summers that have flown ;
Shades o'erclouds the new made field,
And dulls the seasons joy,
Scarce recks us of the bounteous field,
Without our absent boy.

Greater love hath no man than this ;
" He gave his life for his friends."

The Beaumont Hamel Raid

Ever since July the area around Beaumont Hamel had proved an impossible objective for the British Army.[23] On 1st July the 1st Battalion of the Lancashire Fusiliers had been devastated as they attacked out of the Sunken Lane in front of the heavily fortified village. Numerous further assaults towards those fortifications had proved inconclusive, until the Black Watch had taken Y Ravine's formidable shelters and trenches on 13th November. These and other events around the Ancre and Beaumont Hamel, during the third week of November identified the ending of the Battles of the Somme amidst the rain, the overwhelmingly muddy conditions and the sheer exhaustion which would dictate a halt to the sounds of battle.

It did not, however, identify the end of the misery to which the Salford Pals had been subjected, without respite, during all of their time on the Somme.

Before dawn on 18th November, amidst furious blizzard conditions, the 32nd Division opened an attack on the high ground behind Beaumont Hamel towards the Serre Road. The attack was initially successful and many prisoners were taken. However, in the featureless bog of water laden shell holes it proved impossible to locate the objectives and the units in the 97th and 14th Brigades were forced to fall back in the face of heavy counter attacks, losing their prisoners in the process along with many men discovered to be missing from the 16th H.L.I. and 11th Border Regiment.

In reserve to the attack that morning the 1st Salford Pals struggled up from Mailly-Maillet to Beaumont Hamel. Those two and a half miles took eight hours through the most tortuous of conditions. Throughout the move hail and rain lashed across the

Sergeant Enoch Holland M.M., 2nd Salford Pals, sporting his best waxed moustache.

The 1st Battalion of the Lancashire Fusiliers, roll call after their attack at Beaumont Hamel on 1 July 1916. LFM

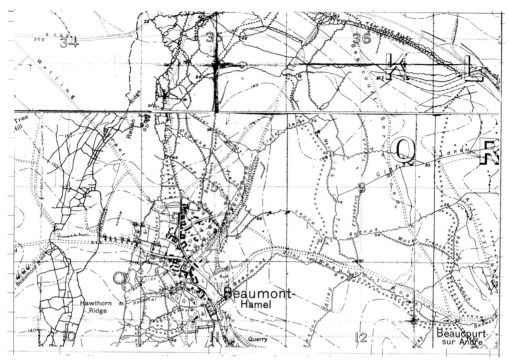

The Beaumont Hamel area showing the location of the Salford Pals' attack on 23 November, 1916, only a few hundred yards from where the 1st Lancashire Fusiliers had been devastated on 1st July during their frontal attack on Beaumont Hamel village, launched from Q4d4/5.

bare landscape almost horizontally. Even in daylight it was deemed easier to risk shellfire by going over the ravaged and torn ground rather than negotiate the sucking quagmires which existed within the communication trenches. Lieutenant Colonel Arthur Stone, recently promoted to command the Battalion, led the way by compass bearing across the naked wasteland which even here was devoid of any recognisable features or landmark. During this awful march up to Beaumont Hamel a Company Commander recorded that one man in his charge, along

> with one or two other craven souls started whining, threatened desertion, and it was only by the menace of a revolver that panic was averted.[24]

By the time the men arrived in the second line trenches behind the Waggon Road they were soaked to the skin. Once in these trenches the men found themselves thigh deep in viscous mud. Parts of the front lines proved to be even worse. That night the luck of some of the fortunate few who had been placed in reserve ran out. These hapless men were killed whilst trying to dry their mud caked clothing. The fire they had made from old mills bomb boxes had exploded. Their disheartened state overcame the caution

Ruins and chaos abounded in the Beaumont Hamel area, above the River Ancre, in the autumn of 1916.

required for safety and these men died for want of a simple check to see that the wooden boxes were empty.

It was, by all accounts, one of the most miserable nights ever spent by the Pals throughout their war.

The following morning, on their way up to the front line trenches at Waggon Road, the men who had spent the night in reserve discovered two English soldiers, sunk down to their armpits in mud. One was dead, the other, facing him, was demented and died soon after being pulled free.

Within hours they were joined in these horrendous circumstances by the 2nd Pals who had dragged themselves up from Colincamps, three miles distant. Their dismal journey had started at 3.00 p.m., on the 19th, when they were relieved by the 16th Northumberland Fusiliers. Through the squalid misery of Mailly-Maillet, Auchonvillers and Beaumont Hamel the men had struggled, leaden footed, to relieve the 2nd K.O.Y.L.I. of the 97th Brigade in the Waggon Road trenches (at Q5b6/5).

From this moment on, every night now saw a desperate struggle as rations were brought up, the journey often taking seven or eight hours after which the rank food was cold, filthy and often inedible. Frequently men had to be taken out of the lines suffering from total exhaustion. During this period two men deserted from the 1st Pals. For Private John Taylor this was not the first time he had seen fit to leave the scene of impending action.

On the very day which marked the first anniversary of their arrival in France the 2nd Pals were called into action at the close of these Somme battles. In their positions in the Waggon Road trenches above Beaumont Hamel the men were experiencing the most inhumane conditions which war had created, amidst terrible mud, water, sickness and death. Since the previous attack on the 18th November the party of men from the 11th Border and 16th Highland Light Infantry had been cut off in Frankfurt Trench (at Q6b1/6) near the Serre Road. Between Waggon Road and Frankfurt the Germans firmly controlled Munich Trench. During the 20th, 21st and 22nd November four men from the besieged party escaped across the German wire with reports that the other 120 men were in a desperate position, with little ammunition, water or food. Although it was believed that, individually, many of the men could have escaped, the Scots were reluctant to leave their wounded behind.

In the first four days since their arrival in the Waggon Road trenches the 16th Lancashire Fusiliers had already lost nearly fifty casualties to the persistent shelling which racked the area around Beaumont Hamel. Whilst this was endured a rescue plan involving three companies of the 2nd Salford Battalion and one company of 2nd Royal Inniskilling Fusiliers was organised, under the command of Captain Charles Merryweather.

The plan involved a dash across the open at dusk (3.30 p.m.) on 23rd November. Four companies, with 80 men in each group, would be involved. The 2nd Pals provided 240 men. It would have been hard to envisage a more arduous and shattered terrain upon which to carry the plan out. When the barrage opened the first wave under the command of Lieutenant D. Robertson and 2nd Lieutenant C. S. Jones swept into Munich trench, between Walker Alley and Crater Trench, with ease. Unfortunately however, their bunching through gaps in the wire had left spaces between these groups and the men of subsequent waves which allowed the German troops to escape from their dugouts and engage the men in close fighting. The combat was severe and it proved impossible to send prisoners back. Twenty German soldiers and their officer, pulled from a dug-out, were bayoneted.

Whilst this was going on Lieutenant George Higginson and his party of men from the second wave pushed on towards Frankfurt Trench in the hope of effecting a rescue of the men believed trapped there. Some of them were cut

The blurred outlines of men of the 1st Pals pass by the wreckage and devastated wire which was once the German fortifications of Beaumont Hamel. Willcock

After the squalid fighting which characterised the Ancre battles in the early winter of 1916 – British troops were often asked to pose, reconstructing "successes" for publications at home. Taylor Library

down as they ran into their own artillery barrage. As what was left of this group sheltered on the ground, awaiting the next lift of the barrage to a line beyond their objective, Higginson and all of his N.C.O.s were shot.

It was already clear that the lack of support on the rescue party's flanks was making their position untenable.

Although 2nd Lieutenant Harold Rylands was then sent forward to take charge the rescue proved incapable of being effected. It was a hopeless cause. Rylands was himself shot immediately. When the barrage lifted only a handful of Higginson's original group were left alive. No sign was seen of the men who it had been planned to liberate and the intensity of fire on the small band of men made forward progress impossible. Captain Charles Merryweather was shot as he stood on the parapet of Munich Trench directing the withdrawal which was now clearly necessary. So desperate was the scene that the chaplain, Rev. Fawkes, worked feverishly, recovering wounded men including three who were lying entangled in the wire at Munich Trench. Three quarters of an hour after the attempt had begun it was over. Under heavy enfilade machine gun fire the survivors made their way back as best they could.

Three of the missing eventually crawled in to safety under cover of darkness. Within three days it was clear that sixty had been killed, three further men dying of their wounds. It was generally believed that the Borders and H.L.I. were, at best, by now taken prisoner. The futility of these events was summarised in Lieutenant Colonel Abercrombie's summary, forwarded to 96th Infantry Brigade headquarters.

> *I have examined all the men who came back and can only find one who got any considerable distance past MUNICH Trench. This is an intelligent man, one of the Battalion snipers, and he was in the left of the wave during the advance. He got up to the Barrage, 150 yards beyond MUNICH but states that he could see nobody else with him and retired when the barrage lifted*

Advanced dressing station at Beaucourt Hamel 24 November 1916.

as there was no one to go forward with him. He states that there was some machine gun fire, mostly from his left, whilst he was advancing and that this became very heavy when he turned to go back and on his way back. He saw no signs of anyone in FRANKFORT [sic] TRENCH, the line of which he could see quite clearly.[25]

It had been what some people called a 'mess up'.

Throughout the long moments which characterise such wretched encounters Sergeant Joe Holland had worked desperately to hold off the German bombers who tried to break through the Salford Pals' blocks in Munich Trench. Along with Lance Corporal G.R. Hughes he was subsequently awarded the Military Medal and joined his brother Enoch, as a proud holder of the honour. Many other original Pals showed their continuing spirit during this action. Of the 15 men commended for their bravery during this action, by Lieutenant Colonel Abercrombie, 12 were original Pals. Of those 12 men, five more would die before the war's end.

For the rest of the men the event had been a shambles. Many, like Rylands, who had survived injury and the experiences of July 1st had now succumbed during an action which had promised much but again achieved nought. Like Lieutenant Rylands, Captain Merryweather was an original officer, and well respected for his bravery and attention to duty.

For others, like Sergeant Healey, it meant the end of a terrible misery on the Somme, and also time with their pals. His leg shattered, James Healey was already en-route to hospital, preparing for amputation. With him was William Tickle, hospitalised for a second time, on this occasion with shrapnel in the back and a bullet through his right wrist. He was the son of Bob Tickle in the 3rd Pals, a former Swinton footballer colleague of Dai Davies who himself had survived the raid unscathed.

Since arriving in Beaumont Hamel, four days of severe action saw the 2nd Pals sacrifice 212 casualties, a third of the Battalion's rifle strength. Writing from hospital in France William Tickle summed it all up,

Christmas decorations in Hope hospital, believed to be 1916. SLHL

It was terrible, and I shall never forget it as long as I live. I am very sorry to say that I lost both of my chums from Eccles, one killed and the other badly wounded.[26]

The postscript to the story concerned the party of Highland Light Infantry and Border soldiers who were marooned. These heroic men maintained themselves at the objectives they captured for eight days after the attack, using water collected from shellholes and one iron ration per man. The party was finally overwhelmed on 25th November when they were down to 15 effectives and practically without ammunition. Although these survivors were taken prisoner having lost many of their comrades to gangrene and septicaemia, members of this distinguished group were later awarded 2 Mentions in Dispatches, 1 D.S.O., 2 M.C.S, N D.C.M.s and 22 M.M.s.[27]

The following day the 1st and 2nd Salford Pals were taken back to Mailly-Maillet and thence back to rest billets in Montrelet and Bonneville. Here they spent the period of Christmas and New Year, as part of six uninterrupted weeks away from the rigours of campaigning on the Somme. The 'rest' however was only from the drudgery of trench life. The men were worked hard and most wished for a 'cushy' sector in the line where working parties for road repair and construction did not exist. The extraordinary thing which galled many was the sight

Portrait of 2nd Lieutenant Harold 'Bi *Rylands, 2nd Salford Pals, K in A 2 November 1916.*

of their German prisoners, carrying out the same tasks, arriving by lorry whilst the Salford lads marched in full kit with packs.

Men engaged in battlefield clearance on the Somme. The salvaged Lee Enfield rifles would be repaired or refurbished and re-issued. During attacks it had often been the habit of soldiers to discard all sorts of equipment, packs, tools and clothing. Throughout late 1918 many of the Salford Pals were used in the horrendous process of battlefield clearance, salvage and burial.

Whilst the 1st Pals worked on their fatigues at Montrelet, an exception was initially made of one company. For ten days these men were treated to the horror of battlefield clearances, salvaging equipment and burying the dead at Beaumont Hamel. In what was described as a 'nightmare' the Salford soldiers found and buried over 400 corpses, often mere skeletons from the July fighting, sometimes the blue, bloated and stinking remains of men killed during the last few days. After the appalling conditions which prevailed along the Waggon Road it seemed inexcusable to the men that they should be expected to carry out these tasks. To these Salford soldiers the burials seemed obscene in view of their intimate knowledge of the locations and many of the soldiers whose bodies they were now expected to identify and inter.

After a week of this half the men were violently sick and ill with the filth and disease which such circumstances propagated. The officers in charge felt compelled to complain, to Divisional HQ, about the lack of replacement footwear which in view of the nature of the work stank unbearably and the lack of proper medical attention for the sickened men.

These were the consequences of war at their most loathsome.

At 10.30 a.m. on 10th December the Remembrance Service at Sacred Trinity church had started. Present were virtually every person who had had any part to play in the original raising and preparation of Salford's Brigade. The most important people there were the many hundreds of grieving parents, wives and children. The most prominent among the congregation were the Mayors and Mayoresses of each community, Montague Barlow M.P., Councillors, the Justices, members of the Old Mancunians Association, the Guardians and Corporation officials, representatives of the many firms and local institutions from which so many had enlisted en masse, parties from local schools and clubs which had also provided young men together with detachments from the local Territorial Units.

During his sermon the Reverend A. E. Cornibeer exhorted his congregation,

> *When we think of them, of what they were. and all they have been prompted to do let us love their memory and imitate their devotion. That, beloved, is the spirit in which our lads met their death. Well then do we set ourselves to love their memory, to imitate their devotion.*[28]

Much was made of the discovery of significant numbers of bodies on the battlefield below Thiepval and the arrangements which were believed to have been made to identify and mark the graves of each and every Salford man. It was a comfort for many who were present to believe that, at some point in the future, it would be possible to visit that grave. The reality would prove far less satisfactory. Before the congregation left, during what must have been a heart rending experience for those present, the Last Post was played.

No Man's Land. The view from Matthew Copse during the January of 1917. Temperatures had fallen to give 15 degrees of frost at this time. Wilcock

The notices which flooded the local newspaper's Roll of Honour that week confirmed that many people would bear the scars of loss. Private E. Thompson, a widow and three children; Private W. Ashton, a widow and three children; Private J. Ward, a widow and five children; Private R. Fensome, 'a popular member of the Boy Scouts'; Private Campbell, a widow and nine children; the lists seemed endlessly poignant and signposted a litany of severe consequences for hundreds of families and communities in the forthcoming years.

Elsewhere, behind the front-line trenches of the Somme, the 1st and 2nd Pals were destined to leave that period of 'rest' for what had already become the most severe of winters on the Western Front. This was a time when the weather tested the resolve of every man and officer. The conditions were unimaginably foul across the length of battlefield upon which so many hopes had faded. Throughout much of the January of 1917 the Pals occupied trenches in front of Serre, a village where thousands of other volunteer Pals from Accrington, Barnsley, Sheffield and elsewhere had died.

A cold snap had set in with three inches of snow, and the trenches were waist deep in water in places. It was so cold at nights that we woke up with our heels frozen to the ground and water carried up in petrol cans was solid at the end of the journey... The firing line was so bad that we could not hold it as a continuous line, but only by a series of posts, and they could only be visited at nights as the communication trenches were washed away with mud.[29]

Edgar Lord in full trench kit at Serre, January 1917. Willcock

The last days of this awful January marked the end of one, perhaps very frightened and inadequate, young man's life. This is one of the saddest episodes in the history of the Salford Pals and reveals the cynicism and heartlessness of war. For six weeks, after he had deserted the previous November, John Taylor had slept out in the confines of the dilapidated and broken buildings which abounded in Albert. On the run, terrified of being caught, horrified by the putrid scenes he had witnessed at Beaumont Hamel, desperate for food and warmth, he presented a sorry sight when he was arrested in early January.

The charge laid against John Taylor was 'Desertion', a capital offence in 1917's British Army. In view of Private Taylor's undistinguished military record the outcome was almost a foregone conclusion. He was already under a suspended sentence for 'quitting his post'. Officers had complained of petty thieving. His behaviour on the march up to Beaumont Hamel, when having to be threatened with a revolver, weighed heavily against him.

In his defence the fact that he was a volunteer who had withstood considerable action in the regions of the Somme and La Bassée stood for naught. Little could be said to prevent the certainty of conviction and the Commander in Chief's confirmation sealed his fate.

The Battalion's Intelligence Officer, Greenhill, was ordered to see the sentence carried out. The firing party of six men was assembled from Taylor's own platoon, on the morning of 27th January in the village of Bertrancourt. It was 7.30 a.m. The temperature was below freezing. He was sat on an old chair with a gas helmet placed back to front over his head. Pinned over his heart was a scrap of white paper. The men had rehearsed to fire on a silent signal. They marched forward to their rifles, one of which was loaded with a blank. One man, more nervous than the rest, fired early. The others quickly followed.

In the company of his pals John Taylor faced death unflinchingly.

Such was the requirement of this volunteer Army. He is buried at Bertrancourt Military Cemetery not far from Mailly-Maillet.

The picture of bleak desolation did not improve when the Pals were taken back to Beaumont Hamel again, in February. Temperatures persisted at well below zero and in a repeat of their previous circumstances at Serre it proved impossible to dig trenches in the rock solid ground. Outposts with picturesque names like 'Plum Post', 'Birdcage', 'Apple' and even 'Last Post' were established, 400 yards in front of the secure defence lines. Any thought of moving forward to these posts during daylight hours proved impossible since communication saps to the outposts were either non-existent or simply filled with ice-encrusted mud. During the days tiny parties of men beyond the security of their own wire shivered in the advanced posts, hoping to hear nothing and waiting the interminable hours before being relieved. On occasions the men in these posts became so disorientated in the darkness that they fired on relief parties, and men returning to the main lines also risked being bombed or shot at.

Later that month the Pals battalions were moved south to take over lines from the French, near Roye on the Amiens-Noyon road. This was a very quiet sector, but there was a great deal of complaint that the sanitary conditions were dreadful and that the fleas in the billets were much more avaricious than those which had ever occupied the British billets further north. Whatever the truth, the men were initially told to wear Blue coats and French helmets in order to deceive their opponents. The barbed wire was so thick as to be quite impenetrable. During the day wiring parties went about their work unhindered and men were able to sit unmolested on the parapet, smoking! It was even rumoured that patrols could pass each other in 'No Man's Land' during the pitch black of night, calling cheery greetings such as 'Pass, friend, all's well!', uttered in any passable German. After the violence of more than a year in much hotter spots this seemed a very 'cushy' place in which to fight a war.

Such an existence was not allowed to continue for long though. Within days of their arrival the Germans opposite were provoked into trench raids by the increased ferocity of shelling and the persistent raids and patrolling which announced the arrival of Salford men in the villages of Le Quesnel and Rouvroy-en-Santerre.

A Mobile Interlude

Incredibly, on 14th March, it became clear that a German retirement was underway.

In the midst of the preceding wintry months the German Army had first planned and was now executing a retirement to a new series of fortifications known as the Hindenburg Line. The purpose was to effect a shortening of their lines and to remove the exposed salient which had been created by the tortuous advances made by the British during the Somme battles of 1916. Before that withdrawal was started any facilities, railway-tracks,

Thomas and Townend of the 1st Pals at their Company HQ near to Serre, during February of 1917. Willcock

orchards, wells and crossroads were destroyed or booby trapped. Bridges were dynamited. Century old poplars, lining the roads since Napoleonic days, were cut down to block traffic. Houses capable of providing shelter were blown up and all military stores withdrawn. Only a few of the larger towns, such as Noyon and Ham, were left relatively intact.

To all intents and purposes the British Army had failed to anticipate the move. At 3.00 a.m. that morning the Pals were given hurried orders to make wills, pack and issue kit ready for a forward advance. Initial patrols found the complexity and seeming permanence of the Germans' defences quite incredible and marvelled that they should have been vacated. Concrete tennis courts were found less than three miles behind the front lines. There were tiled walls, wooden floors, furniture, showers, pianos and pictures. The scenes were like a dream but their opponents had been thorough enough to deny any possibility of the facilities' use to the Pals. Everything had been smashed. Men from the Pals' patrols initially felt irritated at having to return to their own trenches when such a superior billet had so obviously been vacated by their opponents.

Thus, by 17th March the 1st and 2nd Pals began an advance in the direction of St. Quentin from their trenches around Rouvroy-en-Santerre and Fresnoy-en-Chaussee just north west of Roye. At first the scent of wood-smoke from the burning houses made an almost pleasant contrast with the smell of cordite with which everyone was more familiar. The advance was carried out, initially very cautiously, across a wasteland which was soon realised to provide almost no shelter during this the most bitter weather of the war. Just for a few days the conflict seemed to have become mobile and the troops, although filthy, wet and short of rations, soon became elated about what they considered as the possibility of an outcome in sight. Water was in very short supply, one bottle per day per man, plus a petrol can's worth distributed among each company if the supply mules managed the journey each day. Every soldier in these battalions was as louse ridden as they had ever been after their experiences in the

French lines and billets and the total absence of sufficient washing water.

In view of the catalogue of barriers and traps which had been left by the German Army progress had to be circumspect and relatively slow. Nevertheless, forward movements took the men past Rethonvillers and Nesle and on towards the River Somme and its canal. Each night the Pals dug in. Throughout the day they were marched, often tortured by the lack of water. For two complete weeks the men went without sleep or proper rest, the Germans becoming a minor irritation when compared to the men's more immediate obsessions of drink, food, rest and baths. Part of that problem was resolved at Languevoisin, just south of Nesle, when unpoisoned water was found for the first time. Unfortunately this effect was quickly spoilt when it began to rain, heavily. From now on the advance was carried on in sodden boots, just to add to the men's discomfort.

Tank at Serre during February's cold weather. A Salford Pals' officer poses in front of this landmark amidst the snow and frost which took its toll on so many men during the late winter of 1916–1917.
Willcock

Having crossed the Somme, the Pals initially retired back to Canizy where the men received drafts, were deloused and bathed, were refitted with clean clothing and equipment and treated to a period of rest for a few days. They then marched on through Ham, Matigny and Germaine to within sight of Savy Wood, five miles west of St. Quentin.

Here their advance was to stop on the last day of March. They were just short of the huge military engineering which constituted the newly constructed Hindenburg line. Those trenches and bunkers were a formidable collection of strong-points which had benefited from a considered and clinical series of decisions, taking account of every workable fold in the land to ensure as secure a series of defences as was possible to construct. Neither had these been thrown together in a hurry. Whilst the British Army shivered throughout the winter the vast fortifications and impenetrable walls of barbed wire entanglements had taken shape. The German withdrawal was a strategic triumph.

Their shortened line would require thirteen fewer Divisions to maintain it. Better sited and more strongly fortified, it would quickly expose the British Army's obsession with offence as a costly charade. German reserves were now freely available for rest and to counter any threat of breakthrough by British and French forces.

The actions on April Fool's day at Savy Wood

On 31st March the German rearguard made a stand between Savy and Holnon. The period of mobile and open warfare was coming to an end.

By 5.00 a.m. the following morning, the 97th Brigade had attacked and captured Savy village. The 96th Brigade was then ordered to make an attack on the Bois de Savy together with the smaller wood to its south east. The purpose was to harry and prevent the German rearguards from entering St. Quentin unopposed. The Pals'

Edgar Lord and Privates Joe Smith and the 5' 3" tall Hopwood of the 1st Pals have plenty of time to have their photograph taken, three miles in front of the British and French lines, during a patrol which has revealed the extent of the German retreat.
Willcock

assembly points were in the shallow valley at Pommery, three miles to the west of Savy. Whilst waiting in the village one German shell fell among a platoon of 'Skins' causing heavy casualties. Here the men of the Brigade had been assembled at 7.30 a.m. From this position, next to the village's chateau, the 1st and 2nd Pals would advance at 1.00 p.m. in full view of the Germans who were installed on the higher ground south of Holnon. Their objectives were to take the wood and to establish strong-points on the far side in the vicinity of the St. Quentin-Peronne railway.[31]

As the men got under way the gale which was blowing lashed them with rain, sleet and snow. The advance was made in open diamond formation, in companies.

Within minutes, as they crested the rise beyond Pommery chateau, the whole Brigade came under shrapnel fire and the companies split up further into platoons in open diamond or artillery formation. This fire continued to cause some casualties as they marched across open countryside down towards Savy village. In the village numerous German bodies provided a witness to the deadly seriousness with which that rearguard took their duties. As the Pals formed up into their waves they were already being subjected to spasmodic 77mm high explosive and 10.5 howitzer fire, directed from the hill behind Savy Wood.[32] On the right of the attack, as they advanced east from Savy, the 2nd Inniskillings were to the south of the Savy-St. Quentin railway line. On

Men of the 1st Salfords look on as a farmhouse, fired by the retreating German Army, burns. Willcock

the other side of the railway, on the left of the attack, the 1st Salford Pals were supported by their sister battalion.

As the waves moved forward, behind their artillery's creeping barrage, the number of casualties struck down by machine gun rounds rose as a consequence of the fire being brought to bear on their left flank from the direction of Holnon Wood. As they approached Savy Wood another gun opened fire from the

Destruction in the town of Peronne, large parts of which were laid to waste by the retreating German Army. MS

railway halt just beyond the gap between the two woods.

Bullets came in real earnest tearing up the grass and I remember laughing as one hit between my feet. As we advanced I saw my right flank was bunching a little so I sent a runner advising them to spread out and keep to correct direction. Just as I was pointing to something on my left I felt a crash in the left arm and noticed my tunic sleeve with darkening patches of oozing blood in two places six inches apart. I murmured 'I'm hit' but as the pain was not overwhelming, I kept walking with the rest, tearing out my field dressing with the intention of bandaging it, but it was too much trouble, so I kept going. One man,

The bridge at Ham, blown up by the Germans during their withdrawal. Reed

Two photographs show British troops in the village of Nesle, en-route for St. Quentin, March 1917. Reed

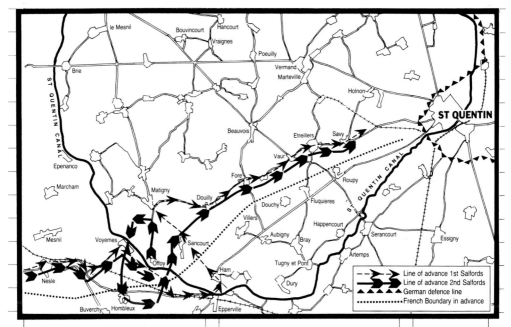

Soldiers move forward during March 1917, as the German army pulled back towards their new lines in front of St. Quentin, the Siegfried Stellung.

seeing I was hit, started to waver and lag behind. I took out my revolver and promised him a dose if he did not keep up. I had reached about 300 to 400 yards from Savy Wood, when I felt a crash in both legs, spun round, and fell flat in the grass. It had been raining and hailing between bursts of sunshine and I felt the grass to be quite wet. My batman was on hand, and whipping out our field dressings, we cut off my right boot and sock, staunched the wound and bound off my right ankle very tightly, as the artery and nerve had been severed. He then slit my left sleeve and we found the bullet had entered and made its exit on the top of the arm appearing at first as if it were

171

Fallen British soldiers. Because of the constant attacks over unfamiliar ground, exposed to the ever present and determined rear-guard machine gunners, heavy casualties were inevitable during the last few days of the German withdrawal. Taylor Library

two wounds. When my batman first came to me he said 'Where are you hit, sir?'. I said 'In the right ankle'. He said 'Thank God, I thought you were hit in the guts'. When the arm and leg were bandaged, I said 'I think I'm hit in the left leg as well'. 'I don't think you are sir.' 'Take off my puttee and look at it.' We found I had a flesh wound in the calf. I got my mackintosh from my equipment and Hopwood placed it under me, and I lay watching the battle, waiting for stretcher bearers. Here and there were groups of men lying down, killed or wounded, and other[s] hobbling about; the remainder had reached our objective at the edge of the wood. Just then the Germans started putting a few shells near us, so Hopwood said 'What about clearing out of this, sir?', but as it would have been almost impossible for me to crawl, I shook my head. As it continued he said 'I shall have to carry you'. I laughed at him as he was only 5'3" and I weighed eleven stones. He hoisted me without further ado and using the fireman's lift, carried me about two hundred yards to the rear, when finding a stretcher, I was lowered painfully on to it. Near us lay a man on a stretcher and being wounded in the stomach cried out piteously, 'Help me, somebody; kill me; put me out of this agony'. I sent over my water bottle and Hopwood made him as comfortable as possible. He then fell unconscious. One of my company, slightly wounded, in the head gave Hopwood a further lift with the stretcher. At one of the halts we came across two dead Bosche, so we 'borrowed' a couple of blankets from them, along with a few souvenirs in a sandbag. Eventually I reached a First Field Ambulance, behind a wall in Savy, this being the only cover and here I was put on a wheeled stretcher.[33]

Meanwhile as the Pals made their way into the southern end of the wood at 3.30 p.m. it was found to be empty. Inside its confines the enemy had left a network of severed trees, obstacles and tangled undergrowth which ensured that any progress made was painstakingly slow. As the men worked along the north west edge of Savy Wood a party of Germans opened fire from the direction of Round Hill, just south of Holnon. They were driven off by Lewis Gun fire. However the machine guns located at The Halt were causing quite a number of casualties amongst the Pals around the southern confines of Savy Wood.

By 4.00 p.m. that afternoon the 1st and 2nd Pals had fought their way round and through Savy Wood. During the next three hours the men began the process of consolidating their advance by establishing a succession of posts in entrenchments to the north and east of the wood. During this process the two machine guns, located at the halt east of Savy Wood, continued causing casualties among men of the 1st Pals whose objectives included that railway junction. For ninety minutes before 8.30 p.m. the halt was heavily shelled before the 1st Pals moved in to capture the guns and their teams. The Salford men of the

1st Pals were, by then, established across the railway line which ran from St. Quentin towards Peronne. These men then began to entrench a series of strong points along a line running from the northern edge of the Bois de Savy towards the higher ground just south of Francilly-Selency (S15c5/9), their strong points then running down past Brown Quarry to join with the Inniskillings' lines at the halt. The 2nd Pals meantime were busy entrenching from the north tip of the wood on a line which ran back westwards towards the railway line where they joined up with the 97th Brigade.[34]

This was by no means a short and sharp engagement, but it was the first occasion during which the Pals experienced open and mobile warfare. The cost to them, in terms of casualties, was severe, almost 230 throughout the two battalions. Of these a total of more than 40 were killed or died from their wounds soon after. However, by contrast with the enormous cost of any advances made through the claustrophobic confines of the Somme's trenches during the summer of 1916, the spring of 1917 had started well for the Pals.

During the next few days the 1st Pals spent their time in the line established in and around Savy Wood. Within the week though the 2nd Pals had been moved into reserve within the village. Evidence exists that their behaviour was less than perfect,

Edgar Lord in hospital at No. 8 General Hospital, Rouen, April 1917.

as men, often recent drafts unaccustomed to the discipline of military service, began a search for loot and the hoarded valuables which had escaped the attention of the German Army during their occupation begun three years earlier. The account of one experienced Regular, detailing his time spent after being

Officers and Sergeants of the 19th Lancashire Fusiliers 1917. Reed.

transferred to the 2nd Pals, describes the events which followed this attack as an opportunity for the men to engage in a series of treasure hunts on the cellars and houses which formed the village of Savy.

> *The boys hacked down walls and dug up floors and passages, working with pick and shovel on anything that seemed to show any kind of unusual mark or sign. Bundles of notes, cash, jewellery, ornaments, musical instruments, cutlery, bundles of bedding and clothes and every conceivable thing of value were found.[35]*

The Pals were now engaged on a period of heavy digging. For the first time in more than two years the Army was engaged in the construction of a totally new system of trenches. The digging went on throughout the day and night, four hours on, eight hours off. The scheme of zone defence was to be the scene of important and almost catastrophic consequences in March 1918 when the German spring offensives utterly over-ran the British lines here outside St. Quentin.

The 16th Northumberlands built the front line trench across Manchester Hill. In front of it a series of wired outposts were constructed. The support lines behind were built by the Salford Pals. The Brigade instructions about the holding of the lines are notable in their willingness to tolerate the giving up of ground in the face of attack and the use of support troops to reinforce or counter-attack in the event of any breach in the front lines.

> *After construction the front line will be held lightly. Its defence will depend mainly on the fire of carefully sighted Machine and Lewis guns, which must bring a cross fire over the whole front. An outpost line will be established in front of the main line of defence. This outpost line will consist of a series of small entrenched posts which will be wired and will be held against attacks by patrols but which will fall back on the front line in the event of a serious attack. Each post will have a supply of bombs. The front line will be the main line of defence, and supporting troops will hold themselves in readiness to reinforce or carry out a counter attack should the enemy penetrate into it.[36]*

Lieutenant Bill Foss, (front left) with his M.C. ribbon, R. Morris and other officers, all wearing distinctive battalion and company recognition patches. Caix May, 1915. LFM

On 11th April the 16th Lancashire Fusiliers left the intrigue and relative comfort of their billets in Savy to take the honour of holding the very right of the British Army's line. At 7.30 p.m. that evening the Pals moved into the outposts near the railway outside St. Quentin (S22d9/4 to S21d9/9). This was the start of a period of relative quiet in the 1st and 2nd Salford Battalions' history as they fulfilled the duties familiar to every infantry line unit in the newly established trenches at Holnon, Fayet and in front of St. Quentin. Good fortune surrounded them for much of this summer of 1917 and the 32nd Division was omitted from the list of units who would be thrown into the start of the Passchendaele offensive.

The Belgian Coast
In early June the 1st and 2nd Salfords were entrained for the Ypres area. However their orders were to bypass the horrors of the salient and, with the onset of high summer, the men found themselves at the extreme northern end of the Western Front, on the Belgian coastline at Nieuport. On 18th June the 15th Lancashire Fusiliers had the

distinction of becoming the holders of the extreme left of the British lines, taking over trenches from the French 165th Infantry Regiment. The area provided the best opportunity for personal cleanliness that anyone could remember. At rest, behind the lines, a brief stroll took the men to the seaside, fishing, bathing and taking the sun. But it was here, behind their trenches close to Nieuport Bains, that the 2nd Salfords' mascot, Bruce, met his end. The man responsible was a shoeing smith with the Battalion's transport.

He was an Irishman, he couldn't read or write. He was a real product from the bog Irish. He used to get me to answer his letters, anything he wanted to write I would write it for him. I'd send it to Mrs D'Arcy. His first letter given me was to tell her, glad to hear she *The 16th LF's mascot, Bruce, who remained with the battalion until the summer of 1917 when his amorous attention towards Private D'Arcy's Belgian 'girlfriend' led D'Arcy t slay the unfortunate animal with his bayonet.* Knott

wasn't in the family way! This old D'Arcy saw the bloodhound off. This girl and he thought it was doing something. She was screaming in panic about the dog. Anyway, it was doing something it shouldn't and Tom D'Arcy saw it off. Put his bayonet on his rifle ... and he buried it quick. Private Frank Holding.

However, the picture in the front line trenches was infinitely more unpleasant. Here the River Yser and a number of associated canals ran through the trench systems. Communication trenches often petered out into hurriedly erected temporary bridges which were themselves the subject of regular and heavy shelling by the German artillery. The landscape had been deliberately flooded by the Belgian Army as a last ditch and successful attempt to stem the German advance in 1914. The high water table meant that deep trenches were impossible to maintain and most of the lines consisted of breastworks, where an embankment was thrown up, without the protection of a parados in the rear. Dugouts were equally impossible.

The whole area was the scene of a sequence of heavy German bombardments, anxiously designed to forestall any build up of agressive intention in this area. July 10th saw extensive German shelling on the 32nd Division's front. The situation began to get heated at 2.00 a.m. that morning, when a raid by the 1st Division, to the left of the 32nd, provoked the initial retaliation. By 4.30 the front lines, supports and access bridges were under heavy calibre H.E. fire. By 10.00 a.m. the 2nd Salford's Diary records that the 'enemy's fire increased to great violence' and Nieuport's houses were ablaze. During the afternoon the bombardment's extent widened, and the 32nd Division came under concentrated fire. Throughout the rest of the day the shelling continued, rolling backwards and forwards from both sides, until an attack was made on both the 1st Division and the 97th Brigade's fronts. Within the 32nd Division 1,000 casualties were suffered, mainly in the 97th Brigade which bore the brunt of these attacks, but the 2nd Salford's toll was still 10 killed and 58 wounded.

Throughout this period much of the Pals' patrolling was done with the intention of exposing the dispositions of German reserve lines in the area. This was considered a

The 'Doc', McGill. LFM

priority since, across the defences opposite, it was planned that a major advance along the coast would be carried out in conjunction with the expected breakout across the Passchendaele Ridge due to take place at the latter end of July. The necessary reconnaissance was often carried out by men who were chosen as much for their expertise as swimmers as by any other criteria.

In pursuit of the policy of constant and matching aggression the 2nd Salfords were engaged in extensive patrolling which turned into heavy fighting around the German saps which extended well into No Man's Land in this area. One of the first of these was by two platoons of B Company under command of Captain C. W. Smith. This particular raid, at 1.30 a.m. on 11th July, failed because of insufficient preparatory work by the artillery which had been unable to cut the wire opposite. The following day, the battalion headquarters were shelled and Captain Powell was killed when the SAA and bomb store was blown up. Throughout the week a constant series of patrols, sent out by both sides, fought for ascendancy in No Man's Land. 2nd Lieutenant McClymont was central in the organisation of a number of these patrols. Often the target was a German sap at N19c3/0. On 17th July at 1.30 a.m. three sections of C and D Companies met a raiding party of 30 Germans in No Man's Land. There followed a sharp fight after which the enemy were driven into their trenches and bombed with what were believed to be heavy casualties.

Batman and observer to C Company Headquarters, Private A. James, (11565), who survived the war. LFM

At night the round of carrying and repairs went on. The waterlogged terrain meant that timber and revetting material was in constant demand. These parties were continually under risk of gas shelling and

The end of the British lines at Nieuport. This photograph shows part of the trench system along the coast which was occupied by the 1st and 2nd Salfords during the summer of 1917. Where the trenches were located close to the sea dunes, as in these pictures, the sandy soil allowed adequate drainage. This was nothing like the infinitely wetter conditions found just a short distance further inland where trenches such as these were utterly impossible to construct or maintain. Paul Reed

a steady stream of men were evacuated for treatment and observation. During this period of July the area continued to witness extensive shelling, that on 24th resulting in a moment of gross mischance for C Company of the 16th LFs, one of whose huts in Kuhn Camp, some miles behind the front lines at Coxyde Bains, received a direct hit.

> *I saw some terrible things. That time they bombarded us on the coast. They must have swivelled some heavy guns from the coast batteries. One of the shells landed on a hut we were in on the dunes. There were about twenty men in the hut. It blew everything to pieces except one end of the hut. Where the shell landed there were sixteen killed. We had a hell of a job sorting it out. The post Corporal gave us four mail bags and we filled them with bits of bodies. There was a tree outside. We were picking bits of body off that. We put them in sandbags, they were just sliced to pieces.* Private Frank Holding.

In fact casualties throughout July in the two senior Salford battalions reflected the constant strain and debilitation of war. The 15th Lancashire Fusiliers' casualties during July amounted to 14 other ranks killed, 91 wounded, 9 gassed and 11 missing. Amongst the officers two were wounded and two gassed. In the 16th LFs, three officers were killed, six wounded and two gassed. 23 men were killed, 109 wounded, 15 gassed and one was missing. A total of 288 casualties in one, single, ordinary month of attrition. However, the life of any units holding the lines had to go on and the two Salford Pals' battalions spent the rest of August, September and almost all of October here, manning the coastal defences and the sodden trenches and dykes around the Nieuport area.

On Sunday, 1st July, 1917, a service was held in Sacred Trinity Church as the town's 'Tribute to Fallen Heroes'. So great were the numbers of people attending that the church was filled to overflowing and many still grieving families were left outside to listen as best as they could. The High Master of Manchester Grammar School J. L. Paton was again present, along with many boys from Salford, marking the demise of so many youthful officers from that institution. Also within the congregation were 80 men of the Reserve Battalion from Prees Heath, Whitchurch, accompanied by two original Pals' officers, Majors Best and Lyon and the Brigade's raising committee. These men and the soldiers' families were present at the first intimation that the dreadful events at Thiepval one year earlier would not be forgotten when the Reverend Cornibeer spoke of the need for a permanent memorial within the walls of the ancient Parish Church, to ensure that the men who had given all must, 'live on in the memory of all who benefit by their self-sacrifice'. It was the origin of the recognition of 1st July as 'Thiepval Day' here in Salford, '... an engagement that will always be perpetuated in our local calendar because of the glorious deeds and heroic deaths of so many of the 1st, 2nd & 3rd Salford Battalions of the Lancashire Fusiliers ...'[37].

Nieuport's stark devastation.

That evening a further Service was held in the Parish Church at Pendleton, St. Thomas', again addressed by Montague Barlow, and where the congregation included a larger number of the relatives of soldiers who had been killed than at any preceding memorial service. J. L. Paton was not present at this service. He had been to St. Clements' Church in Urmston to the service at which the memorial tablet to Captain Geoffrey Heald was unveiled. The depth of feeling surrounding Captain Heald's death was considerable. The brass tablet which the Reverend Cooke revealed included the phrase 'To die for Justice is to die for Christ', a quotation from Manchester Grammar School's Roll of Honour. In reality Geoffrey Heald, 20 years old when killed, had been an active Church member and had found the concept of war distasteful.

Ypern Bogen

By mid October the Lancashire Fusiliers' Bantams had been brought up to Ypres. As part of the 35th Division's 104th Brigade they arrived at the Proven camps, moving up to support in the Langemark area by 16th October. On 17th October the men were visited by the Prince of Wales, then a staff captain at XIVth Corps' headquarters. These Lancashire Bantams[38] were then about to be launched into three and a half months of the most squalid and filthy conditions of warfare which could be imagined. Their location, in an area utterly saturated with the effects of constant shelling, broken drainage and the autumn's persistent rainfall, meant that any attempts to dig shelter were immediately swamped as the water table rose inexorably to fill every ditch, trench or shelter. On the night of 20/21st the Bantams were 'bivouacked' in shell holes at Artillery Wood. The battalion was already very much under strength, details having being drafted to the 241st and 104th Machine Gun Companies as well as the 104th Trench Mortar Battery for duties as carrying parties for ammunition. The following day was spent in working parties before the 4th Salfords moved up into Brigade Reserve on a line between Vee Bend and Pascal Farm, south of Houthulst Forest.

H.R.H. the Prince of Wales.

On October 22nd the 104th Brigade was due to attack in partnership with the 105th on their left and the 101st on their right. The 104th Brigade's objectives included a five hundred yard depth within the southern end of Houthulst Forest. The forest stood in a commanding position to the north of the Ypres salient and capture of this area would provide much improved observation and artillery support for troops still involved in the even more horrendous struggles in the Passchendaele area.

The Brigade's frontage for this attack extended some 800 yards in width from Aden House, just north of the Ypres Staden Railway (at approximately Vlc3/2), then westwards towards the Poelcapelle-Houthulst road, widening out as the forest was approached and entered. The attack was due in the half light of 5.30 a.m. and the men were already assembled at 2.00 a.m. When the attack got underway the right of the assault was held up by poor organisation at the boundary with 101st Brigade and the

In Loving Memory of
PRIVATE SYDNEY SHACKL[...]
No. 21582,
20th Bn. Lancashire Fusili[...]
Who died of wounds re[...]
in Action in Fr[...]
June 21st, 1917.
Aged 21 years.

Memorial silk to Pr[...]
Sydney Shakley, (21582[...]
the 4th Salford Pals,[...]
original battalion men[...]
and one of those who [...]
enlisted from beyond [...]
borough's boundary. Brad[...]

Lancashire Fusiliers cross the Passchendaele landscape. Late 1917. IWM

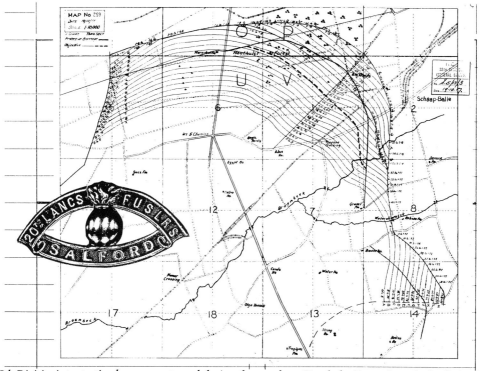

35th Division's protective barrage map used during the attack on Houthulst Forest. Inset is the distinctive shoulder title used by members of the 20th Lancashire Fusiliers, the 4th Salfords.

Bantams of the 23rd Manchesters suffered heavy casualties from a series of untroubled machine guns located in huts in front of the forest (in V1a). On the left however the 17th Lancashire Fusiliers made good progress towards their objectives. The line then bent back where the 18th LFs, the middle of the three assault battalions, had made relatively limited progress.

At 8.38 a.m., three hours after the action began, two companies of the 4th Salford Pals were therefore ordered by the GOC 104th Brigade to fill in the gap which had developed to the right of the 18th Lancashire Fusiliers, where the Manchesters had been repulsed and fallen back. In response W and Z Companies under command of Captain Swarbrick then moved forward to the 23rd Manchesters' headquarters at Egypt House by 10.15 a.m. where Swarbrick's men discovered that the 23rd were back in their start lines, the units on their right were nowhere to be seen and there was no contact with the 18th LFs on their left. In this perilous position W and Z companies then moved further forward under heavy shelling and dug in on the line in front of Les Cinque Chemins (from U6d9/8 to V1c5/4) facing the group of German machine guns which had earlier decimated Manchester's Bantams.

The short sturdy stature of the Bantams is clearly illustrated by this photograph showing a Military Medalist from the 17th Lancashire Fusiliers, Private John Matthew Gregson (36711), standing.
Randall

King George V saw some men and officers of both the 1st and 2nd Pals at Ghyvelde on 5 July 1917. Behind the lines he speaks with the 2nd Pals' C.O., Lieutenant Colonel Abercrombie. Barnes

Swarbrick's men were unable to join up with the 18th LFs but eventually got a patrol even further left to make contact with the 17th LFs (at U6b9/6). A patrol sent out on their right could only find five wounded men belonging to the 101st Brigade. In order to establish less exposed defensible positions the Brigade ordered the remaining men of the 4th Salfords to consolidate and hold the line running between the area of Turenne Crossing to Les Cinque Chemins, just south of the road (V1d2/2 to U6d0/3), behind Captain Swarbrick's group.

By late afternoon the German forces in Houthulst Forest were massing for a counter-attack. As that attack began the British artillery brought a heavy curtain of fire down. Its combination with the rifle and Lewis Gun fire brought to bear by the Bantams forced the Germans back into the forest. To the left however the position was far worse and the collapse of part of the 105th Brigade's position, on the left of the 17th Lancashire Fusiliers, forced the 17ths to pull back and give up a large part of the territory that they had earlier gained.

As darkness fell a flurry of nocturnal activity then saw the lines being properly consolidated and rations and ammunition being brought up. The injured who had lain out all day, often up to their waists in filthy slime, were brought back and an attempt was made to assault and occupy the series of huts which camouflaged the cluster of four machine guns which had held up the Manchesters' attack that morning.

The raiding party, commanded by 2nd Lieutenant H.L. Harris, moved out at 2.00 a.m. on the morning of 23rd, preceded by a team of scouts led by Lance Corporal Grundy. These three men then surprised and captured a machine gun crew, bayonetting the unfortunate gunner and taking the gun and its remaining crew, belonging to the 119th Regiment, prisoner. However, when the main group advanced German SOS flares were sent up. Immediately machine gun fire sprang up from both the flanks as well as the huts. The inevitable artillery shells began to fall thickly and it did not prove possible to occupy the huts.

With the onset of daylight the exposed positions ensured a continuation of the enemy's shelling. It was impossible for the men to scrape effective protective shelter and the position worsened with the decision to locate all three Fusilier Battalions' headquarters at Egypt House. Under direct observation, any movement in the vicinity as casualties were brought in resulted in a deluge of shells. Since the pill box door was too narrow for a stretcher the seriously wounded lay out helplessly whilst the interior became ever more crowded with other wounded men, bearers, medics and HQ staff. Outside the grievously wounded were dying in the most hideous of scenes. It was not until midnight on the 23rd that the 17th and 18th Lancashire Fusiliers were relieved, the men being so exhausted and saturated that the relief took almost five hours of superhuman struggle to complete. The 4th Salfords could only look on enviously. Their relief, by the 7th Northumberland Fusiliers, had to wait through a further 24 hours of utter misery as they endured perpetual shelling, sniping and the mud's penetrating cold.

This attack cost the 104th Brigade roughly 900 casualties of which 213 were suffered by the 4th Salford Pals.[39] For many of the newly arrived drafts who constituted a large portion of the battalion this introduction to the circumstances of 'modern industrial warfare' could hardly have been more symptomatic and typical of the horrors held by Ypres' foul salient that late autumn.

Throughout this later period of battles for Passchendaele village, and the ridge upon which it stood, the 19th Lancashire Fusiliers had continued to labour in their accustomed role as a Pioneer Battalion, servicing the transport and constructional needs of their 49th Division. The Divisional Trench Standing Orders must have made wry reading to the company commanders whose duty it was to ensure,

> ...that their men get exercise and do not stagnate mentally and bodily or live in unnecessary squalor. They must arrange for getting trench boards and other material to make the posts and trenches dry and habitable...There is no disgrace in getting dirty in the performance of a duty which necessitates it, but there is disgrace in remaining dirty longer than necessary or in permitting adverse conditions to excuse slovenliness either in appearance or the performance of duty. All ranks should shave daily whenever this is possible. The moral effect of cleanliness is great. P. Scobell...[40]

By November the 15th and 16th Lancashire Fusiliers had themselves finally been moved south to face the moral challenges of self preservation here in the Salient. Every man who lived through the experience would never forget its evil countenance. In front the rubble and brick coloured stain which marked where Passchendaele village had once stood, where the expected advances, out beyond the Passchendaele ridge, had failed. Any hoped for movement had simply petered out amidst the exhausting, bloodied, inundating mud.

At home in Salford one notable event marking the passing of the original Pals took place with the unveiling of a tablet to the memory of Edgar Hampson.[41] This occasion, on the last Sunday in November, was attended by an enormous number of people, the service at Ascension Church in Lower Broughton

Living conditions in and around the Ypres Salient. As the autumn of 1917 progressed the front line petered out into a swamp of water filled shell holes. Taylor Library

Murray's Newsagents, Bolton Road. Late 1917. The wording under the window reads: 'HAIG'S SUCCESS IN TERRIFIC BATTLE. MILES OF TRENCHES AND MANY PRISONERS TAKEN'. Probably a reference to the Battle of Cambrai, which commenced on 20th November and initially promised great success for the British and Empire troops engaged there. SLHL

being conducted by the Dean of Manchester, Bishop Welldon. In the community's eyes Hampson had come to symbolise all of the 1st Salford Pals' officers who had been obliterated at Thiepval. During his sermon to the congregation the Bishop alluded to the intolerable burden of shock which was suffered by the bereaved fathers whose hopes and aspirations were wrapped up in the lives of their closest sons. In the case of Edgar Hampson's father, Justice of the Peace and proprietor of the town's newspaper, that shock was indeed too much. Within two years he also was dead, although survived by his wife, Edith, and a further brother of Edgar's who served in the 4th Salfords.

In that week which followed the dedication of Lieutenant Hampson's memorial tablet the first two Salford Battalions arrived in the midst of the sea of mud which now surrounded Irish Farm at St. Jean, two miles north east of Ypres on the road towards Westroozebeke and Passchendaele. The glutinous ooze extended northeastwards across a landscape devoid of any feature, save the sickly pools of filth bordering every island of overturned earth. The men's movements into the swamps and shell holes called the front lines had to be undertaken without daylight, along the precarious, slimy duckboards which prevented men being swallowed up. From their positions in the firing lines north of Bellevue, one mile west of Passchendaele, it was planned that the 32nd Division would launch an attack northwards on Westroozebeke which stood at the northern end of the ridge. The objectives were, from right to left, Venison Trench, Volt Farm and, for the 15th LFs, Veal Cottages (at V23c0/2). The area was scattered with the German fortifications and pillboxes which enabled a relatively thinly held front line to be supported in depth by further troops who were expected to counter-attack vigorously in the face of any significant loss of position.

The Brigade chosen for the assault was the 97th, stiffened by the addition of two extra battalions, the 15th Lancashire Fusiliers and the 16th Northumberland Fusiliers who were designated as the 'Counter counter-attack battalion'. Because the whole area was under observation the half-trained conscripts of all six battalions to be used would have to assemble in the pitch black of night. The assault was timed for 1.55 a.m. on the viciously cold morning of 2nd December. In order to avoid alerting the German artillery, no creeping barrage was ordered. The assault was designed to be undertaken as a rush, culminating in the taking of the German posts by the bayonet, only then would a barrage be switched

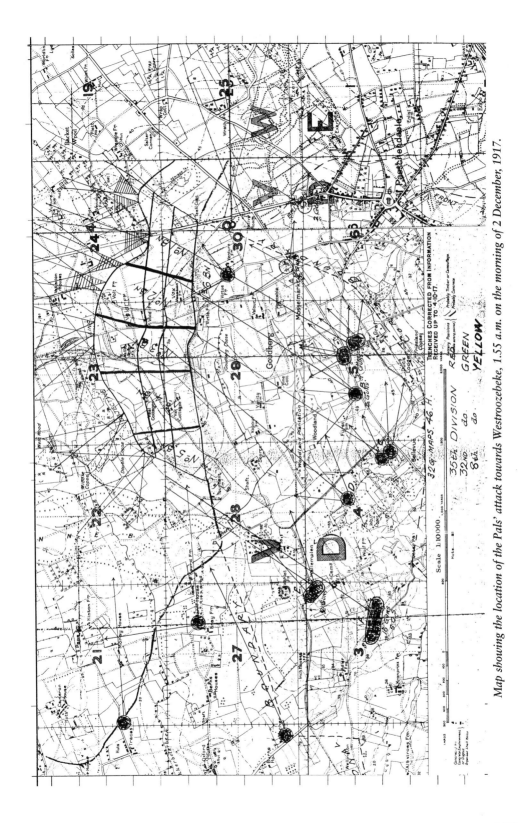

Map showing the location of the Pals' attack towards Westroozebeke, 1.55 a.m. on the morning of 2 December, 1917.

on to the German support lines behind their outpost positions. The 1st Pals were taken up to the front lines on the late evening of 30th November, marching the last seven miles along the duckboards in single file. The role of the 15th Lancashire Fusiliers was to advance as the left flank unit of the 97th Brigade's attack, digging in to consolidate their gains once the objectives were reached. Since any sort of landmark had been utterly obliterated by the colossal weight of shellfire which pulverised this area for months beforehand, the Fusiliers' company objectives were identified by boards at the start lines, each one giving a compass bearing and distance to be covered with the details written in luminous paint.

When the attack was launched it came as a complete surprise to the enemy in their front line outposts. For seven minutes most of the men advanced for once without being assailed by the rattle of machine gun fire. It was nearly fifteen minutes before a weak artillery counter-barrage

Three German soldiers cut down at the rear of the pill box they were manning, located in the Ypres Salient.

was opened, most of which fell behind the British start lines. However, by that time the Germans' forward machine guns had begun to take a heavy toll of men in the 15th LFs' A Company, under 2nd Lieutenant Brockman. All this company's officers and senior NCOs became casualties. For B and C Companies to their left, led by Captain R. F. Greenhill and 2nd Lieutenant G. H. Smith, the going was easier. Throughout the darkness the men pushed forward, surrounding pill boxes and moving up to their required positions which were taken in full in the still complete darkness of 5.00 a.m. that morning. In view of the losses which A Company took, two platoons from the reserve company, led by 2nd Lieutenants Hurst and Pollitt, were pushed up to secure the forward positions.

On the right of the 15th Lancashire Fusiliers the 17th Highland Light Infantry had been unable to make such steady progress, their passage blocked by substantial entanglements of wire at Vat Cottages (V29a5/9) and machine guns. However, to their right the 11th Borders occupied Mallet Copse. To that battalion's right the 16th H.L.I. were at Void Farm and further right the 2nd K.O.Y.L.I. were on Hill 52 and attempting, in the face of very heavy machine gun fire, to consolidate there. Unfortunately, as their attack had got under way the enfilade fire from Venison Trench (at V30b7/7) had caused casualties and killed many of the 2nd K.O.Y.L.I. at Teall Cottage. The remaining ranks now had a very tenuous hold on Hill 52.

Within the area's network of fortified emplacements and pill boxes the German machine guns had now established a real superiority of fire power. Most of the five attacking battalion's officers had become casualties as they were forced to expose themselves to risks when leading attacks on these strongpoints. One of these was 2nd Lieutenant J. S. Scrivener, responsible for the thorough and detailed taping of the forming-up positions which had done so much to ensure that the initial attack was successfully launched from the correct position. Scrivener was killed soon after he and his batman, Private R. H. Poole, had captured one of the pill boxes which took such a heavy toll of men this morning.

By 5.30 a.m., the Salfords were ordered to make contact with the 17th H.L.I. beyond Veal Cottages in order to surround the garrisons there. This move proved impossible in view of the discrepancy between the two battalions' foremost positions, and the 15th LFs then moved their right flank back behind Veal Cottages to join up with the H.L.I., preventing any possibility of the enemy infiltrating between the two units.

However, the situation was about to deteriorate badly.

Before first light the remnants of the 2nd K.O.Y.L.I. were driven back off Hill 52. The 'counter counter-attack battalion', the 16th NFs were immediately ordered to rectify the position. Predictably though, in such featureless surroundings, where even the men on the ground had little if any idea of where they were, it proved impossible to organise an effective protective barrage for the NFs' attack. The position was complicated by the fact that the supporting artillery were located on firmer ground south west and were not able to fire a creeping barrage across a diagonal. It was anyway quite impossible for the Northumberlands to move sideways since no adequate duckboards existed for that purpose. Some ineffective shelling north of the Brigade's objectives was ordered to break up concentrations of German troops at Valuation Houses and Mallet Wood (V24a1/5 and V23 central). Eventually, at 9.20 a.m., the 97th Brigade admitted that it was then unable to make use of the 16th NFs due to 'disorganisation of units and loss of officers'.[42]

The 97th Brigade were now under real pressure from 32nd Division to fix a time to recapture Hill 52. Plans were being drawn up to throw in the 14th Brigade that night if the 97th did not achieve their objectives. After a considerable preparation by artillery and barrage machine guns firing on the area behind Mallet Copse and East of Void Farm the 16th NFs made an attempt in the late afternoon twilight to take Hill 52 at 4.10 p.m.

This was immediately matched by a German counter-attack which inexplicably recovered much of the 97th Brigade's gains around the area of Mallet Copse, apart from a few valueless square yards in the vicinity of Vox Farm, (at V29b9/8), and those locations controlled by the LFs. The initial difficulties seemed to have set in on the 11th Borders' front. Although this battalion had fought through to their objectives they had lost in the process 15 of their Officers and almost all of their NCOs. The 16th H.L.L, on their left, were also pressed by this counter attack and fell back. The 16th NFs, moving up when the Borders and H.L.I. 'retired' soon found itself some three hundred yards in front of the start lines with its flanks in the air. The Divisional Commander said of this,

> I am of the opinion that the O.C. 16th Northumberland Fus. was wrong in the decision he came to, and that he should have advanced at once on VOID FARM and attacked any enemy he encountered.[43]

However, the 1st Salfords were not dislodged at all and they were able to hand over their newly gained territory to the 2nd Manchesters at midnight, on the night of 3/4th December.

Fortunately the plans to use the 14th Brigade to continue these attacks were not approved by Corps.

This futile action cost 102 casualties to the 1st Salford Battalion and 1,063 to the 97th Infantry Brigade as a whole. Their sacrifice had achieved almost nothing which could be spoken of as a tangible gain. Major-General Shute's analysis of the ultimate failure of these operations was specific about the reasons.

> ...it must be realised that we are now dealing with only partially trained troops, whose training and discipline may not be sufficiently good to enable them to surmount the difficulties of control entailed by an attack in the darkness...

Clearing up on Passchendaele Ridge in November 1917.

Menin Road, Hell Fire Corner. Whippy

> *...an intercepted German message shows that an attack by us was expected by the enemy on the night December 1/2nd, and that although his front line of posts had not been warned, his main line of defence had been reinforced, and his machine guns were ready for our advance....*
>
> *...the conditions at this time of the year are very trying to a man's vitality, and that after some hours of fighting in the wet and muddy ground his stamina and powers of resistance are worn out and unless resolute leadership is present he is in no condition to withstand any further high tests on his endurance. The remedy for this is not easy to discover.[44]*

It would have been difficult to speak more clearly of the context within which 1917's campaigns had petered out. The year ended for the Salford Battalions in the debris and corruption of Passchendaele's infamous slopes. The Third Battle of Ypres had become the year's most catastrophic engagement for the British Army, its 250,000 casualties here ensuring that the planned German spring offensives of 1918 would prosper. The December actions here at Westroozebeke were simply a futile sideshow. In this wilderness the vitality and health of the Salford men had indeed been tested to their very limits.

> *I went on leave in December 1917 and had a bath. I showed my father my heels, they were a yellow mass. Father cried when he saw that.* Private Frank Holding.

The rest of December and the New Year saw little reason for good cheer. In the trenches at Gravenstafel one of the 1st Pals' longest serving men fell prey to a random shell which wounded two and killed both he and one other man. John Tonge had enlisted in October 1915, been quickly promoted Sergeant and later 2nd Lieutenant in June 1916. In 1917 he had been made acting Lieutenant and Battalion Signalling Officer to the 15th LFs. His rise from the Pals' ranks was unusual. The reason's simple:

Sans Souce pill box, where many of the 3rd Salfords were quartered in late 1917. Whippy

> *He was popular with both officers and men, and one of the best officers I have known – absolutely fearless and always cheerful and willing to undertake any task however unpleasant or dangerous.[45]*

The men moved from camp to squalid camp in the Ypres area, Hospital Farm, Huddleston Camp, Siege Camp, Dirty Bucket Camp and others. But February of 1918 found the 15th and 16th Lancashire Fusiliers in the lines at Houlthulst Forest, a few miles north of Ypres.[46]

Although the Regiment's Bantams, including the 4th Salfords, had already been directly engaged here in actions at Houlthulst, by the time the 1st and 2nd Salfords arrived those 4th Pals had simply ceased to exist, their officers and men redistributed in equal shares between the 17th and 18th Lancashire Fusiliers.[47] Just as they had been for Salford's now defunct Bantams, the approaches to the forest were still a slough of water-filled holes where movement was confined to a network of duckboards and perilous walk-ways. Throughout February and much of March the 15th and 16th Lancashire Fusiliers lived and fought here, patrolling actively in the optimistic search for signs of weakening resolve on the part of their enemy. On 18th February men from both battalions participated in the Renard Farm raid (at 035c8/l), the purpose of which was to take prisoners, weaponry and examples of food. Whilst this raid was undertaken without loss in achieving all these objectives during a deep penetration of the German lines, the subsequent raid on 27th February was less successful. During that night four patrols from the 16th LFs' A Company, each of platoon strength, searched in Owls Wood. During the course of this patrolling two machine guns were located in an otherwise empty landscape, but an attempt to rush the guns caused casualties, 10 dead and 19 wounded.

During the same night men of the 15th LFs searched in the Marechal Farm area, still deserted after a successful raid by the 2nd Manchesters. Early in the morning these men, under the command of Captain Mandleberg, came in without loss having captured three German soldiers.

The sister Pioneer Battalion was however still here in the Ypres salient, and continued their back-breaking work along the Menin Road throughout the period between mid-November 1917 and early April 1918. Much of their time was spent in the construction of duckboard tracks from near to Zonnebeke church back to the support lines as an aid to evacuating wounded men. Whilst the Battalion's primary task was to engage in this never-ending slog of boarding, road repairs, entrenching and carrying, they were soon to be reminded that they were still, above all else, soldiers who carried a rifle and all the terrible risks and responsibilities which that entailed.

Because of the catastrophic collapse of stability in the St. Quentin area further south, following the Michael offensive launched by the German Army on 21st March, the effective defence and control of the highest points on the ridge which defined the south of the Ypres salient was vital if the British Army's Channel supply routes were not to be threatened or cut.

Disaster at Mount Kemmel
Late March and early April therefore became a testing period in the Allies' titanic struggle for supremacy in this corner of France and Belgium. In a gesture of concern the French had taken over a six mile stretch

Kit and Kat strong points, held by the 3rd Salfords in early April, before their move up to Mount Kemmel.
Whippy

Zonnebeke Village, late 1917. This shows, with terrible clarity, the awful conditions within which the 3rd Pals laboured during late 1917 and early 1918. IWM

of line between Bailleul and Wytschaete, leaving defensive fortification and construction work to two British units in the Kemmel area, the 456th Field Company R.E., and the 19th Lancashire Fusiliers. The British Kemmel Defence Force also had at its disposal a composite company made up of platoons from the 1/5th, 1/6th and 1/7th West Yorkshires, the 146th Trench Mortar Battery and the 149th Machine Gun Battalion. These depleted units totalled just 901 men and were under the command of Lieutenant Colonel H. D. Bousfield of the West Yorkshire Regiment.

Since 11th April Salford's soldier pioneers had been manning outposts here in the Kemmel area amongst their French and British comrades. Mount Kemmel itself was in a commanding position, its 159 metres (at N26a) dominating the area's skyline. German attacks on the morning of 17th April were driven off successfully by men of A Company. Nevertheless, the Battalion's tenure of Mount Kemmel was already proving costly in terms of casualties. Between 15th and 18th the 19th Lancashire Fusiliers lost 94 casualties from their strength. On 18th April the Battalion's outposts were relieved by French troops, enabling the men to begin the digging of new trenches and communications in the rear of the hill. At this point the responsibility for the hill's defence was passed to the French.

For a week this frenetic digging went on as earlier German successes further south were controlled in severe fighting around the Scarpe and Somme rivers. As the pressure and casualties mounted, a start was made on the construction of a new communication trench spanning the 2,500 yards between Mount Kemmel and the Sherpenberg. During the three nights of 22nd, 23rd and 24th work continued as a rota of companies ran the gauntlet of intermittent shrapnel fire to complete the task.

Battalion Headquarters were established within the confines of a tunnel in the rear of the hill, shared by the French Brigade HQ and with the three companies dug in around. In the crowded underground confines the 19th LFs' share of the space doubled as HQ, Orderly Room, Officers' Mess and the Commanding Officer's and Adjutant's bedroom. On 23rd April one of the last men to see his battalion there had finally relocated the unit after recovering from wounds in England.

> *Lt. Col. J. Ambrose Smith is in his shirt sleeves talking volubly with much gesticulation to a French officer. Thomas (acting adjutant) and Mutch (L.G.O.) are also there. We are welcomed, given a drink and pumped for news. One more officer, we discover, is required to complete establishment in the line and Musker is ordered by the C.O. to remain there.[48]*

Ruins on the approaches to Mount Kemmel. Inset: British artillery officers on Mount Kemmel watch the effect of their guns. The advantage of the high ground afforded by Mount Kemmel was lost when the Germans overwhelmed the French 25 April, 1918.

Whilst Clifford Platt returned to the Transport details at Westoutre, the fighting in the area of Mount Kemmel intensified. That night the area was drenched with gas and the surrounding countryside became littered with the bodies of dead farm animals and horses. On the morning of the 24th a party from transport drove down to 'Pop' in pursuit of Croix de Guerre ribbons, due to be presented to a number of men in the battalion by the French Division who shared the defence of Kemmel. At 10.30 a.m. the group left,

> *...with Sheridan and Mick. The former is the driver and the latter his favourite horse, guide, philosopher and friend. When Sheridan - 59 in the shade and rheumatic in both legs - is in an expansive mood, you can learn quite a lot about yourself, your friends and the battalion in general. A wonderful old fellow with two lads in the Army and an old 'Maggie' waiting at home - a fitting object lesson indeed to the genus 'Conchie'. And so I am regaled on my journey with a wealth of anecdotes, some clever, some coarse, many vastly amusing and all entirely whimsical, told in an accent and language by no means fitted for the drawing room, but for a mess cart on a lonely road - bien!*[49]

A major assault against these positions was not unexpected since prisoners, taken by the French 28th Division on the evening of 24th, had stated that a German attack was imminent early the next morning. Unfortunately the French were in some disarray, having tried during the night to move their lines forward in the direction of Lindenhoek. Their losses meant that many reserves were still being installed in the front lines as the German barrage had begun to fall.

At 2.30 a.m. on the morning of 25th April that bombardment was opened by the German artillery. The devastatingly heavy shelling, consisting of lachrymatory and mustard gas as well as high explosive, was initially concentrated on the French field guns and howitzers in the rear positions of the hill where

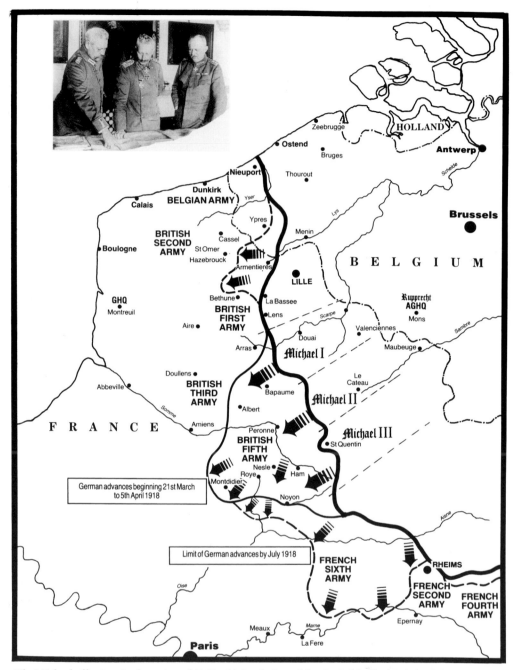

The Michael offensives in the spring of 1918 which culminated for the 3rd Salford Pals in their encirclement on Mount Kemmel. Inset: Hindenberg, the Kaiser and Ludendorff who masterminded this offensive which came close to causing the utter collapse of the British Fifth Army.

the HQ, together with A and C Companies of the 19th LFs were located. At 4.30 a.m. a respite for half an hour occurred, after which the enemy's artillery concentrated on the front lines and highest ground. Throughout this period the men of B Company continued to dig furiously. According to Frenchmen who were present this concentrated bombardment was, 'far worse than anything ever experienced at Verdun'.

Object of the German assault on 25 April – Mount Kemmel – it would give them uninterrupted views over the southern section of the Ypres Salient.

German assault troops occupying former French positions.

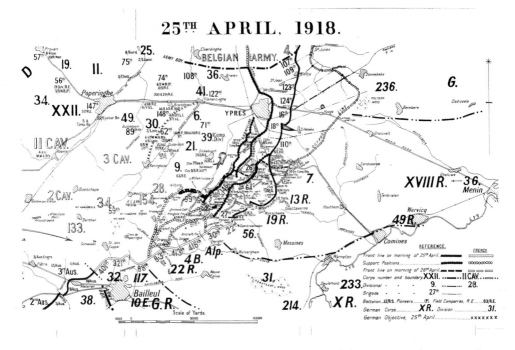

25TH APRIL, 1918.

For three and a half hours the Pals dug, watched and endured until the German infantry assault was launched at 6.00 a.m. Within minutes it was clear that the attack was coming in across a widespread front, the French losing ground to the south and Kemmel village being overrun, quickly leaving Mount Kemmel almost surrounded by the men of the German Alpine Corps. The tightly packed French troops suffered terrible casualties from the shelling of their trenches. By 7.10 a.m. the Germans were on the summit of Kemmel and soon after lines of French soldiers from the 28th Division defending Mount Kemmel were seen running away, down the slopes of the hill in a north westerly direction. The French artillery, located to the rear in the valley running between Mont Rouge and Westoutre, was almost totally hors de combat, silenced by the effects of gas and counter-battery fire and having only one gun per battery still operational at this time. The British artillery was less concentrated but still suffered

German troops storm the Kemmel positions on the morning of 25 April, 1918.

heavy losses. These gunners were still of necessity operating in the clumsy gas masks which they wore throughout the action. Any limited counter-barrage barrage which these isolated guns managed to put up was inadequate to stem the German advance. By the time the summit had been overrun much of A Company's strength had been lost to the terrible shelling. At this point the remaining men of the battalion were sent forward, to a spur on the right of the hill, in an effort to stabilise the situation. In this hopelessly outnumbered position the Pals were progressively outflanked, the Germans surrounding the Battalion's headquarters where the Adjutant's staff, including RSM Walter Garner, were killed, some other men and one

Summit of Kemmel Hill after the severe fighting which followed the German assault. Whippy

officer managing to escape. Only a tiny remnant of the 19th LFs were left to surrender. Soon after 10.00 a.m. the Germans were in pursuit down the northern slopes of Mount Kemmel, halting when they reached the Kemmelbek at approximately 11.00 a.m. By midday it was known that the Fusiliers' Commanding Officer, Lieutenant Colonel Ambrose Smith, was wounded and missing, along with 14 of his fellow officers and 333 other ranks.

As Lieutenant Colonel Bousfield and his fellow prisoners trudged down the southern slopes to captivity their conversation turned to the poor showing of the French troops.

> *From all that I saw personally ... and from what I heard after ... and judging by the state of the ground ... the French can hardly have put in any resistance at all on the forward slopes of the hill. Lieut. Harbord 146 T.M.B. (a fellow prisoner) who was on the forward slopes of Kemmel Hill said that as soon as the barrage lifted the French went forward in large parties, some fifty strong, to surrender to the advancing Germans. This would presumably mask all the fire of the English Machine Guns on the hill...[50]*

To the rear the break up of the telephone lines made communication with Kemmel impossible. Early in the morning the position became a little clearer at the transport lines where,

> *... a couple of men from the battalion arrive and report to C.S.M. Duncanson, who is doing R.S.M. for Details.*
> *They tell of a heavy Bosche attack at about 5 o'clock this morning which, they say, penetrated to their bivvies this side of Kemmel Hill: they add that the hill is captured and the battalion either cut off or scattered; 'B' and 'C' Coys, they say, were out working at the time and suffered very heavily. The men are in 'B' Coy. These tales are discredited as 'panicky' rumours; and the men are put under arrest, as they have no equipment and no rifles. Later more stragglers arrive, but in better order, in parties of five or six, sometimes with an N. C. O. All report more or less the same tale. C. L. Platt*

By 7 p.m. it was clear that Kemmel was lost. This was enormously threatening to the security of the British positions in the Ypres salient, since all the communications and southern defences were now under direct observation. As a consequence a reduction in the length of the Ypres salient's front lines was effected on the night of April 26/27th.

By then the remnants of the 19th Lancashire Fusiliers, made up of the few survivors together with the details and carrying parties who had been behind the lines on the morning of the attack, had moved away to billets in Poperinge. The officers were distributed amongst the 1/4th and 1/5th Yorks and Lancs whose men continued to man the Kemmel area defences.

This was a disastrous loss, but one from which the seeds of catastrophe for the German Army were sown. Their capture of Mount Kemmel on the morning of 25th April[51] proved to be the nadir of Allied territorial losses to this part of the Michael offensives. Whilst the 3rd Salfords had been utterly smashed

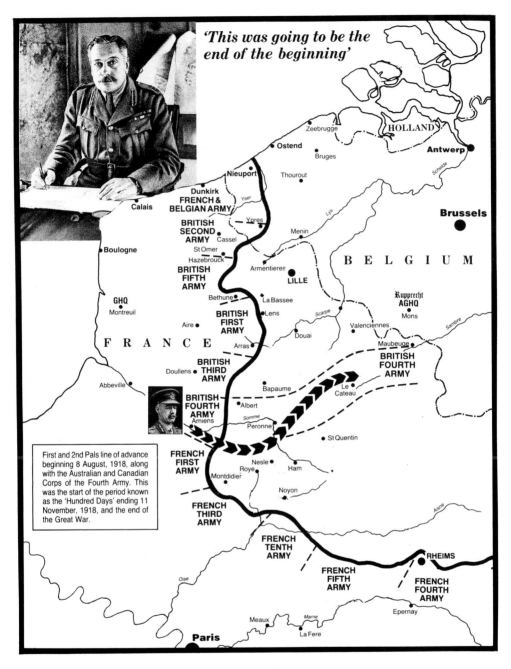

'This was going to be the end of the beginning'

First and 2nd Pals line of advance beginning 8 August, 1918, along with the Australian and Canadian Corps of the Fourth Army. This was the start of the period known as the 'Hundred Days' ending 11 November, 1918, and the end of the Great War.

by the ferocity of the German bombardment and infantry assault, they had stuck to their posts with a tenacity and courage which had proved that their eighteen months as pioneers had not blunted their fighting spirit. For the German Army the sequence of desperate offensives, which both preceded and followed the Kemmel action, would gradually drain the material and moral reserves which were essential to the successful continuance of their campaign. Further south, in the Somme-Amiens region, those German advances which had initially swept them forward from their positions near to St. Quentin had been halted at Villers Bretonneux near to Amiens on 24th April. One month later another vast assault was launched in the Champagne region, the Third Battle of the Aisne, followed two weeks later by an

Second-Lieutenant Lawrence Price. One of the missing on 25th April, later known to have been killed. Whippy

Whilst some of the missing from the Kemmel actions made their way to POW camps in Germany, their replacements continued to be made ready at home. This photograph shows Sergeant Sidney Morgan O'Nions of 3rd Reserve Battalion, LFs, during May 1918. He would be gassed and wounded at the Happegarbes spur actions a week before the War's end, whilst serving with the 2nd Pals. O'Nions

attack towards Compiegne from the direction of Montdidier. The final throw of the German dice came on July 15th when all that country's available manpower and reserves were launched, unsuccessfully, into the Second Battle of the Marne.

In this exhausted atmosphere of high summer an influenza epidemic spreading amongst the enemy's soldiers confirmed what many British soldiers in the Fourth Army already suspected; that a determined and persistent Allied assault might well break their opponent's will-power. Since 14th April a unified Allied Command structure, under control of General Foch, had at last provided the means to ensure this sort of consistent and co-ordinated pressure.

'This was going to be the end of the beginning'
On 18th July the Allied counter attacks began.

That day the 2nd Salfords arrived at Penton Camp in Proven, a few miles north west of Top', near Ypres, followed the next day by the 1st Salfords who occupied Pekin Camp. This period provided an interlude during which the men were rested and refitted in preparation for their part in the anticipated advance. On Minden Day, 1st August[52], the two Battalions celebrated with sports and outrageous humour. People in the town were convulsed with laughter as two couples, of each sex apparently, en route for the sports ground entered the public toilets in the town centre. Although the humour was crude the town's people laughed until tears ran down their faces. Later that morning bareback mule races, tilting the bucket, coconut shies, fancy dress pillow fights on a greasy pole over a huge vat of water and throwing balls at live heads entertained everyone. During the afternoon an inter-battalion football match took place. It was 2-0 to the 16th LFs at half time, and although the 15th Battalion briefly equalized the 16th ran out winners 3-2. The events were rounded off well when the men's evening meal was washed down with plenty of beer and stout. 80 Lancashire Fusiliers officers attended the Regimental Minden Day dinner, given by Brigadier-General Girdwood DSO, at Mieghen camp that evening.

Headquarters of the fourth army, at Flixecourt, on 13 August, 1918, on the occasion of the visit of His Majesty the King.

> *At night the officers of the two battalions with several brass huts from Brigade celebrated with a Minden Day dinner. It cost £120, quite a large portion of which was spent on liquid refreshment. It is regrettable to note that many of the officers were hors-de-combat before the evening ended, six of them spending the night in the fields instead of their beds in billets![53]*

On the 6th August a representative party of the 16th Lancashire Fusiliers were inspected by King George V on this the last day of their preparations in the area of Proven. The following day the Pals were brought down from Proven to Hangest-sur-Somme, thence in lorries; the 15th Battalion to Domart-sur-la-Luce in reserve to the 3rd Canadian Division who would attack towards Ie Quesnel, the 16th to Boves, three miles south east of Amiens.

On 8th August the Allied pressure on the German Army intensified to a new ferocity. A crushing blow was struck at the outset of the Battle of Amiens by the British Fourth Army, in conjunction with the French First Army on their left. These actions induced a catastrophic decay of German morale, the initial telling impact being made by, the divisions of the Australian and Canadian Corps alongside the 32nd Division's men.

As part of the 32nd Division, the 1st and 2nd Salfords then undertook a considerable part in the advances which followed the Battle of Amiens, during what became the last 'Hundred Days' of war. It was however no walk-over and the casualties suffered by the Pals during this period would be very heavy. At 4.00 a.m. on 10th August the 15th and 16th Lancashire Fusiliers were advancing along the Amiens-Roye road towards Bouchoir in the direction of Le Quesnoy-en-Santerre.

> *We were carried towards the front in lorries and then the traffic on the Amiens-Roye road was so terrific coming back from the front, and all the thousands of prisoners that were being marched back, and the ambulances, captured guns and wounded, that we couldn't advance any further in our lorries. We got out and started to march in column of fours and we found that was quite impracticable. We had to march in single file with many halts, in filtering through the oncoming traffic. This took us a great deal longer to get to the front than had been anticipated... We saw vast numbers of them [German prisoners in wire containment 'cages'] which of course made us feel tremendously happy because we saw that a really decisive battle must have taken place and we had a feeling that this was going to be the end of the beginning at any rate.[54]*

In this atmosphere of optimism the two Salford Battalions reached their attack positions at 7.30, between Bouchoir and Folies. Their objectives lay 5,000 yards away, to the south east, Damery village and Damery

Wood. Coincidentally this was the identical location which had seen the start of the Pals' advance, towards the Hindenberg defences, during the Germans' spring withdrawal of 1917 and many of the men and officers were very familiar with both the ground and the depth of German wire in front of Damery. The attack at 8.00 a.m. was led by the 15th LFs with the 16th in support 800 yards behind. The 2nd Manchesters were in Brigade reserve. Within half an hour le Quesnoy-en-Santerre was captured by the 15th LFs with minor casualties. Passing through the village the senior battalion began to take heavy casualties as they became exposed on the line of the crest, east of le Quesnoy. Meanwhile, the French, to the Salfords' south on the other side of the Roye road, had taken Erches. Quickly, by 9.20 a.m., the 15th LFs were reinforced by the support of the 16th Battalion and the combined units took Wood 101 (Bois Sud at L32b9/2), its trench system and a number of machine guns, after very severe fighting. At this moment Major Uniacke ('the human blotting paper', temporarily Officer Commanding the 16th LFs) was wounded by a machine gun round fired from Wood 99, overlooked by the 15th LFs in the speed of their advance.

11 August, 1918, Commander-in-Chief Sir Douglas Haig congratulates the commander of a Canadian battalion of the Fourth Army for the success of his battalion.

By now the situation was critical. From their positions above the old French and British lines the men were looking at huge depths of barbed wire, running east for upwards of 1,000 yards in front of the now derelict 1916 fortifications. The surrounding warren of trenches, already overgrown with summer grasses, hid many snipers and machine gun teams who were still determined to resist to

Captured German artillery.

the last. Although these trenches were crumbling, the wire in front of the old German positions was still 'of a very formidable description'. To complete their misery a very heavy shrapnel barrage was launched on the Salford men's positions at 9.30 a.m. This was a situation which called for considerable initiative on the part of junior officers and NCOs.

That initiative was not lacking and by 10.30 a.m. the two interwoven battalions, 'now greatly reduced in numbers' entered the old German lines at la Cambuse (R3d), south west of Damery under very heavy machine gun fire from Parvillers, Middle Wood (L34c) and from the Bois en Equerre (E3c), fighting their way forward towards Damery Wood. Just yards south of the Bois en Equerre a party of 25 men of the 15th and 16th LFs, led by Lieutenant Brockman and Major Knott, captured a battery of four 4.2" high velocity guns which had been firing at close range over open sights. On the right the French had also been taking heavy casualties and were held up in front of Bois en Z (R1Ob). To their left the 97th Brigade's attack 'had never made any material advance beyond our old front line'.[55] In front of the Salfords continued German resistance, within the Bois en Equerre, ensured that any further progress would be difficult, if not impossible. Orders from Brigade

One of the NCOs in the 2nd Pals this day was Company Sergeant Major Seth Taylor. This postcard, sent home in his post, dated 10 August 1918, clearly shows the youth which characterised many junior officers and NCOs by this stage in the war. Jones

were therefore sent at 11.50, instructing the units to dig in and consolidate the gains already made in preparation for attacks now being planned for the following day. However, before these orders could reach the men, the combined Salford Battalions rushed the Bois en Equerre, taking the pill box known as the 'Tour de Defiance' on its western edge and carrying through to occupy the eastern rim of the wood, overlooking Damery.

"It was soon set on fire and its innards poured out in the shape of ball bearings and molten metal."

A group of the typically English girls who served in the AFDSs and CCSs in 'France 1918'. MS

"Tottles"

"Wem"

"Dot"

The retribution was swift.

The wood was immediately subjected to a heavy German shelling and the LFs were forced back to its eastern edge. However the pill box and the four gun battery, which were the object of the enemy counter-attack, were retained. Here the Lieutenant Colonel of the 15th LFs, Henry Utterson D.S.O., become one of many men who were killed in this action when he was shot dead entering the Bois de la Futaie, just yards to the west of the fighting in the Bois en Equerre.

The situation was both volatile and highly fluid. It had become the scene of an extraordinarily complex amalgam of nations, the combination of whose firepower had been assembled at the Battle of Amiens. At 1.30 p.m., the Brigade frontage was reported as,

> *LA CAMBUSE (R3d) – Western edge of the BOIS en EQUERRE – thence along old German support line to L33d5/7 – thence to old German front line in L27d4/0 – thence along line to SQUARE WOOD inclusive. The O.C. Company of the 16th Bn Lancs Fus. finding that his left flank was in the air formed a defensive flank across NO MAN'S LAND to the old British Front line at L27b0/9 where some Canadians and A. + S. Highlanders were found.[56]*

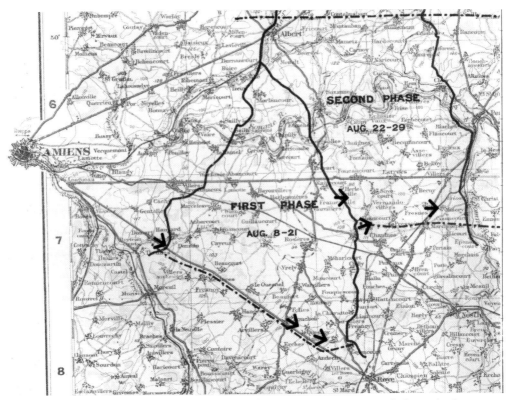

The first and second phases of the Fourth Army's advance following 8 August – "A Black Day for the German Army"

In this middle period of the day a lull in the fighting settled over the battlefield. At 2.00 p.m. four tanks were ordered up to support the attacks on Damery and its wood, lumbering conspicuously forward in an attempt to find where their presence could tip the scales and allow mobility on the battlefield again.

Overhead aeroplanes circled, also desperate to identify their own troops from those of the enemy. Such attempts at operating with a combination of arms proved very difficult in the confusion and smoke of battle. In the midst of this, however, some men of C Company in the 16th LFs had felt secure enough to get out of the depths of their captured trench when,

> *… an RAF plane came over, circled round and began to bomb us. He threw several bombs, I got a piece in the arm, and my men said to me, 'Won't you let us shoot the bugger down? So I said, 'No, not on any account'. My men were carrying little shiny tin discs and we were supposed to catch the reflection of the sun and shine up at any plane which was playing these tricks. This we did and the RAF bloke sheared off and we saw no more of him. We had been up there on top a little time when a solitary tank came up. It stopped and the commander came out and asked what was going on. We said, 'We're held up by a machine gun over on the left'.*[57]

Without hesitation the tank lumbered off in the direction of the gun, straight into the confined depths of the trench lines. The predictable result was that the tank immediately lodged, its nose reared upwards, and became the object of a hail of machine gun and anti tank fire. Whilst its crew managed to clamber out in time,

> *It was soon set on fire and its innards poured out in the shape of ball bearings and molten metal. It became red hot. It was an amazing sight.*[58]

200

Within ten minutes of their crossing the old German lines all four of the tanks suffered the same fate from the curtain of high velocity shellfire which they inevitably attracted. The conspicuous determination and disregard of difficulties shown by the tank crews had been in support of attempts to recapture lost ground within the Bois en Equerre and to push on to take Damery. During the afternoon the LFs succeeded in recapturing the Bois en Equerre, but were again pushed back as the pressure on their flanks, created by the failure of the French on their right and the 97th Brigade on their left to get further forward, told. One disastrous attempt to make progress was witnessed by the Salford men who saw the futile bravery of the Canadian cavalry shattered in front of Bois en Z. The squadron had arrived just south of the Roye road at 5.00 p.m. forming up (in R2 central). Here they were seen by the enemy and shelled. The squadron then galloped forward only to be stopped by wire (about R9 central) where they were shelled and machine gunned, suffering very heavy casualties.

Half an hour later they made a further attack, this time charging down towards the Bois en Z directly along the Amiens-Roye road. It was utterly hopeless. The road was clearly under the closest observation, offering a clean field of fire. In the words of the 96th Brigade's diary,

> ... not a man got within 300 yards of the WOOD as they were swept by M.G. and Artillery fire.[59]

By dusk the remaining men of the 15th Lancashire Fusiliers and the 2nd Manchesters were scattered along a line running roughly 40 yards west of the Bois de la Futaie, across the western border of the Bois en Equerre, then facing towards Damery along a series of posts running in a northerly direction towards

The bodies of determined German rear guards often littered the routes taken by advancing British troops. Although retreating, the German Army's resolve was by no means utterly broken yet.

Parvillers, with little idea of their location in relation to the other companies within either battalion. Behind them, in support, platoons of the 16th Lancashire Fusiliers occupied the old British front line just east of Wood 101. During these hours of the long summer afternoon and evening a succession of carrying parties brought up ammunition to the groups of men forming this fractured front line of outposts.

In view of the death of Lieutenant Colonel Utterson and the wounding of Major Uniacke as well as many other officer casualties, the decision was made to temporarily amalgamate the two Lancashire Fusiliers' Battalions. The following morning it became possible for the remaining junior officers to locate and reorganise the scattered groups in the old German front lines and beyond and these men received rations for the first time in 24 hours. Some were soon cooking breakfast on the hulk of one of the burning tanks whose glowing metal was still amply hot enough to boil a welcome cup of tea. Later that morning the Bois en Equerre was taken following well-orchestrated attacks by the 14th and 97th Brigades and the Salford Battalions were able to form a series of defensive posts on its eastern fringes.

These actions had cost the Lancashire Fusiliers dearly. The 16th Battalion suffered over 240 casualties; three officers and 34 men killed, six officers and 192 men wounded and six men missing. The 15th lost 51 men killed,[60] or died of wounds soon after, as well as more than 200 men wounded.

One of those wounded was 2nd Lieutenant Tobey. His thigh had been penetrated by a bullet during the morning attack on the 10th. Throughout that night he had held on with Captain Watts in the front lines but was now on his way from the battalion's first aid post to the advanced field dressing station. Around his neck the label carried the legend 'WW. GSW. – left thigh'. His first visit to a dressing station behind a major battle amazed him, with the presence of seemingly unflappable English women whose accents and demeanour he found very reassuring.

> We might have been discussing the local flower show... They fortified me with chicken broth which absolutely astounded me, coming at such a place and such a time. I waited there for quite a time and then I was joined by Captain Lord, the man who had got me down to get my wound dressed and had really saved my life by doing so. He had been quite severely wounded and we were taken in a lorry, both of us together, to Amiens... His wound started to bleed in the jolting of the lorry and I had to put pressure on it to stop the bleeding. We got to Amiens and then we got into a hospital train where the doctor joined us who had sent me down with my wound, he'd been gassed, and the three of us went down to Rouen.[61]

Mobile warfare at last!

For Captain Lord this was the end of nearly three years' active service. For 2nd Lieutenant Tobey his front line service had spanned just thirty-six hours.

Throughout the remainder of August the pace of movement and fighting was considerable, the next severe action involving the Salford men taking place on the 23rd August when the 15th Lancashire Fusiliers were holding trenches at Lihons with their sister battalion further north, to the east of Framerville in front of Herleville. In this area and north to the banks of the Somme the 32nd Division and the 1st Australian Division succeeded in pushing forward to capture Herleville, Chuignolles and Chuignes villages. Whilst this action cost the 16th Lancashire Fusiliers few casualties,[62] two days later the still inexperienced men were subjected to a devastatingly heavy mustard-gas shelling, which left 15 officers and 429 men as casualties to its effects. During the course of August 1918 the 16th Lancashire Fusiliers, in so far as they had existed four weeks earlier, had been destroyed by the severity of the actions they were engaged in. However, further drafts continued to be incorporated into the units.

These early phases of the 32nd Division's advance took the 15th and 16th LFs on an easterly march in the direction of St. Quentin and its canal, which formed an integral part of the Hindenberg Line defences. By 30th August the men were encamped at Misery. They were 2,000 yards west of the St. Quentin canal, and roughly five miles south of Peronne.

On 10th September the 2nd Salfords arrived in the front lines at Villeveque, taking Attilly the following day and then moving forward to Holnon Wood, just a stone's throw away from their positions on 1st April 1917. By the 12th the men had advanced to the eastern edge of Holnon and were within sight of the acres of wire which protected the Hindenberg Lines. In preparation for what would be a colossal attack the Pals were rested for two weeks.

If it could be achieved, the storming of the Hindenberg Lines by the Fourth Army would be a monstrous blow to the German power of resistance. The St. Quentin canal, and the slopes above it, were regarded by both sides as a vital natural position of strength, the loss or gain of which would swiftly alter the psychological balance of morale. The attack which the Fourth Army planned against these positions was an extraordinary combination of Allied power, consisting of IX Corps opposite Bellenglise, the Australian-American Corps opposite Bellicourt and III Corps opposite Vendhuille. The French First Army was on IX Corps' left.

During the intensely misty morning of the 29th September, from their positions at Le Verguier, the Salfords heard the 46th Division storming the canal, establishing a bridgehead on the eastern banks by 8.40 a.m. This success was followed up by the men in the 32nd Division's 96th Brigade who crossed the

The St. Quentin Canal, a few days after its crossing by the advancing Salford Pals.

St. Quentin canal lines at 3.00 p.m. en route towards to Magny-la-Fosse, where preparations were undertaken for the attack on the village of Joncourt, which was due to take place within hours. The penetration across a major defensive and water obstacle was almost unprecedented in its speed and depth.

The Attack at Joncourt

The following day the 1st Salfords attacked Joncourt, 2,000 yards north east of Magny la Fosse. The severe nature of the action was described in detail by Lieutenant Platt, now attached to those 15th Lancashire Fusiliers in command of D Company who were in support to the attack delivered by A and B Companies on the village.

> *Amongst other orders that we had received there was one that we must mark all prisoners that we took with the divisional sign on the forehead in indelible pencil in order that the division's captures might be accurately accounted for, thus robbing the Major General of none of the glory due to him.*
>
> *By this time we were at the bottom of a slight slope which stretched upwards to our left front; here a few shells came over and we turned half-left at the same time coming into 'artillery formation' ready to extend when and if we came under rifle or machine-gun fire. I now had a formation roughly diamond shaped with No. 13 platoon at the apex... We advanced like this for some five hundred yards, all the time working up the slope, over the top of which by this time the front line – A and B Coys – had disappeared. On the way we passed several machine gun posts in pits and some infantry posts of the Royal Scots.*
>
> *Almost as soon as the front line appeared on the crest and passed down the other side a fairly hot machine-gun fire broke out at, I judged, a long range, as a good many of the bullets were falling short of us. Also two or three Bosche field guns became active in our vicinity. I then*

Route taken by Fourth Army during August – October 1918.

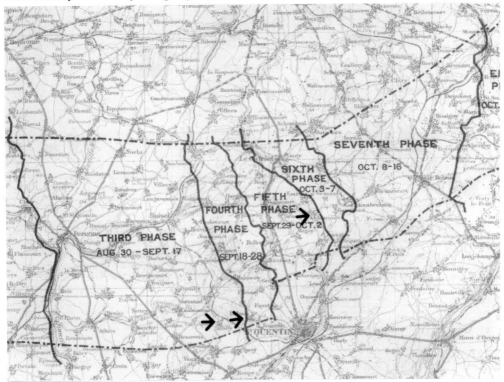

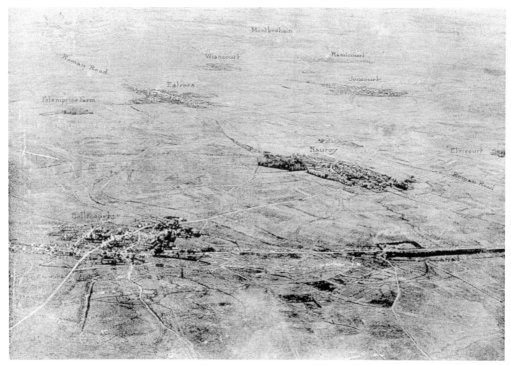

The villages of Bellicourt, Joncourt and Ramicourt.

signalled to the company to fall into 'artillery formation' of sections, that is to say, the four sections of each platoon were to open out in the same way as the platoons themselves had done previously, thus giving an even more scattered target to the Boshe gunners... In this formation we carried on until we were just under the crest, when I extended the company into two single lines. We then went over the crest...

At this point the men of C Company could see that A and B Companies were being badly shot up by machine-gun fire. Platt's own Company began to suffer casualties and he was then ordered to reinforce A and B Companies' attack on the village.

We were now I suppose about four hundred yards from the Bosche, so that it was necessary to advance by fairly short sharp rushes, one line at a time. The first rush was greeted with bursts of machine-gun and rifle fire and I lost several men in the process of advancing about fifty yards. About twenty yards in front of where my first line lay down I suddenly saw a narrow, shallow cable trench running parallel with us and then turning in the direction we had to go. A brain-wave struck me! Why advance over the top – probably at a heavy cost – when we could, by using the trench, make the same amount of ground with a certain amount of cover all the time? The deployment at the other end from Indian file to line would certainly be difficult and probably expensive; but after weighing up the 'pros and cons' I decided to use the trench.

The next rush therefore took the front line – Platoons No. 13 and 14 and Coy HQ – into the trench, which proved to be about waist high, although sometimes deeper and just broad enough to allow a man to walk along it.

We at once moved along to the right, and the second line of the company then joined upon our left in the trench.

The trench almost immediately turned to our front. I was in high hopes of getting along quickly. However I found the trench being the only bit of cover in the neighbourhood – nearly blocked at every step. The infantry who had advanced thus far in the attack the day before were

*holding it more or less as their front line;
casualties of the front two companies of our
battalion had crawled into shelter there, and those
that mere able were attempting to come down it to
the rear. The dead also helped to increase the
congestion; it was with the greatest of difficulty
that we managed to get forward.*

*The machine-guns seemed to be firing harder
than ever and with the upper halves of our bodies
well above ground and moving at a snail's pace,
we no doubt made an excellent target. It was
certainly wise – if it was unsoldierty——to keep
one's head down as low as possible.*

*'The bombardment of the Joncourt defences'
about which we had heard so much in Operation
orders, and so little in the attack, had obviously
made no impression on the Bosche, which never
was likely, considering that our gunners only put
over about 30 or 40 'eighteen pounders'
altogether.*

*"The final act of a German machine-gunner,
always our most formidable opponent."*

*About this time the Bosche 'whizz-bangs'
became increasingly active, and did some very hot shooting at our little trench.*

*About this time the Bosche 'whim-bangs' became increasingly active, and did some very hot
shooting at our little trench.*

*After about half an hour of this I came within about twenty yards of a derelict tank of ours,
which had broken down with one track in our trench. Here were a few men of the Royal Scots,
who told me that there were no more of their men any further forward. They also told me that
our front line had advanced a little further, but of them I could see no sign. Obviously it was here
that our little adventure with the trench ended.*

*I had two out of three subalterns hit on the way up, one with a bullet in the foot and the other
with the loss of a piece of his nose; and as far as I could gather about 20 men were casualties, but
for all intents and purposes I still had an intact company. So far so good; but now the problem
was how to deploy and successfully reinforce 'A' coy with sufficient men and impetus to carry on
the front line to its objective.*

*Obviously the trench was useless any further, as it would have been impossible to go round the
tank, off which the bullets were making sparks fly hard and fast. The only thing to do then was
to deploy into the line to the left by 'driblets' – that is to say one or two men running out at a
time, and then to reinforce those in
front.*

*But the first thing to do was to find
out exactly where 'A' was lying, and so
I decided to go out and see. I sent a
message to the one remaining officer
and the sergeant-major as to my
intentions, collected my 'runner' and
started off at the double to my left
front. The Bosche didn't seem to like
my appearance at all and the air seemed
thick with bullets.*

*As the war reached its end vast quantities of
German material were captured by the
Salford Battalions.*

Also 'whizz-bangs' increased in number and doubtless the Bosche expected a short advance in a rush. I suppose I covered about fifteen yards, when – thump! a bullet hit me, spun me round and hurled me to the ground. Burning pains shot up my back and although for the moment paralysed I found myself studying alternately the sky and the grass by my nose.

Sensations are so numerous and so crowded at such a time that it is utterly impossible to disentangle them. The superstitions inherited from generations of ancestors operated unconsciously but forcibly; I remember wondering whether I had been killed and if my ego was just taking a last look at the thing it had inhabited for so long. Then my common sense re-asserted itself and I thought about getting back to the trench, I wriggled round to face that way – and it hurt like the devil first then a man crawled out of the trench and started running towards me. A 'whizz-bang' pitched under him and he collapsed about five yards away from me. I saw the blood streaming from his leg and a horrible gash in his face.

Then I started to try and crawl but found it a bit too much for me. Another man appeared out of the trench, ran, and flung himself down about a yard in front of me. He refused to go and pull the other man in, but caught hold of my wrists and somehow started crawling backwards, pulling me along with him. I worked as far as I could, with my toes, and after about five minutes we successfully dropped into the trench. I looked at my watch and altogether I had been out about five and twenty minutes.[64]

The man who first attempted to rescue Clifford Platt, a Royal Scot named Foy, had lost a leg but later received a bar to the Military Medal he already possessed. The second man, Vandyne, was at this time under military imprisonment for a Court Martial offence. His many brave actions this day won him release, but no award for his valour.

During these and the further actions conducted this day to take Joncourt, 52 men of the 15th Lancashire Fusiliers had been killed or died of wounds soon after, together with rather more than 150 further casualties.

Within 24 hours the remaining men had cleared the shattered houses of any remaining resistance and by early that afternoon the 1st Salfords established themselves in a defensive position on the east of the village, seeing off counter-attacks from the direction of Waincourt that evening and night. The following morning, the 2nd October, the 16th Lancashire Fusiliers succeeded in crossing the Beaurevoir lines in an attack on Ramicourt village. Early on during this attack one of the 1st Pals' original and most respected officers, Lieutenant Colonel Arthur Stone now commanding the 16th LFs, was killed. His men's success however was short-lived since further to their left progress had failed, leaving their flank totally exposed. Eventually, having suffered heavy casualties, the 16th LFs were ordered to withdraw back to the Beaurevoir lines, from where they were taken back to Lehaucourt, alongside their sister battalion, early on the morning of 3rd October.

This period, immediately up to and following the crossing of the St. Quentin Canal, was necessarily marked by a slowing of the pace of advance. Both the logistical and tactical difficulties to be overcome in planning and executing water crossings were formidable. The immediate and most significant obstacle now to be overcome by the Fourth Army was the Beaurevoir Line, the second line defences some two miles or more behind the Hindenberg defences. The 16th Lancashire Fusiliers had already shown that it was possible to breach these lines and further attacks during the period October 3rd–5th took the Fourth Army past the Beaurevoir lines. From October 8th the pace was picked up again as the advance took a slightly more northerly direction towards Avesnes, before reaching the Sambre-Oise Canal which would itself have to be negotiated. For the 1st and 2nd Salford Battalions the actions at Happegarbes and on the banks of the Sambre-Oise Canal would be their last fighting of the war. In many ways it would also become the most remarkable testimony to their powers of endurance and bravery and shows how disciplined and effective this extraordinary collection of battle-hardened volunteers, Derby scheme drafts, conscripts and nineteen-year-old soldiers could be.

The Happegarbes Spur – actions at Landrecies
As the October of 1918 drew to a close it was becoming clear that the war in France had run its course. The German Army was unable to sustain itself in the field and was desperately reorganising, attempting to shorten their lines and hold together in preparation for winter. One hope of finding a defensible

position lay along the Sambre-Oise Canal. Roughly forty feet wide at water level and seventy-five feet wide from bank to bank, its waters had been diverted to turn the shallow fields on its western banks into quagmires. On the eastern side of the canal a series of low lying hills afforded observation and the chance for German artillery to control any potential bridging points.

In preparation for the forcing of the canal, due to be effected on 4th November, actions were undertaken on the 2nd to take control of the Happegarbes Spur, whose elevated ground caused a steep turn in the canal's course just south west of Landrecies. Control of the spur would allow some British observation over the canal for two miles southwards, past Ors towards Catillon, and northwards for an equal distance. Therefore no crossing could be easily accomplished in this area without the control of this ground and the 15th Lancashire Fusiliers were given the task of its capture. At 6.00 a.m. on the 2nd the battalion attacked the Spur with the support of three tanks, two of which were quickly knocked out. During the next two hours the Spur was gradually taken by the Fusiliers, a particularly brave part in these actions being undertaken by Sergeant (acting CSM) J. Clarke (37721) who was responsible together with men from his platoon for the capture of seven machine guns and many prisoners. In all 62 prisoners belonging to the 6th Cyclist Brigade were taken and a great number of the enemy killed. A defensive line was established on the railway line which cut through the Spur. A counter-attack on the left flank at 9.00 a.m., was initially driven off but gradually, through the position's exposure and its liability to shellfire, the Spur became increasingly untenable. Having previously saturated the area with gas shells and under the protection of a heavy bombardment at 2.00 p.m., the Germans penetrated the Fusiliers' lines and the 15th Lancashire Fusiliers began to fall back towards their starting positions. The SOS barrage and Lewis Gun fire which were quickly brought to bear on the Cyclist Brigade caused terrible casualties amongst them, the enemy showing no lack of commitment even at this late stage in the war. So severe, however, had been the losses to the 15th Lancashire Fusiliers that B, C, and a platoon of D Company from the 16th Battalion were sent up to support their comrades who ended the day back at their original positions.

Twenty-four hours later, at 6.15 a.m., the first of Salford's Battalions made a second attempt on the Happegarbes Spur. This time the higher ground and final objectives were taken within 45 minutes and

The final phase of the Fourth Army's advances.

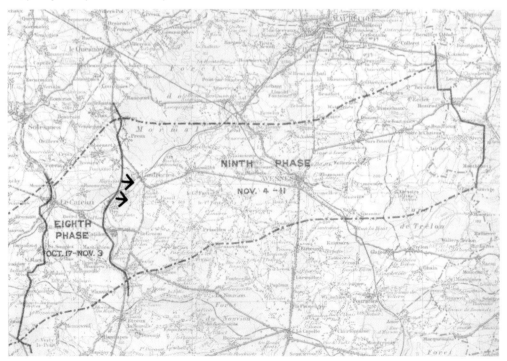

The high ground overlooking the Sambre and Oise Canal.

Sergeant Clarke again showed the greatest of commitment and gallantry in the capture of more prisoners. Immediately a German counter-attack was launched but was repulsed. However, the men's ranks had been terribly thinned by the casualties of this attack and those from the previous day. By 1.00 p.m. the tip of the Spur was being heavily shelled in front of where the railway cutting provided shelter for the German counter-attack to assemble. With one exception all the battalion's machine gun posts and shelters were blown in by this barrage and the German attack from the direction of Happegarbes succeeded in infiltrating between the companies towards the right, crossing the ridge and almost surrounding the battalion's headquarters. This threat was eventually overcome and the enemy were driven back along the railway cutting towards Landrecies. Overnight most of the 15th Lancashire Fusiliers withdrew to spend a further night in the sodden valley west of the Happegarbes Spur, preparing to cross the Sambre-Oise Canal.

Lieutenant-Colonel John Neville Marshall.

The 2nd Salfords cross the Sambre-Oise Canal

Within hours, by 3.30 a.m. on the morning of 4th, the 16th Lancashire Fusiliers were assembled in the orchards opposite la Motte Farm which stood on the far side of the Canal. Their objective was the road running south from Landrecies to la Groise. At 5.50 a.m., after a short artillery barrage, the men dashed down to the banks of the Canal to cover the Royal Engineers who were to erect the bridge here. In half an hour the engineers' work was done and a few men under the command of 2nd Lieutenant Stapley got across. As the next officer, Captain Pemberton, crossed, the anchors holding the floats on the east side gave way. Under heavy machine-gun fire these officers managed to secure the bridge, allowing 2nd Lieutenant Potts and three more men to get across before shells crashed

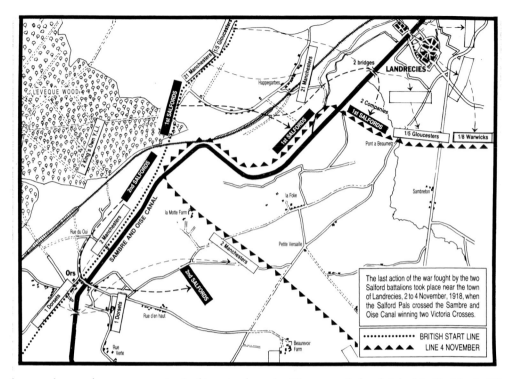

The last action of the war fought by the two Salford battalions took place near the town of Landrecies, 2 to 4 November, 1918, when the Salford Pals crossed the Sambre and Oise Canal winning two Victoria Crosses.

•••••••••••••• BRITISH START LINE
▲▲▲▲▲ LINE 4 NOVEMBER

down to damage the structure again. At this point the acting Lieutenant-Colonel, John Neville Marshall[65], came forward to direct operations personally and to encourage his men. The first group of Engineers and Fusiliers were soon killed or wounded in the intense machine-gun and rifle fire which was being directed on the scene. Nevertheless, other men were willing to risk all and under Marshall's direction and brave example the bridge was repaired.

For his actions here John Marshall was awarded the Victoria Cross. The citation reads:

> *For the most conspicuous bravery, determination and leadership in the attack on the Sambre-Oise Canal, near Catillon, on the 4th November, 1918, when a partly constructed bridge came under concentrated fire and was broken before the advanced troops of his battalion could cross. Lieutenant-Colonel Marshall at once went forward and organized parties to repair the bridge. The first party were soon killed or wounded, but by personal example he inspired his command, and volunteers were instantly forthcoming. Under intense fire and with complete disregard of his own safety, he stood on the bank encouraging his men and assisting in the work, and when the bridge was repaired attempted to rush across at the head of his battalion, and was killed while doing so. The passage of the canal was of vital importance, and the gallantry displayed by all ranks was largely due to the inspiring example set by Lieutenant-Colonel Marshall.[66]*

It was clear that a crossing here was now unlikely and the 16th Lancashire Fusiliers were ordered right, to one of two further bridges erected at Ors, where scattered buildings provided some rudimentary shelter and cover for men protecting the Engineers. Here a crossing was possible and by nightfall the battalion had moved north east towards la Motte Farm, with the Canal on its left flank and the right on the Ors-Landrecies road. By now the fighting

Sergeant James Clarke.

210

strength of the 16th LFs was down to one hundred men, eleven of the battalion's officers having been killed or injured during the previous 48 hours.[67]

Early the following day the Battalion moved forward. Their captures that morning included two complete gun batteries (eight guns) of field artillery, large stores of shells, twenty-six machine guns and a number of transport wagons. The arrival of the 2nd Salfords in their billets at la Folie concluded their remarkable part in the British Army's campaign on the Western Front.

The 1st Salfords crossing of the Sambre-Oise Canal

From their lines west of the Happegarbes spur the 1st Salfords began to move towards the Canal's banks opposite la Folie and Sambreton at 5.45 a.m. In their support two companies of the 2nd King's Own Yorkshire Light Infantry gave covering fire from the lower slopes of the Happegarbes Spur. Again the advance was encouraged by an act of considerable bravery on the part of Sergeant Clarke who brought up a Lewis Gun team through the barrage to engage and silence German gunners on the far banks of the Canal in front of his own right hand companies. By 7.00 a.m. the rest of the Battalion were at the Canal banks, having crossed the Spur and cleared the village of Happegarbes, en route capturing a battery of artillery, more than two hundred prisoners and a number of machine guns at a cost of five men killed. Soon afterwards the two left hand companies were ordered to the north where they crossed the Canal on one of the 25th Division's bridges, just south west of Landrecies, turning immediately south to form the right hand perimeter of the bridgehead there. During the night the remainder of the battalion came across to join these men and the 15th Lancashire Fusiliers advanced towards Sambreton on the road running south of Landrecies. This was the concluding action of the Salford Pals in the war.

For his tenacious and gallant contribution in ensuring a successful outcome to these actions James Clarke was awarded the Victoria Cross. The lengthy citation reads,

> For most conspicuous bravery and initiative during the attack at Happegarbeg on November 2nd, 1918, when in command of a platoon. He led his men forward with great determination, and, on being held up by heavy machine-gun fire, rushed forward through a thick, strongly held hedge, captured in succession four machine-guns, and single handed bayoneted the crews.
>
> Later he led the remnants of his platoon to the capture of three machine-guns and many prisoners.

The lock and bridge at Landrecies.

In the later stages of the attack on the same day, when his platoon was held up by enemy machine guns, he successfully led a tank against them over very exposed ground.

Continuing the attack on November 3rd, after capturing many prisoners and gaining his objective, he organised his line most skilfully and held up the enemy.

On November 4th, in the attack on the Oise-Sambre Canal, under heavy fire from the canal bank, he rushed forward with a Lewis-gun team in the face of an intense barrage, brought the gun into action, effectively silenced the enemy's fire thus enabling his company to advance and gain their objectives.

Throughout the whole of these operations Sergeant Clarke acted with magnificent bravery and total disregard of personal safety and by his gallantry and high sense of duty set an inspiring example to all ranks.[68]

Since the last phase of the war had begun, with the great blow outside Amiens on 8th August, the 15th and 16th Lancashire Fusiliers, the Salford Pals, had seen more than 360 of their number killed or later died from their wounds. On top of these horrific statistics the two battalions also suffered an estimated 1,100 further casualties between them, ranging from those suffering the effects of gas poisoning and the consequences of shell splinters, shrapnel and bullet wounds, which were the men's lot in these final months of warfare, through to the terrible anxiety for the missing. During the actions which were undertaken to cross the Sambre-Oise Canal the 96th Brigade had lost forty officers and 613 other ranks. The figures represented a continuation of an incredibly severe period of mobile warfare and fighting during which the supply and quartermaster's staff had worked an almost miraculous performance in maintaining the surviving men's spirits with a steady and substantial volume of material, rations and ammunition. The notion that the British Army was merely occupying ground given up by a badly beaten foe was folly. This was an interval of atrocious conflict in which the personnel of the 15th and 16th Lancashire Fusiliers gave enormous sacrifice in pursuit of victory. In terms of its contribution to the folklore and history of the First World War these events would never rival the Somme's influence on the nation's consciousness, but in terms of grievous loss the last 100 days were at least its equal in cost to the borough of Salford.

At 3.00 p.m., on the afternoon of 8th November, Lieutenant-Colonel Marshall was buried in the military extension to Ors communal cemetery. Also buried in the same tiny cemetery was Wilfred Owen, killed the same morning as James Marshall, during the same actions whilst serving with the 2nd Manchesters. Present at the funeral were the G.O.C. 32nd Division, Major-General Lambert, Brigadier General Girdwood commanding the 96th Infantry Brigade together with representatives of the two Salford and the 2nd Manchester battalions which, since February of that year, had constituted the 96th Brigade.

Notes

1. S.C.R. 8/7/1916.
2. S.C.R. 8/7/1916.
3. Syndicated, and quoted in the S.C.R. 8/7/1916.
4. S.C.R. 15/7/1916.
5. S.C.R. 15/7/1916.
6. Lieutenant-Colonel Lloyd. Quoted in S.C.R. 29/7/1916.
7. Captain Tweed. E&PJ. 4/8/1916.
8. S.C.R. 29/7/1916.
9. Published by John Long Ltd, London. Not dated. In his introductory note Richard Coke says that, 'certain incidents in the war period have been based upon actual occurences'. I am indebted to Mr Henry Sampson, the son of Captain Coke's batman (J. Sampson 19731) for the initial loan of a copy of *Youth Before the Flood*. After the war Richard Coke became an author,

One officer who did survive, Captain Walton, who as a 2nd Lieutenant had been Captain Tweed's Second in Command at Thiepval on 1 July 1916. Walton

writing scholarly books on the Middle East, The Heart of the Middle East, Baghdad, the City of Peace, The Arab's Place in the Sun and other travel books.

10. *Youth Before the Flood*, pp 267-268.
11. Ibid. p 271.
12. Ibid. pp 271-272.
13. See Trench Map – 36cNW1.
14. 16th LFs' War Diary, 8th August, 1916. P.R.O. WO 95/2397. The 2/8th LFs were the 'second line' of soldiers raised within Salford as part of the borough's Territorial organisation.
15. Captain E. B. Lord.
16. Captain E. B. Lord Sergeant Lawton and Corporal Barlow were buried together within Cuinchy Communal Cemetery Extension.
17. Captain E. B. Lord.
18. Ibid.
19. S.C.R. 9/12/1916.
20. S.C.R. 9/12/1916.
21. Norman Blackett, quoted in S.C.R. 9/12/1916.
22. Quoted in S.C.R. 25/11/1916.
23. See Trench Map 57dSE1 & 2.
24. Captain E. B. Lord.
25. Lt. Col. Abercrombie. Report to 96th Brigade. Document 3457/1. PRO. Reference WO 95/2397. Report attached to the 16th LFs' Battalion War Diary.
26. Private William Tickle. Letter home quoted in SCR 8/12/1916.
27. For a full account of the extraordinary defence of Frankfurt trench throughout the eight days see Ch.V, *History at the 16th Battalion The Highland Light Infantry*. Ed Chalmers. Pub. John M'Callum & Co., Glasgow.
28. S.C.R. 16/12/1916.
29. Captain E. B. Lord.
30. Ibid.
31. PRO WO 95/2395, 96th Brigade Diary.
32. Later known as 'Manchester Hill' and the scene of an heroic action involving men of the 1st Manchester Pals during March 21st, 1918.
33. Captain E. B. Lord.
34. The 32nd Division's 96th Brigade was then the southernmost unit of the British Army on the Western Front. The right of the 'skins' was in touch with the French Army.
35. George Ashurst, *My Bit. A Lancashire Fusilier at War 1914–18*. The Crowood Press. 1987. George Ashurst was a Regular soldier whose experiences during the war included First Ypres, the Gallipoli landings and the first day of the Battle of the Somme.
36. PRO WO 95/2395.
37. S.C.R. 7/7/1917.
38. Strictly speaking the Bantams had already begun to lose their short stature character. Since early 1917 replacement drafts had been made up from men of any appropriate height.
39. 20th Lancashire Fusiliers' War Diary. PRO WO 95/2484.
40. 49th (West Riding) Division's Trench Standing Orders. January 1918.
41. Still standing today in the Church of Ascension, Lower Broughton. The simple inscription reads: "To the Glory of God and in affectionate remembrance of Edgar Hampson, Lieutenant, Lancashire Fusiliers, a Sunday School Teacher of this Parish, who fell in action at Thiepval, France, on July 1, 1916. Aetatis 20 years."
42. 32nd Divisional Diary, Narrative of Events on 1st Dec. 1917. PRO WO 95/2370.
43. PRO. WO 95/2370.
44. PRO. WO 95/2370.
45. Letter to the father of Lieutenant Tongue from Lieutenant-Colonel Utterson. Quoted in S.C.R. 160/1918.
46. At the start of 1918 two men who had been instrumental in the Brigade's origins were identified in the King's New Year's Honours list. Mr G. C. Mandleberg, the secretary to the raising committee, became Sir Charles. Montague Barlow was made a Knight Commander of (he British Empire, 'in recognition of his services in raising the Salford Brigade'.

47. The transfers starting on 7th February whilst the men were at Irish Farm, StJean, below Passchendaele.
48. Lieutenant C. L. Platt.
49. Ibid.
50. Account of Operations at Mount Kemmel from llth to 25th April 1918, compiled from memory by Lieutenant-Colonel H. D. Bousfield C.M.G., D.S.O. as a prisoner in Mainz.
51. The German Army evacuated Mount Kemmel on 31st August, as part of their general retreat at this time.
52. Commemorates an action during the Seven Years' War at Minden, on 1st August, 1759, when the 20th Regiment, who were predecessors of the Lancashire Fusiliers had defeated a considerably superior force of French cavalry.
53. Captain E. B. Lord.
54. Second-Lieutenant Tobey, from Liverpool, had joined the 16th Lancashire Fusiliers during the summer at Proven. This action was therefore his first taste of hostile fire. Imperial War Museum, Department of Sound Records. Tape accession number 567/3.
55. PRO. WO 95/2372.
56. PRO. WO 95/2396.
57. 2nd Lieutenant Tobey.
58. Ibid.
59. PRO. WO 95/2396.
60. This information was not recorded in the battalion's War Diary, but has been taken from 'Soldiers Died in the Great War'. Extrapolating the numbers of injured casualties as a conservative 150, the two battalions suffered approximately 440 casualties on this day.
61. 2nd Lieutenant Tobey. Awarded the Military Cross for his determination and persistence this day.
62. 120 in total. 18 killed, 95 wounded, 5 missing and 2 injured.
63. The sequence of four inter-connecting figures of eight, hence 32nd Div.
64. Clifford Platt survived his wounds to write this account of his last visit to France during April 1920. IWM. 78/72/1.
65. C.O. since the 12th October, John Marshall M.C. was attached to the 16th LFs from the Irish Guards.
66. London Gazette. 13/2/1919. The Battalion's Diary of these events gives a slightly different version: '...Lieutenant-Colonel Marshall M.C. and Bar came forward when his Battalion was held up and fearlessly worked in the Canal Embankment encouraging the men in their efforts to repair the Bridge. Fully exposed to the enemy fire he was shot through the head.'
67. The 2nd Pals' Battalion War Diary, PRO WO 95/2397, records the following names:
Lieutenant-Colonel John N. Marshall. M.C and Bar Killed.
Lieutenant Cecil H.Hulton M. C. Commanding C Company. Killed.
Second-Lieutenant Alan H. Law. Battalion Intelligence Officer. Killed.
Second-Lieutenant Frederick M. Livingston. A
Company. Died of Wounds.
Second-Lieutenant Joseph Morris. C Company. Killed.
Lieutenant J. Treelis. C Company. Wounded.
Second-Lieutenant Scholfield. D Company. Wounded.
Second-Lieutenant R. H. Potts. D Company. Wounded.
Captain G. A. Potts. Adjutant. Wounded.
Second-Lieutenant Schoon. Battalion Signals Officer.
Wounded.
Second-Lieutenant E. Lyons. D Company. Missing.
68. London Gazette. 6/1/1919. During the passage of the Sambre-Oise Canal, in the area of Landrecies, the 32nd Division won five Victoria Crosses, the others being awarded to Major Arnold H. S. Waters, D. S. O., M. C., 218 Field Company R.E.; Second-Lieutenant James Kirk, 2nd Manchesters (killed); Sapper Adam Archibald, 218 Field Company R.E.

Chapter Six

Journey's End

Accounting for the Cost

As soon as the fighting finished both politicians and accountants moved in to weigh the enormous human, financial and political cost of the conflict. The grotesque physical destruction of vast tracts of France, Belgium, Italy, Germany and elsewhere had laid the basis for a generation of ill-will and envy which would take another global war to resolve. The immediate human cost of the war to Salford was considerable, and in some ways disproportionate to the borough's size. Fortunately Salford borough was no stranger to accommodating change since it had always been a magnet for immigrants seeking work in her local industry, and the town now set about coming to terms with its lost manhood.

Since November 1915, when the Pals sailed for France, in excess of 15,000 officers and men had served with the Salford Pals. The bare figures which tell of the story's magnitude are identified over page.

The numbers of men who died had inevitably left a gaping social chasm which the widows and children within this working class community initially found impossible to fill. Quite apart from their own Pals, Salford had raised four active service Territorial battalions, who

Private John Warburton and the scroll issued to him marking both his honourable discharge from the army and the burden of disability which weighed upon many thousands of ex-servicemen. Salford Museum Service

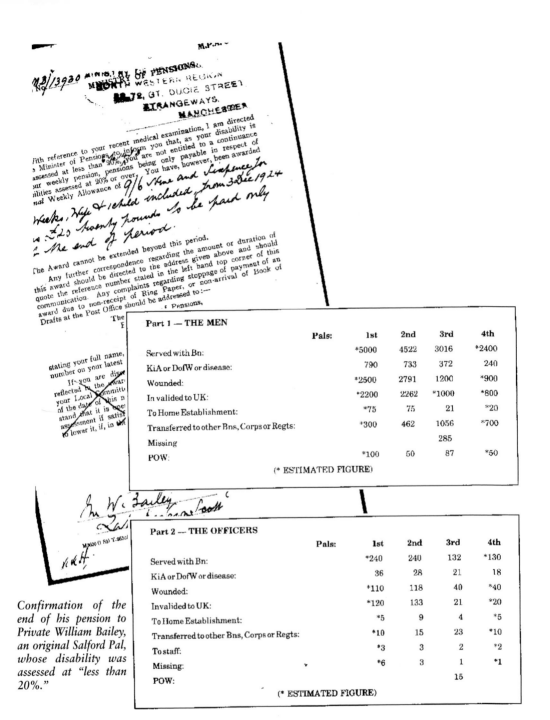

M.P.A.

No. 3/13930 MINISTRY OF PENSIONS.
NORTH WESTERN REGION
72, GT. DUCIE STREET,
STRANGEWAYS,
MANCHESTER.

With reference to your recent medical examination, I am directed
by Minister of Pensions to inform you that, as your disability is
assessed at less than 20%, you are not entitled to a continuance
our weekly pension, pensions being only payable in respect of
ilities assessed at 20% or over. You have, however, been awarded
nal Weekly Allowance of *9/6 nine and sixpence for*

Weeks, Wife & 1 child included from 3 Dec 1924

to £20 twenty pounds to be paid only

to the end of period.

The Award cannot be extended beyond this period.
Any further correspondence regarding the amount or duration of
this award should be directed to the address given above and should
quote the reference number stated in the left hand top corner of this
communication. Any complaints regarding stoppage of payment of an
award due to non-receipt of Ring Paper, or non-arrival of Book of
Drafts at the Post Office should be addressed to:—
Pensions,

stating your full name,
number on your latest

If you are dis
reflected by the war
your Local Committ
of the date of this n
stand that it is ope
assessment if satisf
to lower it, if, in th

W. Bailey

M3609 (I. 53) T.363

H.H.

*Confirmation of the
end of his pension to
Private William Bailey,
an original Salford Pal,
whose disability was
assessed at "less than
20%."*

Part 1 — THE MEN

Pals:	1st	2nd	3rd	4th
Served with Bn:	*5000	4522	3016	*2400
KiA or DofW or disease:	790	733	372	240
Wounded:	*2500	2791	1200	*900
Invalided to UK:	*2200	2262	*1000	*800
To Home Establishment:	*75	75	21	*20
Transferred to other Bns, Corps or Regts:	*300	462	1056	*700
Missing			285	
POW:	*100	50	87	*50

(* ESTIMATED FIGURE)

Part 2 — THE OFFICERS

Pals:	1st	2nd	3rd	4th
Served with Bn:	*240	240	132	*130
KiA or DofW or disease:	36	28	21	18
Wounded:	*110	118	40	*40
Invalided to UK:	*120	133	21	*20
To Home Establishment:	*5	9	4	*5
Transferred to other Bns, Corps or Regts:	*10	15	23	*10
To staff:	*3	3	2	*2
Missing:	*6	3	1	*1
POW:			15	

(* ESTIMATED FIGURE)

themselves suffered substantial numbers of casualties, both at Gallipoli and later in France and Flanders.[2] On top of these forlorn statistics was laid the legion of deaths amongst the locally enlisted Regulars; other men who had joined up in the eagerness of the early general recruitment; the Derby scheme men and the later youthful and aged conscripts who served, often friendless, in any one of the hundreds of distant battalions to which they were drafted.

The watch on the Rhine. Control of the strategically vital Rhine bridges was regarded as an inconspicuous and essential role for the Army of occupation. The Salford battalions' task was centred on the great city of Bonn – astride the Rhine.

Occupation of Germany

Although the fighting had ceased it was by no means clear that the war was over. In the last fortnight of November Germany's people had good cause to think that their army was not defeated. On the signing of the Armistice that German army still occupied large parts of Belgium and parts of France, and Russia's Revolution in 1917 had removed the immediate threat of further conflict in the east. In this context it was vital that a real show of Allied military strength was made to enforce the penalties which the Armistice placed upon Germany's armed forces.

If your unit was destined to be unlucky, Germany beckoned.[3]

Both the 1st and 2nd Salford Battalions drew the short straws.

Throughout the November, December and the January of 1919 both of these battalions initially stayed in north eastern France, clearing wreckage, rebuilding roads and salvaging equipment. During this period some of the original Pals who had survived were demobilized and returned to the essential engineering and coal-based employments which were now desperate for the return of their skilled and experienced employees. The first detachments for demobilization left on December 21st, 1918. Large numbers of young soldiers on short-term engagements were then drafted into the battalions to replace the fortunate men who had gone. Some of the older soldiers had by then established extraordinary records of endurance and commitment which were second to none. Private T. Farrell (10339), who had enlisted into No. 6 platoon of the 1st Pals in September 1914, was an ex-Boer War long service Regular and had completed his period on Army Reserve before the outbreak of war. He had been 50 years old on arrival in France, surviving all to be demobilised in February 1919 when he was at least 52 years old. Not a bad record.

The 3rd Salford Battalion spent their time after the end of hostilities at Douai in France, just east of Vimy Ridge. Here they were billeted amidst the wreckage of the coal mines and slag heaps which had been the scene of so much shelling and fighting throughout the war. The battalion's colours were presented to the men on 9th February. Their service in this dreary situation lasted for six months from 28th November, 1918 to 8th June, 1919 after which the battalion was returned to Dover prior to its disbandment later that month, spared from participation in the Army of Occupation.

Sylvanus Cooper being presented with his Military Medal at a ceremony held in Heaton Park, north east of Salford, during 1919. Greenwood

However, in the very depths of winter's cold the 1st and 2nd Salford Battalions were drafted to Germany.

> We left Natoye at 9.00 a.m., on Thursday Feb. 6th, marching to Namur. A heavy fall of snow made the march difficult. We arrived at the Cavalry Barracks about 3 o'clock, and stayed there the night. On the following day we entrained at 3.30 p.m. for Bonn in Germany. After passing through many places of interest, we arrived at Cologne at 8 a.m. on Saturday and reached our destination about 9.30 a.m. There was not much interest shown as we marched across the Rhine and through the town, probably because English soldiers had been there for some time. But it is an interesting event in the Battalion's history to have crossed the Rhine and we can be numbered as one of the 'great Watchers of the Rhine.' It must be admitted that the birthplace of Beethoven is a lovely spot, and is particularly impressive after the terrible state of devastation in France and Belgium. The inhabitants of Bonn have only realised the meaning of war on account of the shortage of foodstuffs.[4]

Within days of their arrival Major Dunn of the 16th Lancashire Fusiliers established a soup kitchen for hordes of the bedraggled and starved children who abounded. This sort of humanitarian work was no mere gesture. Throughout the final months of the war the allied blockade had led to very real hardship and food for the German civilian population was still in desperately short supply on the men's arrival. In the consequential atmosphere of distrust the 15th and 16th Lancashire Fusiliers were destined to spend a long and unpleasantly tense summer.

Ceremonial duties occupied the young soldiers for relatively short periods of time. Letter writing, sports, concerts, educational and recreational training therefore became the routine of dozens of days throughout the summer. The 15th Battalion were housed in Bonn's municipal museum whilst the 16th were fortunate in occupying a barracks where their canteen facilities were the envy

CSM Suttle of the 3rd Pals, whose record at least matched that of Private Farrell, reunited with his wife in 1919. Jones

of every other unit in the area. Interspersed were long periods of sentry and guard duty whose purpose was to repress the possibility of insurrection and riot. Road blocks and traffic searches were instituted to prevent the surreptitious movement of arms and materiel and to impress the fact of defeat on a disbelieving population.

Whilst here in Bonn the King's Colours, which commemorated the actions and campaigns in which the Pals had been engaged, were presented to the battalions at the Sports Platz. These permanent testimonies to the Borough's willing contribution, service and sacrifice were handed over by General Sir Hubert Plumer, G.C.B., G.C.M.G., G.C.V.O. and A.D.C., to the 1st and 2nd Pals respectively on the 1st and 8th March. On 12th April large drafts of men left the 15th and 16th Lancashire Fusiliers for demobilization. In the case of the 16th this left just two original Pals within the battalions' ranks. On 18th June the 15th and 16th Lancashire Fusiliers were moved to Siegburg and Menden, equipped and ready to advance east, as a threatening insurance in the event of Germany failing to sign the peace terms at Versailles.

During July, 1919, the two figures most active in the raising of Salford's Pals, Sir Montague Barlow and Sir Charles Mandleberg, were entertained in Cologne by the Army of Occupation's Commander-in-Chief, Field Marshal Sir William Robertson. This visit provided one of the last official contacts between

Postcards were the staple diet of communications with home.

the borough and its battalions when Barlow spoke to assemblies of young Salford men who still formed an overwhelming majority within the ranks. The civic party were then present on the occasion of the men's inspection by Robertson on 15th June and watched the men paraded prior to another round of guard and picket duties within Bonn's city centre and on the Rhine bridge.

Apart from the wishes of many at home who looked forward to the men's speedy return, Barlow had brought a considerable quantity of essential equipment: stumps, pads, bats, solid red balls and stubby flags. This enabled a long series of inter-battalion and inter-unit matches to be played out in front of a bemused populace on the sports fields of Bonn that summer. On 1st August, Minden Day, the combined Lancashire Fusiliers' team defeated the rest of the Bonn garrison before retiring to the traditional dinner.

However, the serious purpose of Barlow's visit was a pilgrimage to Thiepval. It was already clear that the fighting in the Somme area during the spring and summer of 1918 had destroyed many of those

The photographer behind the postcards.

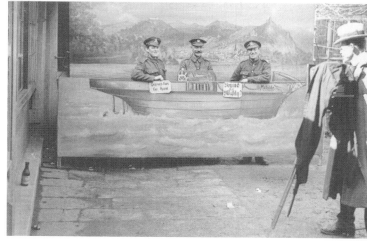

The 32nd Divisional Concert Party. Reed

A group of Pals pose before ceremonial duties. Fisher

The guns of Cologne signal the Signing of Peace, 28 June 1919.

graves so diligently searched for during the November of 1916. On the slopes below Thiepval and Leipzig Redoubt the civic group watched the burial parties at work on the process of interring numerous remains in Authuille, Connaught, Mill Road, Lonsdale and Blighty Valley cemeteries. This was the first of many hundreds of similar visits which marked the final scene of many close friendships blown apart on the battlefields at Thiepval. One such was made by Edgar Hampson's trusted friend, R. H. Royle, who had become curate at St. Silas the Martyr in Kentish Town, London. Royle had been at Mouquet Farm with the 11th Manchesters on the day that Thiepval eventually fell on 26th September, 1916. Three years later he returned to the scarred stumps and smashed stones which marked the site, and penned this optimistic description of the location.

> *Yet the scene is not without its brighter side. Within a mile of poor, devastated Thiepval, shell holes have been filled in, barbed wire removed, and trenches blocked up. Already the French peasants were reaping their harvest, back once more in their own part of their beloved France, living like foxes in holes in the ground, old Nissen huts, trench shelters – anywhere, but full of joy at being home again after nearly five years of exile. At Pozieres a little child was playing on a swing on top of our old battalion H.Q.*[5]

On 24th October the senior Salford Pals battalion was disbanded at Euskirchen, their remaining officers and men being transferred to the 16th Lancashire Fusiliers, the last remaining battalion of the Salford Brigade. The 15th Lancashire Fusiliers' colours were returned to England and handed to 'he Mayor of Salford by 2nd Lieutenant Irlam, M.M., in a ceremony in Bexley Square on 5th November 1919. From Germany the composite battalion then provided an escort, consisting of Captain P. G. Horsler, M. C., together with three N.C.O.'s, who proceeded to Lancashire with the colours of the 16th Battalion which were handed over to the Lancashire Fusiliers' depot at the Wellington Barracks in Bury on 12th November 1919.

D Company of the 15th Lancashire Fusiliers, July 1919, photographed just weeks before this battalion, the senior of Salford's civic battalions ceased to exist. LFM

Back Home

In Salford itself, the contrast with its pre war bustle, tensions and social structure was already becoming very obvious. Gone forever was a substantial proportion of the factory hands, miners, mill-workers, stokers, dockers, clerks and warehousemen who had formed the backbone of the borough's eight active service battalions. More than 2,100 men from the four Pals' battalions had been killed, 1,600 from the Territorials were dead, many thousands more from units not in any way connected with the borough. Far greater numbers were now seeking the part or full disability allowances which were consequential upon their wounds. Temporarily missing from Salford's community were the youthful short service men who formed the bulk of the Army of Occupation's ranks. Their families were already staggering under the impact of an extraordinary upsurge in deaths from pneumonia and influenza. During July and the early stages of the epidemic the poor state of the community's health had shown up in 184 deaths. But now, in November 1918, the figures were disastrous. There were 415 deaths during that month in Salford from pneumonia and flu alone, hundreds more succumbed in Eccles, Swinton and Pendlebury.[6]

One survivor of the war from the 1st Pals, Wilfred Timilty (10130), was a well known local character and at the end of the war had taken to resting upon his crutches at Pendleton tram depot, opposite the bank. Often, when greeting the tram conductors returning their fares, he would joke that he had money both in front and behind him but not much in his pockets. Wilfred Timilty's distinguished active service had been recorded in a citation which reads, 'For Conspicuous gallantry and devotion to duty at all times. His courage, powers of leadership, and his constant cheerfulness under all circumstances have been invaluable in encouraging his men, particularly when they were in action.' Like many other Pals' casualties though, weakened by exposure to gas, wounds, gangrene and amputation, Sergeant Wilfred Timilty, D.C.M. of the 1st Pals did not live long enough to see better times. Like many other crippled and diseased soldiers who had survived the war, Wilfred Timilty became just one further addition to the influenza epidemic's statistics which marked the end of the fighting.

On Saturday 14th December a General Election was contested. It was women's first chance to cast a vote in a Parliamentary election. In Salford the borough's low rateable value and continuing high incidence of social deprivation meant that the previous understandings, which had seen a succession of pre-war Liberal and Conservative MPs returned, were now under threat. Nevertheless, the outcome was still a landslide victory for the raiser of the Salford Brigade, with a vote ten times the size of his nearest challenger. Whilst Barlow's pre-eminence was assured, in the north constituency the Labour activist and sitting member, Ben Tillett, was also returned with a huge majority signalling the town's confirmation of a long association with the organised Labour movement. It was the start of a tortuous

Hohenzollern Bridge, watching fire. MS

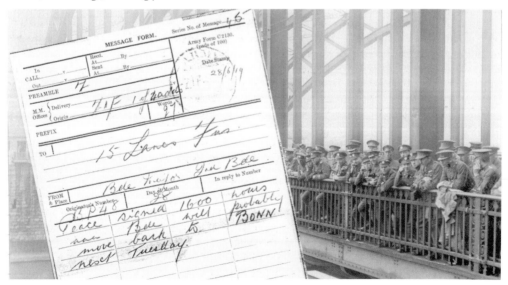

Private Gradwell, just 18 years old and fresh from Salford, engaged on the harrowing work of burials and battlefield clearances conducted by the Imperial War Graves Commission throughout 1919. Sat in the right foreground. Gradwell

decline in the standing of commercial and manufacturing interests as the naturally dominant influences in local affairs.

The progressive return of the survivors, now begun in early 1919, ensured a tense time for many families whose women had become accustomed to doing without their husbands and fathers. The confidence and independence brought about by the franchise and new opportunities to work in the wartime munitions and engineering trades had, rightly, made many women infinitely less deferential in their dealings with men than had been the custom in working class communities before the war. An increase now occurred in the numbers of court cases dealing with marital violence during the months after demobilization, as the men struggled to adjust to these changed circumstances.

Initially there was, as with every other active service battalion, a great groundswell of pride and enthusiasm for the Pals' achievements in victory. Since the summer of 1917 a Salford Brigade Association, with premises at No. 47 on the Crescent provided by Sir Charles Mandleberg, had been in existence. Membership was open to any man or officer who served within the borough's Pals battalions. On 21st February 1919, Sergeant-Major James Clarke, V.C., was admitted as the first honorary life membership of the association. His election was proposed by the 15th Battalion's first Commanding Officer, Colonel Moss, and seconded by Elijah Suttle. Apart from the honour bestowed, the membership also carried a very considerable gift of War Bonds subscribed to by members of the Brigade Association.

Weeks later, a Salford Brigade handbook, detailing every original battalion member's name and regimental number, along with a very hazy platoon photograph was published in the summer of 1919, costing five shillings to the public and two shillings to men who had served in the Pals' Brigade[7]. A first Reunion Dinner for men and officers of the Lancashire Fusiliers took place at the Midland Hotel in Manchester on December 8th, 1919, the forerunner of a series lasting well into the 1960s. Associations of old comrades very quickly sprang up, that of the 16th Lancashire Fusiliers being especially active and having as its motto, 'Pals in war, Pals in Peace'. It charged an annual membership fee of one shilling.

The intensity of interest in the achievements of the battalions flourished during the summer of 1920 when the colours of the battalions, which had all by now been assembled within the borough, were handed into the control of the battalions to be placed for safe keeping in Sacred Trinity Church. Twenty four hours before the Minden Day anniversary the Pals' colours were handed over by the Mayor in the shadow of the Fusilier's memorial statue, on the comer of Oldfield Road, from where they were taken by representatives of the old battalions to their permanent home within the borough's oldest church.

On 17th July, 1922, The Earl of Derby unveiled Salford's cenotaph, built facing the Crescent, which records the contribution made by the borough's people in raising the thousands of men who passed through their own civic battalions, the local territorial units and the many others soldiers who served in further battalions of the Lancashire Fusiliers. The inscription simply reads:

IN MEMORY OF
THE OFFICERS, WARRANT OFFICERS, N.C.Os. AND MEN OF
THE 1/7TH, 2/7TH, 3/7TH, 1/8TH, 2/8TH, 3/8TH 15TH, 16TH, 19TH, 20TH AND 21ST
BATTALIONS THE LANCASHIRE FUSILIERS AND OF
THE OFFICERS, WARRANT OFFICERS, N.C.Os. AND MEN
OF SALFORD SERVING IN OTHER BATTALIONS
OF THE REGIMENT WHO GAVE THEIR LIVES IN THE GREAT WAR 1914–1919

This was the most enduring of the memorials to record the memory of Salford's Pals. Another permanent testament was created at Agecroft by the owners of the area's coal mines, Andrew Knowles and Sons. These mineowner's men had gratefully accepted the opportunity to leave such employment before enlisting in large numbers into the Salford Pals Battalions and the south Lancashire Bantams. The most intimate and telling records of the community's sacrifice lay in the street memorials, hundreds of which were established on the end walls of every terrace throughout the borough. Usually these took the form of a wooden panel, meticulously and beautifully inscribed with the names and regiments of each man from the street who had served. Since early 1917 these communal, almost personal, memorials had sprung up within every part of the borough, usually unveiled at ceremony presided over by the vicar or Mayor.

Each terrible list, set in its hardwood case on the brickwork and visible behind a protective glass screen, made a telling reminder of the calamity which had overwhelmed each impoverished terrace and tenement of Ordsall, the Ellor Street area, Regent, Trinity and the other districts of industrial Salford. The concentration of sacrifice which they recorded, associated with the Lancashire Fusiliers' campaigns at Gallipoli and on the Somme, justified in Salford the end of the British Army's reliance upon locally raised battalions of Pals.[8]

However, the terrible consequences of the '1921 slump in trade were now upon the town. Unemployment in the borough rose rapidly and beggars became an accustomed sight in the streets. Many of the survivors of the Pals were reduced to selling cards, matches and mementos. Soup kitchens and food distribution centres became familiar ports of call for many, even the seriously wounded, who often found that medical tribunals discharged their disability rights far too soon.

Sergeant Wilfred Timilty, DCM. The photographer has carefully disguised the loss of Sergean Timilty's leg. Minogue

Although Lloyd George's Liberal candidates had expressed their full support for the returning soldier's rights and expectations together with the popular sentiment of 'Making Germany Pay', the Labour Party became the beneficiaries of the disillusion which stemmed from the rising unemployment which beset the Government's fortunes in the early 1920s. In 1923 the Labour Party captured all three local Parliamentary seats and the Liberals were confirmed on their irreversible decline as a force in Salford's politics. Two years later, by 1925, the Labour Party was the largest single group in the borough's council.

In the context of widespread economic recession the seeds of disillusion and doubt and the loss of the sense of preservation which had bound this community together before the war were already sown. It was clearly impossible for the older industrial and dock-side districts to absorb the loss of their menfolk easily. Those men who were left now, literally, had to fight for the few jobs which were available at the nearby Trafford Industrial Park. The Great War had created a void in the entrepreneurial spirit of the borough. The death and decline of so many people who would otherwise have striven to overcome the loss of traditional industries was crucial. Salford's failure to actively develop new and vibrant industries during the late 1920s and 1930s meant that employment in the newer food processing, motor vehicle and electronics industries was now concentrated outside the borough's boundaries.

Another group of Salford men return home. This photograph shows the cadre of the 1/8th Battalion, Salford's Territorials, with their battalion's colours amidst a scene quite typical of the return of many men to the borough during early 1919. Concerned about the lack of a formal place for ex-servicemen in the borough's 1919 peace celebrations, the SCR said in June, 'We remember the great reception given to the returning Territorials, full of honours hardly won; the others, alas, came home by ones and twos. Such is the story – five years, the length of its telling' LFM.SCR 28 June 1919.

Dedication of the Colours

1935 saw the final chapter of the Pals' story written.

On Sunday November 10th a service organised by the Salford Brigade's Memorial Committee was held, at which the Pals battalion's colours were finally laid up and displayed over the Nave of Sacred Trinity Church. The church itself was crowded with the surviving veterans of these battalions who listened intently to the prayers in hope of peace and liberty, led by the Reverend W. H. Fawkes who had been chaplain to the 2nd Pals and the 96th Brigade. During the service the beautifully scripted memorial tablets recording the names of every man killed whilst serving in the Brigade were unveiled by the Honorary

The arrival of the colours of the 15th, 16th, 19th and 20th Lancashire Fusiliers at Sacred Trinity Church on 31 July 1920. LFM

Colonel, The Earl of Derby K.G., and dedicated to the men's memory by the Bishop of Manchester, the Right Reverend F. S. Guy Warman.[9] At the end of the service, Derby addressed his old associates, his words were without doubt sage, profound and already being overtaken by events in Nazi Germany:

> *...those who have seen war – those who have experienced war – are the very people who will wish never to see it or experience it again; not only to avoid it for themselves, but to be able to hand on to those who come after a desire for peace. Not peace at any price-you can never ask for that-but that the hearts of men, not only in this country, but every country, may turn to settling their differences not by the arbitration of arms, but by sane and commonsense reasoning.*

'A Memorial to the Lancashire Fusiliers'. Stood in front of the cenotaph is Lord Derby – honorary Colonel to the salford's civic battalions. Surplus funds from subscriptions towards the cost of the cenotaph were used to finance food parcels for destitute soldiers in the Salford area. Manchester Guardian 18 July 1922.

The Knowles memorial at Agecroft.

Two of Salford's street memorials. In the final year of war and during the early 1920s, almost every street in Salford saw one of these memorials erected on the end terrace wall. During the demolition of Salford in the 1950s and 60s almost every one of these remarkable testimonies fell victim to the indiscriminate destruction of social history.

Food distribution amongst Salford War Heroes, 1921. SLHL

'*Two Effects of the Coal Strike'. By 1921 genuine poverty was rife in Salford. Children were reduced to searching amongst pit waste for a few pieces of coal. Food parcels were being distributed to Salford ex-servicemen, paid for by surplus funds left over from the public's over subsription towards the cost of the borough's cenotaph.* Manchester Guard.ian 2 April 1921.

By the 1950s the story of Salford's transformation was complete. The traditional employers in the metals, coal, chemical and textile industries had progressively been eliminated from the manufacturing and commercial maps of the area. Now established with city status after the granting of letters patent in 1926, Salford had returned a local council in 1958 which almost obliterated any sort of Conservative opposition. It was but a short step in the direction of the slum clearances and rehousing programmes which once and for all dispersed the vestiges of community which once gave rise to the town's own Pals, the Salford Brigade.

Notes

1. These are drawn from a variety of sources including Lancashire Fusiliers' Annuals, Regimental History Records, 'Officers Died in the Great War', 'Soldiers Died in the Great War' together with the Sacred Trinity church scrolls. In a few cases I have used estimates where no reliable or official data exists.
2. Apart from their officers the Salford Territorials also lost a very considerable number of men killed and died of wounds or disease:

1/7th Battalion, 560 deaths on active service abroad.

2/7th Battalion, 307 deaths on active service abroad.

11/8th Battalion, 529 deaths on active service abroad.

2/8th Battalion, 264 deaths on active service abroad.

3. Apart from the Pals, the 1st Battalion of the Lancashire Fusiliers, as part of the 29th Division, was also selected as part of the Army of Occupation.

4. S.C.R. 15/3/1919.

5. Reverend R. H. Royle, M.C. 'Visit to Thiepval. A bit of Salford as it is Today.' S.C.R. 4/10/1919.

6. See Medical Officer of Health. Reports 1916–20. SLHL.

7. 'The Lancashire Fusiliers. The roll of Honour of the Salford Brigade.' Published by Sherratt & Hughes. London & Manchester, 1919.

8. Damp weather, and the bulldozers which effected the process of 'slum clearance' in the 1950's and '60's, ensured the destruction of most wooden street memorials. A small number have recently been recovered and are now displayed by Salford's Museum Service.

9. Still carefully preserved on the walls of the Trinity Centre today. Also visible is the memorial triptych to the dead of 1st July, 1916, which includes a remarkable bronze plaque, flanked by the scrolls which list the names of all the officers and men who were killed at Thiepval. This was erected in 1918 and unveiled at the second Thiepval Day service by Montague Barlow on 2nd July that year.

10. Lord Derby, quoted in the *Salford City Reporter*, 15/11/1935.

Members of the 16th Lancashire Fusiliers 'Old Comrades Association' marching down Chapel Street to attend Thiepval Day Service at Sacred Trinity Church, 1932. Their simple motto was 'Pals in War – Pals in Peace'. Walton

Appendix I

Honours and Awards to the 15th, 16th, 19th and 20th Battalions

Victoria Cross
Company-Sergeant-Major J Clarke (15th Battalion):
For most conspicuous bravery and initiative during the attack at Happegarbes on 2 November, 1918, when in command of a platoon. He led his men forward with great determination, and, on being held up by heavy machine-gun fire, rushed forward through a thick, strongly held hedge, captured in succession four machine-guns, and single handed bayoneted the crews. Later he led the remnants of his platoon to the capture of three machine guns and many prisoners. In the later stages of the attack on the same day, when his platoon was held up by enemy machine guns, he successfully led a tank against them over very exposed ground.
London Gazette 6 January 1919

Lieutenant-Colonel John Neville Marshall (Irish Guards attached to 16th Battalion):
For the most conspicuous bravery, determination and leadership in the attack on the Sambre-Oise Canal, near Catillon, on the 4th November, 1918, when a partly constructed bridge came under concentrated fire and was broken before the advanced troops of his Battalion could cross. Lieutenant-Colonel Marshall at once went forward and organised parties to repair the bridge. The first party were soon killed or wounded, but by personal example he inspired his command, and volunteers were instantly forthcoming. Under intense fire and with complete disregard of his own safety, he stood on the bank encouraging his men and assisting in the work, and when the bridge was repaired attempted to rush across at the head of his Battalion, and was killed while doing so. The passage of the canal was of vital importance, and the gallantry displayed by all ranks was largely due to the inspiring example set by Lieutenant-Colonel Marshall.
London Gazette 13 February 1919

Companion of the Order of St. Michael and St. George
Lieutenant-Colonel C. M. Abercrombie (16th Battalion):
London Gazette 3 June 1916

Companion of the Order of the British Empire
Colonel C. M. Abercrombie, CMG (16th Battalion and Staff):
London Gazette 3 June 1919

Clasps to the Companion of the Distinguished Service Order
Lieutenant-Colonel C. E. R. G. Alban, DSO (Liverpool Regiment attached to 15th Brigade mentioned twice):
London Gazette 15 February 1919, 2 April 1919

Liutenant-Colonel J. M. A. Graham, DSO (Attached to 19th Battalion):
London Gazette 1 January 1918

Companion of the Distinguished Service Order
Captain W. J. Brockman (15th Battalion):
London Gazette 2 December 1918

Major W. L. Crawford, VD (20th Battalion):
London Gazette 1 January 1918

Captain J. B. Dunn, MC (15th Highland Light Infantry attached to 16th Battalion):
London Gazette 2 April 1919

Lieutenant-Colonel John Henry Lloyd (Royal Lancaster Regiment attached to 15th Battalion):
London Gazette 4 June 1917

Major L. C. Mandleburg, MC (15th Battalion):
London Gazette 8 March 1919

Captain H. C. Pemberton (16th Battalion):
London Gazette 2 April 1919

Major Arthur Stone (15th Battalion):
London Gazette 22 June 1918

Officer of the Order of the British Empire
Captain W. B. Armitage (15th Battalion and Royal Air Force):
London Gazette 3 June 1919

Captain and Quartermaster G. Holley (19th Battalion):
London Gazette 3 June 1919

Military Cross
Second Lieutenant F. Allcott (16th Battalion):
London Gazette 7 November 1918

Second Lieutenant Gordon Laurie Barclay (15th Battalion):
London Gazette 16 September 1918

Lieutenant E. R. Batho (Royal Army Medical Corps attached to 16th Battalion):
London Gazette 2 April 1919

Second Lieutenant J. W. Bennett (15th Battalion):
For valuable reconnaisance before raid on Houthulst Forest 18-19 February 1918.
London Gazette 22 April 1918

Second Lieutenant R. G. Boden (16th Battalion):
London Gazette 2 April 1919

Second Lieutenant E. J. Brooman (16th Battalion since killed in action):
For conspicuous devotion to duty and gallant work opposite Thiepval. He was wounded three times before he would consent to leave his men.
London Gazette 1 January 1917

Second Lieutenant F. J. Butler (20th Battalion):
For gallantly commanding a raiding party, rushing the enemy wire and bringing back prisoners and valuable information.
London Gazette 18 October 1917

Lieutenant Arthur William Cantwell* (15th Battalion mentioned twice):
This officer during the attack on the Bois de Savy worked indefatigably and though normally in charge of Headquarters' Bombers, went and took charge of a company when the company commander was wounded and led this company to the objective, after which he took a prominent place in helping to clear the enemy out of a strong position where machine-guns were.
London Gazette 26 May 1917, 22 April 1918

Captain R. A. S. Coke (20th Battalion):
For conspicuous gallantry during operations. He took his company out of a wood and dug in in the open under heavy shell fire. When his trench was blown in organised rescue parties, dug the men out, and personally attended to the wounded under heavy shell fire. Though wounded in the back by a shell splinter he stuck to his post for 30 hours till his company was relieved.
London Gazette 20 October 1916

Second Lieutenant J. Cramer (15th Battalion):
London Gazette 2 April 1919

Lieutenant Henry Abraham Davis (15th Battalion):
London Gazette 26 July 1918

Captain A. B. Diplock (15th Battalion):
London Gazette 3 June 1919

Second Lieutenant Ashley Gay Edghill (15th Battalion attached to 96th Mortar Battery):
London Gazette 26 July 1918

Second Lieutenant G. Elding (15th Battalion):
London Gazette 2 April 1919

Reverend Captain W. H. Fawkes (Royal Army Chaplains Department attached to 16th Battalion):
For exceptional bravery and devotion in bringing in wounded men under heavy machine-gun fire. Captain Fawkes brought in three wounded men who had fallen at the wire of the enemy's trench, and several others in from other parts of the field.
London Gazette 13 February 1917

Second Lieutenant P. H. Forman (16th Battalion):
London Gazette 7 November 1918

Lieutenant W. E. Foss (16th Battalion):
For excellent work. Lieutenant Foss's party secured three prisoners, and he shot a German sentry who was about to fire an alarm signal.
London Gazette 20 October 1916

Lieutenant Cecil Henry John Foster (15th Battalion):
London Gazette 22 June 1918

Reverend Captain Reginald French (Royal Army Chaplains Department attached to 15th Battalion):
London Gazette 1 January 1918

Captain H. C. Gill (6th attached to 16th Battalion):
London Gazette 7 November 1918

Captain S. H. Hampson (20th Battalion):
London Gazette 1 January 1918

Lieutenant C. F. Harwood (15th Battalion):
London Gazette 1 January 1919

Lieutenant J. J. Harwood (16th Battalion):
London Gazette 3 June 1919

Captain George Hibbert (19th Battalion):
For conspicuous gallantry in action during an attack, though cut off from his Battalion for many hours he held on to the captured enemy trenches in spite of heavy counter-attacks.
London Gazette 26 September 1916

Second Lieutenant P. G. Harsler (16th Battalion):
London Gazette 2 April 1919

Second Lieutenant T. H. Horspool (5th North Staffordshire Regiment attached to 15th Battalion):
London Gazette 2 April 1919

Second Lieutenant C. H. J. Hulton (16th Battalion):
London Gazette 15 February 1919

Second Lieutenant Joseph Hurst (15th Battalion mentioned twice):
London Gazette 7 November 1918 13 May 1918

Second Lieutenant H. R. E. Irvine (20th Battalion):
For gallantly commanding raiding party. Skilfully rushing a crater under heavy fire from the enemy.
London Gazette 26 July 1917

Captain D. W. John* (Royal Army Medical Corps attached to 15th Battalion):
For remarkable energy and devotion to duty.
London Gazette 6 March 1918

Second Lieutenant R. C. B. Jones (15th Battalion):
London Gazette 2 April 1919

Captain R. B. Knott (16th Battalion):
London Gazette 1 January 1918

Captain Kenneth Ivan Foote Leeming (15th Battalion):
London Gazette 22 June 1918

Lieutenant C. Lees (West Riding Regiment attached 15th Battalion):
London Gazette 2 April 1914

Lieutenant J. W. Lewis* (16th Battalion):
London Gazette 2 April 1919. 8 May 1919.

Second Lieutenant T. Lines, DCM (16th Battalion):
London Gazette 22 April 1918

Captain E. B. Lord (16th Battalion):
London Gazette 16 September 1918

Second Lieutenant J. McClymont (16th Battalion):
London Gazette 22 April 1918

Second Lieutenant Donald Murray Macfarlane (19th Battalion):
For conspicuous gallantry and devotion to duty. Owing to this officer's fine example and devotion to duty, a party organised by him was able to recover six men of the Wireless Detachment who had been buried in the concrete debris, in spite of the heavy fire of hostile artillery, and convey them to the nearest dressing station.
London Gazette 18 January 1918

Captain Ernest Cecil MacLaren (15th Battalion):
For conspicuous coolness and good work when reconnoitring for, and later when guiding a raid on the enemy's trenches. The success of the raid was largely due to his skill and forethought.
London Gazette 31 May 1916

Captain Leonard Charles Mandleberg* (15th Battalion):
London Gazette 7 November 1918 22 June 1918

Captain Ralph Morion (15th Battalion):
London Gazette 1 January 1918

Lieutenant & Adjutant Arthur Rupert Moxsy (19th Battalion):
For most conspicuous gallantry and devotion to duty in the field.
London Gazette 1 January 1917

Captain Hanley Musker (19th Battalion):
For conspicuous gallantry and devotion to duty in the field.
London Gazette 1 January 1918

Second Lieutenant W. J. Nicholson (15th Battalion):
London Gazette 2 April 1919

Lieutenant R. B. Norman (19th Battalion):
London Gazette 2 April 1919

Captain Sidney Arthur Palk (19th Battalion):
For most conspicuous gallantry and devotion to duty in the field.
London Gazette 4 June 1917

Quartermaster & Captain C. W. Patch (15th Battalion):
London Gazette 1 January 1919

Lieutenant A. V. Pegge (Royal Army Medical Corps attached 15th Battalion):
London Gazette 2 April 1919

Second Lieutenant G. H. Potts (16th Battalion)
London Gazette 2 April 1919

Lieutenant G. F. Rigden (Royal Army Medical Corps attached 16th Battalion):
London Gazette 11 January 1919

Captain D. Robertson (16th Battalion):
For bravery and skilful handling of his men. He was in the enemy's trench for about forty minutes, fighting continuously, whilst a rescue party went forward to attempt to extricate some isolated men; when the rescue party came back, he withdrew his men in good order.
London Gazette 4 June 1917

Second Lieutenant Joseph Shiels (19th Battalion):
For most conspicuos gallantry and distinguished service in the field.
London Gazette 1 January 1918

Lieutenant C. W. Smith (16th Battalion):
For skilful direction of a highly successful raid. Lieutenant Smith personally detonated the Bangalore torpedoes and directed the raid from the enemy's parapet.
London Gazette 20 October 1916

Captain G. H. Smith, DCM (15th Battalion):
London Gazette 7 November 1918

Second Lieutenant C. J. Stapley (16th Battalion):
London Gazette 2 April 1919

Captain Charles Alexander Stiebel (19th Battalion attached Kings Own Yorkshire Light Infantry)
Mentioned in Despatches, 7 April 1918, by Field Marshall Sir Douglas Haig, for distinguished service in the field.
London Gazette 24 September 1918

Second Lieutenant W. Tobey (16th Battalion):
London Gazette 7 November 1918

Captain T. F. Tweed (16th Battalion):
For gallant and skilful conduct in commanding his company curing the attack on Thiepval.
London Gazette 1 January 1917

Second Lieutenant Vasey (16th Battalion):
London Gazette 26 July 1918

Major Henry Theodore Wade-Gery (19th Battalion):
For distinguished service in the field.
London Gazette 3 June 1918

Captain Noel Whittles (19th Battalion):
For gallantry. A shell burst on the road, blowing many to pieces. Captain Whittles withdrew his men to a place of safety and then went back with stretchers to attend to the wounded under heavy fire.
London Gazette 17 December 1917

11800 Company Sergeant Major E. Anderson (16th Battalion):
London Gazette 7 November 1918

11110 Regimental Quartermaster Sergeant R. H. Edwards (15th Battalion):
London Gazette 1 January 1918

Albert Medal
Second Lieutenant Douglas Wood (19th Battalion):
For most conspicuous gallantry during bombing practice. This officer risked his own life in picking up and attempting to throw a bomb which had rolled back into the practice trench, therby averting an accident which would otherwise have resulted in the death or serious wounding of the members of his class.
London Gazette

Distinguished Conduct Medal

27849 Sergeant J. Blackledge, MM + Bar, CdG, (15th Battalion):
London Gazette 1 May 1918

27307 Lance Corporal Joseph Brierley (15th Battalion):
London Gazette 3 June 1918

57222 Private A. G. Bunce (15th Battalion):
London Gazette 18 February 1919

2932 Company Sergeant Major F. Capon (16th Battalion):
London Gazette 18 February 1919

11373 Sergeant G. Chandley (16th Battalion):
London Gazette 6 March 1918

12600 Lance Sergeant G. H. Felton (16th Battalion):
London Gazette 3 June 1919

11322 Private W. Fowler (16th Battalion):
London Gazette 1 January 1919

27239 Regimental Sergeant Major W. Garner (19th Battalion):
Mentioned in Despatches, 16 June 1916, by General Sir Douglas Haig for gallantry and devotion to duty in the field.
Mentioned in Despatches, 13 November 1916, by Field-Marshal Sir Douglas Haig for distinguished service in the field.
London Gazette 3 September 1918

11883 Sergeant M. Goodwin (16th Battalion):
London Gazette 1 January 1918

21612 Lance Corporal W. Grundy, MM (20th Battalion):
He showed great determination and did very good work with a raiding party, awarded DCM for gallantly capturing a German machine gun and five prisoners.
London Gazette 4 March 1918

18914 Sergeant Frederick James Haynes (19th Battalion):
For most conspicuous gallantry and devotion to duty in the field.
London Gazette 1 January 1918

10650 Sergeant J. Hughes (15th Battalion):
London Gazette 1 January 1919

17655 Sergeant James Frederick Jackson (19th Battalion):
For gallantry and devotion to duty in the field.
London Gazette 3 September 1918

49289 Company Quartermaster Sergeant F. Logan (15th Battalion):
London Gazette 3 June 1919

19812 Corporal W. McGovern (20th Battalion):
For distinguished conduct and devotion to duty.
London Gazette 1 January 1917

21929 Company Sergeant-Major R. Moyse (20th Battalion):
Mentioned in Despatches 22 May 1917.
London Gazette 4 March 1918

17638 Company Sergeant-Major J. Nuttall (19th Battalion):
London Gazette 3 June 1919

7821 Sergeant H. Parker (19th Battalion):
London Gazette 3 June 1919

17431 Sergeant Thomas Pearce (19th Battalion):
For continuous devotion to duty and gallantry and coolness in action.
London Gazette 3 June 1918

10656 Sergeant J. Pollitt (15th Battalion):
For conspicuous coolness and good work in connection with a raid on the enemy. He reconnoitred the ground on several nights and led the party which covered the advance and withdrawal.
London Gazette 31 May 1916

22843 Corporal Frederick W. Strath (15th Battalion):
London Gazette 26 May 1917

18570 Company Sergeant-Major William Taylor (19th Battalion):
For conspicuous gallantry in action. He showed great courage and determination on several occasions when his company was under fire. He has set a fine example throughout.
Mentioned in Despatches, 13 November 1916, by Field-Marshal Sir Douglas Haig for distinguished service in the field.
London Gazette 25 November 1916

30335 Private F. Thirsk (15th Battalion):
London Gazette 3 October 1918

10130 Sergeant W. Timilty (15th Battalion):
London Gazette 1 January 1918

27240 Company Sergeant-Major Albert Percy West (19th Battalion):
Mentioned in Despatches by Field-Marshal Sir Douglas Haig for distinguished service in the field.
London Gazette 3 June 1917

5320 Private A. Wolfenden (19th Battalion):
London Gazette 18 February 1919

Military Medal
11800 Company Sergeant-Major E. Anderson (16th Battalion):
London Gazette 15 September 1918

39350 Private J. Anderson (15th Battalion):
London Gazette 24 January 1919
52491 Private J. Andrews (15th Battalion):
London Gazette 21 October 1918

47097 Private B. C. Archer (15th Battalion):
London Gazette 24 January 1919

305893 Sergeant J. H. Ashley (15th Battalion):
London Gazette 23 July 1919

18943 Private Ernest Ashurst (19th Battalion):
For conspicuous bravery during heavy hostile bombardment on 8 May 1916.
London Gazette 14 December 1916

282241 Private J. Ashworth (15th Battalion):
London Gazette 14 May 1919

200896 Private H. Atkinson (15th Battalion):
London Gazette 23 July 1919

35736 Private H. V. Atkinson (15th Battalion):
For gallantly carrying messages through the battle 1-2 December 1917.
London Gazette 13 March 1918

17989 Sergeant John Baguley (19th Battalion):
For conspicuous bravery in the field, rescuing wounded from "No Man's Land" under heavy fire.
London Gazette 21 October 1916

18600 Sergeant Alfred Banham* (19th Battalion mentioned twice):
For bravery in the field.
London Gazette 9 December 1916, 23 February 1918

10557 Corporal Joseph Barbossa (15th Battalion):
For gallantry in leading a bombing party in a raid on German trenches.
London Gazette 3 June 1916

37264 Private W. Barton (16th Battalion):
London Gazette 20 August 1919

35792 Private E. Baxendale (15th Battalion):
London Gazette 16 July 1918

305863 Private G. Beardsall (15th Battalion):
For carrying messages and great coolness and fine example during operations 1-3 December 1917.
London Gazette 13 March 1918

39383 Company Sergeant-Major J. Bell (16th Battalion):
London Gazette 23 July 1919

38111 Sergeant C. H. Bellerby (20th Battalion):
During a raid he led his section gallantly in face of heavy fire and kept them well in hand and led them to the enemy's trenches.
London Gazette 2 November 1917

27765 Private S. Beman (16th Battalion):
London Gazette 24 January 1919

18983 Private M. Bergin (19th Battalion):
London Gazette 28 January 1918

11563 Corporal T. Binfield (16th Battalion):
London Gazette 24 January 1919

27849 Corporal J. Blackledge* (9th and 15th Battalion):
London Gazette 2 November 1917

23563 Sergeant H. C. Bolton* (20th Battalion mentioned twice):
During the hours of daylight going across "No Man's Land" and blowing up a chimney.
London Gazette 9 December 1916, 23 February 1918

20039 Private J. E. Booth (15th Battalion):
London Gazette 24 January 1919

202378 Private W. H. Booth (19th Battalion):
For bravery and devotion to duty under heavy shell fire.
London Gazette 13 September 1918

47070 Private J. L. Boschi (15th Battalion):
For courage in cutting wire under fire in raid on Houthulst Forest 18-19 February 1918.
London Gazette 10 April 1918

38215 Private E. Boston (15th Battalion):
London Gazette 14 May 1919

39714 Private L. Brabant* (15th Battalion):
London Gazette 26 May 1917

18595 Private Thomas Bradbury (19th Battalion):
For gallantry and devotion to duty as Stretcher Bearer, attending wounded men in the open under an intense bombardment of H.E. and gas shells.
London Gazette 28 September 1917

11376 Private H. E. Bradford (16th Battalion):
London Gazette 19 February 1917

243393 Private M. Brady (15th Battalion):
London Gazette 24 January 1919

17583 Sergeant J. Brennan (19th Battalion):
London Gazette 23 July 1919

18592 Sergeant C. Brocklebank (20th Battalion since killed in action):
This N.C.O. held on to an advanced post under heavy shell fire and was thus mainly responsible in enabling his company to advance their line about 400 yards. He also carried in several wounded men on his back through a heavy enemy barrage.
London Gazette 23 February 1918

34928 Lance Corporal Fred Chadwick (19th Battalion):
For bravery and devotion to duty under heavy shell fire and rifle fire.
London Gazette 13 September 1918

11373 Sergeant G. Chandley (16th Battalion):
London Gazette 25 April 1918

11267 Sergeant T. Cockayne (16th Battalion):
London Gazette 27 June 1918

25789 Private E. J. Cook (15th Battalion):
London Gazette 12 June 1918

17515 Private Sylvanus Cooper (19th Battalion):
For conspicuous bravery during heavy hostile bombardment on 8 May 1916.
London Gazette 14 December 1916

47102 Lance Corporal D. Coughlan (15th Battalion):
London Gazette 24 January 1919

19145 Lance Corporal W. T. Crabtree (19th Battalion):
For conspicuous gallantry and devotion to duty.
London Gazette 6 August 1918

38108 Lance-Sergeant J. K. Craig (20th Battalion):
During a raid he led the section gallantly in face of heavy fire and kept them together to the enemy's trenches.
London Gazette 2 November 1917

45463 Private A. J. Crawley (16th Battalion):
London Gazette 13 March 1919

38449 Sergeant J. W. Crinigan* (15th Battalion mentioned twice):
London Gazette 14 May 1919, 23 July 1919

12580 Private J. Crossley (16th Battalion):
London Gazette 21 August 1917

22503 Sergeant J. Curran (20th Battalion):
For showing great devotion to duty during a critical period. He and his section dug a new trench when the original was blown in. When the platoon sergeant was wounded he visited all the sections during a heavy barrage and encouraged the men by his fine example.
London Gazette 4 February 1918

49513 Private J. Davies (19th Battalion):
London Gazette 17 June 1919

13755 Private G. Deakin* (15th & 11th Battalion mentioned twice):
London Gazette 27 June 1918, 11 February 1919

10246 Sergeant A. Dean (15th Battalion):
London Gazette 12 June 1918

47938 Corporal H. F. Diprose (16th Battalion):
London Gazette 23 July 1919

37736 Corporal S. Dunbar (15th Battalion):
London Gazette 12 June 1918

12011 Company Quartermaster Sergeant G. Dunning (16th Battalion):
London Gazette 14 May 1919

39688 Corporal C. Eden (15th Battalion):
London Gazette 16 July 1918

25826 Sergeant J. Evans (15th Battalion):
London Gazette 21 October 1918

2983 Private J. E. Farrington (15th Battalion):
London Gazette

38226 Sergeant G. Faulkner (16th Battalion):
London Gazette 21 October 1918

17357 Corporal Arthur Fennell (19th Battalion):
For great gallantry and devotion to duty under heavy shell fire.
London Gazette 13 September 1918

17725 Sergeant G. Fidler (19th Battalion):
London Gazette 20 August 1919

10281 Sergeant R. Finnimore (15th Battalion):
London Gazette 16 July 1918

18332 Lance Corporal J. Fisher (16th Battalion):
London Gazette 24 January 1919

45935 Private V. Fisher (19th Battalion):
For bravery and devotion to duty under heavy shell fire.
London Gazette 13 September 1918

25058 Private C. Fogell (19th Battalion):
For conspicuous gallantry and devotion to duty during an enemy bombardment of our positions.
London Gazette 13 September 1918

21317 Sergeant J. Ford (15th Battalion):
Killed three and took two prisoners at Houthulst Forest.
London Gazette 10 April 1918

36637 Lance Corporal Edward James Foreman* (19th Battalion mentioned twice):
For conspicuous courage and devotion to duty in attending to the wounded under very heavy shell fire.
London Gazette 28 January 1918, 4 February 1918

4495 Sergeant J. Gallagher (15th Battalion):
For gallantry in attack on Houthulst Forest 18-19 February 1918.
London Gazette 10 April 1918

200060 Sergeant A. Gastall (16th Battalion):
London Gazette 14 May 1919

49469 Lance Corporal H. Gear (19th Battalion):
London Gazette 23 July 1919

13239 Private J. Gledhill (16th Battalion):
London Gazette 24 January 1919

38072 Private J. Govier (20th Battalion):
He showed great determination and devotion to duty with a raiding party.
London Gazette 28 September 1917

43439 Private H. C. Green (16th Battalion):
London Gazette 14 May 1919

3403 Sergeant H. Greenwood (16th Battalion):
London Gazette 24 January 1919

63102 Sergeant J. Grundy (15th Battalion):
London Gazette 14 May 1919

21682 Lance Corporal W. Grundy (20th Battalions)
He showed great determination and did very good work with a raiding party.
London Gazette 28 September 1917

23509 Private A. Guest* (20th Battalion mentioned twice):
As a battalion runner he displayed conspicuous gallantry. He repeatedly carried messages through heavy barrages and enabled communication to be maintained at a critical period. He voluntarily attended to the large number of wounded at Battalion Headquarters, often under considerable shell fire.
London Gazette 4 February 1918, 12 June 1918

47715 Private J. Guile (15th Battalion):
London Gazette 14 May 1919

19581 Sergeant W. Hadfield (20th Battalion):
For gallantly leading his section on a raid. He bayonetted a German, and though he could not withdraw his rifle he led his men on.
London Gazette 9 July 1917

57558 Corporal A. E. Hall (16th Battalion):
London Gazette 14 May 1919

32552 Private J. W. Harmer (15th Battalion):
London Gazette 20 August 1919

11604 Corporal H. Harris (16th Battalion):
London Gazette 10 April 1918

3524 Private T. Heald (16th Battalion):
London Gazette 24 January 1919

11978 Sergeant A. Heap (16th Battalion):
For gallant conduct in an attack on Savy Wood. When his platoon sergeant was wounded he assumed command and set a fine example of coolness and courage. Previously he had carried in two wounded officers over a stretch of exposed ground under heavy fire.
London Gazette 26 May 1917

17362 Sergeant Charles Hickinbotham (19th Battalion):
For conspicuous gallantry when in charge of working parties. He was put in charge of a job which had to be completed at all costs. The position came under a very heavy hostile fire, and although direct hits were registered on the work this N.C.O. displayed great courage and set a fine example to his men,

patrolling the work and keeping the men at work. This N.C.O. has always displayed courage in any difficult situation.

London Gazette 23 February 1918

12594 Corporal R. E. Hilton (16th Battalion):
London Gazette 13 September 1918

36442 Corporal George Hird (19th Battalion):
For conspicuous gallantry and devotion to duty. When a pillbox, used as a wireless station, had been hit by a shell, Corporal Hird was in a rescue party organised by his platoon commander. Owing to this N.C.O.'s fine example and devotion to duty, the party was able to recover six of the Wireless Detachment who had been buried in the concrete debris, in spite of the heavy fire of hostile artillery, and convey them to the nearest dressing station.

London Gazette 23 February 1918

202606 Lance Corporal J. Hitchen (19th Battalion):
For great gallantry and devotion to duty during an enemy attack.

London Gazette 13 September 1918

11872 Lance-Sergeant E. Holland (16th Battalion):
Showed great courage and resource in the raid of September 10, and contributed in great measure to its success.

London Gazette 16 November 1916

307245 Lance-Sergeant J. Holland (15th Battalion):
London Gazette 24 January 1919

11915 Company Sergeant Major J. Holland (16th Battalion):
Reported for exceptional courage and bravery during the attack on November 23rd. C.S.M. Holland had shown conspicuous bravery on many previous occasions and had twice been recommended for award.

London Gazette 19 February 1917

27335 Private J. Horridge (19th Battalion):
London Gazette 28 January 1918

39645 Corporal J. W. Horton (15th Battalion):
Carried his wounded officer to rear at Westroosebeke and then organised supply with great credit.

London Gazette 13 March 1918

11348 Corporal G. R. Hughes (16th Battalion):
London Gazette 19 February 1917

11384 Sergeant W. H. Hughes (16th Battalion):
London Gazette 21 October 1918

39646 Lance Corporal J. Ironsides (15th Battalion):
During a heavy bombardment when an enemy attack was anticipated this N.C.O. went along the line inspiring confidence and greatly strengthening the morale of the men by his cool example under very trying circumstances.

London Gazette 19 February 1917

28012 Private R. James (15th Battalion):
London Gazette 23 July 1919

1420 Sergeant Charles Johnson (19th Battalion):
For conspicuous gallantry and devotion to duty. On the camp being shelled and bombed by aeroplanes, he roused his company and marched the men to a place of safety, undoubtedly saving many casualties.

London Gazette 28 January 1918

47061 Sergeant T. A. Johnson (15th Battalion):
London Gazette 24 January 1919

19522 Private E. Jones (20th Battalion):
Stretcher Bearer. For gallant conduct and devotion to duty, carrying in wounded through heavy shell and machine gun fire.
London Gazette 26 May 1917

9556 Private G. V. Jones (16th Battalion):
London Gazette 24 January 1919

235104 Private L. Jones (16th Battalion):
London Gazette 24 January 1919

36820 Corporal Watkin Jones (19th Battalion):
For conspicuous gallantry and devotion to duty. He was instructed to complete a job at all costs (in front of a battery position). The position came under heavy hostile artillery fire, and although direct hits were obtained on the work within a few yards of this N.C.O., he remained at his task until ordered away by the Battery Commander.
London Gazette 23 February 1918

12746 Sergeant W. H. Jones (16th Battalion):
London Gazette 14 May 1919

235449 Private Enoch Leech* (19th Battalion mentioned twice):
For conspicuous gallantry whilst acting as Stretcher Bearer in attending to wounded under heavy shell fire.
London Gazette 28 January 1918, 13 March 1918

15125 Sergeant John William Lewis (19th Battalion):
For conspicuous gallantry and devotion to duty. He showed the greatest coolness and energy under heavy shell fire and by his skillful handling of various parties was able to continue the work without interruption.
London Gazette 28 January 1918

20736 Corporal F. Lewton (15th Battalion):
For courageous leading at Houthulst Forest 18-19 February 1918.

17499 Sergeant Thomas Magee (19th Battalion):
For conspicuous courage and devotion to duty when in command of working parties under heavy shell fire. He showed great devotion to duty and generally inspired the men by his coolness and personal disregard for danger.
London Gazette 28 January 1918

26675 Private J. Maguire (20th Battalion):
For gallant conduct during a raid. He rushed through the enemy wire calling his comrades to follow him and setting a very good example.
London Gazette 2 November 1917

10430 Company Sergeant Major H. Mahon (15th Battalion):
London Gazette 14 May 1919

49136 Private J. T. Malone (15th Battalion):
London Gazette 24 January 1919

13640 Sergeant S. Marior (16th Battalion):
London Gazette 14 May 1919

39434 Private G. Marshall (16th Battalion):
London Gazette 23 July 1919

12035 Lance Corporal G. Mather (16th Battalion):
Was in charge of a Lewis gun and showed both bravery and resource. He was reported as being the first to reach the north point of the wood where he opened fire, thus covering the advance of the rest of the company.
London Gazette 26 May 1917

17572 Corporal Frederick Mayell (19th Battalion attached to Royal Engineers):
For conspicuous gallantry and devotion to duty under heavy shell fire.
London Gazette 13 September 1918

57649 Sergeant H. C. Meddings* (16th Battalion mentioned twice):
London Gazette 14 May 1919, 23 July 1919

17917 Private F. Milligan (19th Battalion):
For conspicuous gallantry and devotion to duty.
London Gazette 13 September 1918

41266 Private J. Mitchell (15th Battalion):
London Gazette 23 July 1919

11849 Private J. Moores (16th Battalion):
London Gazette 23 July 1917

235618 Private F. W. Morton (16th Battalion):
London Gazette 21 October 1918

17779 Company Quartermaster Sergeant John Moulson (19th Battalion):
For gallantry and devotion to duty under heavy shell fire.
London Gazette 13 September 1918

20736 Corporal F. Newton (15th Battalion):
For courageous leading at Houthulst Forest 18-19 February 1918.
London Gazette 10 April 1918

57660 Private F. Orme (16th Battalion):
London Gazette 14 May 1919

36888 Sergeant Enoch Thomas Osmond (19th Battalion):
For conspicuous gallantry and devotion to duty during an enemy attack.
London Gazette 13 September 1918

3688 Sergeant J. Patterson (15th Battalion):
London Gazette 12 June 1918

204716 Private J. W. Pickup (16th Battalion):
London Gazette 10 April 1918

36706 Private Arthur George Pooley (19th Battalion):
For conspicuous bravery and coolness under fire.
London Gazette 13 September 1918

49534 Private H. M. Potter (19th Battalion):
London Gazette 17 June 1919

28903 Private F. Price (20th Battalion):
London Gazette 28 September 1916

29298 Private S. Price (20th Battalion):
He showed great determination and devotion to duty with a raiding party.
London Gazette 28 September 1917

36909 Private T. J. Prosser (19th Battalion attached to Royal Engineers):
For great gallantry and devotion to duty during an enemy attack.
London Gazette 13 September 1919

7999 Private J. E. Quance (20th Battalion):
For gallantry and devotion to duty; though wounded he refused to retire but went forward and carried back a wounded man through a heavy barrage.
London Gazette 2 November 1917

49170 Private A. Riggall (15th Battalion):
London Gazette 24 January 1919

307067 Private T. Robinson (19th Battalion):
For conspicuous gallantry and devotion to duty in the field.
London Gazette

12119 Lance Corporal Harold Rogerson (15th Battalion):
This N.C.O. was ordered to keep in touch during attack on Bois de Savy with the battalion on the right. Despite the enemy's fire he managed to do so, and showed a fine example to duty.
London Gazette 26 May 1917

11672 Private J. H. Rogerson (16th Battalion):
London Gazette 21 October 1918

63206 Private J. W. Rowe (15th Battalion):
London Gazette 24 January 1919

10124 Private Arthur Edmund Roytes (15th Battalion):
This private took charge of his Lewis gun section after the corporal was wounded. Though all the rest of the team were knocked out and under heavy machine gun fire, he managed to bring up the gun and then went back for ammunition, and though exhausted carried on.
London Gazette 26 June 1917

14137 Private F. Ryding (16th Battalion):
London Gazette 24 January 1919

34108 Private F. Salts (15th Battalion):
London Gazette 16 July 1918

201467 Private M. Sawden (16th Battalion):
London Gazette 23 July 1919

33627 Private S. Schofield (15th Battalion):
London Gazette 10 April 1918

27597 Private John Settle (19th Battalion):
For bravery in the field, gallantly maintaining communication under heavy fire.
London Gazette 9 December 1916

51469 Private J. W. Slade (16th Battalion):
London Gazette 14 May 1919

18505 Corporal P. Slamon (20th Battalion):
He showed great determination and did excellent work with a bombing party which accounted for several of the enemy.
London Gazette 28 September 1917

11478 Sergeant A. Smith (16th Battalion):
For digging out under heavy fire three men who were buried in a shelter. He was nearly buried by a shell whilst he was at work, but he stuck to his purpose and got the three men safely away, although they were all injured.
London Gazette 14 December 1916

12019 Sergeant A. Smith (16th Battalion):
For rescuing four men after mine explosion opposite Boisselle, and for gallant effort to bring in a wounded man on the same occasion. He went out under heavy fire more than once, the last time with a rope attached to him. The night after he, with the help of another man, covered the man up who was dead and could not be moved.
London Gazette 3 June 1916

22566 Private C. Smith (20th Battalion attached 104 Infantry Brigade Signal Section):
London Gazette 21 August 1917

11993 Corporal D. Smith (16th Battalion):
Showed great courage and resource in the raid of September 10, and contributed in great measure to its success.
London Gazette 16 November 1916

12244 Sergeant James Patrick George Smith (15th Battalion):
When the company commander was wounded he promptly took charge of the company and brought them up to the objective. He set a fine example to his men at a critical time. During the whole time of the operations until reinforcements were brought up he was hard at work helping the men to consolidate.
London Gazette 26 May 1917

18673 Corporal Joseph Smith (19th Battalion):
For conspicuous bravery in attending to wounded under heavy hostile shell fire.
London Gazette 17 September 1917

11701 Private J. Strapps (16th Battalion):
London Gazette 27 June 1918

53712 Private T. T. Stringman (15th Battalion):
London Gazette 11 February 1919

240308 Private W. Suthers (16th Battalion):
London Gazette 10 April 1918

17866 Private Ebenezer Taylor (19th Battalion):
For conspicuous bravery in the field, rescuing wounded from 'No Man's Land' under heavy fire.
London Gazette 21 October 1916

11794 Sergeant S. Taylor (16th Battalion):
London Gazette 16 July 1918

55066 Private W. Taylor (15th Battalion):
London Gazette 14 May 1919

30781 Sergeant F. Thompson (15th Battalion):
London Gazette 14 May 1919

281195 Private L. Tite (16th Battalion):
London Gazette 10 May 1918

47088 Private B. G. Upton* (15th Battalion mentioned twice):
London Gazette 7 October 1918, 24 January 1919

37283 Corporal G. Vale (15th Battalion):
London Gazette 7 October 1918

10095 Sergeant J. D. Wade (15th Battalion):
In charge of group raiding Leason Farm, Houthulst Forest 18-19 February 1918, killing a number of the enemy.
London Gazette 10 April 1918

238153 Private W. Wainwright (19th Battalion):
London Gazette 23 July 1919

34976 Private W. Walker (16th Battalion):
London Gazette 24 January 1919

12046 Private J. Walsh (16th Battalion):
London Gazette 23 July 1919

34941 Private S. Warburton (19th Battalion):
London Gazette 17 June 1919

3380 Private H. Ward (16th Battalion):
London Gazette 24 January 1919

202213 Private J. Ward (16th Battalion):
London Gazette 11 February 1919

11667 Lance Corporal J. Welch (16th Battalion):
Was reported by his company commander as acting with great dash and gallantry, affecting all near him by his fearless behaviour. He was wounded later carrying in an officer who was wounded and unable to walk.
26 May 1917

21504 Private J. A. Whitwam (20th Battalion):
London Gazette 2 April 1918

12431 Sergeant J. Wilkinson (16th Battalion):
Showed great courage and resource in the raid of September 10, and contributed in great measure to its success.
London Gazette 16 November 1916

201491 Private J. Williams (16th Battalion):
London Gazette 23 July 1917

10956 Private J. Wood* (15th Battalion):
London Gazette 24 January 1919

38162 Lance Corporal J. H. Wood (15th Battalion):
London Gazette 10 April 1918

66113 Private J. Worrall (15th Battalion):
London Gazette 23 July 1919

10751 Sergeant Harold Worsnup (15th Battalion):
During a heavy bombardment when an enemy attack was anticipated this N.C.O. went along the line inspiring confidence and greatly strengthening the morale of the men by his cool example under very trying circumstances.
London Gazette 14 December 1916

40304 Corporal R. G. Young (15th Battalion):
London Gazette 7 October 1918

Meritorious Service Medal
11800 Company Sergeant Major E. Anderson (16th Battalion):
London Gazette 17 June 1918

10090 Company Quartermaster Sergeant T. Ayres (15th Battalion):
London Gazette 3 June 1919

2932 Regimental Sergeant Major F. Capon, DCM (16th Battalion):
London Gazette 3 June 1919

286 Corporal H. Chaston (16th Battalion):
London Gazette

17392 Company Sergeant Major A. Cheney (19th Battalion):
London Gazette 18 January 1919

10893 Sergeant Thos. Cowen (15th Battalion):
Especially for work at Houthulst Forest.
London Gazette 17 June 1918

11235 Sergeant H. Eccles (16th Battalion):
London Gazette 17 June 1918

1586 Sergeant A. E. V. Fossey (19th Battalion):
For devotion to duty in the field.
London Gazette 17 June 1918

11788 Regimental Sergeant Major F. W. Hailwood (16th Battalion):
London Gazette 17 June 1918

10676 Company Quartermaster Sergeant Reginald Hodson (15th Battalion):
London Gazette 17 June 1918

11753 Corporal J. Kelleher (16th Battalion):
London Gazette 18 January 1919

13640 Company Sergeant Major S. Marior (16th Battalion):
London Gazette 18 January 1919

17387 Sergeant J. Matthews (19th Battalion):
London Gazette 18 January 1919

10189 Sergeant G. Norbury (15th Battalion):
London Gazette 18 January 1919

10482 Sergeant Oscar Pheasey (15th Battalion):
Especially for organising food supplies at Passchendaele Ridge, December 1917.
London Gazette 17 June 1918

11443 Sergeant J. Shore (16th Battalion):
London Gazette 18 January 1919

17781 Quartermaster Sergeant W. Timperley (19th Battalion):
London Gazette 18 January 1919

11066 Sergeant H. Williamson (15th Battalion):
London Gazette 3 June 1919

Croix de Guerre – France
Captain J. Hewitt (19th Battalion):
London Gazette 15 December 1919

Captain H. C. Pemberton (20th Battalion):
London Gazette 15 December 1912

Lieutenant Colonel J. Ambrose Smith (19th Battalion):
London Gazette 10 October 1918

Captain W. S. Wrinch (20th Battalion):
London Gazette 18 April 1918

25663 Captain T. M. Atkinson (19th Battalion):
For gallantry and devotion to duty in the field.
London Gazette 10 October 1918

18911 Private Leonard Christian (19th Battalion):
For gallantry in carrying his gun across "No Man's Land" and working it after all the remainder of the machine gunners had been killed or wounded.
London Gazette 1 May 1917

27239 Regimental Sergeant Major Walter Garner (19th Battalion):
Mentioned in Despatches, 16 June 1916, by General Sir Douglas Haig for gallantry and devotion to duty in the field.
Mentioned in Despatches, 13 November 1916, by Field-Marshal Sir Douglas Haig for distinguished service in the field.
London Gazette 10 October 1918

19691 Private Alfred Ham (20th Battalion):
London Gazette 18 April 1918

203188 Private C. W. J. Thomas (19th Battalion):
For gallantry and devotion to duty in the field.
London Gazette 10 October 1918

Croix De Guerre – Belgium
235551 Private Albert Bradburn (15th Battalion):
For repairing wires during attack 1-3 December 1917.
London Gazette 15 April 1918

27511 Corporal A. Burgess (15th Battalion):
London Gazette 15 April 1918

19940 Corporal H. T. Cornish (20th Battalion):
London Gazette 15 April 1918

39645 Lance Corporal J. W. Horton (15th Battalion):
Carried his wounded officer to rear at Westroosebeke and then organised supply with great credit.
London Gazette 15 April 1918

19754 Sergeant J. McCann (20th Battalion):
London Gazette 15 April 1918

22282 Private J. Ogden (20th Battalion):
London Gazette 15 April 1918

16390 Lance Corporal A. Webb (16th Battalion attached to Headquarters 104 Infantry Brigade):
London Gazette 16 January 1920

* Indicates awarded Clasp to the Cross or Medal.

Many men were also awarded and granted Promotions in the Field and Mentioned in Despatches. To these and all the others whose service so merited more reward we regret that space does not allow a fuller representation of their bravery and sacrifice.

Appendix II

Battalion Rolls 1915 – The Lancashire Fusiliers, The Salford Brigade

Roll of Officers

Colonel	Moss, H. B., V.D.		Lieutenant	Teague, H. G
Major	Stone, A.		2nd Lieut.	Wright, C. H.
,,	Thomas, R. A.		,,	Harwood, C. F.
,,	Hartland, H.		,,	Sharratt, W.
Capt. & Adjt.	Best, A.		,,	Lowe, W. H.
Captain	Smith, R. J.		,,	Hampson, E.
,,	Howe, G. A.		,,	Robinson, H. F.
,,	McLeod, E. R.		,,	Wrong, H. V.
Chaplain	Farnworth, Rev. C. R.		,,	Younger, J. R.
Lieutenant	Heald, G. Y.		,,	Morton, R.
,,	Yeld, R. N.		,,	Noyes, C. R. B.
,,	Beyts, L. S.		,,	Inglis, A. W.
,,	Armitage, W. B.		,,	Darlow, A. P.
,,	Mandleberg, L. C.		,,	Rowson, S.
,,	Lee Wood, A.		,,	Lloyd, P. P.
,,	O'Hanlon, S. E.		Lieut. & Q.M.	Tomlinson, J. H.
Captain	Maclaren, E. C.		Lieutenant	Wilson, R.
,,	Broadbent, S.		Lt. R.A.M.C.	Norman, B. N.
Lieutenant	Sutcliffe, W		2nd Lieut.	Schill, E. M.

Non-Commissioned Officers' (Sergeants) Roll.

Warrant Officer.
Act. S.M. Shaw, A. W.

11110	R.Q.M.S. Edwards, R. H.
10132	R.O.R.S. Hickman, N.

Roll No.	Rank and Name.		Roll No.	Rank and Name.	
10082	C.S.M.	Joynt, J.	10534	Sergeant	Henney, H.
10020	,,	Ryan, C. E.	10839	,,	Brady, A.
10697	,,	Carnall, J. A.	10997	,,	Moyse, W.
10314	,,	Rowlett, J.	10279	,,	Sutcliffe, A.
10062	C.Q.M.S.	Boyle, B.	10316	,,	Lewis, H.
10355	,,	Carroll, P.	10231	,,	Chantler, R.
10676	,,	Hodson, R.	10463	,,	Willcock, R.
10231	,,	Chantler, T. O. W.	10527	,,	Creegan, F.
11072	,,	Spence, R.	10718	,,	Fletcher, J.
10210	Sgt. Cook	Hendy, W.	11150	,,	Muir, A.
10112	Pion. Sgt.	Burden, W.	13076	,,	Probert, D.
10138	M.G.Sgt.	Renshaw, C. W.	10604	,,	Fielding, A.
11035	,,	Brooks, T.	10212	,,	King, A. E.
10673	Trns. Sgt.	Stirrup, C. H.	10828	,,	Mumford, A.
10645	Sig. Sgt.	Frewin, A.	11143	,,	Young, W.
13066	Sgt. M.T.	Andrews, J. H.	13160	,,	Stowell, A. E.
10007	Sergeant	Brown, A. E.	10153	,,	Anderson, E. J.
10028	,,	Turner, H.	13264	,,	Green, J. S.
10013	,,	Richardson, R.	10315	,,	Hoggarth, R.
10363	,,	Alexander, H. D.	10179	,,	Knox, R.
10392	,,	Chapman, J.	11111	L.-Sergt.	Savage, F. C.
10434	,,	Bowden, E. A.	11182	,,	Hesketh, W.
10782	,,	Williams, E. J.	10758	,,	Preston, J. R.
10078	,,	Cotton, J. H.	10045	,,	Spencer, H. V.
10021	,,	Skevey, C.	10738	,,	Greenhalgh, C.
10103	,,	Stafford, J.	10881	,,	Kennedy, M.
10229	,,	Pickering, E.	10094	,,	Wilding, J. A.
10524	,,	Bowler, J.	10108	,,	Goring, J. M.
10801	,,	Darbyshire, G.	10587	,,	Unsworth, J.
10135	Sergeant	Hickman, H.	10272	Sergeant	Nelson, J.
10157	,,	McGarry, J.	11029	L.-Sergt.	Fogell, A.
10817	,,	Thompson, W.	10631	,,	Meakin, J.
10555	,,	Barbossa, J.	10260	,,	Hancock, W.

15th (Service) Battalion Lancashire Fusiliers.

"A" COMPANY.

Officer Commanding Company - Major H. HARTLAND.
Second in Command - - - Capt. E. R. McLEOD.
Company Sergeant Major - - JOYNT, J.
Company Quartermaster Sergeant - BOYLE, B.

PLATOON NO. I.

Platoon Commander - - - 2nd Lieut. C. R. B. NOYES.
Platoon Sergeant - - - BROWN, A. E.

No.	Rank	Name	No.	Rank	Name	No.	Rank	Name
10112	Sergeant	BURDEN, W.	10040	„	EMLEY, H.	10006	„	PARKINSON, J. H.
10021	„	SKEVEY, C.	10484	„	FULHAM, T.	10024	„	PRESTON, W.
10094	L.-Sergt.	WILDING, J. A.	11171	„	GREEN, J.	10477	„	ROBINSON, W.
10479	Corporal	WILLIAMS, C. B.	10044	„	GRIMES, L.	10053	„	SEABRIDGE, A.
10037	L.-Corpl.	MAWER, E. W.	10018	„	HAYTON, H.	11126	„	SLATER, J.
10130	„	TIMILTY, W.	10210	Sergeant	HENDY, W.	10035	„	SMITH, R.
10105	„	VIRGO, C. O.	10145	Corporal	THOMPSON, A. H.	10389	„	SMITH, W. H.
10005	„	WALKER, H.	10059	Private	BIRTWISTLE, E.	10482	„	SULLIVAN, C. B.
10391	„	CLAYTON, J.	13159	„	DUDDLE, D.	10052	„	TWIST, H.
10490	Private	ATHERTON, W. B.	10107	„	HEAP, J.	10048	„	WARD, W. A.
11124	„	BAGSHAW, J.	10058	„	MORAN, W.	10008	„	WILLIAMS, J.
11125	„	BAGSHAW, J.	13220	Private	HARRISON, W.	10011	„	WOODWARD, J.
10401	„	BAGULEY, H.	10036	„	HOUGH, H.	10090	„	AYRES, T.
10478	„	BERRY, J.	10029	„	JONES, A.	10022	„	HANKEY, E.
10032	„	BIRTWISTLE, A.	13166	„	JONES, I.	10403	„	HOLLINGS, H.
10046	„	BEALE, C.	13068	„	KIELTY, M.	10409	„	MORRIS, J.
10485	„	CALLENDER, A.	10019	„	KNOWLES, J.	10041	Private	THOMAS, A.
10042	„	CLEMINSON, R.	10411	„	LAUDER, R.	10039	„	TOMLINSON, J. E.
10054	„	DAVIES, F.	11077	„	MAWER, R.	10017	„	WALKER, H.
10034	„	DAVIES, G. P.	10025	„	MULLEN, W.	10057	„	WILLIAMS, W.
10016	„	DOWNIE, J.	11093	„	OXLEY, T. A. W.	10060	„	WOOD, J.
10004	„	EATON, J. W.						

PLATOON NO. II.

Platoon Commander - - - 2nd Lieut. C. F. HARWOOD.
Platoon Sergeant - - - TURNER, H.

No.	Rank	Name	No.	Rank	Name	No.	Rank	Name
10103	Sergeant	STAFFORD, J.	11137	„	EDWARDS, J.	10072	„	PRESTON, P. G.
11111	L.-Sergt.	SAVAGE, F. C.	10064	„	EDWARDS, W.	10114	„	PROBERTS, W.
10015	Corporal	COPE, F.	10498	„	GRAY, J.	11084	„	REGAN, J.
10066	„	NUTTALL, A. E.	10063	„	GREENHALGH, W. H.	10081	„	ROBINSON, A.
10264	„	WINSTANLEY, J.	10104	„	HALLIGAN, N.	10091	„	SHEEN, T. H.
10073	L.-Corpl.	HEALEY, H.	10120	„	HALSALL, R.	13071	„	SMITH, S.
10509	„	NESBITT, A.	10033	„	HARPER, W.	10002	„	SPILLING, J. B.
10458	„	FOX, W.	10101	Private	GRIFFITHS, W.	10395	„	STEWART, J.
10106	„	EUSTON, H.	10080	„	HORRIDGE, B. A.	10076	„	SUTTON, J.
10116	Private	BAILEY, W.	10084	„	LYNCH, J.	10087	„	TURNER, R.
10400	„	BARKER, H.	13143	„	RAWSTERNE, W.	10493	„	THOMPSON, R.
10092	„	BATES, T.	10068	Private	HESTON, L.	11079	„	TWIGG, J.
10055	„	BEVAN, J.	10069	„	HOWARD, J.	10095	„	WADE, J. D.
10098	„	BRADLEY, H.	10087	„	JENKINS, R.	10110	„	WHINFIELD, W. H.
10277	„	BRIERLEY, J.	10086	„	KYTE, H.	10115	„	GERRARD, H.
10492	„	BROWNING, E.	10096	„	LEEMING, G.	11132	„	CLARKE, M.
10065	„	COOPER, J.	10075	„	McGUINNESS, A.	10086	„	ROBB, J. J.
10077	„	COXON, C.	11082	„	MINSHALL, L.	10123	Private	TURNER, T.
10119	„	CREEGAN, J.	10093	„	MORRIS, J.	11090	„	VINALL, T. A.
10113	„	CULLIS, W.	11159	„	NOLAN, M. J.	10010	„	WOLSTENCROFT, T.
13209	„	DEACEY, D.	10495	„	ORAM, H.	10511	„	NUTTALL, A. E.
10396	„	DELVIN, G.	11081	„	PARSONS, J.			

15th (Service) Battalion Lancashire Fusiliers.

"A" COMPANY.

Officer Commanding Company - Major H. Hartland.
Second in Command - Capt. E. R. McLeod.
Company Sergeant Major - Joynt, J.
Company Quartermaster Sergeant - Boyle, B.

PLATOON NO. III.

Platoon Commander - Lieut. W. B. Armitage.
Platoon Sergeant - King, A. E.

No.	Rank	Name	No.	Rank	Name	No.	Rank	Name
10128	Sergeant	Mumford, A.	10206	,,	Gahon, J.	10177	,,	Platt, L.
10138	,,	Renshaw, C. W.	10185	,,	Grayson, J.	10472	,,	Price, J.
10102	Corporal	Flynn, A.	11107	,,	Grundy, W.	11151	,,	Pursglove, W.
10009	L.-Corpl.	Worthington, W.	11127	,,	Harper, J.	11129	,,	Riddell, H.
10122	,,	Hoey, J. E.	11170	,,	Henshall, R.	10124	,,	Royles, A. E.
10131	,,	Hanlon, L. W.	13177	,,	Hedley, A.	13167	,,	Smith, C. F.
10038	,,	Ellis, E. A.	10181	,,	Hill, J.	10184	,,	Stanley, P.
11080	,,	Charnock, F.	10270	,,	Hunter, C.	10125	,,	Swinbourne, T. H.
10138	Private	Anderson, J.	10137	,,	Husband, W.	10183	,,	Turnbull, R.
11114	,,	Ashton, W.	10045	L.-Corpl.	Grant, J.	10175	,,	Vaughan, J.
10125	,,	Barker, T.	10190	Private	Carrole, C. H.	10129	,,	Wilcock, R.
13124	,,	Barrett, H. P.	10189	,,	Norbury, G.	10180	,,	Wood, C. G.
10186	,,	Birch, A.	10454	Private	Hopwood, G.	11122	,,	Worswick, W. J.
10176	,,	Blackshaw, P. D.	10474	,,	Jennings, T.	10140	,,	Davenport, C.
13114	,,	Booth, W.	11158	,,	Kinsey, W.	10111	,,	Cole, J.
10136	,,	Brennan, W. O.	10192	,,	Kirkman, M.	13114	,,	Devine, J.
10127	,,	Brown, A.	10126	,,	Lees, A.	10398	,,	Creighton, J. E.
11130	,,	Brown, S.	10141	,,	Longfield, H.	13115	,,	Ainsworth, S.
11149	,,	Byrne, T.	10188	,,	McWilliams, E.	11083	,,	Cartwright, C.
10173	,,	Cain, P.	10191	,,	Mumford, G. A.	10118	,,	Seddon, A.
11094	,,	Charnock, J.	13094	,,	Murray, J. W.	11197	,,	Casey, E. J.
10174	,,	Ditchfield, A.	10144	,,	O'Hara, E.	10211	Private	Walton, W.
10187	,,	Dunning, J.	11118	,,	Peddigrew, F.	10222	,,	Worthington, T.
13045	,,	Farrell, E.	10134	,,	Pilkington, T.	10142	,,	Clague, F.

PLATOON NO. IV.

Platoon Commander - Lieut. L. S. Beyts.
Platoon Sergeant - Pickering, E.

No.	Rank	Name	No.	Rank	Name	No.	Rank	Name
10179	Sergeant	Knox, R.	10167	,,	Harrison, R.	10207	,,	Pendlebury, J.
10108	L.-Sergt.	Goring, J. M.	10160	,,	Hartley, G.	10203	,,	Ratcliffe, H.
10051	Corporal	Shanks, J. W.	10204	,,	Hutton, G.	11174	,,	Royle, C.
10159	L.-Corpl.	Whittle, F.	10199	,,	Isherwood, J.	10150	,,	Royle, W.
10014	,,	Graham, J.	11075	,,	Hope, H.	10171	,,	Smith, D.
10148	,,	Dennell, R.	10218	Private	Brennan, J.	10194	,,	Smith, G.
10056	,,	Morris, E.	10205	,,	Calderbank, J.	10172	,,	Spence, W.
10143	,,	Sidebottom, H.	10410	,,	Gollins, S.	13270	,,	Taylor, J.
11156	Private	Allen, J.	10156	,,	Harding, G.	10201	,,	Topping, W.
10209	,,	Armstrong, W.	10170	,,	Hargreaves, B.	13174	,,	Whiteley, T.
10164	,,	Ashworth, J. H.	10146	,,	Jones, J.	11155	,,	Gallagher, J. W.
10154	,,	Atkinson, G.	10200	,,	Landers, T.	10151	,,	Devine, J. C.
10195	,,	Beaumont, E.	10155	Private	Howells, J.	10213	,,	Nettleton, R. A.
10455	,,	Brierley, R.	10161	,,	Jennings, R.	11112	,,	Knight, J.
10470	,,	Brierley, W.	10390	,,	Jones, E.	10158	,,	Hooley, A.
11134	,,	Brown, G. H.	11138	,,	Jones, H.	10397	,,	Shakespeare, D.
11145	,,	Corcoran, M.	10163	,,	Kight, G. E.	10219	Private	Makin, C. A.
13105	,,	Davies, W. H.	10218	,,	Lincoln, H.	10197	,,	Millington, F.
10149	,,	Dentith, R.	10402	,,	Llewellyn, E.	10473	,,	Musgrove, J.
10196	,,	Earnshaw, E.	11173	,,	Martell, J.	10074	,,	Olive, T. W.
13039	,,	Goodier, J.	11154	,,	McElroy, H.	10162	,,	Stafford, E.
10203	,,	Griffiths, I.	13064	,,	Morris, H.	10402	,,	Ward, J.
10193	,,	Guest, A.	10198	,,	Norman, H. J. E.	10214	,,	Wright, W. J.
10202	,,	Hadcock, D. E.	10166	,,	Oliver, S.			

15th (Service) Battalion Lancashire Fusiliers.

"B" COMPANY.

Officer Commanding Company	- Major R. A. Thomas.
Second in Command	- Capt. G. A. Howe.
Company Sergeant Major	- Ryan, C. E.
Company Quartermaster Sergeant	- Carroll, P.

PLATOON NO. V.

Platoon Commander	- Lieut. R. N. Yeld.
Platoon Sergeant	- Lewis, H.

10245	Corporal	Delve, W.	10247	„	Taylor, R.	11065	„	Bellis, T.
10275	L.-Corpl.	Jones, D. H.	10741	„	Brett, T.	13237	„	Taylor, J.
10375	„	Williamson, D.	11166	„	Riley, G.	11062	„	Bates, C. F.
11177	„	Fairburn, F.	13088	„	Whalley, W.	13216	„	Hill, D.
10246	„	Dean, A. T.	10272	Sergeant	Nelson, J	10261	„	Harrison, A.
10236	Private	King, P.	10260	L.-Sergt.	Hancock, W.	10262	„	Jolly, S.
10228	„	Greenhalgh, J.	10230	Private	McMahon, J.	10254	„	Baker, S.
10501	„	Doherty, E.	13023	„	Roberts, T.	10253	„	Timmis, J.
10240	„	Broughton, A. V.	10234	„	Savage, W.	10263	„	Spiers, W.
10736	„	Partington, J.	11086	„	Horrocks, J.	10268	„	Finnimore, R.
10238	„	Page, J. E.	10226	„	Greenhalgh, T.	10776	„	Knowles, A.
10257	„	Fitzgerald, J. E.	10225	„	Jones, J. H.	13181	„	Watson, H.
10735	„	Fenlon, J.	10265	Private	Vickers, H.	13211	„	Houghton, T.
10233	„	Bonnar, C.	13218	„	Eldridge, E.	11121	„	Wright, S. S.
10239	„	Gerrard, E.	10249	„	Gilbody, F.	11116	„	Williams, F.
13200	„	Brocklehurst, E.	10271	„	Timbs, J.	10282	Private	Simmonds, A.
10237	„	Tunnicliffe, F.	10283	„	Houghton, W.	13212	„	Hanson, E.
10366	„	Simpson, O.	10278	„	Sheffield, C.	13238	„	Bennett, A.
10232	„	Seddon, S.	10273	„	Wilkinson, J.	10742	„	Percival, A.
10248	„	Dickens, J.	10241	„	Evans, R.	13095	„	Wilson, J.
10250	„	Robinson, A.	10739	„	Henry, J.	10242	„	Matthews, G.
10251	„	Holme, A. G.	11092	„	Hunt, J.	10258	„	Donegan, J.
10235	„	Kay, J.	11074	„	Corris, H.	10255	„	Wilson, C. H.

PLATOON NO. VI.

Platoon Commander	- 2nd Lieut. R. Morton.
Platoon Sergeant	- Sutcliffe, A.

10315	Sergeant	Hoggarth, R.	10294	„	Candland, J.	10749	„	Chapman, G.
10317	L.-Corpl.	Mulleady, P.	10290	„	Speakman, T.	11066	„	Williamson, H.
10227	„	Thorpe, W.	10746	„	Crosby, J.	11059	„	Bentley, H.
10327	„	Latham, D.	10745	„	Pilling, G.	11058	„	Evans, A.
10280	„	Hallam, T.	11091	„	Crofts, W.	13199	„	Edge, A.
10274	Private	Jones, J.	11068	„	Hill, J. J.	13003	„	Soar, W.
10286	„	Leech, F. —	13110	„	Walker, T.	13067	„	Bucktrout, E.
10298	„	Bluer, J. B.	10135	Sergeant	Hickman, H.	13182	„	Burgess, A.
10301	„	Jackson, C.	10300	L.-Corpl.	Edge, J. H.	11061	„	Dawson, A.
10307	„	Thompson, E.	10267	Private	Wright, T.	10326	„	Fay, P.
10289	„	Harding, H.	10310	„	Stewart, J.	10321	„	Garlick, B.
10744	„	Dawson, S. C.	13233	Private	Hudson, J.	10330	„	Jones, W.
10775	„	Atkinson, S.	13090	„	Swindells, S.	10323	„	Ryan, J.
11063	„	McKenzie, J. D.	10343	„	Rawsthorne, S.	10324	„	Wallace, J.
11067	„	Higgins, J.	10303	„	McWilliams, J.	11161	„	Hickson, W.
10292	„	Duffy, E.	10311	„	Taylor, G.	11136	„	Underwood, J.
13179	„	Jones, J. B.	10312	„	Evans, W.	13052	„	Burrows, T.
13234	„	Goode, J. W.	10302	„	Beckett, W.	13046	„	Ditchfield, C. F.
13109	„	Griffin, J.	10305	„	Samuels, W.	10320	Private	Conway, T.
10288	„	Burke, J.	10344	„	Parkin, W.	10757	„	Askew, H.
10295	„	Fincham, A.	10339	„	Farrell, T.	10322	„	Morris, T.
10293	„	Clarke, S.	10747	„	Jenkins, T.	10319	„	Watson, A.

15th (Service) Battalion Lancashire Fusiliers.

"B" COMPANY.

Officer Commanding Company - Major R. A. THOMAS.
Second in Command - - - Capt. G. A. HOWE.
Company Sergeant Major - - RYAN, C. E.
Company Quartermaster Sergeant - CARROLL, P.

PLATOON NO. VII.

Platoon Commander - - - Lieut. G. Y. HEALD.
Platoon Sergeant - - - CHANTLER, R.

10434	Sergeant	BOWDEN, A. E.	10332	„	BROADLEY, A.	10358	„	YATES, W. A.
10758	L.-Sergt.	PRESTON, J. R.	10357	„	LANDALE, A.	10764	„	VIPOND, W. H.
10377	Corporal	DARLINGTON, F.	10330	„	FAULKNER, C.	10351	„	CARNEY, J.
10328	„	WARD, T.	10220	„	RYLANCE, W.	13229	„	SOUTH, J.
10348	L.-Corpl.	SPENCER, F.	10341	„	PHILLIPS, J.	10347	„	EVANS, P.
10353	„	TAYLOR, W. H.	10755	„	GARNER, J.	13086	„	SMITH, H.
10753	„	OMAN, H.	13279	Sergeant	GORDON, R.	13060	„	HALL, C.
10384	„	WALSH, A.	10373	Private	PRESCOTT, G.	10412	„	BARLOW, G.
10359	„	MYCOCK, T.	10337	„	LEES, H.	10760	„	SHERIDAN, D.
10387	Private	JONES, A.	13186	„	MORETON, W.	10342	„	HORFORD, R.
10372	„	BRIDGE, T.	10365	„	HIGSON, H.	10345	„	PRINCE, J.
10221	„	LEWIS, J.	10334	Private	BOWNESS, A.	11060	„	MAHON, J.
10380	„	FANNING, L. A.	13203	„	WALL, S.	10385	„	CATTERALL, E.
10069	„	ELLABY, F.	10333	„	CONNOLLY, M.	10362	„	DICKENSON, T.
10379	„	HENRY, J.	13140	„	FINCH, J. E.	10428	„	PHEASEY, O.
10489	„	WASHINGTON, C. H.	13100	„	SEARLE, W. J.	13136	„	WHALLEY, E.
10752	„	ROBSON, A.	10369	„	HESKETH, J.	10762	Private	HODSON, J.
10335	„	DIGGLE, J.	10370	„	ASHLEY, E.	13144	„	HOLROYD, H.
10375	„	MOCKRIDGE, C. W.	10354	„	HIVES, W.	10381	„	THOMAS, J.
13057	„	FILKIN, R.	10350	„	CHARLESON, A.	10349	„	WILKINSON, H.
13129	„	LUPTON, J.	10376	„	DIGGLE, W.	10338	„	ROSTRON, J.
13116	„	HOLT, A. E.	10356	„	RADFORD, H.			
10346	„	BARLOW, G.	10763	„	MAKEPEACE, S.			

PLATOON NO. VIII.

Platoon Commander - - - 2nd Lieut. C. H. WRIGHT.
Platoon Sergeant - - - WILLCOCK, R.

10465	Sergeant	FREWIN, A.	10433	„	JERVIS, W.	10436	„	CARTWRIGHT, J.
10432	Corporal	TONKIN, J.	10459	„	EASTWOOD, J.	10435	„	HIBBERT, J. T.
10430	„	MAHON, H.	10771	„	LAMB, A.	11113	„	LEONARD, T.
13230	L.-Corpl.	CORE, A.	10768	„	HINDLEY, L.	11115	„	RICHARDSON, J.
10405	„	GREENHALGH, J.	10561	Corporal	GUEST, S.	11147	„	KITCHEN, R.
10456	Private	BRADY, C.	11057	L.-Corpl.	SALTHOUSE, H.	11162	„	DERBYSHIRE, F.
10419	„	DOLMAN, C. T.	10424	Private	SEDDON, T.	10407	„	GLOVER, W.
10466	„	WRIGHT, J.	10460	„	ROSS, W.	13219	„	NICHOLLS, G.
10450	„	WILSON, E.	10467	„	BURNS, J.	10774	„	RIDDLE, J.
10468	„	WARBURTON, J.	13145	„	FORD, J.	10426	„	LEABODY, A.
10404	„	DANIELS, W.	11071	„	DIXON, F.	10408	„	WEAVER, E.
10761	„	CUNLIFFE, T.	10772	Private	CRAVEN, F.	10418	„	SILCOCK, J.
10759	„	DANN, J.	13084	„	RIDGWAY, B. W.	11054	„	MURPHY, F.
10422	„	WOODINGS, T.	13165	„	CASH, W.	13047	„	GREENHALGH, J.
13051	„	THORNTON, J. T.	13181	„	WILDING, C.	13065	„	SWINDELLS, G.
13032	„	GRAY, A.	10429	„	BURNS, G. F.	10442	Private	TURNER, S.
13097	„	JONES, J.	10431	„	BOSTON, F.	10441	„	BRENNAN, W.
13127	„	ROBERTS, H.	10427	„	DAWSON, F.	10448	„	LAFFIN, F.
10444	„	PICKUP, J.	10452	„	BURLING, J.	10420	„	GOULDIN, H.
10443	„	NASH, M. J.	10449	„	CHAPMAN, J.	10406	„	GREGORY, C. E.
10447	„	BLEARS, R.	11053	„	DAWSON, A.	13073	„	COE, J. E.
10451	„	ELLISON, J. G.	10425	„	MUGRIDGE, H.	10438	„	REDFERN, W.
10446	„	METCALF, R.	10421	„	BIRD, R.			

"C" COMPANY.

Officer Commanding Company	Capt. R. J. SMITH.
Second in Command	Lieut. A. LEE WOOD.
Company Sergeant Major	CARNALL, J.
Company Quartermaster Sergeant	HODSON, R.

PLATOON NO. IX.

Platoon Commander	2nd Lieut. W. SHARRATT.
Platoon Sergeant	FIELDING, A.

No.	Rank	Name	No.	Rank	Name	No.	Rank	Name
10013	Sgt. Dr.	RICHARDSON, R.	10529	„	TAYLOR, S.	13104	„	ALLEN, J.
10534	Sergeant	HENNEY, H.	10519	„	WORTHINGTON, W.	13069	„	MINSHULL, G.
10508	Corporal	MOSSFORD, J.	10518	„	WARD, H.	13091	„	WHARTON, H.
10339	L.-Corpl.	NEAL, L.	10506	„	HAMER, E.	13037	„	GOSTRIDGE, G.
10568	„	OLLERTON, H.	10513	„	LOCKWOOD, J. E.	10533	„	DUXBURY, R.
10494	Private	SMITH, J.	10833	„	COOKSON, J.	10546	„	PLATT, J. W.
10500	„	ROBERTS, J.	10539	Corporal	WILSON, J. H.	10553	„	GRAHAM, R.
10567	„	GARDNER, H.	10502	Private	HANKEY, W. H.	10549	„	UNDERWOOD, E. W.
10499	„	FERNLEY, W.	10513	„	WEBSTER, S.	10541	„	WORSWICK, C. J.
10512	„	KING, T.	10530	„	LOMAX, S.	10544	„	HOLROYD, J.
10503	„	JAMES, T. D.	10548	„	McCARTHY, J.	10538	„	HOLDEN, J. W.
10528	„	CARTER, W.	11193	„	JONES, H.	11051	„	SMITH, T.
10682	„	KENYON, W.	10285	Private	HENNEY, H. E.	10805	„	JONES, G. J.
10728	„	BURNS, J.	11184	„	WATTS, G. R.	13178	„	McCABE, J.
13187	„	GREENHALGH, H.	10504	„	BRADY, O.	13085	„	KIRKMAN, F.
10785	„	BRADFORD, A.	10522	„	BAKER, J.	13202	„	BOSTOCK, T.
11179	„	CARR, A.	10487	„	DUNBAR, T.		„	HUGHES, J.
13016	„	LANE, E.	10491	„	IRELAND, W.	13054	Private	WANE, E.
13018	„	FILKIN, J. W.	10526	„	PALMER, J.	10516	„	NUGENT, J.
10517	„	BRAITHWAITE, J.	10525	„	TAYLOR, W.	10547	„	RIDGWAY, C.
10515	„	BORRICK, R.	10521	„	FARRELL, J.	10835	„	HOLT, S.
10532	„	STOREY, W.	10838	„	BURGESS, F. R.	10626	„	CAPELLA, A.

PLATOON NO. X.

Platoon Commander	2nd Lieut. A. P. DARLOW.
Platoon Sergeant	UNSWORTH, G.

No.	Rank	Name	No.	Rank	Name	No.	Rank	Name
10577	Corporal	MITCHELL, J.	10608	„	EVANS, C.	10556	„	MULLHEARN, T.
10616	L.-Corpl.	BIRCHALL, E.	13201	„	MURPHY, J.	10543	„	DANKS, H.
10147	„	EATON, G.	11029	L.-Sergt.	FOGELL, A.	10553	„	GRAHAM, R.
10557	„	BARBOSA, J.	10579	L.-Corpl.	DICKSON, W.	10558	„	STEVENS, H.
10580	„	PATRICK, B.	10565	„	JONES, F.	10570	„	ROBERTS, J. E.
10571	Private	ROBERTS, J. R.	10595	Private	BODEN, W.	10562	„	CAMPBELL, W.
10583	„	SHORTMANN, G.	10576	„	GEARY, J.	10552	„	BERRY, J.
10584	„	HUMPHRIES, J.	10575	„	TAYLOR, J.	10563	„	HEATHCOTE, W.
10581	„	WEBB, D.	13173	„	BEAVER, G.	10551	„	WATERHOUSE, A.
10594	„	WRIGLEY, T.	13210	„	HUGHES, W.	11102	„	MORRISSEY, J.
11056	„	SCOFFIN, P.	11073	„	NAPPEY, E.	13213	„	LAWRENCE, J.
13232	„	ROSENTHAL, M.	13204	Private	BOWKER, H.	11191	„	WARRENER, E.
10591	„	MADDOCKS, A.	11198	„	BOURING, R.	10588	„	ECKERSLEY, J.
10573	„	JACKSON, A.	13151	„	WHITWORTH, T. W.	11096	Private	GALLAGHER, P.
10574	„	GREEN, F.	10605	„	COOPER, J.	11097	„	WRIGHT, H. F.
10593	„	McFADGEN, R.	10602	„	BLORE, S.	13221	„	WHITTHAM, R.
10586	„	NEYLON, E.	11095	„	COMERFORD, A.	10559	„	WATSON, H.
10600	„	COLLINS, W.	13119	„	ANDREWS, J.	10599	„	SCREETON, R.
10589	„	LAMBE, J. P.	13131	„	LEVER, W.	10544	„	NUTT, J.
10572	„	DONOHUE, W. G.	13130	„	DANIELS, E.	10566	„	ORR, G.
11098	„	HAYES, H.	13134	„	HOUGHTON, A.	10560	„	PARKER, E.

15th (Service) Battalion Lancashire Fusiliers.

"C" COMPANY.

Officer Commanding Company	- Capt. R. J. SMITH.
Second in Command	- Lieut. A. LEE WOOD.
Company Sergeant Major	- CARNALL, J.
Company Quartermaster Sergeant	- HODSON, R.

PLATOON NO. XI.

Platoon Commander	- 2nd Lieut. W. H. LOWE.
Platoon Sergeant	- CREEGAN, F.

No.	Rank	Name	No.	Rank	Name	No.	Rank	Name
10600	Corporal	TEE, L. B.	13014	„	NASH, T.	13164	„	HOPWOOD, H.
10394	„	ADAMS, N.	13024	„	MARRS, D.	13185	„	SHEDLOCK, J.
10672	„	McKINNELL, A.	13026	„	SMITH, A.	10657	„	GILL, S.
10619	L.-Corpl.	COLLINS, R.	13241	„	MYERS, L. W.	10662	„	ECKERSLEY, R.
10665	„	MILLS, S.	13280	„	DODD, S.	10661	„	WEBB, J.
10615	Private	BIRCHALL, H.	10312	R.O.R.S.	HICKMAN, N.	10663	„	WINSTANLEY, H.
10612	„	THOMAS, R.	11072	C.Q.M.S.	SPENCE, R.	10668	„	CONWAY, F.
10617	„	TAYLOR, A.	10613	L.-Sergt.	MEAKIN, J.	10669	„	GREENHALGH, H.
10624	„	YATES, C.	10613	Private	MOSS, J.	10664	„	TAYLOR, J.
10622	„	CRENNEL, F.	10621	„	MOHAN, E. H.	10730	„	BUCKLEY, T.
10618	„	HARGREAVES, S.	10628	„	SHENTON, R.	13195	„	STEPHENSON, H.
11045	„	SNAITH, H.	10633	„	DODD, A.	13030	„	SMITH, C.
11100	„	LEE, R.	10540	Private	HOWARTH, W.	11199	„	HOWARTH, H.
13098	„	BURKE, R.	10610	„	ATHERTON, S.	11192	„	EMBURY, T.
13005	„	JONES, I.	10644	„	DORNING, W.	10886	„	AVERY, A.
10632	„	SHENTON, E.	10643	„	BARCROFT, T.		„	SHARPLES, E.
10638	„	ARCHER, S.	10642	„	McKIERNAN, J.	10648	Private	CRAM, J.
10637	„	CODLIN, J.	10641	„	SEVILLE, H.	10654	„	COURTIS, C.
10635	„	WALLACE, R.	10645	„	COWBURN, C.	10658	„	BEGLEY, F.
10639	„	BRIGGS, A.	10651	„	CRENNEL, W.	10660	„	BATES, W.
10646	„	DUNNE, E. J.	10650	„	HUGHES, J.	10731	„	SHAW, J.
11099	„	LEWIS, E.	10649	„	HUFTON, C.	10647	„	BARROW, R. H.
13012	„	FEENEY, T.	10729	„	HILL, F.			

PLATOON NO. XII.

Platoon Commander	- 2nd Lieut. J. R. YOUNGER.
Platoon Sergeant	- BOWLER, J.

No.	Rank	Name	No.	Rank	Name	No.	Rank	Name
10718	Sergeant	FLETCHER, J.	10690	„	FODEN, E.	13197	„	HUGHES, J.
10392	„	CHAPMAN, J.	10687	„	GREGORY, E.	13217	„	HUGHES, J.
10667	Corporal	BURGESS, C.	10688	„	O'BRIEN, J. H.	13015	„	HOWARD, J.
10671	L.-Corpl.	MOUNTAIN, W.	10700	„	BUNN, C.	13117	„	DAVIES, J. W.
10712	„	DAWSON, W.	11106	„	GREGORY, H.	11050	„	BUCKLEY, J.
10678	„	CONNOR, H.	13049	„	TOOLAN, J.	10719	„	WILLIAMS, S.
10675	Private	LAWTON, W.	10673	Sergeant	STIRRUP, A.	10717	„	HAWTHORNE, W.
10684	„	CHAMBERS, W.	10677	Corporal	DOOLEY, J.	10721	„	CHAMBERS, T.
10683	„	McDERMOTT, T.	10680	Private	BODEN, T.	10720	„	KIRBY, W.
10685	„	BOWER, T.	10696	„	BRANNICK, W.	10722	„	SMITH, T. H.
10679	„	HAYWARD, C.	10691	„	BROADHEAD, A.	10726	„	MUNDY, H.
10681	„	DAVIES, J. T.	13092	Private	CORBETT, T.	10725	„	McCARTHY, R.
10694	„	JOHNSON, J. D.	10636	„	CRAWFORD, J.	10724	„	SHATTOCK, C.
11052	„	PEACOCK, C. A.	10701	„	SMITH, W. H.	10732	„	SHOREMAN, R.
13224	„	HUMPHRIES, J.	10702	„	SMITH, A.	13231	„	PAUL, W.
13089	„	CONGLETON, J.	10705	„	CUNNINGHAM, S.	10955	„	WILLIAMS, R.
13061	„	RICHARDS, A.	10706	„	NICKLIN, C.	10703	Private	ROBINSON, J. A.
13157	„	MITCHELL, M.	10711	„	RAWLINSON, S.	13050	„	HOLDEN, J.
10695	„	DICK, A.	10709	„	PRINCE, A.	13196	„	THOMAS, W. H.
10698	„	ELLABY, J.	10710	„	LEONARD, J. H.	11049	„	RICHINGS, H.
10692	„	MATTHEWS, T.	11105	„	FITZSIMMONS, J.	10713	„	GARNETT, W.

15th (Service) Battalion Lancashire Fusiliers.

"D" COMPANY.

Officer Commanding Company -	Capt. E. C. MACLAREN.
Second in Command - - -	Lieut. L. C. MANDLEBERG.
Company Sergeant Major - -	ROWLETT, J.
Company Quartermaster Sergeant -	SPENCER, H. V.

PLATOON NO. XIII.

Platoon Commander - - -	2nd Lieut. H. V. WRONG.
Platoon Sergeant - - - -	ALEXANDER, H. D.

No.	Rank	Name	No.	Rank	Name	No.	Rank	Name
10078	Sergeant	COTTON, J. H.	10797	„	McMAHON, D.	10825	„	COOK, A.
13066	„	ANDREWS, J. H.	10806	„	ROTHWELL, J.	10804	„	JACKSON, W.
10738	L.-Sergt.	GREENHALGH, C.	10807	„	PRITT, F.	10836	„	BUTLER, J.
10793	Corporal	WRIGHT, J.	10784	„	JONES, W. J.	10837	„	JONES, F. G.
13125	L.-Corpl.	PICKERSGILL, C. H.	10796	„	PIXTON, W.	10840	„	BIRD, G.
10754	„	TOMLINSON, B.	10787	Corporal	BAKER, J.	10842	„	TITLEY, S.
10832	„	LLOYD, F.	10832	L.-Corpl.	BATES, H.	10844	„	BOWMAN, H.
10765	Private	TAAFE, J.	10802	Private	RAFFO, J.	10845	„	WITHERS, H.
10766	„	MORRISS, J.	10788	„	MOCKLOW, J.	10847	„	WALSH, H.
10767	„	GOODWIN, W.	10831	„	DEAN, T.	10848	„	WALSH, J. H.
10792	„	POLLITT, H.	10800	„	HINGSTON, S.	10849	„	WITHERS, J.
10770	„	WILSON, R.	10810	Private	STATHAM, J.	10850	„	LEWIS, S.
10789	„	SCOTT, J. W.	13000	„	ROBINSON, H.	10853	„	REID, T.
10790	„	ANDERTON, J.	10777	„	GRUNDY, F.	10854	„	GORTON, A.
10780	„	PAGE, W. H.	13010	„	SUNLEY, J.	11009	„	GORE, J.
10740	„	TAYLOR, W.	10811	„	SPELLMAN, J.	10786	„	PICKTHALL, S.
13128	„	BRAZELL, A.	10818	„	BATTY, J.	10819	Private	HUNT, W.
13008	„	MOORE, J. H.	10826	„	BURKE, W.	10829	„	HOEY, J.
11188	„	GROVES, J. H.	10815	„	SPENCER, A.	10828	„	BARKER, T.
10808	„	MIDGLEY, E.	10822	„	BLOOMFIELD, J. A.	10830	„	FISH, T.
10794	„	CHARLES, G.	10827	„	DARBY, A.	10843	„	HODSON, W.
10795	„	OLDHAM, I.	10823	„	GEMMELL, H.			

PLATOON NO. XIV.

Platoon Commander - - -	Lieut. W. SUTCLIFFE.
Platoon Sergeant - - -	WILLIAMS, E. J.

No.	Rank	Name	No.	Rank	Name	No.	Rank	Name
10881	L.-Sergt.	KENNEDY, M.	10915	„	CAHILL, P.	10859	„	MULLEN, M.
10809	Corporal	BARTON, R.	10897	„	DUTTON, W.	10893	„	COWEN, T.
10909	L.-Corpl.	LAWLESS, J.	13050	„	HAMILTON, M.	10895	„	WARDLE, C. E.
10901	„	DEAKIN, E.	10887	„	SMITH, S.	10870	„	TAYLOR, J.
10879	„	PARKER, H.	10873	„	SHAW, F.	11183	„	NIGHTINGALE, J.
10888	„	SIMPSON, W.	10875	„	FALLON, T.	10877	„	HOLDEN, J.
10863	Private	ALLCOCK, L.	10883	„	WILSON, S. A.	10872	„	COOPER, S. V.
10592	„	HANSON, H.	10157	Sergeant	McGARREY, J.	10885	„	JONES, E. L.
11036	„	SCANLON, M.	10857	L.-Corpl.	BOLGER, E.	10861	„	HUGHES, T. G.
10906	„	ATKINSON, T. W.	10912	Private	BEARMAN, D. T.	10869	„	LEACH, H.
10911	„	BOTHWELL, J.	10857	„	O'BRIEN, W.	10904	„	RAMSDEN, W.
10896	„	BRERETON, G.	10905	„	VALENTINE, H.	10862	„	WEBB, R.
10891	„	EGERTON, J.	10864	Private	HADDOCK, J.	10913	„	DONE, A.
10869	„	JOHNSON, T.	10890	„	HUMPHRIES, H.	13123	„	JONES, S.
10898	„	KILGOUR, J.	10914	„	REYNOLDS, W.	13168	„	GEE, T.
10851	„	LEWIS, S.	10903	„	SCHOFIELD, A.	13001	„	BERRY, H.
10882	„	MANOCK, J.	10899	„	GREENWOOD, J.	10894	„	WILSON, R.
10858	„	STELLFOX, F.	10887	„	CROSSLAND, R.		„	FOGG, E.
10902	„	MOULDING, J. R.	10860	„	BROOKS, H.	10856	Private	LAFFIN, A.
10914	„	WATSON, W.	10855	„	LONGWORTH, G.	10814	„	JARVIS, J.
11172	„	FRANCIS, C.	10892	„	EDWARDS, E.	10865	„	HASKELL, H.
10852	„	BRASSINGTON, T.	10908	„	POWER, W.	10878	„	EVANS, G.

15th (Service) Battalion Lancashire Fusiliers.

"D" COMPANY.

Officer Commanding Company	- Capt. E. C. MACLAREN.
Second in Command - -	- Lieut. L. C. MANDLEBERG.
Company Sergeant Major -	- ROWLETT, J.
Company Quartermaster Sergeant	- SPENCER, H. V.

PLATOON NO. XV.

Platoon Commander - -	- 2nd Lieut. E. HAMPSON.
Platoon Sergeant - -	- BRADY, A.

No.	Rank	Name	No.	Rank	Name	No.	Rank	Name
10841	Corporal	WALSH, T.	10976	,,	GEE, J.	13228	,,	SOUTHALL, J.
10940	,,	TONGE, J. R.	10964	,,	HOPWOOD, W.	13009	,,	STEVENSON, S.
10905	L.-Corpl.	MOLINEUX, J. H.	13099	,,	SHORTLAND, H.	10944	,,	CRAWFORD, J.
10812	,,	APPLEYARD, J.	10923	,,	ANGLESEA, T.	10934	,,	DUMAKIN, J.
10919	,,	GRADY, J.	10817	Sergeant	THOMPSON, W.	10938	,,	GRIFFIN, J.
			10827	Corporal	RUSHTON, W.	10947	,,	HEWITT, W.
10963	Private	BROWN, A.	10953	Private	HEANEY, F.	10946	,,	MOSS, H.
10751	,,	WORSNUP, H.	10982	,,	DIDLER, F.	10950	,,	MYCOCK, H.
10961	,,	HALL, A.	10972	,,	GOULD, R.	10952	,,	PEARCE, R.
10959	,,	HATTON, W.	10966	,,	JACKSON, J.	10937	,,	PRITCHETT, W.
10948	,,	LLOYD, F.	10960	,,	WHITELEY, J.	10936	,,	WOODWARD, J. A.
10962	,,	MORRISON, J. W.	10967	,,	ALLEN, W. S.	10939	,,	DONELLY, T.
10957	,,	MULROONEY, E.				10931	,,	DOWNING, J. E.
10958	,,	SMITH, W.	10978	Private	ROBERTS, J.	10834	,,	COTTAM, W. H.
10956	,,	WILLETTS, W.	10925	,,	BUCKLEY, J. H.	13267	,,	LEA, W.
13024	,,	WOOD, J.	10927	,,	DORNING, E.	10074	Private	SOUTHWARD, J.
11190	,,	SIDDONS, B.	10929	,,	HARRISON, F.	10933	,,	STEVENSON, W.
13031	,,	HALL, W.	10920	,,	HUDSON, W.	10935	,,	WILSON, W.
13002	,,	STANLEY, W.	10930	,,	RODWELL, R.	10932	,,	MORGAN, J.
10969	,,	PEARCE, W.	10917	,,	STAPLETON, J.	10921	,,	LEES, H.
10973	,,	BOWEN, J.	10924	,,	WALL, E.	13191	,,	SCHOLES, D. S.
10975	,,	CAMPBELL, A.	10916	,,	WALSH, W.	10949	,,	CAMPBELL, W.
10971	,,	DUFF, H.	10918	,,	WHITE, J. A.	10968	,,	CONNOR, J.

PLATOON NO. XVI.

Platoon Commander - -	- 2nd Lieut. H. F. ROBINSON.
Platoon Sergeant - -	- DARBYSHIRE, G.

No.	Rank	Name	No.	Rank	Name	No.	Rank	Name
10997	Sergeant	MOYSE, W.	10983	,,	TURNER, H.	11181	,,	MASSEY, J.
11035	L.-Sergt.	BROOKS, T.	13236	,,	GEMMELL, J.	13028	,,	KNOTT, C.
11021	Corporal	RICHARDSON, W.	11041	,,	FINN, T.	13038	,,	PENDLEBURY, T.
10980	,,	McCLENAN, J.	11030	,,	BRADY, T.	13033	,,	WILLIAMS, T.
11031	L.-Corpl.	BARBOSA, L.	11189	,,	PURVIS, W.	13020	,,	MORAN, J.
10996	,,	STAFFORD, J.	11185	,,	JEPSON, H.	11000	,,	EASTWOOD, W.
11014	Private	BURTON, J. H.	11186	,,	GIBBONS, H.	11048	,,	LOWTHIAN, F.
10799	,,	DAVIS, A.	11006	L.-Corpl.	HALL, E.	10988	,,	McBRIDE, B. E.
13075	,,	CLARKE, J.	11027	Private	FURPHY, N. W.	11024	,,	CARROLL, M.
13080	,,	BUCKLEY, J. H.	11043	,,	BURNS, J.	10986	,,	TAYLOR, J. G.
10979	,,	PETERS, M. W.	10999	,,	HENSHAW.	11038	,,	LORD, R.
11009	,,	SEERS, G.	10992	,,	AINSCOW, J. E.	10993	,,	SPILSBURY, E.
10981	,,	HOLT, E. D.	11040	Private	DOUGLAS, R. W.	11015	,,	BAILEY, W.
11037	,,	WARDEN, R.	10985	,,	STONES, A.	11020	,,	RENSHAW, J.
11023	,,	BANHAM, J. B.	11007	,,	HORTON, H.	11031	,,	AINSCOW, R.
11010	,,	WATSON, B.	11001	,,	HOLME, R.	13226	,,	REDFORD, R.
11011	,,	ADAMS, C.	11002	,,	HOME, J.	13025	,,	CARTER, J.
10984	,,	DEAVILLE, C.	11046	,,	WILLIAMS, T. G.	13027	,,	FENSOME, P.
11039	,,	HADDOCK, W.	11013	,,	HIGGINS, A.	11017	Private	SHIELDS, W.
10998	,,	BUDGE, G. F.	10457	,,	HARWOOD, W. E.	11044	,,	ROBINSON, G. H.
10991	,,	JACOBS, W.	11042	,,	GALLAGHER, J.	10995	,,	RUSSELL, J.
11088	,,	CLIFFE, H.	11072	,,	DORNEY, J.	11012	,,	JONES, R.
10990	,,	GURLING, T.	11022	,,	BURKE, J.			

15th (Service) Battalion Lancashire Fusiliers.

"E" COMPANY.

Officer Commanding Company - Capt. S. BROADBENT.
Second in Command - - - Lieut. R. WILSON.
Company Sergeant Major - SHAW, A.(Acting).
Company Quartermaster Sergeant - CHANTLER, T. O. W.

PLATOON NO. XVII.

Platoon Commander - - - 2nd Lieut. A. W. INGLIS.
Platoon Sergeant - - - - MUIR, A.†

11143	Sergeant	YOUNG, W.	13147	„	TAYLOR, S.	13141	„	MYERS, F. W.
13160	„	STOWELL, A. E.	13021	„	TRIMBLE, S.	13183	„	ASHMAN, J.
11182	L.-Sergt.	HESKETH, W.	13153	„	MONKS, W.	13128	„	BOYER, A.
11135	Corporal	BARKER, T.	13118	„	TAYLOR, A.	11176	„	LYDIATE, T.
11117	„	MADDOCKS, A.	13152	„	SCHOLFIELD, J.	11175	„	McALPINE, D.
13246	„	PILGRIM, G.	13146	„	SHAW, W.	11157	„	CULLY, J.
13070	„	NEVIN, J. A.	13055	„	CHADWICK, W.	11164	„	DOWLING, A.
11142	L.-Corpl.	CHRISTIE, J.	11200	Corporal	GREAVES, J.	13133	„	CRABSTICK, E.
13043	„	GRUNDY, F.	13222	L.-Corpl.	WILSON, J.	13979	„	TAYLOR, H.
11160	„	WEST, G.	13042	Private	APPLEYARD, S.	13083	„	McALEER, P.
13044	„	BERRY, J. R.	13040	Private	MORRIS, N.	13205	„	CHEETHAM, J. J.
13162	„	BARRAND, C.	13096	„	SMITH, J.	13111	„	ROPER, R. F.
13172	„	BEAVER, J.	13137	„	ALDRIDGE, W.	13171	„	HAMER, F.
13252	„	CRANE, G.	13156	„	BUXTON, F. D.	13087	„	TAYLOR, A.
13112	„	JONES, W. E.	13296	„	HARPER, J.	13120	„	BOYD, H.
11133	„	KEANE, E.	13316	„	SIMM, S. H.	13103	„	FEENEY, H.
13006	„	MULVEY, H.	13154	„	WARBURTON, A.	13101	Private	SLATER, C.
13176	„	SHAW, A.	11139	„	CLAYTON, R.	13163	„	LLOYD, T.
13126	Private	THORPE, R.	13139	„	PARKER, J.	11194	„	BARNES, T.
13149	„	BARLOW, A.	13142	„	DALY, T.			

PLATOON NO. XVIII.

Platoon Commander - - -
Platoon Sergeant - - - - PROBERT, D.

10153	Sergeant	ANDERSON, J. E.	13295	„	BOARDMAN, H.	13335	„	McDOWELL, W.
11119	Corporal	O'BRIEN, W.	13300	„	KING, F.	13336	„	ROGERS, A.
13148	„	GRIMSLEY, H.	13288	„	DUTTON, J.	13314	„	HURINE, S.
13312	Private	HAMER, S.	13303	„	LEWIS, J. D.	13337	„	MILLINGTON, B.
13311	„	McKEWAN, T.	13293	„	BESSEL, J. A.	13326	„	WILLIAMS, T.
13302	„	COURTNEY, J.	13285	„	WILDING, L.	13325	„	HAINES, G.
13310	„	KELLY, P.	13313	„	CUNLIFFE, J.	13339	„	GARNER, J.
13314	„	HUDSON, T. A.	13292	„	HUGHES, G.	13327	„	WINNARD, J.
13309	„	PICKERING, E.	13287	Private	HAMMOND, J.	13331	„	PLATT, J.
13324	„	POTTS, W. C.	13289	„	GRIFFITHS, W.	13321	„	ANGUS, J.
13298	„	CHESTER, E.	13323	„	SMITH, F.	13305	„	MAY, J.
13286	„	SIMPSON, M.	13319	„	NOLAN, P.	13307	„	POLLITT, J.
13291	„	MORRIS, J. R.	13284	„	ENTWISTLE, W.	13306	„	MASON, W.
13294	„	GLEAVES, J.	13328	„	CROSSLEY, C.	13315	„	CLITHEROE, M.
13290	„	CROMPTON, W.	13283	„	WOODCOCK, J. W.	13322	„	HEAP, F.

15th (Service) Battalion Lancashire Fusiliers.

" E " COMPANY.

Officer Commanding Company - Capt. S. BROADBENT.
Second in Command - - - Lieut. R. WILSON.
Company Sergeant Major - - SHAW, A.(Acting).
Company Quartermaster Sergeant - CHANTLER, T. O. W.

PLATOON NO. XIX.

Platoon Commander - - -
Platoon Sergeant - - - - GREEN, J. S.

13362	Private	WOODCOCK, J. W.	13318	Private	BARRETT, W.
13352	,,	DAVIES, J. L.	13320	,,	DAWSON, J.
13353	,,	WRIGHT, J.	13361	,,	MURPHY, P.
13354	,,	TOOLE, D.	13342	,,	O'ROURKE, H.
13351	,,	EGAN, D. M.	13345	,,	WARREN, H.
13365	,,	HAY, R.	13366	,,	WILLIAMS, W.
13346	,,	WELCH, W.	13348	,,	WOOD, H.
13364	,,	NAVIN, P.	13360	,,	HILTON, H.
13363	,,	CARTLEDGE, J.	13333	,,	SOWERBY, E.
13357	,,	O'TOOLE, A.	13344	,,	PAGE, J. E.
13349	,,	FARNWORTH, N.	13367	,,	OWEN, H.
13343	,,	GREEN, W.	13359	,,	RADCLIFFE, T.
13352	,,	MADDOCKS, J.	13358	,,	BAINBRIDGE, P.
13340	,,	McCAULEY, J. H.	13347	,,	PARKIN, L.
13356	,,	ROWLAND, T.	13350	,,	STEPHENSON, C.
13317	,,	KENT, S.	13338	,,	BRENNAN, J.

Bugle Band.

10013	Sergt. Drmr.	RICHARDSON, R.	10158	Drummer	HOOLEY, A.
10245	Corpl. Drmr.	DELVE, W.	11036	,,	SCANLON, M.
10317	L.-Cpl. Drmr.	MULLEADY, P.	13087	,,	TAYLOR, A.
10353	,,	TAYLOR, W. H.	10354	,,	HIVES, W.
10090	Drummer	AYRES, T.	10140	,,	DEVONPORT, C.
10397	,,	SHAKESPEARE, D.	10248	,,	DICKENS, J.
10428	,,	PHEASEY, O.	10022	,,	HANKEY, E.
10553	,,	GRAHAM, R.	11112	,,	KNIGHT, J.
10955	,,	WILLIAMS, R.	10115	,,	GERRARD, H.
10886	,,	AVERY, A.	10785	,,	BRADFORD, A.
10786	,,	PICKTHALL, S.	10419	,,	DOLMAN, C.
10592	,,	HANSON, H.	10819	,,	STATHAM, J. H.
10751	,,	WORSNUP, H.	10811	,,	SPELLMAN, J.
10799	,,	DAVIS, A.		,,	ECKERSLEY.
10343	,,	RAWSTHORNE, S.		,,	FOGG, E
			10511	Drummer	NUTTALL, A.

Roll of Officers.

Lieut.-Col.	ABERCROMBIE, C. M.	Lieutenant	McCANN, J.
Major	WALLACE, C. C.	2nd Lieut.	HARWOOD, J. J.
Capt. & Adjt.	MUMFORD, E. M.	,,	SHARRATT, R. W.
Captain	SMITH, W. O.	,,	CUNLIFFE, E. G.
,,	TWEED, T. F.	,,	JARVIS, A. W.
,,	MERRYWEATHER, C. W.	,,	BARON, E.
,,	CROMPTON, E.	,,	LEWTAS, J.
,,	KNOTT, R. B.	,,	BREAR, B. H.
Lieutenant	MORRIS, C. F.	,,	HIGSON, R. H.
,,	ALLEN, W. H.	,,	JONES, D. L.
,,	MORGAN, J. S.	,,	RYLANDS, H. B.
,,	WAUGH, F. F.	,,	HICK, F. J.
,,	TATTERSALL, J.	,,	ELLISON, J. B. R.
,,	SMITH, A. M.	,,	OWEN, E. A.
,,	ROBERTSON, D.	,,	SWAIN, M. E.
,,	SMITH, C. W.	,,	MARTINDALE, J. B.
,,	ALLEN, A. N.	Lieutenant	BUTCHER, A. H.
,,	WARD, R. W.	(R.A.M.C.)	
Lieutenant	CROSSLEY, S.	2nd Lieut.	WALTON, W.
,,	ROTH, J. B.	,,	SCOTT, J. G. A.
,,	CRAN, A. H. (R.A.M.C.)		

Non-Commissioned Officers' (Sergeants) Roll.

Warrant Officer.

7667   S.M. HARGREAVES, H

11967   R.Q.M.S. WALCH, J. W
11449   C.Q.M.S. ANDREWS, H. W.
(O.R.S.)

Roll No.	Rank and Name.		Roll No.	Rank and Name.	
11435	C.S.M.	FORD, F. A.	11241	Sergeant	BROADHURST, B.
11788	,,	HAILWOOD, F.	11899	,,	HOWCROFT, W.
12534	,,	HASTINGS, J.	12497	,,	BRADSHAW, S. J.
11256	,,	ROBINSON, W.	11379	,,	CARROLL, S.
369	,,	HOLDING, B.	11972	,,	THOMPSON, A.
11308	C.Q.M.S.	WALLSWORTH, J. J.	12019	,,	SMITH, A.
10716	,,	CHAPMAN, D.	11383	,,	JOHNSON, G.
12535	,,	DOUGLAS, W. J.	11882	,,	RIDDELL, A. E.
11766	,,	WATSON, C.	15201	,,	MASTERSON, R.
15202	Sgt. Cook	BROOKS, W.	11801	,,	BREWSTER, A.
11235	Pion. Sgt.	ECCLES, H.	12187	,,	RYLANCE, G.
12088	M.G.Sgt.	SIGHE, J.	12589	,,	MACHELL, P.
11716	,, L.Sgt.	BOURNE, L.	12440	,,	MITCHELL, J. E. D.
11512	Sig. Sgt.	SULLIVAN, F. W.	12069	,,	BROOKS, J.
11787	Sergeant	BARDSLEY, J.	12587	,,	LORD, M.
11885	,,	RIDDELL, W. J.	15198	,,	SANT, T. J.
11800	,,	ANDERSON, E.	11968	,,	BARNES, W. J.
11227	,,	WILSON, G.	11391	,,	ANDREWS, W.
11228	,,	BETTS, F.	11977	,,	OSBORNE, A. K.
11399	,,	M'CARDLE, R.	11791	,,	GIBSON, F.
11352	,,	BULMER, A.	11415	L.-Sergt.	MACHIN, J.
11487	,,	MOORE, J.	15200	,,	GOODIER, J.
11798	,,	TAYLOR, J. E.	11973	,,	GRIFFITHS, E.
11799	,,	FLEMING, J.	11915	,,	HOLLAND, J.
11287	,,	TAYLOR, W.	12068	,,	PUNG, H. O.
12071	,,	GROVE, J.	15006	,,	BRAIME, A. J.
11765	,,	RICE, H.	12572	,,	DUDLEY, G.
11312	,,	MORAN, D.	15101	,,	POTTS, P. W.
12197	,,	ARMSTRONG, T.	12011	,,	DUNNING, G.
11775	,,	BELL, J.	12553	,,	HULME, W.
7174	C.S.M.	GREENOUGH, P.	12437	Sergeant	BLACK, M.
11773	C.Q.M.S.	WINTERTON, C.	12533	,,	BURNS, T.
11516	Sergeant	STORR, T.	11466	,,	MILNER, O.
11539	,,	MARTIN, J. E.			

"A" COMPANY.

Officer Commanding Company -	Capt. C. W. MERRYWEATHER.
Second in Command - - -	Lieut. J. McCANN.
Company Sergeant Major - -	HAILWOOD, F.
Company Quartermaster Sergeant -	CHAPMAN, D.

PLATOON NO. I.

Platoon Commander - - -	Lieut. S. CROSSLEY.
Platoon Sergeant - - -	BARDSLEY, J.

12572	L.-Sergt.	DUDLEY, G.	15017	,,	READ, J.	12152	,,	McDONALD, P.
12148	Corporal	SAVILLE, J. W.	15011	,,	LAMB, D.	12165	,,	WRIGHT, S.
12103	L.-Corpl.	SMITH, J. R.	15165	,,	CUNLIFFE, J.	12118	,,	ENGLISH, D.
12164	,,	BURTON, J.	15059	,,	EVANS, J. R.	12183	,,	LOGAN, J.
12179	,,	HUGHES, W. H.	15086	,,	HUNT, W. H.	12163	,,	LEE, F.
12159	,,	HOLT, J. A.	15110	,,	DAMMERY, B.	12112	,,	LEIGH, H. E.
11349	,,	TIMPERLEY, J.	15016	,,	CHAPMAN, P.	12154	,,	METCALFE, J.
12140	Private	HORSFIELD, E.	15018	,,	BARNES, J.	11339	,,	JOHNSON, H. G.
12111	,,	KELLY, T.	12137	Corporal	TURNER, J. E.	15140	,,	JOYCE, E.
12108	,,	WHITEHEAD, H. H.	12167	L.-Corpl.	WILD, E.	11724	,,	HOBSON, G.
12185	,,	FLANAGAN, J.	12156	Private	STAFFORD, J. E.	11348	,,	HUGHES, G.
12149	,,	THOMPSON, S.	15053	Private	BROADHURST, P.	12140	,,	MURPHY, G.
12422	,,	MORRIS, J.	15116	,,	JAMESON, A.	11336	,,	MALONE, T.
12104	,,	STANLEY, P.	12131	,,	KING, T.	11394	,,	MOTTESHEAD, H.
11204	,,	JACKSON, S.	12132	,,	BURNETT, B.	11343	,,	PRITCHARD, S.
12133	,,	CROWDEN, J.	12116	,,	BOOTH, O. W.	11335	,,	SALTER, E.
12171	,,	FRANCE, J.	12147	,,	GIBBONS, T.	11296	,,	GORE, C.
12114	,,	GREENWOOD, J.	12115	,,	GRIMSHAW, W. E.	11307	,,	HARGREAVES, J.
12157	,,	HARDMAN, J.	12129	,,	SIBLEY, R.	12182	Private	HOWELLS, W.
12123	,,	McDONALD, J.	12177	,,	WINKSWORTH, B.	12425	,,	EASTHORPE, A.
12175	,,	PATTEN, J.	12172	,,	SHEPLEY, A.	12180	,,	BROMLEY, E.
12109	,,	ROBERTS, A.	11215	,,	O'KELL, I.			
12119	,,	ROGERSON, H.	12188	,,	RUSSELL, E. W.			

PLATOON NO. II.

Platoon Commander - - -	2nd Lieut. J. LEWTAS.
Platoon Sergeant - - -	PUNG, H. O.

11309	Corporal	GLOVER, J.	12170	,,	WINSKILL, T.	11237	,,	JACKSON, A.
11252	,,	JEFFERSON, A.	11244	,,	WITHERS, C.	11248	,,	JACKSON, W.
11205	,,	BOWCOCK, C. B.	12454	,,	TYRER, H.	11333	,,	KING, T. H.
12193	L.-Corpl.	BERTRAM, H.	11251	,,	ALLEN, W.	11226	,,	CHRISTY, J.
12426	,,	VANN, A.	12419	,,	CLARKE, R.	11231	,,	GRETRIX, C.
12113	,,	SUCH, W. E.	12124	Private	McKAY, J.	11255	,,	HOWARTH, J. R.
11243	,,	KELLY, M.	12169	,,	WROE, E.	11298	,,	JONES, T.
11208	,,	McLEAN, F.	11746	,,	BORRICK, J.	11216	,,	STEWART, J.
11202	Private	DERBYSHIRE, A.	11301	,,	KELLY, F.	11246	,,	BURROWS, J.
11322	,,	FOWLER, W.	12125	,,	ASTON, T.	11201	,,	WILKINSON, H.
12155	,,	HODGINS, J.				11245	,,	ORTON, H.
12181	,,	HARRISON, F.	12189	Private	HOWARD, E.	11330	,,	THOMAS, H.
12176	,,	PALMER, T.	12418	,,	HILL, E.	12110	,,	BENT, W.
12162	,,	TWIGG, W.	12428	,,	WALKER, H.	12141	,,	MURPHY, P.
11332	,,	MULHALL, M.	12523	,,	HOWES, J.	12166	,,	MIDDLETON, H.
12453	,,	HOWARTH, T.	11232	,,	BALL, A.	11320	,,	BARNES, A. E.
11712	,,	WIGHTMAN, R.	11222	,,	BRADSHAW, E.	11238	Private	COOK, R.
11211	,,	FELTON, G.	11217	,,	BAILEY, T.	11219	,,	RUSSELL, V. W.
12200	,,	GARTON, J.	11207	,,	CHEADLE, J.	11212	,,	CROWTHER, F.
11213	,,	HALL, S.	11220	,,	FLYNN, N.	12196	,,	BOON, W.
11203	,,	MATLEY, R.	11717	,,	CHAPMAN, J.	12184	,,	MILLS, F.
12149	,,	McCAW, J.	11229	,,	GOLDSMITH, J. J.			
11206	,,	MORRIS, S.	11223	,,	HETTRICK, A.			

16th (Service) Battalion Lancashire Fusiliers.

"A" COMPANY.

Officer Commanding Company   -   Capt. C. W. MERRYWEATHER.
Second in Command   -   -   Lieut. J. McCANN.
Company Sergeant Major   -   HAILWOOD, F.
Company Quartermaster Sergeant -   CHAPMAN, D.

PLATOON NO. III.

Platoon Commander   -   -   -   2nd Lieut. E. G. CUNLIFFE.
Platoon Sergeant   -   -   -   BETTS, F.

No.	Rank	Name	No.	Rank	Name	No.	Rank	Name
11235	Sergeant	ECCLES, H.	11744	„	ROBERTS, W.	11752	„	WRIGHTHOUSE, S. H.
12440	„	MITCHELL, J. E. D.	11295	„	SIMON, R.	11748	„	BROWN, M.
11723	L.-Sergt.	CAWDREY, C.	11745	„	TURNER, E. G.	12418	„	HILL, F.
11716	Corporal	BOURNE, L.	12460	„	BLAKEMORE, H.	11341	„	JACKSON, H.
11713	L.-Corpl.	BROADY, H.	11292	„	ROBERTS, S.	11331	„	LAWSON, F.
12146	„	REDFERN, H.	11218	„	ROWLANDS, J. W.	12424	„	CURRE, H.
11729	„	TIMPERLEY, A.	12153	L.-Corpl.	CAMPBELL, R.	11285	„	HEALEY, J. A.
11240	Private	BATES, J.	11714	Private	NUGENT, W.	11315	„	COTTAM, J.
11747	„	BARNES, W.	11292	„	PHIPPS, G.	11303	„	DUTTON, J.
11730	„	BUCKLEY, E.	11224	„	TUDOR, J. W.	11281	„	LEEK, G.
11717	„	CHAPMAN, C.	11719	„	IRVING, H.	11297	„	OLDFIELD, G.
11711	„	HUGHES, J.	12174	Private	HEYWOOD, W.	11288	„	SMITH, H.
11726	„	MILNER, T.	11750	„	MATHER, L.	11278	„	UNSWORTH, F. W.
11725	„	MELLER, A.	11751	„	PENNINGTON, W.	11286	„	WOODS, R.
11247	„	O'NEILL, H.	11741	„	ROE, J.	11284	„	YOUNG, H.
15207	„	PHIPPS, H.	12160	„	BURGESS, S.	11753	„	KELLEHER, J.
11236	„	POWELL, C.	11334	„	BOOTH, J.	11311	„	KILCOURSE, J.
12459	„	BILLINGHAM, J.	11759	„	BARNES, T.	11221	Private	HUNT, H.
11758	„	AKISTER, W.	11319	„	ENGLAND, J.	11763	„	CLEMENS, J.
11769	„	BOWDEN, R.	11723	„	HEARTWELL, J. C.	12461	„	POMFRET, A.
11735	„	HODGES, W.	11249	„	MINOR, W.	11749	„	FAULKNER, B.
11718	„	McDONALD, S.	11763	„	RIGG, A. P.	11767	„	BURGESS, J. S.

PLATOON NO. IV.

Platoon Commander   -   -   -   2nd Lieut. H. B. RYLANDS.
Platoon Sergeant   -   -   -   CARROLL, S.

No.	Rank	Name	No.	Rank	Name	No.	Rank	Name
12589	Sergeant	MACHELL, P. S.	12577	„	THOMPSON, W.	15005	„	MAINE, J.
12076	Corporal	HALL, E.	12581	„	ROWLEY, T.	15032	„	MOORE, R.
12512	„	LEMMON, H.	15038	„	SAVAGE, W.	15044	„	WRAY, J.
12431	„	WILKINSON, J.	15151	„	LAWLER, A.	15046	„	ALDIS, B.
11344	L.-Corpl.	PURSER, E.	15007	„	BROWN, E.	15063	„	DAINTY, J.
12569	„	O'BRIEN, L.	15141	„	KNIGHT, J.	15138	„	DYKE, E.
15045	Private	BARLOW, B.	11466	Sergeant	MILNER, O.	15126	„	OLDFIELD, T.
15035	„	COOK, J.	15146	Private	GARRY, J.	15132	„	SHARPLES, H.
15033	„	ERKAMP, J.	15030	„	GREATOREX, W.	15093	„	TATLEY, G.
15042	„	FREEMAN, J.	12530	„	JONES, B. T.	15013	„	WOLRENDEN, J.
15139	„	LAWTON, F.	15147	„	McKENNA, J.	15135	„	NUTTALL, A.
15028	„	LYMAN, J.				15113	„	WOLSTENHOLME, H.
15142	„	VOST, T.	12513	Private	JENKINS, J.	15095	„	HOWARTH, A.
15025	„	BURNETT, J. W.	15149	„	McCLACHLAN, F.	12591	„	HIGHAM, A. E.
15143	„	McNALLY, J.	12500	„	PARKER, W. H.	15071	„	SEDDON, S.
15022	„	RADFORD, J.	15153	„	TURNER, F.	15057	„	BROOME, A.
12510	„	RICHARDS, J.	12578	„	BEVENS, S.	11321	„	RATCLIFFE, H.
15026	„	WILSON, A.	12580	„	CROSSLEY, J.	12511	Private	ROWLANDS, J.
12549	„	WORTHINGTON, F.	15025	„	DAY, W.	12496	„	SWARBRICK, B.
15023	„	YARDLEY, C.	12495	„	GEE, R.	12408	„	TOMPHALL, J. C.
12507	„	OLIVER, A.	15039	„	HALL, A. E.	15060	„	SMETHURST, W.
15154	„	KETTLE, P.	12499	„	HORTON, J. W.	12540	„	BANNER, A.
15140	„	JOYCE, H.	15021	„	COXON, T.			

"B" COMPANY.

Officer Commanding Company - Capt. T. F. TWEED.
Second in Command - - Lieut. W. WALTON.
Company Sergeant Major - ROBINSON, W.
Company Quartermaster Sergeant - WINTERTON, C. H.

PLATOON NO. V.

Platoon Commander - - 2nd Lieut. E. BARON.
Platoon Sergeant - - McCARDELL, R.

No.	Rank	Name	No.	Rank	Name	No.	Rank	Name
11241	Sergeant	BROADHURST, B.	11665	,,	GRINDLEY, S.	11510	,,	PARKER, G.
11275	Corporal	CORLESS, N.	11259	,,	HAIGH, G.	11398	,,	PIERCE, T. W.
11624	,,	CROFT, J.	12517	,,	HARROP, A. E.	11422	,,	REDFORD, R.
12563	L.-Corpl.	POLE, N.	11408	,,	HIGGINS, J.	11261	,,	RICHMOND, C. H.
11378	,,	SUMMERFOLD, F.	11324	,,	HOLLAND, F.	11504	,,	ROBINSON, J.
11238	,,	ELLISON, R.	11407	,,	HOLDING, F.	11272	,,	SCOTT, J. E.
11316	Private	BARRY, J.	11410	,,	HOUGHTON, E.	11380	,,	SIMPSON, H.
11654	,,	BOWKER, F. E.	11266	,,	HOWELL, H.	11239	,,	STOTT, A.
11362	,,	BUNTING, E.	12541	,,	HULMES, J.	11254	,,	STRACHAN, H. D.
11472	,,	BURCH, H.	11655	,,	JACKSON, J.	11701	,,	STRAPPS, J.
12526	,,	BURTON, J. W.	11279	,,	JOHN, W.	11260	,,	SULLIVAN, W.
12525	,,	BURTONWOOD, P.	12516	Private	JOHNSON, J. H.	11270	,,	TOWN, J.
11491	,,	BUTTERFIELD, S.	11277	,,	KENYON, A.	11266	,,	WAKEFIELD, H.
11253	,,	CHIPCHASE, R. H.	11328	,,	LOMAX, R.	11290	,,	WHARMBY, A.
11267	,,	COCKAYNE, T.	11377	,,	MARRIN, J.	11464	,,	WILSON, G.
11274	,,	CRONIN, W.	11273	,,	McCANN, T.	11250	,,	WILSON, J.
11258	,,	CUTHBERT, D.	11506	,,	McDERMOTT, E.	11269	,,	WILSON, T.
11620	,,	DARBY, B.	11262	,,	MEEK, J. H.	11473	,,	WILSON, T.
11325	,,	DYKE, W.	11263	,,	MILLER, J. H.	11329	,,	TOMS, H.
11265	,,	EGGINTON, H.	11362	,,	MOODY, J.	11359	,,	LAYTON, S.
11490	,,	FIELDHOUSE, J.	11853	,,	ORLEDGE, J.	11366	,,	SWINBURNE, E.
11453	,,	FISHWICK, W.	12544	,,	ORR, C.	11659	,,	MELLER, W.
12156	,,	FOWLER, N.	11486	,,	OWEN, H.			

PLATOON NO. VI.

Platoon Commander - - 2nd Lieut. A. W. JARVIS.
Platoon Sergeant - - TAYLOR, W.

No.	Rank	Name	No.	Rank	Name	No.	Rank	Name
12069	Sergeant	BROOKS, J. H.	11578	,,	FIDDES, J. S. S.	11602	,,	SMITH, W.
11973	L.-Sergt.	GRIFFITHS, E.	11687	,,	FISH, W.	11682	,,	STANLEY, J. E.
11237	Corporal	CURRIE, W.	11685	,,	GREENHALGH, E.	11611	,,	STOREY, S.
11976	,,	MYERS, J. S.	11538	,,	HARRISON, G.	11532	,,	TAYLOR, W.
15210	L.-Corpl.	CROFT, E.	11518	,,	HIGHAM, J.	11638	,,	TAYLOR, J. W.
11736	Private	GREENWOOD, A.	11891	,,	HOLMES, H.	11467	,,	THORLEY, J. S.
12556	,,	ALLCOCK, W.	11694	,,	HOUGHTON, S.	11281	,,	TROTT, J. A.
12536	,,	ASHTON, G.	11619	,,	JONES, D. W.	11693	,,	TROTT, H.
12423	,,	BEASLEY, J. L.	15211	,,	JONES, J.	11707	,,	WARMISHAM, W.
11381	,,	BESWICK, W. H.	12460	,,	LEES, W. H.	11618	,,	WEBB, V.
11692	,,	BOARDMAN, E.	11684	Private	LYNAGH, T.	11667	,,	WELCH, J.
11376	,,	BRADFORD, A. E.	12486	,,	MASON, A.	11409	,,	WOOD, A.
11452	,,	BROADBENT, J.	11699	,,	MOORE, H.	11493	,,	WORTHINGTON, H.
11686	,,	BROWNLOW, H.	11643	,,	MOORHEAD, H.	12538	,,	YATES, A.
11534	,,	BURY, J.	11543	,,	MORAN, J.	11524	,,	ROYLE, J.
11502	,,	BUTTERWORTH, H.	11531	,,	PERCIVAL, F.	11568	,,	LEIGH, R.
11621	,,	CHAPMAN, J. E.	11545	,,	PLATT, J.	11438	,,	MAGILL, J.
12514	,,	CLAYTON, S.	11492	,,	PYKE, J.	11581	,,	HAMILTON, W.
11697	,,	CRAGGS, W.	11593	,,	ROBERTS, H.	11264	,,	BOGG, C.
11688	,,	DAVIES, F.	11672	,,	ROGERSON, J. H.	11523	,,	RIGBY, R.
12521	,,	EDWARDS, A.	11691	,,	ROYLE, W. M.			
12537	,,	ELLISON, A.	11535	,,	SLATER, E. W.			
11681	,,	EVANS, A.	11536	,,	SMITH, F.			

"B" COMPANY.

Officer Commanding Company - Capt. T. F. TWEED.
Second in Command - - - Lieut. W. WALTON.
Company Sergeant Major - ROBINSON, W.
Company Quartermaster Sergeant - WINTERTON, C. H.

PLATOON NO. VII.

Platoon Commander - - - 2nd Lieut. R. H. HIGSON.
Platoon Sergeant - - - THOMPSON, A.

No.	Rank	Name	No.	Rank	Name	No.	Rank	Name
15006	L.-Sergt.	BRAME, A. J.	11837	„	COWAN, J. D.	11804	„	RENNISON, J. H.
11680	Corporal	BLAKELEY, F.	12067	„	CROFT, G.	11397	„	RHODES, H.
11537	„	JOHNSON, F.	11704	„	CROFT, W.	12539	„	RIDGWAY, A.
11779	„	PENDLEBURY, A.	11645	„	CRANE, H.	11838	„	RIGBY, G. W.
11512	L.-Corpl.	COLLEY, T. H.	11951	„	CROOK, T.	11874	„	RIGBY, S.
11276	„	WORSLEY, L.	11836	„	FORREST, A.	11840	„	RIMMERS, W. F.
11883	„	GOODWIN, W. H.	11841	„	GRANT, W. H.	12545	„	ROBERTS, H.
11963	Private	ANDREWS, T.	11644	„	HAMBLETON, W.	11754	„	ROUTLEDGE, J. L.
11317	„	ANKERS, H.	11614	„	HAMER, S.	11656	„	ROYLE, J.
11933	„	BANKS, A.	12016	„	HEATH, S.	11757	„	SHARPLES, S.
11615	„	BARRETT.	11633	„	HENNESSEY, W.	11689	„	SMITH, C. A.
11732	„	BLEARS, L.	11700	Private	HOEY, G. L.	11708	„	SWARBRICK, A.
11764	„	BETHEL, A.	11762	„	JOHNSON, J.	12012	„	SWINDELLS, C.
11835	„	BOON, T.	11705	„	JOHNSON, W.	11956	„	STREET, S.
11666	„	BOOTH, A.	11828	„	JONES, F.	11761	„	TWIGG, E.
11612	„	BROOKS, T.	11739	„	LEESON, F.	11704	„	WARNER, H.
11703	„	BROOKSBANK, J. G.	11839	„	MARCHMENT, R.	12017	„	WELCH, H. K.
11809	„	BULL, F.	11810	„	MATTOCK, E. T.	11906	„	WHINFIELD, F.
12540	„	BURGESS, F.	11702	„	MILLINGTON, A. V.	11852	„	WINN, E. H.
11934	„	CARTER, S. J.	11673	„	MURDEN, W.	11372	„	GREGSON, T.
11755	„	CLARKE, A.	11857	„	OWENS, S.	11600	„	DEAKIN, W.
11552	„	COTTERELL, J. G.	11706	„	RATCLIFFE, J. J.	11470	„	HARDMAN, W.

PLATOON NO. VIII.

Platoon Commander - - - Lieut. C. W. SMITH.
Platoon Sergeant - - - GROVE, J.

No.	Rank	Name	No.	Rank	Name	No.	Rank	Name
12019	Sergeant	SMITH, A.	12003	„	GRUNDY, W.	11994	„	NUTTALL, E.
12432	Corporal	HARRISON, C.	12084	„	HINDLEY, W.	12488	„	PARRISH, J.
11834	L.-Corpl.	MELLER, T. E.	11695	„	HOLT, J.	12449	„	PETERS, E.
12515	Private	BATEMAN, E.	12008	„	HOLT, R. B.	12485	„	SHAW, W. H.
12411	„	BENT, J.	11922	„	HOOLEY, A.	12510	„	SIMCOCK, H. F.
12427	„	BLACKWELL, J.	11622	L.-Corpl.	RADCLIFFE, J.	11993	„	SMITH, D.
12026	„	BOWKER, W.	12412	Private	BELLIS, W.	11731	„	SMITH, A.
11989	„	BRITTAIN, E.	12451	„	GRIFFITHS, J.	11931	„	TOWNSHEND, N.
12053	„	BROOK, M.	12504	„	PINDERS, I. W.	12023	„	THORLEY, J. T.
12050	„	CARTER, B.	12467	„	SLOAN, N.	11997	„	VALENTINE, J.
12036	„	CASSIN, W.	12018	„	TRACEY, A.	11530	„	WALLWORK, R.
11663	„	COLDWELL, A. H.	12484	„	WAGGESTAFFE, J.	12555	„	WHITTLE, F.
12024	„	COLLINS, J.	12055	Private	JONES, F.	12455	„	WHYATT, G.
12051	„	CROSS, I. H.	12033	„	KIRWIN, W.	12524	„	WITHERS, J.
12404	„	DEAN, J.	12052	„	LEATHER, F.	12476	„	WORRALL, W. E.
11974	„	DIXON, F.	11698	„	MAHER, W.	11639	„	BRABIN, H.
12136	„	DWYER, A.	11847	„	MATHER, T.	12191	„	BARNES, O. G.
12487	„	FARRELL, M. J.	12035	„	MATHER, G.	12554	Private	WORTHINGTON, J.
12470	„	FEARNELEY, W.	12079	„	McCOMBS, J.	11431	„	YOUNG, W. H.
12491	„	FIDDES, W. G.	12054	„	MAYBURY, G.	11668	„	PEARSON, W.
11683	„	FISHWICK, J.	12438	„	NEWELL, J.	11501	„	ISMAY, B.
12518	„	GRANT, D.	12021	„	NIGHTINGALE, J.	11637	„	CRAWSHAW.
12049	„	GRUNDY, H. D.	12415	„	NORTON, R.	11534	„	BURY, J.

"C" COMPANY.

Officer Commanding Company - Capt. R. B. Knott.
Second in Command - - Capt. A. Macdonald-Smith.
Company Sergeant Major - - Ford, F. A.
Company Quartermaster Sergeant - Wallsworth, J. J.

PLATOON NO. IX.

Platoon Commander - - - Lieut. A. Nelson Allen.
Platoon Sergeant - - - Bradshaw, S. J.

No.	Rank	Name	No.	Rank	Name	No.	Rank	Name
12550	Corporal	Carruthers, D.	15065	„	Greenhalgh, W.	15100	„	Parker, R.
11893	„	Croft, J. W.	12548	„	Hardman, W.	12583	„	Philips, H.
15204	L.-Corpl.	Barrett, H.	15088	„	Harrison, J. A.	12565	„	Pilkington, A.
12508	„	Colclough, J.	12594	„	Hilton, E.	12528	„	Riley, J.
12217	„	Harrison, F.	12560	„	Hayman, W.	15188	„	Rothwell, H.
11594	„	Tench, H.	12503	„	Hill, T. F.	15089	„	Rushton, W.
12527	Private	Ball, T.				15119	„	Ryder, J.
12505	„	Bate, W.	11539	Sergeant	Martin, J. E.	15156	„	Savage, J. H.
12531	„	Bates, R.	12588	Corporal	Thompson, C.	15103	„	Schofield, J. T.
12595	„	Bluer, H.	15052	Private	Atherton, F.	12493	„	Senior, R.
12584	„	Booth, A.	11372	„	Parry, E.	15083	„	Sydall, J.
15155	„	Broughton, J.	12443	„	Lovatt, W.	15054	„	Tomlinson, J. H.
15188	„	Buck, H.				15045	„	Wakeley, E. F.
12576	„	Clements, C.	15067	Private	Hughes, A.	15160	„	Watson, W. H.
11380	„	Dick, G. W.	15815	„	Hughes, W.	12566	„	Wolstenholme, F.
15061	„	Dunne, T.	12592	„	Jackson, H.	12565	„	Bottomley, G.
15003	„	Edwards, R.	15205	„	Kane, F.	12597	„	Smith, T.
15048	„	Egan, J.	15068	„	Kilgariff, J.	12006	Private	Taylor, J.
12570	„	Egerton, J.	12543	„	Kilburn, J.	15014	„	Whalley, J.
12600	„	Felton, G. H.	15050	„	Lawley, E.	11471	„	D'Arcy, T.
12598	„	Ferber, W.	12557	„	Leish, W.	15012	„	Basson, A.
15002	„	Greenhalgh, A.	15117	„	Marsh, W.	12394	„	Jenkinson, C.
15066	„	Greenhalgh, T.	12509	„	Naylor, W. H.			
			12575	„	Ormrod, F.			

PLATOON NO. X.

Platoon Commander - - - 2nd Lieut. J. J. Harwood.
Platoon Sergeant - - - Fleming, J. R.

No.	Rank	Name	No.	Rank	Name	No.	Rank	Name
11391	Sergeant	Andrew, W.	16074	„	Fairhurst, J.	11448	„	Naylor, R.
11461	Corporal	Daber, C.	11401	„	Fitzsimmons, J.	11451	„	Pearson, J.
11627	L.-Corpl.	Hendley, A.	11439	„	Forrester, H.	11650	„	Pearson, J.
11384	„	Hughes, W. H.	15072	„	Glover, J. T.	11468	„	Pimlott, W.
11505	„	Jackson, B.	11441	„	Guinan, W.	11522	„	Pollitt, J.
11476	„	Lawton, F.	11457	„	Hart, R.	12568	„	Preston, C.
11460	„	Whiteley, A.	10047	„	James, A.	11475	„	Roscoe, A.
12596	Private	Baker, C.	11449	C.Q.M.S.	Andrews, W. H.	11641	„	Seddon, J.
11616	„	Bate, A. P.	11631	Corporal	Worrall, T.	11478	„	Smith, A.
15079	„	Berisford, J.	11443	L.-Corpl.	Shore, J.	11479	„	Smith, A.
11495	„	Birch, W.	11433	Private	Chidgey, R.	11458	„	Taylor, J.
11647	„	Bowker, F.	11450	Private	Ingham, J.	11474	„	Weardon, J.
11629	„	Brassington, H.	11455	„	James, S. H.	11454	„	Williams, C.
11649	„	Brown, G.	12464	„	Kirwin, W.	11928	„	Young, G.
11632	„	Clarke, J.	15004	„	Lawrence, G.	11517	„	Young, M.
11456	„	Connely, J.	12465	„	Lomas, E.	11462	„	Pass, W.
11369	„	Coupe, E.	11411	„	Lowndes, A.	11387	„	Walshe, G. E.
11447	„	Coulter, J.	12439	„	Lowe, W.	11653	„	Winterbottom, F.
15075	„	Cordwell, J.	11437	„	Marsden, H.	11426	Private	Clements, E.
12559	„	Davenport, A.	11652	„	Mayer, J. D.	11628	„	Jarvis, W.
11420	„	Doyle, T. J.	11469	„	McDermott, P.	11459	„	Vanden, V.
15074	„	Eastwood, M.	11651	„	Montier, F.	11431	„	Young, W. H.
11627	„	Edwards, H.	11463	„	Morrican, J.			

16th (Service) Battalion Lancashire Fusiliers.

"C" COMPANY.

Officer Commanding Company - Capt. R. B. Knott.
Second in Command - - - Capt. A. Macdonald-Smith.
Company Sergeant Major - - Ford, F. A.
Company Quartermaster Sergeant - Wallsworth, J. J.

PLATOON NO. XI.

Platoon Commander - - - 2nd Lieut. R. W. Sharratt.
Platoon Sergeant - - - - Bulmer, A.

11487	Sergeant	Moore, J.	11428	,,	Greenhalgh, H.	11412	,,	Redford, W.
15200	,,	Goodier, J.	11405	,,	Hand, R. H.	11465	,,	Risby, H.
11515	Corporal	Hayes, J. J.	12442	,,	Hardman, J.	11424	,,	Roberts, E.
11605	L.-Corpl.	Broe, L.	11604	,,	Harris, H.	11430	,,	Rothwell, T.
11606	,,	Murray, J.	11369	,,	Holgate, J. E.	11482	,,	Rushton, A.
11610	,,	Almand, A.	12463	,,	Holland, J. F.	11371	,,	Shanley, M.
12462	,,	Brown, J. J.	11579	,,	Holmes, J. W.	11418	,,	Shaw, E.
11406	Private	Andrew, J. S.	11388	,,	Holt, T.	12433	,,	Taylor, J. H.
11414	,,	Barnes, J.	11480	Corporal	Rostron, C.	11419	,,	Thompson, W.
11382	,,	Barrow, A.	11373	L.-Corpl.	Chandley, G.	11607	,,	Tonge, W.
11385	,,	Barry, W.	11427	Private	Dudson, A.	11590	,,	Towers, E.
11527	,,	Beeson, W.	11565	Private	James, A.	11576	,,	Weatherby, F.
11429	,,	Bostock, E.	11569	,,	Hughes, J.	11421	,,	Wheeler, E.
11426	,,	Burton, H.	11368	,,	Johnson, J.	11609	,,	Wilkes, J.
11634	,,	Channon, J.	15101	,,	Kelly, J. D.	11351	,,	Woodford, W.
11608	,,	Davidson, J. A.	11392	,,	Kilgariff, J.	11586	,,	Baker, M.
11375	,,	Dewhurst, J.	11416	,,	Mackey, M.	11402	,,	Heany, B.
11374	,,	Digan, D.	12441	,,	McKale, C.	11417	,,	Shaw, J.
11575	,,	Ellison, R. A.	11458	,,	Milligan, G.	12435	Private	Roberts, G.
11404	,,	Foster, W.	10186	,,	Pearson, J.	11393	,,	Wilcox, W.
11477	,,	Garner, A.	11413	,,	Pendlebury, W. H.	11573	,,	Williams, R.
11386	,,	Gettins, R.	11588	,,	Pepper, J. A.			
12564	,,	Gilmore, J.	12434	,,	Redford, J.			

PLATOON NO. XII.

Platoon Commander - - - Lieut. F. J. Hick.
Platoon Sergeant - - - - Johnson, G.

11191	Sergeant	Gibson, F.	12468	,,	Davidson, J.	11558	,,	McKie, H.
11562	,,	Sullivan, F. W.	11541	,,	Davies, T.	11355	,,	Moores, J.
11798	,,	Taylor, J. T.	12452	,,	Davies, W.	11360	,,	Murphy, M.
11630	Corporal	Farrell, G.	11356	,,	Derbyshire, W. W.	11589	,,	Nixon, W.
11446	,,	Mills, W.	11601	,,	Ellary, B.	11585	,,	Oulten, T. H.
11678	,,	Ostick, J.	11503	,,	Gunn, A.	11595	,,	Proctor, F. H.
11357	L.-Corpl.	Ingham, A. E.	12007	,,	Hardman, J.	11592	,,	Raby, T.
15193	,,	Seddon, F.	11367	,,	Hindle, H.	11358	,,	Rostron, W. H.
11540	,,	Walker, E.	11496	,,	Housley, G.	11483	,,	Seddon, H.
11561	,,	Robinson, W.	11499	,,	Hughes, J.	11556	,,	Shaw, W.
11551	Private	Bancroft, A.	11656	Private	Briggs, W.	11559	,,	Sharples, A. V.
11670	,,	Anson, J. W.				11365	,,	Sloane, F.
11354	,,	Bebbington, J.	11350	Private	Hunter, A.	11662	,,	Smith, H.
11495	,,	Birch, W.	11484	,,	James, E.	11661	,,	Sutherland, J. K.
11664	,,	Bird, E.	11557	,,	Jardine, J.	11505	,,	Taylor, R.
11519	,,	Bowden, S.	11574	,,	Jones, J. E.	11596	,,	Tonge, J.
12466	,,	Bowden, W.	11488	,,	Jones, H.	12447	,,	Wharmley, H.
11542	,,	Bracken, J.	11658	,,	Jones, W.	11577	,,	White, H. A.
11521	,,	Brighton, F.	11500	,,	Lakin, E.	11514	,,	Winstanley, J.
11660	,,	Caffrey, P.	11669	,,	Lord, A.	11507	,,	Woodward, E.
11676	,,	Cowper, J.	11674	,,	Martin, A.	12444	,,	Mudd, W.
11597	,,	Currie, H.	12448	,,	Mason, J.	11544	Private	Taylor, W.

16th (Service) Battalion Lancashire Fusiliers.
"D" COMPANY.

Officer Commanding Company -	Capt. W. Owen Smith.
Second in Command -	Capt. J. Tattersall.
Company Sergeant Major -	Greenough, P.
Company Quartermaster Sergeant -	Watson, C.

PLATOON NO. XIII.

Platoon Commander - - -	Lieut. D. Robertson.
Platoon Sergeant - - -	Anderson, E.

11967	R.Q.M.S.	Walsh, J. W.	12473	„	Farnsworth, H. S.	11829	„	McDonald, A.
11882	Sergeant	Riddell, A. E.	11640	„	Flitcroft, J.	11871	„	McQuade, J.
11785	Corporal	Baker, A.	11780	„	Gallagher, A.	12479	„	Procter, A.
11776	„	Davies, J. A.	11878	„	Gibson, J. W.	11833	„	Reeves, J.
12480	L.-Corpl.	Black, J.	11860	„	Hellis, J.	11802	„	Rigby, J.
11794	„	Taylor, S.	11876	„	Hobson, T.	11873	„	Riley, T.
11323	Private	Allison, F.	11813	„	Horton, S.	11879	„	Robinson, S.
11862	„	Barker, J. E. H.	11864	„	Howarth, R.	11796	„	Roche, G.
11823	„	Bartlett, F.	11851	Corporal	Kenyon, W. F.	11866	„	Rogers, W. T.
11806	„	Bettress, D.	11792	Private	Egan, A.	11816	„	Shaw, A.
11446	„	Bevins, F.	11432	„	Gorton, L.	11880	„	Smith, C.
12590	„	Bidmead, H. L.	11814	„	Gent, W.	11822	„	Sproston, H.
11778	„	Bleese, C.	11863	Private	Hopwood, J.	12478	„	Sumner, F.
11786	„	Brearley, A.	12558	„	Hyland, J. C.	11818	„	Tarrant, H.
11795	„	Campbell, T.	11790	„	Jackson, W.	11634	„	Thorne, J. J.
11797	„	Chapman, J.	11827	„	Jones, F.	11824	„	Wade, A.
11845	„	Craig, J.	11861	„	Lees, J.	11777	„	Wallace, T.
11870	„	Crow, W.	11831	„	Leman, A.	12414	„	Williamson, J.
11859	„	Culler, P.	11803	„	Matthews, W.	11817	„	Young, C.
11868	„	Davies, E. S.	11812	„	Molden, C.	11872	Private	Holland, E.
11881	„	Davies, W.	12472	„	Mollard, E.	11875	„	Lawton, F.
11793	„	Edge, W.	11789	„	Mottershead, H.	11434	„	Wood, W.

PLATOON NO. XIV.

Platoon Commander - - -	2nd Lieut. E. A. Owen.
Platoon Sergeant - - -	Brewster, A.

11885	Sergeant	Riddell, W. J.	11942	„	Fox, W.	11918	„	Maycox, T.
15084	Corporal	Harrison, P.	11902	„	Goodwin, J.	11849	„	Moores, J.
11805	„	Kirkwood, R.	11938	„	Hall, C. R.	11895	„	Morrow, T.
11923	L.-Corpl.	Unsworth, J.	11925	„	Hardy, J.	11932	„	Oakes, T. A.
11598	Private	Anderson, C. N.	11907	„	Heywood, J.	11485	„	O'Donnell, A.
11599	„	Ashcroft, A.	11919	„	Hodgkiss, B.	11858	„	Parker, L.
11563	„	Binfield, T.	12522	„	Holland, T.	11930	„	Phillips, C. E.
11425	„	Birmingham, J.	11855	„	Hopkins, J.	11924	„	Poole, H.
11555	„	Booth, H.	11850	Private	Barrington, C.	11742	„	Reeks, H.
11553	„	Brooks, J. G.	11904	„	Cottrill, H.	11361	„	Smith, T.
11854	„	Cartledge, F. J.	11856	Private	Howard, A.	11911	„	Swift, H.
11901	„	Clarke, F.	11943	„	Howell, R.	12416	„	Sykes, D.
11913	„	Clarke, J. G.	11946	„	Hubbard, F.	11897	„	Timperley, A.
11914	„	Collier, O. G.	12065	„	Hulmes, J.	11892	„	Watts, W.
11940	„	Costain, A.	11887	„	Hurine, G.	11846	„	Widdows, H.
11917	„	Crook, H.	11842	„	Ingham, E.	11929	„	Withington, A.
11843	„	Currie, J.	11920	„	Jeffs, J.	11947	„	Wohlters, I. H.
11908	„	Daber, W.	11890	„	Jones, W.	11926	„	Wolstenholme, A.
11888	„	Diggle, A.	11910	„	Lawson, S.	11912	Private	Matley, A.
11909	„	Donnelly, F.	11886	„	Lawton, W.	12099	„	Withers, A.
11921	„	Eite, H.	12482	„	Leech, J.			
11939	„	Evans, J. W.	11889	„	Marshall, H.			

16th (Service) Battalion Lancashire Fusiliers.

"D" COMPANY.

Officer Commanding Company - Capt. W. OWEN SMITH.
Second in Command - - - Capt. J. TATTERSALL.
Company Sergeant Major - GREENOUGH, P.
Company Quartermaster Sergeant - WATSON, C.

PLATOON NO. XV.

Platoon Commander - - - Lieut. F. F. WAUGH.
Platoon Sergeant - - - BARNES, W. J.

No.	Rank	Name	No.	Rank	Name	No.	Rank	Name
11899	Sergeant	HOWCROFT, W.	11953	„	GARTLAND, B.	12022	„	QUINN, L. H.
11977	„	OSBORNE, A. K.	11957	„	GILMARTIN, T.	11961	„	RABY, F.
12011	L.-Sergt.	DUNNING, G.	11988	„	HAMBLETT, H.	11560	„	ROWBOTTOM, R.
11807	Corporal	BEGLEY, C. J.	11903	„	HARTLAND, W.	11965	„	ROGERS, T.
11959	L.-Corpl.	DALZIEL, A.	11960	„	HETHERINGTON, J.	11980	„	RUSSELL, T. P.
11978	„	HEAP, A.	12040	„	HEWSON, G.	11583	„	SIDLOW, R. A.
12005	Private	BENNETT, J.	11954	„	HOLT, G.	12039	„	STANNEY, J.
12474	„	BRADLEY, A.	12048	„	HULMES, A.	12445	„	STEWART, J.
11529	„	BEGGS, P.	11962	„	JOLLY, E.	12015	„	SUTCLIFFE, T.
11935	„	BRIERLEY, E.	11566	Private	CASWELL, J. W.	12032	„	TABBRON, S.
11983	„	BROWN, S.	11955	„	DAVIES, J.	11513	„	TAYLOR, H.
11996	„	CHORLTON, N.	12020	Private	HOWARD, W.	12014	„	THOMPSON, J.
12475	„	CONWAY, R.	11984	„	KENDAL, S.	11986	„	TURNER, W.
11975	„	DAVENPORT, J.	11969	„	LENORD, J.	11865	„	WADDINGTON, J.
11995	„	DONACHIE, E.	11998	„	LINDLEY, J.	12046	„	WALSH, J.
11950	„	DRIVER, J.	11987	„	LUCAS, T.	11991	„	WALTON, S.
11936	„	DURKIN, H.	11992	„	MAXWELL, H.	11571	„	WHITEHEAD, J.
11815	„	ELLERAY, T.	12031	„	MAXWELL, A.	11820	„	WHITELEY, A.
11981	„	ELLIOTT, H.	11985	„	OATES, J.	11964	„	YOUNG, W.
11533	„	FIELDING, F.	11971	„	PARSONS, L. E.	11511	Private	HINCHCLIFFE, J.
12042	„	FROST, E.	12013	„	QUIGLEY, T.	11944	„	HORNBY, T.

PLATOON NO. XVI.

Platoon Commander - - - 2nd Lieut. B. H. BREAR.

No.	Rank	Name	No.	Rank	Name	No.	Rank	Name
7667	B.S.M.	HARGREAVES, H.	12093	„	EMMETT, E. A.	12167	„	O'GARR, W.
11771	Corporal	HAYHURST, J.	12009	„	EVISON, A. W.	11722	„	QUINN, C. A.
12494	„	LEE, H.	12087	„	FALLOWS, J.	12092	„	SAMSON, E. C.
12081	L.-Corpl.	CABLE, A. E.	12056	„	FRANCES, R.	12063	„	SCOTT, A.
12030	„	JONES, A.	12407	„	GIFFORD, H.	12098	„	SEERS, F.
12025	Private	BARKER, E.	12058	„	HADCOCK, G.	12064	„	SHELDRICK, W.
12408	„	BECKETT, W.	12010	„	HOLT, T.	12403	„	STEAD, B.
12029	„	BLACKSTONE, M.	12088	Sergeant	SIGHE, J.	11781	„	STOCKTON, P.
12406	„	BOOTH, A.	11915	L.-Sergt.	HOLLAND, J.	12072	„	STRAFFORD, W.
11342	„	BRETT, J.	12074	Private	ATHERTON, F.	12028	„	TONGE, J.
12002	„	BROWN, J.	12401	„	BARTLEY, J.	12077	„	WELLBORN, F.
12086	„	BROWN, R.	15208	„	CASEY, E.	12060	„	WESTHEAD, C.
12405	„	BURGHALL, W.	12090	Private	HORROCKS, H.	12120	„	WHEELDON, H.
11970	„	CAMPBELL, R.	12409	„	HOWARD, T.	11737	„	WHITEHILL, W. H.
12059	„	CAWLEY, F.	11884	„	HULME, J.	11314	„	WHITTLE, J.
12192	„	CONNER, J.	12420	„	HUNTER, J.	12417	„	WINTERBURN, A.
12094	„	DAVIES, Dan.	12413	„	JONES, T.	12000	„	WOODACRE, J. R.
12095	„	DAVIES, Dai.	12091	„	KELLY, J.	12070	„	WORSLEY, W.
12062	„	DEAN, A.	12073	„	KNIGHT, J. W.	12075	Private	HOPWOOD, W.
12004	„	DIBLEY, F. W.	12117	„	LEE, J. W.	11999	„	JONES, H.
12006	„	DIBLEY, A. E.	12057	„	MOORE, W.	12402	„	McDERMOTT, T.
11743	„	DORSAY, W.	15209	„	MORLEY, C. T.	12083	„	RAGGETT, F.
12085	„	EDWARDS, J.	12001	„	MOSS, J. T.	12080	„	RIGBY, E.
15029	„	EDWARDS, A.	12066	„	NIGHTINGALE, W.			

16th (Service) Battalion Lancashire Fusiliers.

"E" COMPANY.

Officer Commanding Company - Capt. E. CROMPTON.
Second in Command - - - Lieut. R. W. WARD.
Company Sergeant Major - - HASTINGS, J.
Company Quartermaster Sergeant - DOUGLAS, W. J.

PLATOON NO. XIX.

Platoon Commander - - - 2nd Lieut. M. E. SWAIN.
Platoon Sergeant - - - BELL, J.

12197	Sergeant	ARMSTRONG, J.	11525	,,	DOWLER, J.	11844	,,	ROSCOE, G.
11312	,,	MORAN, W.	11294	,,	GALVIN, J.	12033	,,	KIRWIN, W.
11765	,,	RICE, H.	11509	,,	GUTHRIE, F.	11528	,,	SHUTTLEWORTH, E.
11442	Private	ATHERTON, T.	12457	,,	HASLAM, H.	11635	,,	SYKES, H.
12458	,,	BEAMISH, G.	12016	,,	HEATH, E.	11738	,,	SIMPSON, R.
12412	,,	BELLIS, W.	11756	,,	FORSHAW, W.	11782	,,	SHORE, C.
11520	,,	BEBBINGTON, C.	11306	,,	JONES, E.	12122	,,	TONGUE, J.
11423	,,	BOOTH, C.	12178	Private	MARTIN, C.	11710	,,	TAYLOR, T.
11330	,,	BOWDEN, G.	11291	,,	PRESTON, J.	11894	,,	TAW, H.
11772	,,	BROWN, L.	11696	,,	PENNINGTON, J. W.	12106	,,	WATERWORTH, J.
11389	,,	BAGRIDGE, W. H.	12134	,,	PHILIPS, E.	12102	,,	WATSON, G.
11347	,,	CULSHAW, A.	11353	,,	POLLITT, J.	11225	,,	WALSH, W.
11675	,,	DAVIDSON, E.	11340	,,	ROBINSON, D.	11363	,,	WHITEHEAD, W.
12436	,,	DAVIES, D.	12105	,,	RATCLIFFE, J.			

PLATOON NO. XX.

Platoon Commander - - - 2nd Lieut. A. LINDSAY-JONES.
Platoon Sergeant - - - SANT, T. J.

15101	L.-Sergt.	POTTS, P. W.	15159	,,	GRIFFITHS, W.	15092	,,	PYE, W.
12553	,,	HULME, W.	15031	,,	GREATOREX, W.	15144	,,	ROWLANDS, E.
15069	Corporal	TAYLOR, S.	12492	,,	GRIMSHAW, W.	15182	,,	SAMBROOK, H.
12505	L.-Corpl.	CASHIN, J.	15170	,,	GRIME, H.	15192	,,	SHARPLES, A.
15189	Private	BAILEY, T.	15130	,,	HARRISON, P.	15058	,,	SHARPLES, S.
15107	,,	BARNSLEY, T.	15158	,,	HESFORD, J.	15161	,,	SIDDONS, W.
15051	,,	BARNES, A.	15055	,,	HUTCHINSON, C. I.	15191	,,	SWEENEY, T.
15076	,,	BESWICK, W.	15062	,,	JONES, M.	15049	,,	TAYLOR, T.
15081	,,	BESWICK, W.	15212	,,	JOHNSTONE, R.	15047	,,	TICKLE, W.
15109	,,	BOLAND, J.	15125	Private	LEWIS, J. W.	15115	,,	TOMKINSON, A. E.
15180	,,	BOWLING, A.	15087	,,	LLOYD, P.	15206	,,	WALKDEN, J.
15121	,,	CHILTON, J.	15174	,,	LEWIS, R.	15190	,,	WALLWORK, R.
15102	,,	CORDWELL, P.	15199	,,	MATHER, C.	15163	,,	WAINWRIGHT, J.
15120	,,	DAVIES, R.	15183	,,	MORTON, F.	12127	,,	WALSH, H.
15213	,,	DOUGLAS, W. A.	15178	,,	MEE, J. W.	15094	,,	WILKES, U.
15127	,,	EVANS, W.	15186	,,	ORMROD, E.	15176	,,	WOLSTENCROFT, H.
15123	,,	FENNY, J. T.	15136	,,	PEARSON, J. R.	12127	,,	WALSH, H.
12599	,,	GOSTRIDGE, J.	15162	,,	PRICE, S.	15197	,,	YATES, A.

Bugle Band.

11885	Sergeant	RIDDELL, W. J.	11240	,,	BATES, J.	11742	,,	REEKS, H.
11976	Corporal	MYERS, J.	11264	,,	BOGG, C.	12104	,,	STANLEY, T.
11208	L.-Corpl.	MCLEAN, F.	12531	,,	BATES, R.	12577	,,	THOMPSON, W.
12529	,,	DERBYSHIRE, W.	12136	,,	DYWER, A.	15111	,,	WALSH, P.
11561	,,	ROBINSON, W.	11221	S.Act.Dr.	HUNT, H.	15179	,,	YOUNGMAN, S.
11546	Drummer	ALDRED, G.	11815	Drummer	ELLERAY, T.	11222	S.Act.Dr.	BRADSHAW, E.
11323	,,	ALLISON, F.	12558	,,	HYLAND, J. C.	11319	,,	ENGLAND, J. T.
11670	,,	ANSON, J. W.	11536	,,	MALONE, F.	11388	,,	HOLT, T.
11495	,,	BIRCH, W.	11321	,,	RATCLIFFE, C.	11781	,,	STOCKTON, P.

Roll of Officers.

Brevet-Col.	STAINFORTH, L. C. H.		Lieutenant	WALLERS, F.
Major	BARTLETT, ERIC O.		2nd Lieut.	WOOD, D.
,,	AMBROSE SMITH, J.		,,	DIXON, A. C.
Captain	THOMAS, A. E.		,,	STIEBEL, C. A.
,,	LYON, E. W.		,,	CRESSY, C. C.
,,	EVANS, F. W.		,,	WHITTLES, N.
,,	WADE-GERY, H. T.		,,	JACKSON, F. D.
Lieut. & Adjt.	HEWITT, J.		,,	GUILLAUME, A.
Lieutenant	BARSTOW, H. H. A.		,,	SMITH, G. B.
,,	FREEMAN, J. L.		,,	SMITH, H. A.
,,	WOOD, R. T.		—,,	NIGHTINGALE, W. R.
,,	PALK, S. A.		,,	WILLETT, J. C.
,,	EVANS, K. R.		,,	HILL, E. ST. L.
,,	MUSKER, H.		,,	LAMBERT, H.
,,	WHITEHEAD, J. G.		2nd Lieut.	MIDGLEY, L. B.
Lieut.-Col.	HUGHES, R. G. H.		,,	ATKINSON, F. W.
Lieutenant	HAYWOOD, W. G.			*Attached.*
,,	PILLING, F. W.		Lieutenant	KENNY, E. H.
Lieut. & Q.M.	PATCH, C. W.			(R.A.M.C.)

Non-Commissioned Officers' (Sergeants) Roll.

17348 War. Off. BOND, T. H.

17425 R.Q.M.S. PENKETH, J. C.
17685 R.O.R.S. FOWLER, F.

Roll No.	Rank and Name.		Roll No.	Rank and Name.	
17653	C.S.M.	DUNKINSON, H.	18655	Sergeant	SUTTLE, E.
18570	,,	TAYLOR, W.	17492	,,	MACKAY, J.
6858	,,	GREEN, J.	18656	,,	MORRIS, A.
18508	,,	REARDEN, D.	17616	,,	PRESTWICH, W.
18540	,,	VALENTINE, W. H.	17797	,,	WILDMAN, W. J.
17392	C.Q.M.S.	CHENEY, A.	17290	,,	SHARPLES, T.
17557	,,	WALLWORK, P.	17634	,,	SMITH, J. E.
10693	,,	BRADFORD, J. J.	17608	,,	HURD, A. E.
6379	,,	MILNE, F. A.	17617	,,	MULRANEY, F.
17474	Sgt. Cook	BIRTWISTLE, J.	17886	,,	LOOKER, J.
18617	Sig. Sgt.	CARTER, H.	17784	,,	HARLAND, J.
17406	Sergeant	BRANDISH, J.	17777	,,	FRASER, J. B.
17361	,,	BLACKSHAW, J.	18586	,,	GIBSON, F. T.
17410	,,	HUNTER, J. W.	18600	,,	BANHAM, A.
17445	,,	SMEDLEY, H. A.	17733	,,	NEYLON, J.
17480	,,	LEDGER, H.	17778	L.-Sergt.	SMITH, C.
17534	,,	KNOWLES, J.	17459	,,	BROWN, A.
17372	,,	ANDERSON, T.	17527	,,	HOOLEY, F. E.
10109	,,	SPIERS, S.	17781	,,	TIMPERLY, W.
17514	,,	FRAY, R.	18780	,,	CUNNINGHAM, W.
17297	,,	WILKINSON, T.	17945	,,	LOMAS, J. W.
17262	,,	KNIGHT, T.	18528	,,	HABERSHON, W.
18985	,,	FITZGERALD, T.	17380	,,	HESKETH, W.
17355	,,	ORAM, A.	17791	,,	HODGSON, R.
6362	,,	BOOTH, T.	17465	Sergeant	MULLINS, W.
17779	C.Q.M.S.	MOULSON, J.	17400	,,	TYSON, J.
10168	Sergeant	CUNNINGHAM, T.	18986	L.-Sergt.	PITTS, J. E.
17989	,,	BAGULEY, T.			
17845	,,	DAWSON, P.			

19th (Service) Battalion Lancashire Fusiliers.

"A" COMPANY.

Officer Commanding Company - Major J. Ambrose Smith.
Second in Command - - - Lieut. W. G. Haywood.
Company Sergeant Major - Dunkinson, H.
Company Quartermaster Sergeant - Cheney, Arthur.

PLATOON NO. I.

Platoon Commander - - - 2nd Lieut. W. Roocroft Nightingale.
Platoon Sergeant - - - - Ledger, H.

13268	Corporal	Robinson, J.	13214	,,	Wilkinson, A.	17363	,,	Aston, J.
13170	L.-Corpl.	Jobson, R.	13244	,,	Billington, A.	13263	,,	Boyd, T.
17388	Private	Davies, C. E.	17465	Sergeant	Mullins, W.	17375	,,	Birtles, E.
13121	,,	Ogden, J.	13251	L.-Corpl.	Cochrane, H.	13036	,,	Campbell, J.
13108	,,	Dodd, R.	13271	,,	Taylor, R.	17268	,,	Greensmith, R.
13260	,,	Hope, J.	17543	Private	Nixon, E. H.	17267	,,	Heywood, W.
13250	,,	Horridge, J.	13259	,,	Pennington, N. H.	13242	,,	Hamblett, J.
13374	,,	Hiley, L.	13223	,,	Ashton, T.	13007	,,	Mulvey, J. H.
17304	,,	Littler, W.	17526	,,	Crimes, C.	17381	,,	Pennington, J.
13245	,,	McGuinness, A. J.	17879	,,	Coldhill, H.	13247	,,	Parry, T.
17378	,,	Whittaker, J.	13256	Private	Beard, J.	13255	,,	Stott, J. T.
13225	,,	Aspden, G.	17369	,,	Bridge, W. J.	13235	Private	Poole, R.
17411	,,	Black, J.	17365	,,	Crook, C. E.	13277	,,	Tomlinson, W.
13254	,,	Caldwell, T.	13253	,,	Downie, J.	13265	,,	Wainright, C.
17540	,,	Gregory, H.	13240	,,	Keyes, C.	13248	,,	Smallman, W.
13249	,,	Jenkinson, H.	13257	,,	Luttmann, A. E.	17899	,,	Fleury, J.
13278	,,	Jones, T. H.	13274	,,	Mills, J.	13227	,,	Foster, W. H.
17382	,,	Lancelot, R.	17383	,,	McKiernan, T.	13272	,,	Kelly, W.
13275	,,	Muir, J.	17364	,,	Thompson, H.	13266	,,	Williams, R.
17373	,,	Taylor, J. C.	13262	,,	Walsh, A.			
17339	,,	Wainright, C. W.	17368	,,	Poland, W.			

PLATOON NO. II.

Platoon Commander - - - 2nd Lieut. C. A. Stiebel.
Platoon Sergeant - - - - Brandish, J.

17100	Sergeant	Hunter, J. W.	17413	,,	Glenny, S.	17469	,,	Ditchfield, D.
17360	Corporal	Astle, W.	17808	,,	Gardiner, H.	17938	,,	Carew, W.
17372	,,	Anderson, T.	17391	,,	Plumbly, W.	17370	,,	Allen, A.
17396	L.-Corpl.	Tinsley, W.	17405	,,	Scott, J.	17423	,,	Baines, J.
17386	,,	Croden, J. E.	17398	,,	Wardle, J.	17427	,,	Constantine, H.
17428	Private	Branagan, J.	17389	L.-Corpl.	Greaves, S.	17434	,,	Cole, J. P.
17437	,,	Connor, R.	17436	Private	Ashworth, S.	17415	,,	Ellis, J.
17422	,,	Davies, G.	17432	,,	Heywood, T. M.	17424	,,	Hawthorn, J. T.
17385	,,	Farthing, G. P.	17390	,,	Doyle, J.	17628	,,	Horsbrough, D.
17358	,,	Hammett, W.	17842	,,	Evans, J.	17362	,,	Hickinbotham, C.
17453	,,	Irving, G. E.	17871	,,	Finney, C.	17416	,,	Jackson, W.
17572	,,	Mayell, F.	17417	Private	White, J.	17433	,,	North, E. J.
17402	,,	McCann, A.	17401	,,	Bromley, W.	17418	,,	Steell, F.
17421	,,	Pearce, T.	17438	,,	Barry, J.	17393	,,	Wood, F.
17446	,,	Stones, L. C.	17793	,,	Bullough, W.	17841	,,	Walton, T.
17394	,,	Armstrong, T.	17414	,,	Cooke, W.	17395	Private	Sharrocks, J.
17397	,,	Crook, W.	17347	,,	Greenhalgh, T.	17426	,,	Norman, W. H.
17466	,,	Crook, G. A.	17582	,,	Leigh, J.	17767	,,	Shaw, A.
17403	,,	Dillon, W.	17419	,,	Sinclair, J.	17454	,,	Lillas, P.
17404	,,	Foulkes, W.	17366	,,	Shelmerdine, W.	17439	,,	Partington, E.
17376	,,	Fletcher, D. W.	17441	,,	Wall, R.			

19th (Service) Battalion Lancashire Fusiliers.

"A" COMPANY.

Officer Commanding Company	- Major J. AMBROSE SMITH.
Second in Command	- Lieut. W. G. HAYWOOD.
Company Sergeant Major	- DUNKINSON, H.
Company Quartermaster Sergeant	- CHENEY, ARTHUR.

PLATOON NO. III.

Platoon Commander	- Lieut. J. HEWITT.
Platoon Sergeant	- SMEDLEY, H.

17496	Sergeant	PARKINSON, A.	17671	,,	DUCKWORTH, T.	17461	,,	ROBINSON, T.
17614	,,	ISAACS, L.	17764	,,	ENTWISTLE, W.	17306	,,	RUDD, W.
17501	Corporal	BROWN, A.	17579	,,	FARRELL, R.	17457	,,	WEBB, C.
17677	L.-Corpl.	RUDD, J. J.	17493	,,	FEENEY, J.	17679	,,	SCHOFIELD, D.
17442	,,	STAPELY, W.	17475	L.-Corpl.	RAVENSCROFT, J. C.	17678	,,	CREWE, D.
17464	,,	JOHNSON, W.	17477	,,	BRADY, C.	17447	,,	DUFFY, C.
			17576	Private	CUNLIFFE, A.	17770	,,	ENTWISTLE, E.
17654	Private	AVERY, W.	17494	,,	CLEARY, A.	17430	,,	JONES, T.
17471	,,	BATTY, C. E.	17470	,,	WEBSTER, W.	17443	,,	KITE, J.
17577	,,	CUNLIFFE, W.	17408	,,	DOOLEY, C.	17482	,,	MAJOR, J. A.
17703	,,	CARTER, T.	17895	,,	ROGER, C.	17476	,,	RILEY, W.
17658	,,	HATTON, P. T.	17581	Private	HARRIS, J.	17723	,,	SMITH, J.
17637	,,	JONES, A.	17491	,,	FLANNAGAN, D.	17502	,,	WILLIAMS, I. A.
17657	,,	JONES, E.	17655	,,	JACKSON, J. F.	17488	,,	WINSTANLEY, T.
17698	,,	MOLLARD, E.	17837	,,	BUCKLEY, F.	17452	Private	ROOKE, H.
17373	,,	SIMON, G.	17583	,,	BRENNAN, J.	17495	,,	KENNY, J.
17450	,,	SMITH, G.	17612	,,	CLARKSON, D.	17440	,,	WALL, A.
17877	,,	TOMLINSON, W.	17570	,,	FLANAGAN, J.	17789	,,	HESTEN, W.
17618	,,	BARNES, J.	17504	,,	FLYNNE, D.	17490	,,	POTTS, C. F.
17656	,,	BURTINSHAW, J.	17571	,,	FRASER, W.	17336	,,	SMITH, W.
17702	,,	CARTER, T.	17769	,,	HOOK, I.			
17705	,,	COLE, A.	17768	,,	NESBITT, T.			

PLATOON NO. IV.

Platoon Commander	- 2nd Lieut. DOUGLAS WOOD.
Platoon Sergeant	- BLACKSHAW, J.

17534	Sergeant	KNOWLES, J.	13273	,,	WITHNELL, F.	17343	,,	ASHTONHURST, J.
17776	,,	WOOD, W.	13276	,,	GRUNDY, S.	17538	,,	HASTINGS, W.
17926	Corporal	HIBBERT, F.	17299	L.-Corpl.	APPLEBY, G.	17788	,,	GOODIER, B.
17544	Private	BERRY, W.	17507	Private	BUCKLEY, J.	17311	,,	MORRIS, W.
17449	,,	BATE, S.	17518	,,	DAVIES, D.	17302	,,	RODELEY, A.
17342	,,	DARWELL, W.	17286	,,	MASON, A.	17529	,,	ROYLANCE, A.
17539	,,	BARRATT, P.	17519	,,	PEACE, J.	17454	,,	LILLAS, P.
17517	,,	HOWARTH, S. T.	17533	,,	MORRIS, T.	17528	,,	SKEGG, D.
17613	,,	HARPER, W.	17269	,,	SHERIDAN, B.	17334	,,	WILLIAMSON, B.
17271	,,	JEFFRIES, J.	17503	,,	DAVIES, J.	17535	,,	PRATTLEY, J.
18512	,,	JACKSON, A.	17326	,,	FERBER, H.	17509	Private	JONES, W. H.
17508	,,	BROWNHILL, A.	17338	,,	HANSBURY, P.	17352	,,	PRICE, A.
17337	,,	BOOTH, G. W.	17536	Private	JOHNSON, G.	17277	,,	TAYLOR, J.
17843	,,	DARBYSHIRE, H.	17349	,,	HOLDEN, T.	17300	,,	WALSH, F.
17285	,,	GOULDBOURN, J.	17809	,,	NORTON, G.	17532	,,	BOWDEN, J.
17554	,,	ROGERS, W.	17576	,,	SYKES, T.	17530	,,	CARMAN, J.
17832	,,	SCOTT, J.	17771	,,	WHEATLEY, W.	13239	,,	DUCKER, W.
17505	,,	VALENTINE, R.	17726	,,	JONES, W.	17891	,,	HARVEY, W.
17250	,,	WHITEHEAD, W.	17335	,,	BYRNE, J.	17545	,,	INCE, T.
17810	,,	ASTON, F.	17636	,,	BOAK, D.	17870	,,	KENYON, T.
17275	,,	DALY, W.	17251	,,	CROOK, D.	17455	,,	WOLSTENHOLME, T
17542	Corporal	O'CONNOR, J.	13132	,,	DOWNES, S.	17699	,,	DIXON, J.
						17473	,,	DUNN, D.

"B" COMPANY.

Officer Commanding Company - Capt. E. W. Lyon.
Second in Command - - - Lieut. H. H. A. Barstow.
Company Sergeant Major - - Taylor, W.
Company Quartermaster Sergeant - Moulson, J.

PLATOON NO. V.

Platoon Commander - - - Lieut. J. L. Freeman.
Platoon Sergeant - - - Oram, A.

17380	L.-Sergt.	Hesketh, W.	17498	,,	Steeples, E.	17325	,,	Johnson, W.
17708	Corporal	Robertson, D.	17500	,,	Tandy, D.	17513	,,	Salmon, C.
17264	,,	Carter, J.	17265	,,	Parks, G.	17550	,,	Oldfield, H.
17958	L.-Corpl.	Dunn, J.	17667	,,	Thompson, W.	17266	,,	Powell, B.
17665	,,	Lomas, A.	17745	,,	Lee, C. W.	17585	,,	Oakley, J.
17295	,,	Mather, A.	17796	Corporal	Potts, S.	17511	,,	Reynolds, W.
18885	Private	Banfield, A.	17896	Private	Broadbent, T.	17956	,,	Dorrington, S.
18520	,,	Megus, G.	17479	,,	Cooper, R.	17668	,,	Smith, G. A.
18504	,,	Bromley, G.	17261	Private	Carson, H.	17512	,,	Mason, J.
17344	,,	Bronson, H.	17584	,,	Harrison, J. E.	18518	,,	Evans, W.
17270	,,	Bamby, W. H.	18503	,,	Hall, J.	17681	,,	Peel, P.
17282	,,	Chaderton, E.	17736	Private	Hornby, J.	18505	,,	Slamon, P.
18515	,,	Evans, W.	17408	,,	Duffy, A.	17897	,,	Weaver, J.
17552	,,	Forshaw, J.	17837	,,	Sapsead, H.	17917	,,	Story, W.
17522	,,	Gaskell, H.	17523	,,	Lea, J. E.	17510	,,	Roe, E.
17856	,,	Grindley, J. W.	17953	,,	Fryer, T.	17497	,,	McGee, T.
18530	,,	Goldstrong, J.	17520	,,	Newton, A.		,,	Hadfield, W.
17549	,,	Higham, H.	17322	,,	Johnson, J.			
17282	,,	Hayes, W.						

PLATOON NO. VI.

Platoon Commander - - - 2nd Lieut. J. G. Whitehead.
Platoon Sergeant - - - Cunningham, J.

17297	Sergeant	Wilkinson, T.	17663	,,	Campbell, W.	17713	,,	McCarthy, T.
17912	Corporal	Taylor, W. A.	17920	,,	Garside, W.	17934	,,	Pendleton, D.
17715	L.-Corpl.	Rodgers, J.	17341	,,	Pennington, A.	17686	,,	Edwards, C.
17534	Private	Burgess, S.	17619	,,	Helps, E.	17711	,,	Clunie, C.
17347	,,	Harrop, J.	17688	,,	Hallsworth, F.	17857	,,	Grey, E.
17710	,,	Kempton, J.	17384	L.-Corpl.	Battersby, J.	17882	,,	Ridgway, G.
17672	,,	Gregory, J.	17918	,,	Lee, T.	17894	,,	Watkins, J.
17915	,,	Hall, G.	17707	Private	Holt, D.	17908	,,	Eccles, A.
17683	,,	Ferguson, S.	17740	,,	Potts, W.	17858	,,	Concanon, S.
17738	,,	Fryatt, W.	17969	,,	Birkenhead, J.	17935	,,	McDermott, T.
17743	,,	Lynch, P.	17260	Private	Scott, H.	17833	,,	Barnes, W.
17838	,,	Beswick, L.	17706	,,	Gandy, J.	17913	,,	Thorpe, G.
17340	,,	Rigby, G.	17883	,,	Sutcliffe, H. J.	17907	,,	Royle, E.
17279	,,	Tevnan, J.	17916	,,	Milligan, F.	17524	,,	Morgan, J.
17741	,,	Stark, S.	17861	,,	Dootson, W.	17737	Private	Emmitt, W.
17739	,,	Murray, W.	17862	,,	Pilling, F.	17539	,,	Stabler, H.
17742	,,	Knight, J. W.	17863	,,	Tyler, T.	17885	,,	Baron, T.
17499	,,	Pinchers, T.	17880	,,	Foster, J.	17664	,,	Fallows, S.
17324	,,	Jones, J.	17881	,,	Cox, H.	17552	,,	Quinlan, M.
17744	,,	Pollard, H.	17855	,,	Edwards, R.			

3

"B" COMPANY.

Officer Commanding Company -	Capt. E. W. Lyon.
Second in Command - - -	Lieut. H. H. A. Barstow.
Company Sergeant Major - -	Taylor, W.
Company Quartermaster Sergeant -	Moulson, J.

PLATOON NO. VII.

Platoon Commander - - -	2nd Lieut. N. Whittles.
Platoon Sergeant - - -	Fray, R.

18655	Sergeant	SUTTLE, C.	18648	,,	DEANE, R.	18983	,,	BERGIN, M.
17791	L.-Sergt.	HODGSON, R.	18062	,,	PENNELL, J.	18647	,,	EVANS, F. C.
18537	Corporal	WHEELDON, A.	18660	,,	BENNETT, J.	18754	,,	ALLEN, C.
17814	L.-Corpl.	WORTHINGTON, S.	18773	,,	BARSTOW, W.	17919	,,	CROMPTON, F.
18519	Private	SAVILLE, E.	18603	,,	BOLLESTY, H.	18790	,,	JONES, J.
18542	,,	WALKER, A.	17993	,,	COY, C.	18833	,,	THORNTON, H.
17547	,,	HAMILTON, W.	17646	Corporal	HAZEL, F.	18649	,,	SMETHURST, W.
17984	,,	TAYLOR, J.	17548	L.-Corpl.	LEE, J.	18945	,,	BAILEY, J.
17684	,,	HARROP, T.	17884	Private	McCAW, W.	18612	,,	HAUGHTON, J.
17716	,,	HAUGHEY, J.	17669	Private	ROYLE, J.	18680	,,	EMMS, H.
17921	,,	CRAMER, J.	17980	,,	ROGERS, J.	17671	,,	LEE, F.
17483	,,	BROWNBILL, H.	18941	,,	LEIGH, J.	18521	,,	MOIR, G.
17983	,,	BENNETT, G.	17478	,,	MUSKER, W.	18043	,,	ASHURST, E.
18531	,,	BROOKS, J.	17854	,,	CLEGG, J.	17709	,,	NEWTON, J.
18541	,,	SMITH, P.	18794	,,	HOPE, F.	18838	,,	THOMPSON, R.
17831	,,	SALMON, C.	18942	,,	HIRSHMURGH, S.	17796	Private	POTTS, S.
18761	,,	TAYLOR, O.	18750	,,	RUSTAGE, T.	17054	,,	MELLOR, W.
18785	,,	CULLITON, W.	18561	,, —	NICHOLSON, J.			
18615	,,	ROYLE, J.	18587	,,	TROW, T.			

PLATOON NO. VIII.

Platoon Commander - - -	2nd Lieut. F. D. Jackson.
Platoon Sergeant - - -	Spiers, S.

17685	O.R. Sgt.	FOWLER, F.	18961	,,	LEE, W.	17996	,,	CONNER, A.
17444	Corporal	HIRST, V.	18834	,,	JENKINSON, F.	18567	,,	BEDDOWS, T.
18841	L.-Corpl.	DALEY, J.	18714	,,	HINKS, W.	18571	,,	CANN, C.
18538	,,	CHESTER, W.	18662	,,	CROMPTON, E.	18781	,,	MAYO, T.
18560	,,	DUNN, J.	18783	,,	BONSALL, W.	18761	,,	SHEPARD, J.
18641	Private	POWER, J.	18555	,,	COLLANTINE, W.	18782	,,	WALTERS, W.
18626	,,	ROBINSON, F. H. J.	18717	,,	MEE, E.	18539	,,	BROOKS, B.
18787	,,	WIDDOWS, W.	18896	Private	CAFFERY, T.	18842	,,	CARSON, R.
18616	,,	RODGERS, W.	17844	,,	BURGESS, A.	17591	,,	CONNER, M.
18880	,,	BALL, H.	18568	Private	THOMPSON, R. A.	18597	,,	IRLAM, A.
17937	,,	HARVEY, J.	18838	,,	PURSALL, H.	18613	,,	BUTLER, C.
18944	,,	BARNETT, W.	18559	,,	REID, W.	17951	,,	CHADWICK, S.
18789	,,	HOYLE, W.	18753	,,	SMITH, H.	17892	,,	BARBER, A.
18730	,,	SIMISTER, H.	18759	,,	EGERTON, S.	18748	,,	SMITH, A.
18661	,,	ROBINSON, F.	18926	,,	HERITY, T.	18637	,,	HANDLEY, W.
18853	,,	CLARE, E.	18749	,,	GOODWIN, F.	18784	,,	KELLY, S.
18869	,,	McGARRY, J.	18523	,,	HIRSHMURGH, J. W.	18881	Private	CONNOR, T.

19th (Service) Battalion Lancashire Fusiliers.

"C" COMPANY.

Officer Commanding Company	- Capt. H. T. WADE GERY.
Second in Command - -	- Lieut. F. W. PILLING.
Company Sergeant Major -	- GREEN, J.
Company Quartermaster Sergeant -	WALLWORK, P. E.

PLATOON NO. IX.

Platoon Commander - -	- 2nd Lieut. J. C. WILLETT.
Platoon Sergeant - - -	- BOOTH, T.

17608	Sergeant	HURD, A. E.	17645	,,	THORPE, G.	17977	,,	HEAPS, W.
17487	L.-Corpl.	SACKFIELD, W.	17821	,,	PARKER, H.	17307	,,	McGARRY, F.
17629	,,	AUSTIN, J. H.	17749	,,	EVANS, A.	18874	,,	DAVIES, J. W.
17877	,,	DICKENSON, A.	17556	,,	TINSLEY, T.	17693	,,	HODGKINSON, C. W.
17333	Private	BERRY, W.	17802	,,	WINSTANLEY, A.	17627	,,	TOWNSEND, G.
17607	,,	POTTS, G. H.	17371	Corporal	ELLIS, J.	17853	,,	DOLMAN, J.
17754	,,	WALLWORK, J. J.	17358	Private	KYNASTON, G. P.	17310	,,	HARRIS, G.
17647	,,	DAVIES, J.	17760	,,	NICHOLLS, J.	17923	,,	DOLMAN, F.
17254	,,	RYDINGS, E.	17873	,,	WALLWORK, G.	17925	,,	DENNELL, G. H.
17765	,,	LLOYD, W.	17605	,,	POLLITT, J.	21047	,,	DEWHIRST, G. P.
17751	,,	BROUGH, C. W.				17650	,,	JONES, S.
17604	,,	TATLOCK, W.	17626	Private	WOLSTENCROFT, O.	18524	,,	CUMMINGS, D.
17597	,,	CORRESTINE, J. B.	17697	,,	WALKER, J.	17889	,,	OARE, J. T.
17758	,,	EVANS, W.	17599	,,	STEVENS, M.	17682	,,	REID, R.
17825	,,	STAPLETON, G.	17255	,,	ATKINSON, J.	17800	,,	CASKELL, H.
17753	,,	ANDREWS, J.	17772	,,	GLOVER, J.	17803	Private	WINSTANLEY, E.
17756	,,	SMITH, A.	17762	,,	PLATT, G.	17259	,,	LOWE, A.
17903	,,	SMETHURST, B.	17823	,,	PARTON, W. H.	17489	,,	LEE, H.
17652	,,	PRESTWICH, M.	17563	,,	KIRTON, R.		,,	YOUNG, J.
17851	,,	GRIFFIN, F.	17646	,,	HASLAM, W.			

PLATOON NO. X.

Platoon Commander - -	- 2nd Lieut. H. MUSKER.
Platoon Sergeant - - -	- SMITH, J. E.

17290	Sergeant	SHARPLES, T.	17307	,,	KIRKMAN, J.	17822	,,	ARNOLD, J.
17790	Corporal	SMITH, T.	17525	,,	EVANS, J. W.	17806	,,	BARNES, H.
17272	L.-Corpl.	WRAY, F.	17696	,,	WILD, F.	17318	,,	HALL, R.
17284	,,	WHALLEY, H.	17933	,,	HORSEFIELD, J.	17319	,,	EVANS, J.
17601	Private	EGAN, P.	17721	,,	CROOK, W. H.	17720	,,	JONES, J. L.
17827	,,	GIBBONS, C.	17289	,,	BENNETT, J.	17878	,,	PEARSON, R.
17561	,,	HILTON, J.	17310	Corporal	HARRISON, H.	17757	,,	TALBOT, J.
17905	,,	SILVER, F.	17692	Private	WILLIAMS, W.	17747	,,	WALLWORK, H.
17296	,,	POWER, J. H.	17236	,,	BOOTH, M.	17804	,,	HAYES, J.
17633	,,	CURETON, T.	17660	Private	HUGHES, J.	17976	,,	HARGREAVES, L.
17596	,,	BARNES, T.	17561	,,	STINCHCOMBE, W.	17799	,,	LUMB, L.
17558	,,	WALLWORK, G. R.	17562	,,	HARGREAVES, J.	17924	,,	WHALLEY, E.
17577	,,	KELLY, C.	17625	,,	SAVAGE, S.	17565	,,	BEDDOWS, T.
17825	,,	ATKINSON, W.	17694	,,	EDGE, A.	17719	,,	MILLINGTON, J.
17632	,,	SEDDON, W.	17643	,,	HOLDEN, J.	17718	Private	COX, J. B.
17876	,,	BROWN, J.	17966	,,	JONES, C.	17978	,,	FRYER, S.
17662	,,	TATE, S. H.	17331	,,	TOWNSEND, J. H.	17695	,,	ASHCROFT, J.
17274	,,	RYAN, T.	17689	,,	WILSON, W.			

19th (Service) Battalion Lancashire Fusiliers.

"C" COMPANY.

Officer Commanding Company - Capt. H. T. WADE GERY.
Second in Command - - - Lieut. F. W. PILLING.
Company Sergeant Major - - GREEN, J.
Company Quartermaster Sergeant - WALLWORK, P. E.

PLATOON NO. XI.

Platoon Commander - - - 2nd Lieut. C. C. CRESSY.
Platoon Sergeant - - - MACKAY, J.

17778	L.-Sergt.	SMITH, C.	17690	,,	RAWLINSON, F.	21041	,,	RILEY, M.
21038	Corporal	BLEACKLEY, T.	17863	,,	WALKER, J. W.	17763	,,	BIRMINGHAM, A.
17486	,,	TURNER, W.	18566	,,	JONES, T.	17365	,,	WRIGHT, J.
17332	L.-Corpl.	MACKAY, E.	18907	,,	GREENHALGH, H. E.	17748	,,	WOLSTENHOLME, T.
17826	,,	KELLY, N.	17906	,,	PHEASEY, T.	17875	,,	WRAY, S.
17774	Private	PURCELL, E.	17968	,,	BROWN, G.	17775	,,	McGURK, W.
17603	,,	ROBERTS, G.	17761	,,	LLOYD, J.	17564	,,	BERRY, J.
17764	,,	DAWSON, H.	17661	Private	SEDDON, G.	17650	,,	BLEARS, J.
18738	,,	POSTLE, T.	17900	,,	WOOD, J. W.	21046	,,	RYAN, H.
17965	,,	MITCHELL, M.	17801	Private	HUGHES, J.	21043	,,	SETTLE, J.
17962	,,	POWELL, S. W.	17906	,,	COOPER, J.	21042	,,	DUNCAN, J.
17807	,,	MUNDY, J.	18901	,,	WILLIAMS, J. C.	21045	,,	BUNTING, H.
18832	,,	JONES, F.	21008	,,	FARADAY, W.	18953	,,	SUTCLIFFE, H.
17961	,,	EVANS, F. W.	18966	,,	GROOME, G.	18807	,,	RUSSELL, W.
17253	,,	NICHOLLS, H.	18954	,,	JONES, L.	18874	,,	BOLESWORTH, R.
18576	,,	JONES, J. H.	18981	,,	BAILEY, H.	18535	,,	KENYON, F.
18911	,,	CHRISTIAN, L.	18912	,,	JONES, R.	17967	Private	MOSS, J.
18974	,,	BAILEY, W. H.	17598	,,	STEWARDSON, J.	21040	,,	ASHWORTH, R. B.

PLATOON NO. XII.

Platoon Commander - - - 2nd Lieut. L. B. MIDGLEY.
Platoon Sergeant - - - MORRIS, J.

17497	Sergeant	BROWN, A.	18904	,,	MOORES, S.	18994	,,	WALKER, W.
17616	,,	PRESTWICH, W.	18830	,,	CHAPMAN, H.	18585	,,	HEYWOOD, G.
17797	,,	WILDMAN, W. J.	18879	,,	NUGENT, A.	18946	,,	LOADER, A.
17691	Corporal	COOPER, W. F.	18831	,,	TICKLE, R.	18905	,,	RITCHIE, R.
17485	L.-Corpl.	BLUER, A.	17600	,,	POTTS, J.	17555	,,	ROTHWELL, J.
17850	Private	LEWIS, W. H.	21004	,,	RIMMER, J.	18557	,,	OAKLEY, E.
17814	,,	WINNARD, J.	18654	,,	EGAN, P.	18534	,,	HALL, T.
17273	,,	GARNER, R.	17798	,,	THOMAS, W.	18565	,,	RADCLIFFE, R.
17963	,,	BAUGH, A.	18903	Corporal	VIPOND, J.	18903	,,	BAILEY, W. H.
17722	,,	PRICE, J. S.	17824	Private	BOUSTEAD, A.	18978	,,	CLARKE, J.
18902	,,	BRAY, A.	18526	,,	MATHER, P.	18757	,,	ASTBURY, J.
21001	,,	WOOD, W. J.	17852	Private	RIDINGS, W.	18963	,,	ENTWISTLE, P.
17904	,,	JONES, W.	18876	,,	REYNOLDS, W.	18558	,,	PARKINSON, W.
17828	,,	COLLEY, E.	21007	,,	BROWN, S.	17775	,,	BATEMAN, H.
17560	,,	BOSWELL, J.	18564	Private	CROWTHER, J.	21003	,,	HOOKWAY, W. H.
17766	,,	LOWE, G.	18909	,,	DYSON, W.	18756	,,	FORSHAW, J.
17974	,,	PLATTIN, L.	18711	,,	SHEEN, W.	18932	,,	WILDE, T.
18543	,,	OSTICK, J.	21025	,,	SOUTHERN, R.	20014	,,	PATTERSON, W.
18652	,,	CROWTHER, J. J.	18910	,,	COTTRILL, S.	18875	,,	JARVIS, S.
18948	,,	WADSWORTH, B.	18874	,,	EDWARDS, J.	18556	,,	THOMPSON, R.
21012	,,	HOWARTH, R.	18511	,,	BLEASE, J.		,,	JONES, R.

19th (Service) Battalion Lancashire Fusiliers.

"D" COMPANY.

Officer Commanding Company - Capt. A. E. Thomas.
Second in Command - - - Lieut. J. L. Freeman.
Company Sergeant Major - - Reardon, D.
Company Quartermaster Sergeant - Bradford, J. J.

PLATOON NO. XIII.

Platoon Commander - - - Lieut. J. L. Freeman.
Platoon Sergeant - - - Mulraney, F.

17784	Sergeant	Harland, J.	17357	,,	Fennell, A.	17975	,,	Kenyon, W.
17781	L.-Sergt.	Timperley, W.	17865	,,	Haines, J. G.	17969	,,	Lyno, W. F.
17293	Corporal	Jones, G. P.	17630	,,	Hulme, E.	17864	,,	McHugh, J.
17315	L.-Corpl.	Jones, H. E.	17356	,,	Marlow, R.	17869	,,	Owen, J.
17587	,,	Taylor, F.	17973	,,	Mather, J.	17567	,,	Pearson, J.
17328	,,	Radway, R.	17316	,,	Monk, W.	17829	,,	Lord, J.
17638	,,	Nuttall, J.	17623	,,	Price, J. W.	17819	,,	Weaver, J.
17817	Private	Kelly, J.	18986	L.-Sergt.	Pitts, J. E.	17591	,,	Baxter, J.
17519	,,	Mills, E.	17705	Private	Collings, J.	17782	,,	Bolton, A.
17834	,,	Overton, G.	17252	,,	Worthington, D.	17718	,,	Carroll, J.
17566	,,	Hope, S. P.	17700	,,	Gleave, W.	17317	,,	Glynn, M.
17868	,,	Lomax, J.	17830	Private	Southern, J.	17589	,,	Gray, P.
17291	,,	Pollitt, E. K.	17676	,,	Stephenson, G.	17815	,,	Harrop, J. H.
17624	,,	Silver, W.	17816	,,	Williams, G.	17622	,,	Ogden, B.
17292	,,	Smith, T.	17590	,,	Berry, J.	17621	,,	Ogden, H.
17735	,,	Smethurst, R.	17867	,,	Boydell, H.	17592	,,	Stone, G.
17588	,,	Stevenson, G.	17568	,,	Gregory, J.	17569	,,	Wright, H. L.
17866	,,	Taylor, E.	17783	,,	Hope, R.	7568	Private	Hetherington, C.
17970	,,	Twist, L.	17640	,,	Hunt, W.	17831	,,	Ridings, A.
17620	,,	Davies, A.	17922	,,	Kelly, T.	17972	,,	Walsh, P.

PLATOON NO. XIV.

Platoon Commander - - - 2nd Lieut. A. C. Dixon.
Platoon Sergeant - - - Looker, J.

17329	Corporal	Morris, J.	18632	,,	Haworth, J.	18533	,,	Rothwell, J. W.
18684	,,	Byrne, C.	18848	,,	Henry, T.	18777	,,	Braithwaite, G. W.
18507	L.-Corpl.	Ashworth, R.	18500	,,	Horridge, J.	18770	,,	Blackburn, A.
18574	Private	Barlow, S.	18545	,,	Kennedy, E.	17999	,,	Diggle, D.
18578	,,	Lyon, H.	18846	,,	Leather, E.	18638	,,	Stoboff, I.
18779	,,	Sharman, H.	18877	,,	Smith, J.	18588	,,	Grumley, J.
18659	,,	Rigby, T.	18510	,,	Fox, J.	18609	,,	Stanley, R.
18776	,,	Green, E.	17330	,,	Vose, J.	18889	,,	Cowan, E.
18878	,,	Morris, S.	17578	Private	Roberts, S.	18532	,,	Hilton, T.
17593	,,	Wolstenholme, J.	17527	,,	Sinclair, R.	18607	,,	Leighton, J.
18786	,,	Hamer, S.	18775	,,	Morris, L.	18611	,,	Colley, J.
21009	,,	Corkindale, H.	18569	Private	Wilson, T.	18847	,,	Perry, T.
18850	,,	Markland, J. W.	17990	,,	Wardle, H.	18509	,,	Chantler, T.
18849	,,	Johnson, D.	18843	,,	Sheppard, T.	17586	,,	Rogerson, C.
18939	,,	Bolton, T.	18810	,,	Harrison, W.	18650	,,	Lord, H.
17974	,,	Ogden, H.	18608	,,	Moss, A.	18697	,,	Grimshaw, R.
18554	,,	Halliwell, R.	18515	,,	Harrington, H.	18940	,,	Byron, A.
18589	,,	Wright, G. W.	18618	,,	Clough, J.	18570	,,	Eccles, H.
18506	,,	Smith, H.	18908	,,	Barlow, S.	18652	Private	Small, B.
18792	,,	Clarke, W.	17785	,,	Derbyshire, J.	17327	,,	Brown, J.

"D" COMPANY.

Officer Commanding Company - Capt. A. E. THOMAS.
Second in Command - - - Lieut. J. L. FREEMAN.
Company Sergeant Major - - REARDON, D.
Company Quartermaster Sergeant - BRADFORD, J. J.

PLATOON NO. XV.

Platoon Commander - - - 2nd Lieut. G. B. SMITH.
Platoon Sergeant - - - - HOOLEY, F. E.

18866	L.-Corpl.	WATSON, J.	18811	,,	GRAHAM, F.	18731	,,	KIRKPATRICK, S.
18799	,,	HADFIELD, H.	18721	,,	KELLY, T.	18844	,,	SEARING, L. W.
18854	,,	PEARSON, W. E.	18763	,,	HARTLEY, F.	18862	,,	CLOUGH, T.
18819	,,	GILLIGAN, T.	18920	,,	GRIMSHAW, J.	18949	,,	GRIMSHAW, W.
18795	Private	MOORES, G.	18767	,,	McROY, H.	18808	,,	ASHTON, T.
18858	,,	TYLDESLEY, G.	17314	Corporal	DUDLEY, E.	18812	,,	RUSH, H.
18707	,,	RIDINGS, J.	18766	Private	FINERAN, J. E.	18852	,,	BARLOW, A.
18803	,,	SLATER, J.	18798	,,	HAWTHORNTHWAITE, F.	18837	,,	CONNELL, J.
18923	,,	TORRANCE, T.	18988	,,	GORDON, G.	18890	,,	SANGSTER, H.
18829	,,	TAPP, G.	18529	,,	SHELMERDINE, W. C.	18872	,,	DOWD, J.
18778	,,	STEPHENS, C. R.	18505	,,	LYNCH, T.	18762	,,	CARTAIN, J.
18835	,,	WILLIAMS, W. R.	18809	Private	TAYLOR, H.	18827	,,	BANKS, A.
18975	,,	KINSEY, J.	18885	,,	SMALLWOOD, W.	18887	,,	GILL, M.
18860	,,	ROPER, J.	18824	,,	JACKSON, T.	18800	,,	WALLWORK, W.
18921	,,	ROBERTSON, H.	18793	,,	MARTIN, T.	18882	,,	ROGERS, J.
18859	,,	COOK, J. W.	18870	,,	GARRATT, J.	18801	Private	THOMPSON, J.
18765	,,	ROBERTSON, J.	18823	,,	GANZEMAN, A.	18886	,,	RILEY, W.
18821	,,	BARNES, H.	18884	,,	LOMAS, J.	18760	,,	KEARNEY, E.
18764	,,	TAYLOR, J.	18865	,,	BUCKLEY, F.	18867	,,	McGOWAN, A.
18828	,,	PARKINSON, G.	18768	,,	STOKES, A.	18935	,,	GRADY, M.

PLATOON NO. XVI.

Platoon Commander - - - 2nd Lieut. K. R. EVANS.
Platoon Sergeant - - - - CUNNINGHAM, W.

18861	L.-Corpl.	HOLLORN, J.	18864	,,	HAYWOOD, W.	18928	,,	MAGUIRE, A.
18797	,,	COLLINGE, W.	18922	,,	DANIELS, J.	18918	,,	HELLEWELL, W.
18919	,,	JONES, T.	18899	,,	TASKER, R.	18931	,,	YATES, H.
18959	Private	HARRIS, J.	18925	,,	WARD, A.	18805	,,	SMITH, J. J.
18913	,,	TISSINGTON, J.	18938	,,	HOPKINS, W.	18888	,,	KENDALL, S.
18915	,,	LAMBERT, F.	18772	,,	DOWNS, J.	18826	,,	MURRAY, P.
18960	,,	CHAPMAN, J.	17400	Sergeant	TYSON, J. E.	18863	,,	ASHCROFT, R. E.
18891	,,	LAWTON, E.	18804	Private	FULLER, J.	18840	,,	BROOKES, W.
18815	,,	NESBITT, R.	17615	,,	BRIGGS, A.	18796	,,	McINTOSH, J.
18933	,,	ROSE, F.	17298	,,	MARSDEN, P.	18822	,,	COPPLE, E.
18820	,,	WRIGHT, J.	18950	Private	BRISTOL, C.	18825	,,	WADE, G.
18893	,,	COLLETT, J.	18900	,,	SHIELDS, A.	18927	,,	EAST, P.
18895	,,	CONNOR, J.	18817	,,	BROCKLEY, J.	18898	,,	WARD, T.
18894	,,	DAVENPORT, F.	18853	,,	BROWN, E.	18930	,,	CHEETHAM, R.
18968	,,	FITZGIBBON, F.	18851	,,	WOODWORTH, A.	18816	,,	WITTER, G. W.
18914	,,	HAYNES, F. J.	18856	,,	STOKES, J.	18883	,,	NIGHTINGALE, W.
18917	,,	SMITH, R.	18769	,,	CARR, F. E.	21020	Private	McMAHON, F.
18807	,,	TURNER, A.	18932	,,	GREENWOOD, W.	18871	,,	FILDES, J. H.
18813	,,	WAGG, J.	18927	,,	MOSS, W.	18814	,,	ALLMARK, W.
18802	,,	CARR, T.	18257	,,	CONNOR, L.	18934	,,	UNDERWOOD, E.

"E" COMPANY.

Officer Commanding Company - Capt. F. W. Evans.
Second in Command - - - Lieut. R. T. Wood.
Company Sergeant Major - - Valentine, W. H.
Company Quartermaster Sergeant - Millne, F. A.

PLATOON NO. XVII.

Platoon Commander - - - Lieut. R. T. Wood.
Platoon Sergeant - - - - Dawson, P.

17348	R.S.M.	Bond, T. H.	17940	,,	Scott, W.	18723	,,	Pritchard, E.
18985	Sergeant	Fitzgerald, T.	18513	,,	Day, H.	17943	,,	Costella, P.
17807	L.-Corpl.	Jones, A.	17902	,,	Powell, J.	17729	,,	Woodcock, H.
17909	Private	Aldcroft, H.	17845	Sergeant	Dawson, P.	17484	,,	Chapman, W.
17789	,,	Dilworth.	17733	,,	Neylon, J.	17944	,,	Barnes, J.
17942	,,	Whiteside, G.	17949	Corporal	Emsley, J.	18501	,,	Day, J. E.
17730	,,	Scott, A.	17872	,,	Cooper, S.	17987	,,	Clavering, J.
18522	,,	Jackson, J. S.	18604	,,	Richmond, J.	18582	,,	Delaney, J.
17728	,,	Cosgrove, W.	17950	L.-Corpl.	Hyde, A. E.	18548	,,	Taylor, M.
18572	,,	Schofield, J.		,,	Fidler.	18516	,,	Murphy, D.
17997	,,	Long, J.	18995	Private	Ball, H.	17086	,,	Etchells, E.
17989	,,	Tatton, A.	18547	,,	Holt, A. E.		,,	Pilkington.
17995	,,	Marriot, J.	17952	,,	Wilcock, R.		,,	Heath.
18571	,,	Schofield, H.	18550	,,	McCall, W.	17839	L.-Corpl.	Jeyes.
18517	,,	Paxton, G.	21027	,,	Bolland, A.		,,	Cooke.
21013	,,	Dale, J.	17812	,,	Miller.	17994	Private	Coyle, J.
18989	,,	Dawson, H.	21057	,,	Thomas, A.	17734	,,	Roberts, W.
21005	,,	Hall, R.	17927	,,	Morris, F.	17979	,,	Smith, D.
21030	,,	Lamb, H.	17928	,,	Morris, T.	17910	,,	Pope, F.
18540	,,	Leigh, J.	17946	,,	Webster, W.	18584	,,	Bowley, A. E.

PLATOON NO. XVIII.

Platoon Commander - - - Lieut. S. A. Palk.
Platoon Sergeant - - - - Fraser, J. B.

18600	Act. Sgt.	Banham, A.	18735	,,	Rogers, J.	17811	,,	Clunie, J.
	Corporal	Williams.	18606	,,	Moss, E.	21021	,,	Smith, J. A.
	,,	Denton.	18663	,,	Cross, A.	18593	,,	Hart, T.
	L.-Corpl.	Dodd.	18709	,,	Charleson, F.	18636	,,	Hall, T. F.
	,,	Lee.	18635	,,	Taaffe, G.	18596	,,	Sullivan, J.
			18679	,,	Rawlinson, W.	18997	,,	Parkinson.
18577	Private	Howard, R. S.	18694	,,	Smith, J.	18733	,,	Francis, J.
18595	,,	Bradbury, T.	18639	,,	Howard, G.	18676	,,	Thomasson, J.
18629	,,	Chapman, R.	17888	,,	Madden, E.	18729	,,	Jameson, J.
18592	,,	Brocklebank, C.				21024	,,	Thompson, A.
18644	,,	Thornton, H. E.	18713	Private	Williams, G.	18606	,,	Bassant, G.
18712	,,	Corey, E.	18665	,,	Davies, M.	21031	,,	Roberts, R.
18023	,,	-Bellerby, R.	18590	,,	Bromley, J.	21010	,,	Dixon, W.
18624	,,	Williams, C.	18591	,,	Holgate, A.	18657	,,	Heenan, J.
18633	,,	Wright, W.	18622	,,	McGillivray, J.	21003	,,	Wallace, A. F.
18706	,,	Greasby, C.	18581	,,	Wilson, A.		,,	Jarvis.
21011	,,	Callega, M.	18622	,,	Wiseley, W.		,,	Ogden.
21017	,,	Smethurst, R.	18598	,,	Wright, J.		,,	Phythian.
18670	,,	Waller, W.	18671	,,	Jones, H.		L.-Corpl.	Schofield, C.
18678	,,	Fraser, G.	18720	,,	Brooks, J.		L.-Corpl.	Scott, C.

"E" COMPANY.

Officer Commanding Company	-	Capt. F. W. EVANS.
Second in Command	-	Lieut. R. T. WOOD.
Company Sergeant Major	-	VALENTINE, W. H
Company Quartermaster Sergeant -		MILLNE, F. A

PLATOON NO. XIX.

Platoon Commander	- -	2nd Lieut. F. WALLERS.
Platoon Sergeant	- -	BAGULEY, J.

18528	L.-Sergt.	HABERSHON, W. H.	18686	,,	DAY, J.	18552	,,	BURNS, W.
17731	Corporal	HUTCHINSON, J.	18580	,,	HAUGHEY.	18573	,,	ASPIN, J.
17938	,,	WEBB.	18967	,,	GARNER, T.	18705	,,	SHAW, R.
18601	,,	JONES, C. L.	18744	,,	JOLLEY.	18732	,,	FEYMER, T.
18741	Private	BAILEY, J.	18718	,,	ALLCOCK, H.	18675	,,	CROMPTON, T.
18642	,,	OAKLEY, E.	18745	Private	THORPE, S.	18689	,,	PENKETH, J.
18646	,,	THOMAS, R.	18687	,,	JOYNSON, J.	18690	,,	BUTT, T.
18668	,,	HABORSHON, J.	18743	,,	SYKES, J.	17991	,,	BROWN, E.
18711	,,	McKEE, T.	18737	,,	BEST, D.	18673	,,	SMITH, J.
18722	,,	LEWIS, W.	18674	,,	AMBLER, C.	18979	,,	BARRY, W.
18698	,,	PULLETT, J. H.	18740	Private	KEYES, W.	18799	,,	GRIMSHAW.
18724	,,	HARRISON, J.	18700	,,	HERBERT, W.	18651	,,	RICHMOND, J.
18688	,,	JEFFERS.	18682	,,	DICKENSON, J		,,	MATTHEWS.
18734	,,	WALKER, S.	18970	,,	HORROCKS, W.		,,	POMPET, J.
18666	,,	WASS, T.	18640	,,	JACKSON.		,,	COLLIER.
18704	,,	LEACH, W.	18736	,,	WORTHINGTON.	18971	Private	EMSLEY.
18726	,,	KEYES, C.	18710	,,	GEE, W.	18738	,,	GORTON, F.
18658	,,	HANAVAY, J.	18699	,,	WRIGHT, T. N.	18999	,,	HEALD, J.
18727	,,	GREGG, W.	21015	,,	TITE, T.	18645	,,	JONES, J.

PLATOON NO. XX.

Platoon Commander	- -	Lieut. SMITH.
Platoon Sergeant	- -	GIBSON, F. T.

17945	L.-Sergt.	LOMAS.	18677	,,	OLIVER, J.	18672	,,	LAING, J.
18984	Corporal	MOORES, J.	18742	,,	MILLS, C.	18747	,,	WILKINSON, R.
18603	,,	WORRALL.	18708	,,	HASLAM, W.	18575	,,	ALDCROFT, T.
18964	L.-Corpl.	ELLIS.	18739	,,	WHITE, J.	18956	,,	LACEY, J.
18620	,,	GERBER.	21034	,,	BOSTOCK, T.	21001	,,	TENNANT, S.
18621	,,	FELDMAN.	21035	,,	ELLIS, C.	21016	,,	ATHERTON, F.
18634	,,	FITTON, R.	18972	,,	PERRETT, J.	18955	,,	SHAW, H.
18546	Private	ALLEN, W.	17948	Private	COCKSEY, J.	18957	,,	DOWDALL, C.
17782	,,	CONNOR, T.	18951	,,	GARNER, J. D.	21010	,,	GREENWOOD, W.
17506	,,	HEMSWORTH.		,,	KELLY, P.	18965	,,	DOWD, J.
13261	,,	ROSE, J.	18987	Private	DIXON, H.	21023	,,	GRIMSHAW, C. H
17910	,,	KELLY, J.	21021	,,	RUSH, J.	21020	,,	HALSWORTH, A.
18988	,,	COUNSELL, W.	17458	,,	STRETCH.	18594	,,	MOULES, J.
21036	,,	WALSH.	18991	,,	WELSH, P.	18880	,,	HOUGHTON, W.
21022	,,	SCULLY.	18992	,,	RUSSELL, W.	21002	,,	BOULGER, T.
21028	,,	BURKE, J.	18973	,,	HOLLAND, T.	18976	,,	BILLINGS, T. W.
18996	,,	KELLY, J. J.	18958	,,	MANLEY, S.	18977	Private	FORSTER, R.
21000	,,	LIVESEY.	21032	,,	BAINES, W.		,,	CLEWES.
18551	,,	PEPWORTH.	18990	,,	ATKINSON, C.		,,	WALSH, J.
18601	,,	ECKERSLEY.	18681	,,	LIGHTFOOT, C.			

Bugle Band.

Rank and Name.		Rank and Name.	
Sergeant	GROVES, C. E.	Drummer	SINCLAIR, R.
Corporal	BAILEY, T.	„	WORTHINGTON, D.
„	BRIGGS, R.	„	BRIGGS, A.
L.-Corpl.	HARTLAND, E.	„	MARSDEN, P.
„	ALLEN, W. A.	„	GLEAVE, W.
Drummer	BALE, T.	„	JACKSON, H.
„	ARMSTRONG, W.	„	CREWDSON, H.
„	HERSEY, G. H.	„	ROBINSON, C.
„	McKUNE, F.	„	BROOME, G.
„	ASHWORTH, J.	„	BROGAN, J.
„	CHETTOE, E.	„	FISH, R.
„	SAVAGE, J.	„	GREENWOOD, G.
„	HIGNETT, E.	„	BREARLEY, A.
„	BAYLEY, G.	„	HARRISON, S.
„	KING, H.	„	HICKSON, J.
„	MOSSEY, F.	„	DONOHUE, S.
„	MANN, G.	„	HINDS, C.
„	WALLWORK, W.	„	DEWHIRST, S.
„	ROBERTS, S.	„	HAWTHORNTHWAITE, F.
		Drummer	ROSE, G.

Roll of Officers.

Lieut.-Col.	REID, A., D.S.O., V.D,		2nd Lieut.	BERRY, A. J.
Capt. & Adj.	YATES, H. W. M.		„	CRESSY, R.
Captain	LIAS, W. J.		„	BARLOW, H. C.
„	PARKINSON, R. H.		„	HODGKINSON, G. W.
„	PEET, J. T.		„	BARKER, A. M.
„	PHELPS, W.		„	DUCKWORTH, W. H.
„	LOWE, W. H.		„	HELLICAR, G. H.
Chaplain	SCOTT, Rev. A. T.		„	MORLEY, R. M.
Lieutenant	SHAND, W. G., R.A.M.C.		„	GRIFFIN, T.
„	TURNEUR, I.		„	PEMBERTON, H. C.
„	CROSSLEY, S.		„	QUINNEY, H.
„	COKE, R. A. S.		„	BUCKLEY, C. F.
„	SALT, C. W.		„	ROTHWELL, W. E.
„	CRESSY, C. C.		„	McKEVITT, P. J.
„	DOBSON, H. N.		„	SWARBRICK, W. A.
„	YATES, J. M. ST. J.		Lieut. & Q.M.	JOLLEY, S.
Captain	EVANS HUGHES, H.		2nd Lieut.	BARLOW, S. G.
„	SHAW, J. T.		„	GUEST, J. H.
Lieutenant	LINDSEY JONES, H.		„	HUGHES, R.
„	ROBERTSON, F. P.		„	ILLINGWORTH, J.
„	HAMPSON, S. H.		„	DERWENT, F. R.
2nd Lieut.	HARTLEY, B. H.		„	HEWITT, E. N.

Non-Commissioned Officers' (Sergeants) Roll.

7174   War. Off. GREEENOUGH, P.

22463   R.Q.M.S. BOOTH, F.

Roll No.	Rank and Name.		Roll No.	Rank and Name.	
7667	C.S.M.	HARGREAVES, H.	21835	Sergeant	MEEHAN, J.
10697	„	CARNALL, J. A.	22464	„	PARKINS, S.
21545	„	PLATT, J.	19724	„	CHAMBERLAIN, C. W.
960	„	HEDGECOCK, F.	19588	„	RUTTER, S.
19821	C.Q.M.S.	HARGREAVES, J. A.	19645	„	ECCLES, E.
10363	Sgt. Dr.	ALEXANDER, H. D.	19861	„	SHELDON, J. H.
11312	Sergeant	MORAN, W.	19154	„	WILDING, J.
11785	„	RICE, H.	19507	„	CASTLEDINE, J.
21920	„	MORRIS, F.	21625	„	SMITH, F. F.
19570	„	BROWNBILL, A. E.	21505	„	NIELD, J.
21845	C.Q.M.S.	ATHERTON, F.	21630	Sergeant	ADAMSON, J.
21921	„	WILSON, T. T.	19807	„	ORCHARD, E.
22555	„	JAMES, F. H	19833	„	SNOW, F.
22556	„	STEEN, F.	21613	„	RIGG, J.
11415	Sergeant	MACHIN, J. T.	21730	„	TALBOT, S.
11194	„	BARNES, T.	19764	„	BOOTHROYD, W.
19618	„	SCOTT, W.	21541	„	HOLLAND, R.
21888	„	HIGGINS, M. T.	21598	„	HARRIS, G.
21699	„	DEAN, W.	19655	„	DAVIES, E.
21929	„	MOYSE, R.	21732	„	WILKES, J. S.
19598	„	SOUTHERN, R.	21715	„	FAZACKERLEY, T. V.
19903	„	ODENRODE, E.			

20th (Service) Battalion Lancashire Fusiliers.

"A" COMPANY.

Officer Commanding Company -	Capt. J. T. PEET.
Second in Command -	Lieut. W. H. LOWE.
Company Sergeant Major -	CARNALL, J. A.
Company Quartermaster Sergeant -	WILSON, T. T.

PLATOON NO. I.

Platoon Commander - - -	2nd Lieut. G. W. HODGKINSON.
Platoon Sergeant - - -	MORAN, W.

7174	R.S.M.	GREENOUGH, P.	19577	,,	DOWNIE, J.	19588	,,	ROWBOTHAM, A.
19724	Sergeant	CHAMBERLAIN, C.	19556	,,	OFFICER, R.	19641	,,	GORTON, F.
19509	Corporal	JACKSON, F.	19815	,,	TIDSEY, F.	19679	,,	PLATT, T.
17399	,,	WILD, F.	19570	Sergeant	BROWNBILL, A. E.	19634	,,	WILSON, A.
19591	L.-Corpl.	KIRKHAM, F.	19782	L.-Corpl.	MILLS, R.	19635	,,	SMITH, F. C.
19501	Private	McCARTNEY, L.	19511	Private	BOOTH, A.	19625	,,	BROOKES, C.
19527	,,	JOHNSON, H.	19572	,,	GATCLIFFE, J.	19809	,,	KNEEN, A.
19633	,,	MURRAY, J.	19587	,,	GARTON, F.	19522	,,	JONES, E.
19512	,,	WORRALL, H.	19638	,,	McFARLANE, J.	19557	,,	LEE, J. T.
19523	,,	CARROLL, F.	19526	,,	KENNEY, T.	19669	,,	HUGHES, J. A.
19525	,,	CARTER, W. E.				·19555	,,	WOOD, F.
19536	,,	BLACKBURN, R.	19688	Private	BOWDEN, R.	19521	,,	GREGORY, T.
19510	,,	TAYLOR, T. -	19690	,,	OWEN, J.	19640	,,	GROCOTT, H.
19517	,,	LLOYD, A.	19504	,,	POWELL, P.	19826	,,	SMITH, A.
19560	,,	WILSON, A.	19676	,,	FELLOWS, C.	19502	Private	WHITTAKER, T.
19535	,,	GOODWIN, J.	19505	,,	LEADBETTER, J. V.	19554	,,	MORTON, W. H.
19558	,,	WARDLE, W.	19604	,,	WILLIAMS, J.	19539	,,	LOCKETT, R.
19551	,,	ECCLES, R.	19594	,,	O'GARR, T.	19622	,,	DONOHUE, P.
19541	,,	OAKES, E.	19548	,,	WARBURTON, H.	19553	,,	SLAVIN, T.
19568	,,	DOWNIE, C.	19590	,,	MALPASS, R. E.	19518	,,	HOPE, E.
19536	,,	SILCOCK, W.	19630	,,	DEE, W.	19631	,,	ROURKE, J. W.
19712	,,	LUCAS, T.	19550	,,	ROBERTS, E.			

PLATOON NO. II.

Platoon Commander - - -	2nd Lieut. R. CRESSY.
Platoon Sergeant - - -	MACHIN, J. T.

19507	Sergeant	CASTLEDINE, J.	19749	,,	HARPER, F.	19753	,,	HYDE, G.
19616	Corporal	WHITHAM, C.	19543	,,	CAMPBELL, R.	19617	,,	McALPINE, A.
19500	,,	DOHERTY, B.	19747	,,	JACKSON, W.	19721	,,	IRVIN, J.
19810	L.-Corpl.	BRADBURY, H.	19587	,,	DISKIN, J. P.	19772	,,	SHARP, M.
19799	,,	MULLANS, S. V.	17491	Corporal	CASTLEDINE, H.	19658	,,	EDMONDSON, E.
19600	,,	CRABBE, R.	19544	Private	FREDRICKSON, J.	19689	,,	SMITH, F.
19661	,,	ROSCOE, T.	19599	,,	GAULT, W.	19686	,,	BELL, S.
19756	Private	DIXON, H.	19700	,,	GOSLING, J.	19620	,,	BROOKS, C.
19698	,,	SAUNDERS, J.	19748	,,	NIXON, T.	19605	,,	WRIGHT, H.
19603	,,	ELEY, J.	19719	,,	WRIGHT, W. G.	19530	,,	EDGE, G.
19687	,,	BERRA, A.				19659	,,	TURNER, J.
19684	,,	DULSON, W.	19678	Private	NICHOLSON, R.	19615	,,	SMITH, J.
19706	,,	WILLIAMS, J.	19672	,,	ELLISON, G.	19629	,,	BURNS, W.
19683	,,	KNOWLES, W.	19571	,,	ELDRIDGE, J.	19609	,,	HOWARD, F.
19602	,,	GRESWELL, J.	19578	,,	WARBURTON, A.	19632	,,	CRELLIN, G.
19733	,,	WELLS, W.	19713	,,	HILTON, R.	19742	Private	MILLS, T. W.
19612	,,	HURST, H.	19538	,,	LOCKETT, A.	19776	,,	MOSS, T.
19628	,,	DODD, J.	19739	,,	UGLOW, F.	19528	,,	TOBIN, A.
19668	,,	TRAVIS, J.	19736	,,	ELLIS, C.	19580	,,	COOMBES, C.
19680	,,	LANG, J.	19704	,,	JONES, A.	19699	,,	BERESFORD, G.
19752	,,	MANSFIELD, S.	19613	,,-	CHAPMAN, W.			
19619	,,	BROWN, W.	19636	,,	SULLIVAN, W.			

20th (Service) Battalion Lancashire Fusiliers.

"A" COMPANY.

Officer Commanding Company - Capt. J. T. PEET.
Second in Command - - - Lieut. W. H. LOWE.
Company Sergeant Major - - CARNALL, J. A.†
Company Quartermaster Sergeant - WILSON, T. T.

PLATOON NO. III.

Platoon Commander - - - 2nd Lieut. H. C. BARLOW.
Platoon Sergeant - - - - RUTTER, S.

No.	Rank	Name	No.	Rank	Name	No.	Rank	Name
19626	Corporal	KENNEDY, J.	19788	,,	ARMSTRONG, H.	19791	,,	GREEN, F.
19790	,,	TESTER, L.	19743	Private	GORMAN, H.	19774	,,	SEVILLE, H.
19681	L.-Corpl.	RAIN, W.	19718	,,	SHEARD, W. E.	19800	,,	MULLANS, L.
19705	,,	BRAY, C.	19802	,,	JENNINGS, J.	19769	,,	DOWNING, T. M.
19833	,,	SNOW, F.	19738	,,	RYAN, M.	19789	,,	ASPRAY, J.
19729	Private	FRASER, T.	19772	,,	ALDRIDGE, W.	19763	,,	LAKIN, J.
19755	,,	HOWARTH, J.	19740	,,	POTTS, T. H.	19759	,,	DOYLE, J.
19818	,,	WALKER, W.	19540	,,	BARKER, A.	19795	,,	LUKE, J.
19794	,,	LAWSON, T.	19775	,,	WATTS, W.	19534	,,	WEST, W.
19785	,,	DEVONSHIRE, G.	19730	Private	HIGGINS, J.	19760	,,	HUGHES, W.
19723	,,	HULSE, W.	19746	,,	HOPKINSON, H.	19773	Private	HATTON, J.
19808	,,	TUCKER, H.	19777	,,	SHAWCROSS, J.	19778	,,	HANKINSON, C.
19770	,,	GOLDSBOROUGH, W. C.	19786	,,	LITTLE, R. B.	19797	,,	HOUGHTON, A.
19610	,,	BEARD, G. J.	19783	,,	HUMPHREYS, W.	19784	,,	TAYLOR, S.
19503	,,	MONAGHAN, P.	19792	,,	TAYLOR, T.	19673	,,	SMITH, W.
19765	,,	BURKE, C.	19793	,,	WILLIAMS, J.	19768	,,	HOLMES, H.
19751	,,	FITZPATRICK, J.	19798	,,	DICKINSON, W.	19766	,,	SLATER, J. T.
19750	,,	OWEN, J.	19803	,,	MILLS, H.			

PLATOON NO. IV.

Platoon Sergeant - - - - MACHIN, T.

No.	Rank	Name	No.	Rank	Name	No.	Rank	Name
19618	Corporal	SCOTT, W.	19575	,,	HOWARD, G.	19757	,,	SEYMOUR, G.
19812	L.-Corpl.	McGOVERN, W.	19806	,,	PARFITT, A.	19832	,,	JONES, J.
19579	,,	FORD, J.	19761	,,	GLYNN, W.	19754	,,	McCANN, J.
19542	,,	EATON, W.	19524	Corporal	WALSH, H.	19745	,,	DYSON, C.
19674	,,	WATERHOUSE, A.	19762	Private	WHELAN, J.	19816	,,	WARD, F.
19807	Private	ORCHARD, E.	19508	,,	KENYON, R.	19819	,,	KILLORAN, P.
19830	,,	HARGREAVES, H.	19529	,,	GAFNEY, F.	19639	,,	TROW, J.
19805	,,	FENNIMORE, A. E.	19829	,,	ARDREY, J.	19586	,,	PRICHARD, J.
19796	,,	HILL, J.	19779	,,	MULLAN, J.	19828	,,	KNOWLES, R.
19735	,,	STUBBS, W.	19820	Private	CULLEN, R.	19520	,,	CHAPMAN, H.
19714	,,	LEWISS, H.	19624	,,	LIPTROTT, A.	19720	,,	GEORGE, J.
19823	,,	OWEN, J.	19787	,,	PEATFIELD, C.	19637	,,	OLIVER, J.
19825	,,	MATHER, H.	19685	,,	KING, W. T.	19824	Private	ROACH, R.
19734	,,	STROUD, G. A.	19702	,,	APPLETON, J.	19814	,,	O'NEILL, D.
19822	,,	SMITH, A.	19758	,,	BOWLES, F.	19592	,,	TURNER, W.
19708	,,	SINCLAIR, J.	19771	,,	LUDLOW, W.	19817	,,	BERRY, E.
19801	,,	SIMS, J.	19811	,,	JONES, W. T.	19831	,,	BROWN, J.
19725	,,	HUNT, J.	19813	,,	HAGGAS, E.	19767	,,	DOLAN, J.

20th (Service) Battalion Lancashire Fusiliers.

"B" COMPANY.

Officer Commanding Company	- Capt. R. H. PARKINSON.
Second in Command - -	- Lieut. C. C. CRESSY.
Company Sergeant Major -	- PLATT, J.
Company Quartermaster Sergeant ·	ATHERTON, F.

PLATOON NO. V.

Platoon Commander - -	- Lieut. C. C. CRESSY.
Platoon Sergeant - - . -	ODENRODE, E.

21621	Corporal	NUTTALL, J.	19843	,,	MAWSON, A.	21577	,,	MURPHY, W.
19956	,,	SEWELL, W.	19903	,,	WYATT, H.	19904	,,	DAWSON, W.
19884	L.-Corpl.	HASLAM, C.	19845	,,	TAIT, J.	19837	,,	THOMOND, E
21612	,,	RICE, R.	19910	,,	LEES, J.	19841	,,	MAWSON, J.
11693	,,	OAKES, J.	19887	,,	PHILIPS, T.	21520	,,	BOUGHTON, H.
19940	,,	CORNISH, H.	19838	Private	ROBINSON, A.	19914	,,	POOLE, R.
19883	Private	JEMMETT, J.	19853	,,	PRYME, H.	19849	,,	GILMARTIN, B.
19907	,,	RUSSELL, J.	19856	,,	PLANT, E.	19915	,,	THORPE, J.
19855	,,	ENTWISTLE, A.	19858	,,	WALKER, G. S.	19919	,,	ALLEN, J.
19943	,,	HOLT, J.	19869	,,	TOWNLEY, E.	19862	,,	TIMPERLEY, W.
19875	,,	MAINE, J.	19870	,,	BATES, J. L.	19912	,,	JONES, E.
19860	,,	POOLE, A.	19876	,,	BURROWS, G.	19926	,,	HEALEY, J.
19859	,,	PARKIN, H.	19877	Private	TODD, H.	19834	,,	HOLROYD, H.
19839	,,	MOORES, J.	19886	,,	PIPER, W.	19902	,,	FISH, R.
19893	,,	CASH, H.	21507	,,	PEACOCK, R.	19895	,,	EGAN, J.
19909	,,	JONES, J.	19911	,,	YEOMANS, E.	19913	,,	EMBLETON, W.
19879	,,	HARRISON, J.	21516	,,	WORTHINGTON, J.	19889	Private	CRITCHLEY, H.
19990	,,	KEEFE, J.	19901	,,	CARTER, D.	19898	,,	LAVENDER, J.
19922	,,	WALKER, C.	19878	,,	BARTON, R.	19906	,,	LEE, J.
19872	,,	GENT, W.	19846	,,	BINGHAM, W.	19916	,,	GILLBODY, J.
19888	,,	VERNON, J.	19908	,,	JONES, T.	19921	,,	MULLEN, R.
						19924	,,	WILKES, A.

PLATOON NO. VI.

Platoon Commander - -	- 2nd Lieut. R. M. MORLEY.
Platoon Sergeant - -	- SHELDON, J. H.

19868	L.-Corpl.	EVANS, F.	21506	,,	ALLSWORTH, H.	21508	,,	MULROY, M.
19931	,,	DAWES, C.	19986	,,	HOLT, J.	21503	,,	MARSDEN, E.
19966	,,	BASFORD, F.	19967	,,	HAIGH, M.	19985	,,	OWEN, J.
21522	Private	ANDREWS, J.	19951	,,	HEY, R.	19970	,,	— PULLEN, J.
19988	,,	ALLEN, W.	19949	,,	HAMPTON, J.	19925	,,	RAWSON, A.
19983	,,	ASPIN, F.	21509	,,	HOLLINSHEAD.	19969	,,	RUDDEN, O.
19939	,,	BATES, E.	19854	,,	HORRIDGE, A.	21502	,,	RIMMER, R.
19990	,,	BARTHOLOMEW, J.	19986	L.-Corpl.	SWINDLES, H.	19950	,,	SANDERSON, R.
19952	,,	BUCKLEY, W.	19955	Private	BRANDON, A.	19996	,,	TAYLOR, H.
21512	,,	BELL, W.	19984	,,	FIRTH, F.	19987	,,	THOMAS, T.
21510	,,	BAINES, F.	19901	,,	HACKING, T.	19930	,,	TIPLADY, J.
19894	,,	BARNES, F.				19978	,,	WILLIAMS, M.
19944	,,	BARKER, F.	19995	Private	HENRY, R.	21504	,,	WHITWAM, J.
19994	,,	COTTRILL, W.	19979	,,	JONES, R.	19999	,,	WILSON, T.
19980	,,	CARTWRIGHT, J.	19991	,,	KELLY, T.	19958	,,	WILD, G.
19959	,,	DOWNING, P.	19962	,,	KAUFMAN, J.	19989	,,	WATERWORTH.
21500	,,	DICKENSON, H.	19928	,,	KEAN, W.	19960	,,	WARREN, J.
19938	,,	DOLON, J.	19907	,,	LEWIS, A.	19946	,,	YEWDALE, H.
19964	,,	ELLIS, A.	19961	,,	LUND, S.	19977	Private	HAMILTON, J.
19997	,,	FULLER, W.	19993	,,	MIDDLETON, H.	19937	,,	POWER, R.
19941	,,	HUNTER, R.	19955	,,	McDONALD, J.	19998	,,	WALMSLEY, T.

"B" COMPANY.

Officer Commanding Company	- Capt. R. H. Parkinson.
Second in Command - -	- Lieut. C. C. Cressy.
Company Sergeant Major -	- Platt, J.†
Company Quartermaster Sergeant -	Atherton, F.

PLATOON NO. VII.

Platoon Commander - -	- 2nd Lieut. H. M. Dobson.
Platoon Sergeant - -	- Smith, F. F.

21613	L.-Corpl.	Rigg, J.	19885	,,	Backhouse, H.	19929	,,	Boustead, W.
21607	,,	Gartside, A.	21564	,,	Barnes, E.	21547	,,	McAllister, F.
21517	Private	Chew, T.	21560	,,	Whitby, T. A.	21536	,,	Unwin, T.
21523	,,	O'Brien, B.	21543	,,	Walsh, E.	21622	,,	Blackstone, G.
21528	,,	Burclark, W.	19863	,,	Bradbury, F.	21550	,,	Fisher, H.
21608	,,	Smith, J.	21555	,,	Wood, J.	21540	,,	Pimlett, P.
21539	,,	Lancaster, J. A.	21558	Private	Hart, F.	21529	,,	Kelly, J.
21550	,,	Hind, A.	21539	,,	Brown, A.	21514	,,	Rigney, J. J.
21538	,,	Watkins, G.	19896	,,	Gough, R.	21553	,,	Billington, J.
21566	,,	Walton, W.	21544	,,	Foxcroft, T.	21533	,,	Graves, J.
19917	,,	Dance, H.	21568	,,	Salmon, H.	21537	,,	Nightingale, J.
19982	,,	Avis, H.	21515	,,	Holt, R.	19916	,,	Gilbody, J.
21554	,,	Anderton, J.	21623	,,	Metcalf, B.			

PLATOON NO. VIII.

Platoon Commander - -	- 2nd Lieut. T. Griffin.
Platoon Sergeant - -	- Nield, J.

19923	L.-Corpl.	Potter, T.	21592	,,	Simmons, J.	21587	,,	Lloyd, G.
21578	,,	Taylor, J. H.	21591	,,	Thompson, A.	21631	,,	Pilkington, S.
21618	,,	Gray, W.	21582	,,	Shackley, S.	21565	,,	Marsh, C.
21557	,,	Wattleworth, L.	19874	,,	Mason, F. E.	21626	,,	Nuttall, A.
19932	,,	Mitchell, H.	19927	,,	Gilbody, F.	21632	,,	Mawdsley, J. H.
21627	,,	McIntyre, J. F.	21604	,,	Robinson, J.	19890	,,	Graham, W.
21531	Private	Howarth, H.	21585	Private	Whitworth, J.	21530	,,	Webster, W.
19945	,,	Summerell, S.	21586	,,	Broadbent, F.	19933	,,	Needham, E.
19948	,,	Heminsley, W.	19971	,,	Pelham, H.	19891	,,	Pelham, E.
21628	,,	Burns, P.	21584	,,	Jones, W.	21619	,,	Rawcliffe, J.
21588	,,	Taylor, T.	19954	,,	Dagnall, T.	21606	,,	Johanson, M.
21574	,,	Price, E.	21569	,,	Walsh, H.			
21570	,,	Hammil, J.	21610	,,	Taylor, W.			

20th (Service) Battalion Lancashire Fusiliers.

"C" COMPANY.

Officer Commanding Company - - Capt. W. Phelps.
Second in Command - - - Lieut. R. A. S. Coke.
Company Sergeant Major - - Hedgecock, F. H.
Company Quartermaster Sergeant - James, F. H.

PLATOON NO. IX.

Platoon Commander - - - 2nd Lieut. W. H. Duckworth.
Platoon Sergeant - - - - Moyse, R.

22411	L.-Corpl.	Ashworth, F.	22453	,,	Gannon, H.	22431	,,	Pilgrim, P.
19643	,,	Wroe, W.	21998	,,	Hartley, R.	22425	,,	Prestwich, R.
19644	,,	Milliken, J.	21982	,,	Kelsall, J.	22420	,,	Pope, G.
22437	,,	Parr, J. S.	21541	Corporal	Holland, R.	22409	,,	Singleton, H.
21942	Private	Bowen, R.	21948	Private	Abraham, W.	22443	,,	Sumner, P.
22478	,,	Bowker, G.	21985	,,	Cullen, J.	21996	,,	Sommerville, A. T.
22417	,,	Barlow, W. H.	21940	,,	Fothergill, R.	21054	,,	Thomas, A.
21973	,,	Bolton, T.	21984	,,	Kenyon, R.	22428	,,	Toole, W.
22421	,,	Bowers, A.	21999	,,	Knowles, B.	21051	,,	Williams, J.
21975	,,	Blundell, H.	21941	,,	Langley, N.	22474	,,	Walsh, R.
21952	,,	Cooke, S.	21946	Private	Hughes, C.	22446	,,	Glossop, R.
21941	,,	Cholton, G.	22450	,,	Lane, S. H.	22475	,,	Burke, J.
22413	,,	Cooper, J. J.	21974	,,	Langley, H.	22431	Private	Routledge, G.
22430	,,	Crank, G.	21979	,,	McDonald, W.	22445	,,	Thornton, N.
22419	,,	Cooper, H. C.	21991	,,	Metcalf, J.	21971	,,	Tierney, C.
21943	,,	Downing, R.	21953	,,	Morris, R.	21944	,,	Thelwell, E.
22438	,,	Davies, C.	22458	,,	McCormack, J.	22461	,,	Watson, J.
22455	,,	Deakin, R.	22436	,,	McDonald, J.	21978	,,	Walsh, J.
22462	,,	Diamond, A.	21980	,,	O'Donnell, J.			

PLATOON NO. X.

Platoon Commander - - - 2nd Lieut. G. W. Salt.
Platoon Sergeant - - - - Eccles, E.

19648	Corporal	James, T.	21849	,,	Gallimore, J.	22427	,,	Oldham, J.
19606	L.-Corpl.	Rennil, J.	22469	,,	Grant, F.	22424	,,	Palmer, Hd.
19537	,,	Grayson, T.	21977	,,	Green, W.	22468	,,	Palmer, Hy.
21947	,,	Carr, B. J.	21989	,,	Greer, J. H.	21997	,,	Price, C. A.
22489	Private	Allott, C.	21966	,,	Graham, H.	22451	,,	Romans, B.
21705	,,	Allen, G.	22472	,,	Horton, W.	21959	,,	Ripley, N.
22490	,,	Beaumont, P.	21963	Private	Chapman, R.	22406	,,	Smith, T.
22447	,,	Billingham, R.	22429	,,	Holt, T.	22432	,,	Sewell, J.
21995	,,	Burns, F.	19651	,,	Jones, J.	21065	,,	Stewart, H. S.
21964	,,	Broadhead, C.	19654	,,	Morris, C.	21912	,,	Taylor, J.
21895	,,	Buckley, F.				22470	,,	Thompson, A. M.
21896	,,	Barton, H.	22435	Private	Howard, F.	21976	,,	Wells, G. E.
19693	,,	Brannan, J.	21969	,,	Lyno, G.	21950	,,	Wilson, G.
21889	,,	Clark, H.	21986	,,	Lonsdale, J. A.	21992	,,	Woods, E.
21760	,,	Cumberbatch, J.	21761	,,	Mather, J.	21852	,,	Whitfield, W.
21983	,,	Collier, J.	21878	,,	Muldoon.	21990	,,	Walsh, B.
22422	,,	Durham, H.	21960	,,	Maginn, J.	21968	Private	Smith, A.
22442	,,	Dewhurst, J.	22449	,,	Meaden, J. H.	21933	,,	Stott, J.
19566	,,	Dawson, N.	22452	,,	McGlassen, J.	19992	,,	Walker, R.
21857	,,	Davies, E.	21961	,,	McCarthy, J. J.			
22460	,,	Early, W.	21987	,,	Newton, J. A.			

20th (Service) Battalion Lancashire Fusiliers.

"C" COMPANY.

Officer Commanding Company - Capt. W. Phelps.
Second in Command - Lieut. R. A. S. Coke.
Company Sergeant Major - Hedgecock, F. H.
Company Quartermaster Sergeant - James, F. H.

PLATOON NO. XI.

Platoon Commander - 2nd Lieut. A. M. Barker.
Platoon Sergeant - Mason, J.

No.	Rank	Name	No.	Rank	Name	No.	Rank	Name
22464	Act. T. S.	Parkins, S.	19607	„	Hamilton, S.	21765	„	Ogden, S.
19531	L.-Corpl.	Myerscough, J.	19920	„	Howard, W.	21956	„	Paterson, C.
19780	„	Reid, G. W.	21722	„	Higginbotham, J.	21595	„	Potts, J.
19882	„	Eccles, A.	21820	„	Hatton, A.	21832	„	Perkins, M.
21723	Private	Alexander, T.	21890	„	Heath, J.	19703	„	Race, A.
21837	„	Bowen, R.	19598	Corporal	Southern, R.	19975	„	Ridgwell, G.
19850	„	Billing, C.	21898	Private	Corrigan, J. H.	19881	„	Reid, G.
21843	„	Bromley, C.	19847	„	Edwards, J. R.	22467	„	Sellers, J.
21962	„	Broughton, P.	21836	„	Gerrard, W.	19621	„	Stubbs, E.
21915	„	Bond, J.	22491	„	Hadfield, J.	22408	„	Seale, A.
21657	„	Butterworth, A.	21726	Private	Hayes, W.	22499	„	Stephenson, E.
22412	„	Beck, J.	22457	„	Heffernan, W.	21899	„	Spir, W. A.
21786	„	Berry, J.	19596	„	Jones, W.	19569	„	Trotman, A.
22415	„	Collins, J.	21766	„	Jackson, W.	19976	„	Wilson, J. K.
22486	„	Collier, A.	21597	„	Kershaw, H.	22456	„	Worrall, G.
19597	„	Devenport, F.	21822	„	Leonard, J.	21785	Private	Mennell, G.
21816	„	Grimshaw, J.	19601	„	Moore, C.	22416	„	Nolan, J.
21803	„	Graham, T.	21994	„	Musgrave, J.	21540	„	Offer, B. E.
21655	„	Halls, W.	19576	„	McLoughlin, E.	19726	„	Royle, G.
22414	„	Hall, R.	21955	„	Millington, J.	22483	„	Smith, J.

PLATOON NO. XII.

Platoon Commander - 2nd Lieut. A. J. Berry.
Platoon Sergeant - Harris, G.

No.	Rank	Name	No.	Rank	Name	No.	Rank	Name
19655	Corporal	Davies, E.	22429	„	Harris, S.	19663	„	Stott, H.
19546	„	Collier, W.	19972	„	Keane, J.	19731	„	Sampson, J.
19827	L.-Corpl.	Williamson, H.	22497	„	Kershaw, J.	19717	„	Smethurst, W.
21858	Private	Abbott, W.	19650	„	Lingard, W.	19696	„	Schofield, E.
21967	„	Ashworth, A.	19552	„	Lawton, E.	21883	„	Stevenson, J. C.
19899	„	Barnes, A.	19583	Corporal	Chapman, G.	19664	„	Taylor, W.
19608	„	Chapman, J.	19666	Private	Chadwick, G.	21856	„	Teasdale, J.
19692	„	Colpitts, J.	19662	„	Cox, W.	19744	„	Thorpe, J.
21664	„	Davies, A.	21758	„	Gregory, H.	19973	„	Thompson, A.
19646	„	Derbyshire, A. B.	21669	„	Gallagher, A.	19671	„	Valentine, H.
19716	„	Derbyshire, T.	22440	„	Groves, E.	19623	„	Welch, W.
21842	„	Dix, W.				19697	„	Wells, H.
21727	„	Everett, N.	19880	Private	Mack, J.	19700	„	Williamson, J.
21828	„	Finn, D.	19867	„	Marren, J.	21780	„	Woodford, W.
21913	„	Farrell, G.	19649	„	McBean, C.	19864	„	Woodier, F.
19865	„	Flannery, T.	21784	„	Marsh, H.	19677	„	Yates, E.
21829	„	Gallagher, J.	19513	„	Pearson, W.	21750	Private	Hale, A.
19647	„	Garlick, A.	19781	„	Parry, T.	19694	„	Isherwood, D.
19653	„	Harris, G. A.	19582	„	Partington, F.	21706	„	Parr, C.
22410	„	Holgate, W. H.	21704	„	Parr, W.	19840	„	Ryder, J. J.
19866	„	Heywood, G. R.	22423	„	Quigley, T.	19565	„	Shortman, J.
19974	„	Hastle, J.	21914	„	Sale, W.	19695	„	Wray, P.

20th (Service) Battalion Lancashire Fusiliers.

" D " COMPANY.

Officer Commanding Company	- Capt. W. J. Lias.
Second in Command - -	- Capt. H. Evans Hughes.
Company Sergeant Major -	- Hargreaves, H.†
Company Quartermaster Sergeant -	Steen, F.

PLATOON NO. XIII.

Platoon Commander - -	- 2nd Lieut. H. C. Pemberton.
Platoon Sergeant - - -	- Dean, W.

19514	Sergeant	Wilding, J.	21649	„	Fielding, C.	21687	„	Fallon, F.
22448	Corporal	Sullivan, D.	21639	„	Willcocks, T.	21663	„	Coyle, C.
21636	L.-Corpl.	Hagan, J. W.	21653	„	Clegg, J.	21670	„	Ogden, J.
21680	„	Kenyon, J.	21654	„	Farnworth, W. H.	21674	„	Bamber, J.
21681	„	Nuttall, F.	21661	„	Bamber, W.	21679	„	Pendlebury, T.
			21660	„	Young, F.	21666	„	Woodhouse, E.
19652	Private	Reece, W.	21682	„	Grundy, W.	21678	„	Coombes, A.
19667	„	Pollitt, W.	21689	„	Myerscough, T.	21637	„	O'Neill, W.
19727	„	Berry, J.				21646	„	Davies, W.
21615	„	Simms, J.	21694	Private	Hughes, G.	21650	„	Coulson, J.
21677	„	Haw, J.	21691	„	Pickup, H.	21645	„	Cookson, F.
19728	„	Phillips, W.	21685	„	Highway, E.	21641	„	Phipps, G.
21638	„	Tracey, J.	21690	„	Waddington, G.	21634	„	McLaren, W.
21651	„	Leach, J.	21659	„	McGawley, R.	21633	„	Noble, W.
21647	„	Dawson, F.	21684	„	Whittaker, A.	21535	„	Larner, J.
21640	„	Eastham, J.	21686	„	Barker, J.	21616	„	Brown, C.

PLATOON NO. XIV.

Platoon Commander - -	- 2nd Lieut. H. Quinney.
Platoon Sergeant - - -	- Morris, F.

21730	L.-Corpl.	Talbot, S.	21751	„	Gill, C. P.	21716	„	McGreavy, J.
21752	„	Topping, J.	21739	„	Rollinson, S.	21717	„	Fox, W. J.
21715	„	Fazackerley, W.	21767	„	Whitehead, R.	21711	„	Chadderton, J. W. 1
19710	„	Barnes, T.	21749	„	Graham, G. F.	21732	„	Wilks, J. S.
19711	„	McGuire, J.	21755	Private	Aitkenhead, J. B.	21719	„	Barlow, J.
21753	Private	Aitherton, J.	21743	„	Foden, W.	21716	„	Threlfall, W.
21756	„	Brierley, H.	21738	„	Spencer, J. W.	21731	„	Memory, J.
21757	„	Brown, C.	21744	„	O'Brien, J. E.	21777	„	Walsh, W.
21768	„	Wild, W.	21746	„	Thacker, G.	21712	„	Ward, A. W.
21764	„	Street, H. L.	21745	„	McLoughlin, J.	21736	„	Bradshaw, J.
21773	„	Jones, T. W.	21771	Private	Shaw, J. W.	21721	„	Wilson, J.
21774	„	Hornby, T. V.	21724	„	Garside, B.	21720	„	Wetherall, R.
21754	„	Errington, T.	21697	„	Young, W.	21733	„	Winstanley, S.
21737	„	Gorman, W.	21700	„	Rothwell, J.	21735	„	Sankey, E.
21770	„	Roscoe, J.	21701	„	Read, J.	21750	Private	Waddington, J. W.
21742	„	Prescott, G.	21702	„	Duff, W.	21741	„	Ruberry, J. P.
21762	„	Whillins, F.	21703	„	Walsh, F.	21698	„	Barrett, J. W.
21772	„	Martin, D.	21707	„	O'Brien, E.	21729	„	Blunt, G.
21769	„	Mawdsley, H.	21709	„	Fulham, N.	21734	„	Duckworth, J.
21775	„	O'Niel, P.	21710	„	Bearder, H.			
21747	„	Winterbottom, H.	21713	„	Hughes, H.			

20th (Service) Battalion Lancashire Fusiliers.

"D" COMPANY.

Officer Commanding Company - - Capt. W. J. Lias.
Second in Command - - - Capt. H. Evans Hughes.
Company Sergeant Major - - Hargreaves, H.†
Company Quartermaster Sergeant - Steen, F.

PLATOON NO. XV.

Platoon Commander - - - 2nd Lieut. C. F. Buckley.
Platoon Sergeant - - - - Meehan, J.

10363	Sergeant	Alexander, H. D.	22541	,,	Lee, J.	21839	,,	Black, A.
21865	Corporal	Price, W.	22540	,,	Broome, P. J.	21840	,,	Reed, H.
21501	L.-Corpl.	Cunliffe, S.	21825	,,	Litherland, W.	21841	,,	Derbyshire, J.
21859	,,	Jepson, W.	21834	,,	Preston, F.	21665	,,	Hall, C.
21782	Private	Hutton, J. E.	22547	,,	O'Brien, F. O.	21847	,,	Hall, W. G.
21783	,,	Brown, G.	21864	,,	Griffen, A.	21853	,,	Brooks, A.
21787	,,	Ireland, D.	22511	,,	Lonsdale, W. H.	21854	,,	Riley, W.
21791	,,	Beckham, J. S.	21812	,,	Seal, J.	21855	,,	Jones, F. H.
21798	,,	Higham, J.	21824	,,	McGuire, J.	21861	,,	Lawler, C.
21795	,,	Keighley, A.	21866	,,	Bruce, J.	21863	Private	Riley, J.
21797	,,	Williams, T. V.	21805	Private	Monks, J. E.	21833	,,	Hammond, S.
21790	,,	Mawdsley, C.	21807	,,	Harris, J. H.	21809	,,	McDermott, J. M
21794	,,	Woods, T. A.	21806	,,	Martin, E.	21848	,,	Morbey, J.
21793	– ,,	Keegan, T. E.	21808	,,	Leigh, A. C.	21860	,,	Morris, R. F.
21799	,,	Bennett, A.	21811	,,	Mudie, F. W.	21838	,,	Maher, T.
21800	,,	Flynn, J.	21814	,,	Broadhurst, H.	21817	,,	Crooks, A.
21801	,,	Brown, A. E.	21818	,,	Walsh, W.	21810	,,	Lewis, G.
21802	,,	Newton, J.	21823	,,	Plant, E.	21844	,,	Waterworth, J.
21796	,,	Pettigrew, W.	21827	,,	Heywood, T. A.	21868	,,	Spencer, T.
21804	,,	Wood, W.	21821	,,	Lewis, T. J.	21792	,,	Quinn, J.
21779	Private	Thickett, J.	21830	,,	Ward, A.			

PLATOON NO. XVI.

Platoon Commander - - - 2nd Lieut. J. M. St. J. Yates.
Platoon Sergeant - - - - Higgins, M.

21882	L.-Corpl.	Beaver, A.	21897	,,	Allen, W.	21924	,,	Nelson, C.
21932	,,	Schofield, J.	21892	,,	Pickup, R.	21675	,,	Tavener, H.
19574	Private	Fitzgerald, W.	21901	,,	Barrett, S.	21696	,,	Ripley, E.
21900	,,	Linford, E.	21881	,,	Longworth, J.	21919	,,	Lomas, W.
21879	,,	Hinds, E.	21905	Private	Marshall, P.	21918	,,	Carroll, S.
21873	,,	Knight, J.	21875	,,	Pevitt, H.	21927	,,	Hackland, J.
21902	,,	Jones, T. E.	21911	,,	Shaw, W. H.	21910	,,	Bentley, W.
21891	,,	Burns, R.	21930	,,	Marsh, J.	21815	,,	Ogarr, T. H.
21893	,,	Bordaky, F.	21874	Private	Pattinson, J.	21909	,,	Hopkins, J. C.
21907	,,	Riley, T. E.	21935	,,	Barrie, P.	21931	,,	Duxbury, W. D.
21904	,,	Whitehead, W.	21894	,,	Spiller, H.	21928	,,	Mawdesley, J.
21906	,,	McKettrick, S.	21922	,,	Williams, W.	21926	Private	McHugh, G.
21903	,,	Swift, T. H.	21936	,,	Crowther, A.	21873	,,	McKnight, J.
21917	,,	Gould, E.	21938	,,	Wallsworth, R.	21876	,,	Weston, O.
21908	,,	Booth, A.	21880	,,	Thompson, L.	21887	,,	Whitfield, J.

20th (Service) Battalion Lancashire Fusiliers.

" E " COMPANY.

Officer Commanding Company - Capt. W. H. LOWE.
Company Quartermaster Sergeant - HARGREAVES, J. A.

PLATOON NO. XVII.

Platoon Commander - - - 2nd Lieut. W. E. ROTHWELL.

21541	Corporal	HOLLAND, R.	22542	,,	BURGESS, W. R.	22565	,,	KAY, G. E.
19563	,,	ASHURST, R. H.	22540	,,	BROOME, P. J.	22559	,,	CONLON, F.
22498	Private	EDWARDS, H.	22541	,,	LEE, J.	22560	,,	PHILLIPS, F.
22466	,,	HOLLAND, J.	22546	,,	PERCIVAL, W.	22561	,,	COTTRILL, R.
22494	,,	FARRINGTON, A. F.	22548	,,	CHARLTON, T.	22562	,,	WILSON, W. G.
22426	,,	WARDLE, C.	22547	,,	O'BRIEN, F.	22563	,,	HODGKIS, J. F.
22418	,,	RATCLIFFE, F.	22550	,,	DALE, J.	22566	,,	SMITH, C.
21988	,,	WILSON, A.	22549	Private	HODGSON, W.	22568	,,	STOCKER, W.
21972	,,	WALKER, H.	22551	,,	WILSON, S.	22569	,,	CROFT, T.
22433	,,	WELCH, A.	22545	,,	RILEY, W.	22570	,,	LIVESEY, A. M.
22535	,,	FARRINGTON, J.	22553	,,	ELLISON, J.	22571	,,	DAVIES, E. C.
22537	,,	CARR, J.	22554	,,	CROWE, T. A.	22572	,,	EALEY, R.
22538	,,	HUDSON, H.	22552	,,	LEIGH, A.	22573	,,	PORTER, J.
22539	,,	LOCKING, S.	22557	,,	CONNELLY, G.			
22544	,,	SIDEBOTHAM, A.	22558	,,	CAFFERTY, M.			

PLATOON NO. XVIII.

21505	Sergeant	NIELD, J.	22521	,,	VAIL, S.	22476	,,	TRAYERS, T.
19524	Corporal	WALSH, H.	22522	,,	POWER, R.	22477	,,	ROWE, T.
22501	Private	MORGAN, W. A.	22523	,,	FALLOWS, H.	22479	,,	GILLIBRAND, J.
22505	,,	BUTLER, A.	22524	,,	CARR, W.	22480	,,	JOHNSTONE, M.
22506	,,	RIDHOUGH, T. H.	22526	,,	COUNSELL, H.	22481	,,	FLETCHER, J.
22507	,,	SMITH, H.	22527	,,	BROWN, J.	22482	,,	MASON, E.
22508	,,	CLYNES, T.	22529	,,	WILLIAMSON, W.	22484	,,	FINCH, J.
22509	,,	PARKER, L. H.	22528	Private	BAKER, T.	22485	,,	McCARTY, T.
22515	,,	ROWEN, P.	22530	,,	GRIFFITHS, S.	22488	,,	CORRIGGAN, J. H.
22517	,,	ATKINSON, J.	22531	,,	FIRTH, E.	22407	,,	DONOGH, H.
22518	,,	CHADD, J.	22534	,,	ROYLANCE, J. M.	22492	,,	VAUGHAN, J.
22519	,,	WILLIAMSON, E.	22471	,,	PRICE, C.	22493	,,	BESWICK, G.
22520	,,	SHELDON, J.	22444	,,	KNIGHT, A.	22496	,,	WATCHORNE, J.

Bugle Band.

10363	Sgt. Dr.	ALEXANDER, H. D.	19567	,,	COOPER, R.	21680	,,	PITT, G.
19871	Corporal	TITTLEY, A.	19665	,,	CAMPBELL, W.	21668	,,	WELSH, G.
19675	L.-Corpl.	BAY, J.	19962	,,	HULME, G. H.	21615	,,	SIMMS, J.
19674	,,	WATERHOUSE, A.	19965	,,	SIMPSON, G. W.	22468	,,	PALMER, H.
19561	Drummer	CLARKSON, C.	21596	Drummer	COX, J.	21829	,,	GALLAGHER, J.
19516	,,	HILLIER, H.	22513	,,	CONNOR, P.	22439	,,	HARRIS, S.
19691	,,	HAM, A.	21677	,,	HAW, J.	19916	,,	GILBODY, J.
19624	,,	LIPTROTT, A.	21665	,,	HALL, C.	21537	,,	NIGHTINGALE, J.
19741	,,	McCOY, D.	21676	,,	MAYERS, V.	19573	Drummer	WOODWARD, R.
19627	,,	TARRANT, D.	21810	,,	HANLEY, J. E.			

Appendix III

90 Years On

Leipzig Redouby. This photograph shows the quarry around which the German front line trench ran. clearly visible past the once German strongpit is the massive memorial to the missing, designed by Sir Edward Lutyens. The memorial is located on the site of Thiepval Chateau, which overlooks the slopws where the 1st and 2nd Salford Pals were cut down on the morning of 1 July, 1916. Later the same morning the 3rd Salford Pals were stopped at this point by concentrated machine-gun fire. This track was then known as Track Number Two. (See Chapter 4)

The area of ground known as "The Ilot" is situated in front of the village of La Boisselle, on the Albert to Bapaume road. It was here where the Salford Pals received their first taste of action when they entered the trenches in December 1915. As can be seen the area has not fully recovered from the devastation caused by the impact of mining in this location, where the opposing lines were little more than 30 yards apart. (See map on page 83 and picture on page 86). Author's collection

The slope towards Thiepval where the 15th Lancashire (1st Salford Pals) were shot down during the opening minutes of the Battle of the Somme. Beyond them Irishmen of the 35th (Ulster) Division were initially successful in their advance into the German defensive stronghold known as the Schwaben Redoubt, once situated on the right of the skyline. To the left is Thiepval Wood, hiding a maze of trenches within which the Salfords assembled on the night of 31st June, 1916, ready for the big attack at 7.30 the following Saturday morning. Author's collection

Mailly-Maillet church. The village lay behind the British lines during the spring and summer of 1916. Engineers sandbagged the ornate entrance to protect it from the ravages of shellfire. During the foul winter weather of November, 1916, the Salford Pals left here en-route for their terrible experiences above Beaumont Hamel, on Waggon Road. Sleigh

Behind the lines in the village of Watloy Baillon many barns still exist, which once served as shelter to the Pals during their periods in divisional Reserve, and throughout the few final days of training prior to their disastrous part in the events of July 1sr. (See chapter 3) Author's collection

Still shrouded in thick woodland and the summit and slopes of Mount Kemmel (south of Ypres) are scarred by trenches and interlaced shell holes, which bear witness to the severity of the fighting for this dominant hill. In the Spring of 1918 positions on Mount Kemmel held by the 19th Lancashire Fusiliers were overrun by a German assault from the South. The Germans occupied the hill and advanced across country towards Ypres, the limit of their advance defined by the marker stone in the foreground. Sleigh

Sambre-Oise Canal was the scene of determined fighting in the closing days of the war. The 32nd Division crossed at two points, Landrecies and Ors, under fire and won five Victoria Crosses two of which were awarded to men serving with the 15th and 16th Lancashire Fusiliers. A week later hostilities ended. The famous war poet Wilfred Owen, who was serving with the 2nd Manchesters, was also killed in this action.

Trones Wood, facing the village of Guillemont and Waterlot Farm, was the scene of horrific and intense fighting during July 1916. The trenches occupied by Salford's Bantams ran to the left of this farmer's track. To the right the woodland still gives up a regular harvest of grenades, unexploded shells and other debris of war. The photograph was taken at map reference S24c3/4 printed on page 147 (See pages 146 to 149 Author's collection

Ors Communal Cemetery and military extension is much visited by people for whom Wilfred Owne's grave is a powerful symbol of the tragedy of war. (See pages 208 to 212) Sleigh

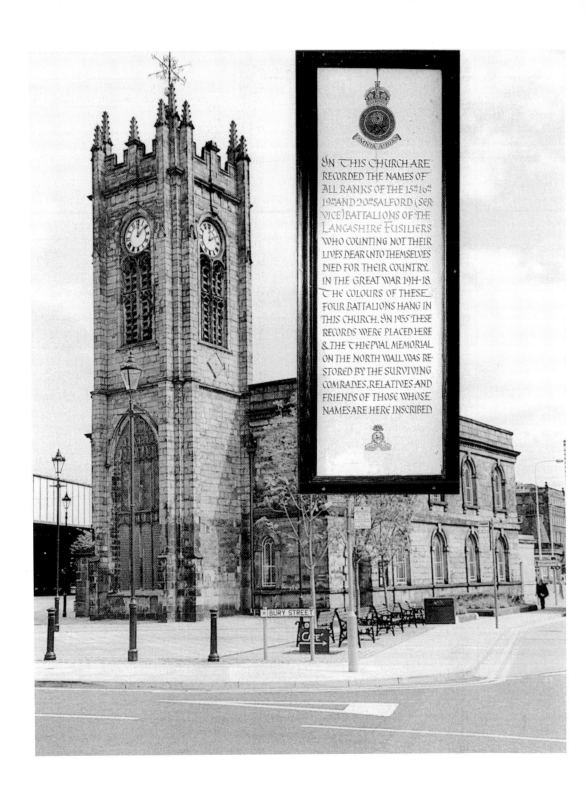

ed Trinity Church,
e to the Lancashire
iers' memorial scrools
e of which are
res here) and the
alion Colours. For
y years the church was
nerative services each
val Day, until age
ered the congregation
rehousing took its toll
e church's position in
rd's life.

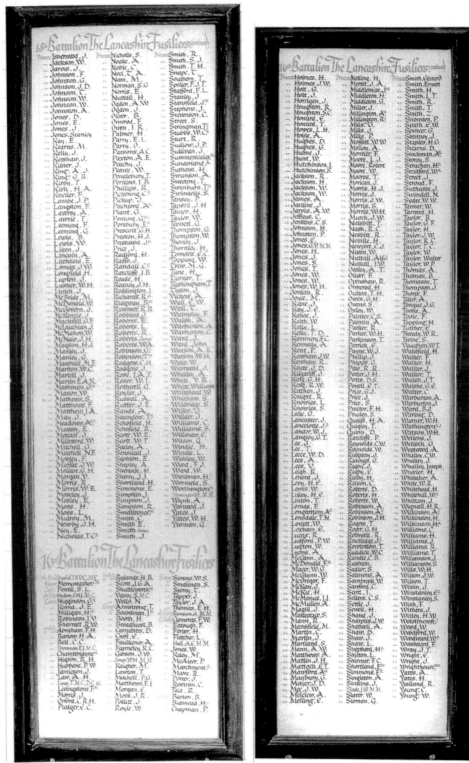

19th Battalion The Lancashire Fusiliers

19th Battalion The Lancashire Fusiliers (continued)

20th Battalion The Lancashire Fusiliers

Pte. A. SMITH,
6, Vicarage-rd., Eccles,
Lancashire Fusiliers.

Sec.-Lt. A. ...
West Dene, ...
Lancashire ...

Sergt. A. E. HURD,
26, Deans-rd., Swinton,
Lancs. Fusiliers.

Sergt. A. ...
16, Ellesmere-...
Lancashire ...

Pte. E. ROE,
23, Myrtle-kr., P'croft,
Lancashire Fusiliers.

Pte. W. BA...
Cemetery-rd., ...
Lancashire Fu...

Pte. B. MILLINGTON,
The Crescent, Worsley,
Lancashire Fusiliers.

The Thiepval casualties are recorded on this remarkable tribute to Salford's Pals, unveiled on Thiepval Day, 1918, by Sir Montague Barlow, raiser of the Salford Brigade.